The Works of
Katherine
Davis Chapman
Tillman

THE SCHOMBURG LIBRARY OF
NINETEENTH-CENTURY BLACK WOMEN WRITERS

Henry Louis Gates, Jr.
General Editor

Titles are listed chronologically; collections that
include works published over a span of years are listed according to
the publication date of their initial work.

Phillis Wheatley, *The Collected Works of Phillis Wheatley*
Six Women's Slave Narratives: M. Prince; Old Elizabeth;
    M. J. Jackson; L. A. Delaney; K. Drumgoold; A. L. Burton
Spiritual Narratives: M. W. Stewart; J. Lee; J. A. J. Foote;
    V. W. Broughton
Ann Plato, *Essays*
Collected Black Women's Narratives: N. Prince; L. Picquet;
    B. Veney; S. K. Taylor
Sojourner Truth, *Narrative of Sojourner Truth; A Bondswoman
    of Olden Time, With a History of Her Labors and Correspondence
    Drawn from Her "Book of Life"*
Frances E. W. Harper, *Complete Poems of Frances E. W. Harper*
Charlotte Forten Grimké, *The Journals of Charlotte Forten Grimké*
Two Biographies by African-American Women: J. Brown; F. A. Rollin
Mary Seacole, *Wonderful Adventures of Mrs. Seacole in Many Lands*
Eliza Potter, *A Hairdresser's Experience in High Life*
Harriet Jacobs, *Incidents in the Life of a Slave Girl*
Collected Black Women's Poetry, Volumes 1–4: M. E. Tucker;
    A. I. Menken; M. W. Fordham; P. J. Thompson;
    C. A. Thompson; H. C. Ray; L. A. J. Moorer; J. D. Heard; E. Bibb;
    M. P. Johnson; Mrs. H. Linden
Elizabeth Keckley, *Behind the Scenes. Or, Thirty Years a Slave,
    and Four Years in the White House*
C. W. Larison, M.D., *Silvia Dubois, A Biografy of the Slav
    Who Whipt Her Mistres and Gand Her Fredom*

KATHERINE DAVIS CHAPMAN TILLMAN

The Works

of

Katherine
Davis Chapman
Tillman

Edited by
CLAUDIA TATE

～ ～ ～

～ ～ ～

New York   Oxford
OXFORD UNIVERSITY PRESS
1991

Oxford University Press

Oxford   New York   Toronto
Delhi   Bombay   Calcutta   Madras   Karachi
Petaling Jaya   Singapore   Hong Kong   Tokyo
Nairobi   Dar es Salaam   Cape Town
Melbourne   Auckland

and associated companies in
Berlin   Ibadan

Library of Congress Cataloging-in-Publication Data
Tillman, Katherine Davis Chapman.
[Works. 1991]
The works of Katherine Davis Chapman Tillman / edited by Claudia Tate.
p.   cm.—(Schomburg library of nineteenth-century Black women writers)
ISBN 978-0-19-506200-7
1. Afro-American women—Literary collections.
2. Afro-Americans—Literary collections.
I. Tate, Claudia.   II. Title.   III. Series.
PS3068.T63 1991
818'.409—dc20   90-7420

Frontispiece: Katherine Davis Chapman Tillman. From "The Negro
Among Anglo-Saxon Poets," *A.M.E. Church Review* 14 (July 1898): 106.

Printed in the United States of America
on acid-free paper

The
Schomburg Library
of
Nineteenth-Century
Black Women Writers
Is
Dedicated
in Memory
of
PAULINE AUGUSTA COLEMAN GATES

1916–1987

PUBLISHER'S NOTE

FOREWORD TO THE SCHOMBURG SUPPLEMENT

Henry Louis Gates, Jr.

The enthusiastic reception by students, scholars, and the general public to the 1988 publication of the Schomburg Library of Nineteenth-Century Black Women Writers more than justified the efforts of twenty-five scholars and the staff of the Black Periodical Literature Project to piece together the fragments of knowledge about the writings of African-American women between 1773 and 1910. The Library's republication of those writings in thirty volumes—ranging from the poetry of Phillis Wheatley to the enormous body of work that emerged out of the "Black Woman's Era" at the turn of this century—was a *beginning* for the restoration of the written sensibilities of a group of writers who confronted the twin barriers of racism and sexism in America. Through their poetry, diaries, speeches, biographies, essays, fictional narratives, and autobiographies, these writers transcended the boundaries of racial prejudice and sexual discrimination by recording the thoughts and feelings of Americans who were, at once, black *and* female. Taken together, these works configure into a literary tradition because their authors read, critiqued, and revised each other's words, in textual groundings with their sisters.

Indeed, by publishing these texts together as a "library," and by presenting them as part of a larger discourse on race and gender, we hoped to enable readers to chart the formal specificities of this tradition and to trace its origins. As a whole, the works in the Schomburg Library demonstrate that the contemporary literary movement of African-American women writers is heir to a legacy that was born in 1773, when Phillis Wheatley's *Poems on Various Subjects, Religious and Moral* first unveiled the mind of a black woman to the world. The fact that the Wheatley volume has proven to be the most popular in the Schomburg set is a testament to her role as the "founder" of both the black American's and the black woman's literary tradition.

Even before the Library was published, however, I began to receive queries about producing a supplement that would incorporate works that had not been included initially. Often these exchanges were quite dramatic. For instance, shortly before a lecture I was about to deliver at the University of Cincinnati, Professor Sharon Dean asked me if the Library would be reprinting the 1859 autobiography of Eliza Potter, a black hairdresser who had lived and worked in Cincinnati. I had never heard of Potter, I replied. Did Dean have a copy of her book? No, but there *was* a copy at the Cincinnati Historical Society. As I delivered my lecture, I could not help thinking about this "lost" text and its great significance. In fact, after the lecture, Dean and I rushed from the building and drove to the Historical Society, arriving just a few moments before closing time. A patient librarian brought us the book, and as I leafed through it, I was once again confronted with the realization that so often accompanied the research behind the Library's first thirty volumes—the exciting, yet poignant awareness that there probably exist *dozens* of works like Potter's, buried in research libraries, waiting only to be uncovered through an accident of contiguity like that which placed Sharon Dean in Cincinnati, roaming the shelves of its Historical Society. Another scholar wrote to me about work being done on the poet Effie Waller Smith. Several other scholars also wrote to share their research on other authors and their works. A supplement to the Library clearly was necessary.

Thus we have now added ten volumes, among them Potter's autobiography and Smith's collected poetry, as well as a narrative by Sojourner Truth, several pamphlets by Ida B. Wells-Barnett, and two biographies by Josephine Brown and Frances Rollin. Also included are books consisting of various essays, stories, poems, and plays whose authors did not, or could not, collect their writings into a full-length volume. The works of Olivia Ward Bush-Banks, Angelina Weld Grimké, and Katherine Davis Chapman Tillman are in this category. A related volume is an anthology of short fiction published by black women in the *Colored American Magazine* and *Crisis* magazine—a collection that reveals the shaping influence which certain periodicals had upon the generation of specific genres within the black women's literary tradition. Both types of collected books are intended to kindle an interest in still another series of works that bring together for the first time either the complete *oeuvre* of one writer or that of one genre within the periodical press. Indeed, there are several authors whose collected works will establish them as major forces in the nineteenth- and early twentieth-century black women's intellectual community. Compiling, editing, and publishing these volumes will be as important a factor in constructing the black women's literary tradition as has been the republication of books long out of print.

Finally, the Library now includes a detailed bibliography of the writings of black women in the nineteenth and early twentieth centuries. Prepared by Jean Fagan Yellin and Cynthia Bond, this bibliography is the result of years of research and will serve as an indispensable resource in future investigations of black women writers, particularly those whose works appeared frequently throughout the nineteenth century in the principal conduit of writing for black women *or* men, the African-American periodical press.

The publication of this ten-volume supplement, we hope, will make a sound contribution toward reestablishing the importance of the creative works of African-American women and reevaluating the relation of these works not only to each other but also to African-American *and* American literature and history as a whole. These works are invaluable sources for readers intent upon understanding the complex interplay of ethnicity and gender, of racism and sexism—of how "race" becomes gendered and how gender becomes racialized—in American society.

FOREWORD
In Her Own Write

Henry Louis Gates, Jr.

One muffled strain in the Silent South, a jarring chord and
a vague and uncomprehended cadenza has been and still is
the Negro. And of that muffled chord, the one mute and
voiceless note has been the sadly expectant Black
Women, ...

The "other side" has not been represented by one who "lives
there." And not many can more sensibly realize and more
accurately tell the weight and the fret of the "long dull pain"
than the open-eyed but hitherto voiceless Black Woman of
America.

. . . as our Caucasian barristers are not to blame if they
cannot *quite* put themselves in the dark man's place, neither
should the dark man be wholly expected fully and adequately
to reproduce the exact Voice of the Black Woman.

—ANNA JULIA COOPER
A Voice From the South (1892)

The birth of the African-American literary tradition occurred
in 1773, when Phillis Wheatley published a book of poetry.
Despite the fact that her book garnered for her a remarkable
amount of attention, Wheatley's journey to the printer had
been a most arduous one. Sometime in 1772, a young African girl walked demurely into a room in Boston to undergo
an oral examination, the results of which would determine
the direction of her life and work. Perhaps she was shocked

upon entering the appointed room. For there, perhaps gathered in a semicircle, sat eighteen of Boston's most notable citizens. Among them were John Erving, a prominent Boston merchant; the Reverend Charles Chauncy, pastor of the Tenth Congregational Church; and John Hancock, who would later gain fame for his signature on the Declaration of Independence. At the center of this group was His Excellency, Thomas Hutchinson, governor of Massachusetts, with Andrew Oliver, his lieutenant governor, close by his side.

Why had this august group been assembled? Why had it seen fit to summon this young African girl, scarcely eighteen years old, before it? This group of "the most respectable Characters in *Boston*," as it would define itself, had assembled to question closely the African adolescent on the slender sheaf of poems that she claimed to have "written by herself." We can only speculate on the nature of the questions posed to the fledgling poet. Perhaps they asked her to identify and explain—for all to hear—exactly who were the Greek and Latin gods and poets alluded to so frequently in her work. Perhaps they asked her to conjugate a verb in Latin or even to translate randomly selected passages from the Latin, which she and her master, John Wheatley, claimed that she "had made some Progress in." Or perhaps they asked her to recite from memory key passages from the texts of John Milton and Alexander Pope, the two poets by whom the African claimed to be most directly influenced. We do not know.

We do know, however, that the African poet's responses were more than sufficient to prompt the eighteen august gentlemen to compose, sign, and publish a two-paragraph "Attestation," an open letter "To the Publick" that prefaces Phillis Wheatley's book and that reads in part:

> We whose Names are under-written, do assure the World,
> that the Poems specified in the following Page, were (as we

verily believe) written by Phillis, a young Negro Girl, who was but a few Years since, brought an uncultivated Barbarian from *Africa,* and has ever since been, and now is, under the Disadvantage of serving as a Slave in a Family in this Town. She has been examined by some of the best Judges, and is thought qualified to write them.

So important was this document in securing a publisher for Wheatley's poems that it forms the signal element in the prefatory matter preceding her *Poems on Various Subjects, Religious and Moral,* published in London in 1773.

Without the published "Attestation," Wheatley's publisher claimed, few would believe that an African could possibly have written poetry all by herself. As the eighteen put the matter clearly in their letter, "Numbers would be ready to suspect they were not really the Writings of Phillis." Wheatley and her master, John Wheatley, had attempted to publish a similar volume in 1772 in Boston, but Boston publishers had been incredulous. One year later, "Attestation" in hand, Phillis Wheatley and her master's son, Nathaniel Wheatley, sailed for England, where they completed arrangements for the publication of a volume of her poems with the aid of the Countess of Huntington and the Earl of Dartmouth.

This curious anecdote, surely one of the oddest oral examinations on record, is only a tiny part of a larger, and even more curious, episode in the Enlightenment. Since the beginning of the sixteenth century, Europeans had wondered aloud whether or not the African "species of men," as they were most commonly called, *could* ever create formal literature, could ever master "the arts and sciences." If they could, the argument ran, then the African variety of humanity was fundamentally related to the European variety. If not, then it seemed clear that the African was destined by nature to be a slave. This was the burden shouldered by Phillis Wheatley when she successfully defended herself and the authorship of her book against counterclaims and doubts.

Indeed, with her successful defense, Wheatley launched two traditions at once—the black American literary tradition *and* the black woman's literary tradition. If it is extraordinary that not just one but both of these traditions were founded simultaneously by a black woman—certainly an event unique in the history of literature—it is also ironic that this important fact of common, coterminous literary origins seems to have escaped most scholars.

That the progenitor of the black literary tradition was a woman means, in the most strictly literal sense, that all subsequent black writers have evolved in a matrilinear line of descent, and that each, consciously or unconsciously, has extended and revised a canon whose foundation was the poetry of a black woman. Early black writers seem to have been keenly aware of Wheatley's founding role, even if most of her white reviewers were more concerned with the implications of her race than her gender. Jupiter Hammon, for example, whose 1760 broadside "An Evening Thought. Salvation by Christ, With Penitential Cries" was the first individual poem published by a black American, acknowledged Wheatley's influence by selecting her as the subject of his second broadside, "An Address to Miss Phillis Wheatly [*sic*], Ethiopian Poetess, in Boston," which was published in Hartford in 1778. And George Moses Horton, the second African American to publish a book of poetry in English (1829), brought out in 1838 an edition of his *Poems By A Slave* bound together with Wheatley's work. Indeed, for fifty-six years, between 1773 and 1829, when Horton published *The Hope of Liberty*, Wheatley was the *only* black person to have published a book of imaginative literature in English. So central was this black woman's role in the shaping of the

African-American literary tradition that, as one historian has maintained, the history of the reception of Phillis Wheatley's poetry *is* the history of African-American literary criticism. Well into the nineteenth century, Wheatley and the black literary tradition were the same entity.

But Wheatley is not the only black woman writer who stands as a pioneering figure in African-American literature. Just as Wheatley gave birth to the genre of black poetry, Ann Plato was the first African American to publish a book of essays (1841) and Harriet E. Wilson was the first black person to publish a novel in the United States (1859).

Despite this pioneering role of black women in the tradition, however, many of their contributions before this century have been all but lost or unrecognized. As Hortense Spillers observed as recently as 1983,

> With the exception of a handful of autobiographical narratives from the nineteenth century, the black woman's realities are virtually suppressed until the period of the Harlem Renaissance and later. Essentially the black woman as artist, as intellectual spokesperson for her own cultural apprenticeship, has not existed before, for anyone. At the source of [their] own symbol-making task, [the community of black women writers] confronts, therefore, a tradition of work that is quite recent, its continuities, broken and sporadic.

Until now, it has been extraordinarily difficult to establish the formal connections between early black women's writing and that of the present, precisely because our knowledge of their work has been broken and sporadic. Phillis Wheatley, for example, while certainly the most reprinted and discussed poet in the tradition, is also one of the least understood. Ann Plato's seminal work, *Essays* (which includes biographies and poems), has not been reprinted since it was published a century and a half ago. And Harriet Wilson's *Our Nig*, her

compelling novel of a black woman's expanding consciousness in a racist Northern antebellum environment, never received even *one* review or comment at a time when virtually
all works written by black people were heralded by abolitionists as salient arguments against the existence of human slavery. Many of the books reprinted in this set experienced a
similar fate, the most dreadful fate for an author: that of
being ignored then relegated to the obscurity of the rare book
section of a university library. We can only wonder how
many other texts in the black woman's tradition have been
lost to this generation of readers or remain unclassified or
uncatalogued and, hence, unread.

This was not always so, however. Black women writers
dominated the final decade of the nineteenth century, perhaps
spurred to publish by an 1886 essay entitled "The Coming
American Novelist," which was published in *Lippincott's
Monthly Magazine* and written by "A Lady From Philadelphia." This pseudonymous essay argued that the "Great
American Novel" would be written by a black person. Her
argument is so curious that it deserves to be repeated:

> When we come to formulate our demands of the Coming
> American Novelist, we will agree that he must be native-
> born. His ancestors may come from where they will, but we
> must give him a birthplace and have the raising of him.
> Still, the longer his family has been here the better he will
> represent us. Suppose he should have no country but ours,
> no traditions but those he has learned here, no longings apart
> from us, no future except in our future—the orphan of the
> world, he finds with us his home. And with all this, suppose
> he refuses to be fused into that grand conglomerate we call
> the "American type." With us, he is not of us. He is origi-
> nal, he has humor, he is tender, he is passive and fiery, he
> has been taught what we call justice, and he has his own
> opinion about it. He has suffered everything a poet, a dra-

matist, a novelist need suffer before he comes to have his lips
anointed. And with it all he is in one sense a spectator, a
little out of the race. How would these conditions go towards
forming an original development? In a word, suppose the
coming novelist is of African origin? When one comes to
consider the subject, there is no improbability in it. One
thing is certain,—our great novel will not be written by the
typical American.

An atypical American, indeed. Not only would the great
American novel be written by an African American, it would
be written by an African-American *woman:*

> Yet farther: I have used the generic masculine pronoun be-
> cause it is convenient; but Fate keeps revenge in store. It was
> a woman who, taking the wrongs of the African as her theme,
> wrote the novel that awakened the world to their reality, and
> why should not the coming novelist be a woman as well as
> an African? She—the woman of that race—has some claims
> on Fate which are not yet paid up.

It is these claims on fate that we seek to pay by publishing
The Schomburg Library of Nineteenth-Century Black Women
Writers.

This theme would be repeated by several black women
authors, most notably by Anna Julia Cooper, a prototypical
black feminist whose 1892 *A Voice From the South* can be
considered to be one of the original texts of the black feminist
movement. It was Cooper who first analyzed the fallacy of
referring to "the Black man" when speaking of black people
and who argued that just as white men cannot speak through
the consciousness of black men, neither can black *men* "fully
and adequately . . . reproduce the exact Voice of the Black
Woman." Gender and race, she argues, cannot be conflated,
except in the instance of a black woman's voice, and it is this
voice which must be uttered and to which we must listen. As
Cooper puts the matter so compellingly:

It is not the intelligent woman vs. the ignorant woman; nor the white woman vs. the black, the brown, and the red,—it is not even the cause of woman vs. man. Nay, 'tis woman's strongest vindication for speaking that *the world needs to hear her voice*. It would be subversive of every human interest that the cry of one-half the human family be stifled. Woman in stepping from the pedestal of statue-like inactivity in the domestic shrine, and daring to think and move and speak,—to undertake to help shape, mold, and direct the thought of her age, is merely completing the circle of the world's vision. Hers is every interest that has lacked an interpreter and a defender. Her cause is linked with that of every agony that has been dumb—every wrong that needs a voice.

It is no fault of man's that he has not been able to see truth from her standpoint. It does credit both to his head and heart that no greater mistakes have been committed or even wrongs perpetrated while she sat making tatting and snipping paper flowers. Man's own innate chivalry and the mutual interdependence of their interests have insured his treating her cause, in the main at least, as his own. And he is pardonably surprised and even a little chagrined, perhaps, to find his legislation not considered "perfectly lovely" in every respect. But in any case his work is only impoverished by her remaining dumb. The world has had to limp along with the wobbling gait and one-sided hesitancy of a man with one eye. Suddenly the bandage is removed from the other eye and the whole body is filled with light. It sees a circle where before it saw a segment. The darkened eye restored, every member rejoices with it.

The myopic sight of the darkened eye can only be restored when the full range of the black woman's voice, with its own special timbres and shadings, remains mute no longer.

Similarly, Victoria Earle Matthews, an author of short stories and essays, and a cofounder in 1896 of the National Association of Colored Women, wrote in her stunning essay,

"The Value of Race Literature" (1895), that "when the literature of our race is developed, it will of necessity be different in all essential points of greatness, true heroism and real Christianity from what we may at the present time, for convenience, call American literature." Matthews argued that this great tradition of African-American literature would be the textual outlet "for the unnaturally suppressed inner lives which our people have been compelled to lead." Once these "unnaturally suppressed inner lives" of black people are unveiled, no "grander diffusion of mental light" will shine more brightly, she concludes, than that of the articulate African-American woman:

> And now comes the question, What part shall we women play in the Race Literature of the future? . . . within the compass of one small journal ["Woman's Era"] we have struck out a new line of departure—a journal, a record of Race interests gathered from all parts of the United States, carefully selected, moistened, winnowed and garnered by the ablest intellects of educated colored women, shrinking at no lofty theme, shirking no serious duty, aiming at every possible excellence, and determined to do their part in the future uplifting of the race.
>
> If twenty women, by their concentrated efforts in one literary movement, can meet with such success as has engendered, planned out, and so successfully consummated this convention, what much more glorious results, what wider spread success, what grander diffusion of mental light will not come forth at the bidding of the enlarged hosts of women writers, already called into being by the stimulus of your efforts?
>
> And here let me speak one word for my journalistic sisters who have already entered the broad arena of journalism. Before the "Woman's Era" had come into existence, no one except themselves can appreciate the bitter experience and sore

disappointments under which they have at all times been compelled to pursue their chosen vocations.

If their brothers of the press have had their difficulties to contend with, I am here as a sister journalist to state, from the fullness of knowledge, that their task has been an easy one compared with that of the colored woman in journalism.

Woman's part in Race Literature, as in Race building, is the most important part and has been so in all ages. . . . All through the most remote epochs she has done her share in literature. . . .

One of the most important aspects of this set is the republication of the salient texts from 1890 to 1910, which literary historians could well call the "Black Woman's Era." In addition to Mary Helen Washington's definitive edition of Cooper's *A Voice From the South,* we have reprinted two novels by Amelia Johnson, Frances Harper's *Iola Leroy,* two novels by Emma Dunham Kelley, Alice Dunbar-Nelson's two impressive collections of short stories, and Pauline Hopkins's three serialized novels as well as her monumental novel, *Contending Forces*—all published between 1890 and 1910. Indeed, black women published more works of fiction in these two decades than black men had published in the previous half century. Nevertheless, this great achievement has been ignored.

Moreover, the writings of nineteenth-century African-American women in general have remained buried in obscurity, accessible only in research libraries or in overpriced and poorly edited reprints. Many of these books have never been reprinted at all; in some instances only one or two copies are extant. In these works of fiction, poetry, autobiography, biography, essays, and journalism resides the mind of the nineteenth-century African-American woman. Until these works are made readily available to teachers and their students, a significant segment of the black tradition will remain silent.

Oxford University Press, in collaboration with the Schomburg Center for Research in Black Culture, is publishing thirty volumes of these compelling works, each of which contains an introduction by an expert in the field. The set includes such rare texts as Johnson's *The Hazeley Family* and *Clarence and Corinne*, Plato's *Essays*, the most complete edition of Phillis Wheatley's poems and letters, Emma Dunham Kelley's pioneering novel *Megda*, several previously unpublished stories and a novel by Alice Dunbar-Nelson, and the first collected volumes of Pauline Hopkins's three serialized novels and Frances Harper's poetry. We also present four volumes of poetry by such women as Henrietta Cordelia Ray, Adah Menken, Josephine Heard, and Maggie Johnson. Numerous slave and spiritual narratives, a newly discovered novel—*Four Girls at Cottage City*—by Emma Dunham Kelley (-Hawkins), and the first American edition of *Wonderful Adventures of Mrs. Seacole in Many Lands* are also among the texts included.

In addition to resurrecting the works of black women authors, it is our hope that this set will facilitate the resurrection of the African-American woman's literary tradition itself by unearthing its nineteenth-century roots. In the works of Nella Larsen and Jessie Fauset, Zora Neale Hurston and Ann Petry, Lorraine Hansberry and Gwendolyn Brooks, Paule Marshall and Toni Cade Bambara, Audre Lorde and Rita Dove, Toni Morrison and Alice Walker, Gloria Naylor and Jamaica Kincaid, these roots have branched luxuriantly. The eighteenth- and nineteenth-century authors whose works are presented in this set founded and nurtured the black women's literary tradition, which must be revived, explicated, analyzed, and debated before we can understand more completely the formal shaping of this tradition within a tradition, a coded literary universe through which, regrettably, we are only just beginning to navigate our way. As Anna Cooper said nearly one hundred years ago, we have been blinded by the loss of sight in one eye and have therefore been unable to detect the full *shape* of the African-American literary tradition.

Literary works configure into a tradition not because of some mystical collective unconscious determined by the biology of race or gender, but because writers read other writers and *ground* their representations of experience in models of language provided largely by other writers to whom they feel akin. It is through this mode of literary revision, amply evident in the *texts* themselves—in formal echoes, recast metaphors, even in parody—that a "tradition" emerges and defines itself.

This is formal bonding, and it is only through formal bonding that we can know a literary tradition. The collective publication of these works by black women now, for the first time, makes it possible for scholars and critics, male and female, black and white, to *demonstrate* that black women writers read, and revised, other black women writers. To demonstrate this set of formal literary relations is to demonstrate that sexuality, race, and gender are both the condition and the basis of *tradition*—but tradition as found in discrete acts of language use.

A word is in order about the history of this set. For the past decade, I have taught a course, first at Yale and then at Cornell, entitled "Black Woman and Their Fictions," a course that I inherited from Toni Morrison, who developed it in the mid-1970s for Yale's Program in Afro-American Studies. Although the course was inspired by the remarkable accomplishments of black women novelists since 1970, I gradually extended its beginning date to the late nineteenth century, studying Frances Harper's *Iola Leroy* and Anna Julia Cooper's *A Voice From the South*, both published in 1892. With the discovery of Harriet E. Wilson's seminal novel, *Our Nig* (1859), and Jean Yellin's authentication of Harriet Jacobs's brilliant slave narrative, *Incidents in the Life of a Slave Girl* (1861), a survey course spanning over a century and a quarter emerged.

But the discovery of *Our Nig*, as well as the interest in nineteenth-century black women's writing that this discovery generated, convinced me that even the most curious and diligent scholars knew very little of the extensive history of the creative writings of African-American women before 1900. Indeed, most scholars of African-American literature had never even read most of the books published by black women, simply because these books—of poetry, novels, short stories, essays, and autobiography—were mostly accessible only in rare book sections of university libraries. For reasons unclear to me even today, few of these marvelous renderings of the African-American woman's consciousness were reprinted in the late 1960s and early 1970s, when so many other texts of the African-American literary tradition were resurrected from the dark and silent graveyard of the out-of-print and were reissued in facsimile editions aimed at the hungry readership for canonical texts in the nascent field of black studies.

So, with the help of several superb research assistants—including David Curtis, Nicola Shilliam, Wendy Jones, Sam Otter, Janadas Devan, Suvir Kaul, Cynthia Bond, Elizabeth Alexander, and Adele Alexander—and with the expert advice of scholars such as William Robinson, William Andrews, Mary Helen Washington, Maryemma Graham, Jean Yellin, Houston A. Baker, Jr., Richard Yarborough, Hazel Carby, Joan R. Sherman, Frances Foster, and William French, dozens of bibliographies were used to compile a list of books written or narrated by black women mostly before 1910. Without the assistance provided through this shared experience of scholarship, the scholar's true legacy, this project would not have been conceived. As the list grew, I was struck by how very many of these titles that I, for example, had never even heard of, let alone read, such as Ann Plato's *Essays,* Louisa Picquet's slave narrative, or Amelia Johnson's two novels, *Clarence and Corinne* and *The Hazeley Family.* Through our research with the Black Periodical Fiction and Poetry Project (funded by NEH and the Ford Foundation), I also realized that several novels by black women, including three works of fiction by Pauline Hopkins, had been serialized in black periodicals, but had never been collected and published as books. Nor had the several books of poetry published by black women, such as the prolific Frances E. W. Harper, been collected and edited. When I discovered still another "lost" novel by an African-American woman (*Four Girls at Cottage City,* published in 1898 by Emma Dunham Kelley-Hawkins), I decided to attempt to edit a collection of reprints of these works and to publish them as a "library" of black women's writings, in part so that I could read them myself.

Convincing university and trade publishers to undertake this project proved to be a difficult task. Despite the commercial success of *Our Nig* and of the several reprint series of women's works (such as Virago, the Beacon Black Women Writers Series, and Rutgers' American Women Writers Series), several presses rejected the project as "too large," "too limited," or as "commercially unviable." Only two publishers recognized the viability and the import of the project and, of these, Oxford's commitment to publish the titles simultaneously as a set made the press's offer irresistible.

While attempting to locate original copies of these exceedingly rare books, I discovered that most of the texts were housed at the Schomburg Center for Research in Black Culture, a branch of The New York Public Library, under the direction of Howard Dodson. Dodson's infectious enthusiasm for the project and his generous collaboration, as well as that of his stellar staff (especially Diana Lachatanere, Sharon Howard, Ellis Haizip, Richard Newman, and Betty Gubert), led to a joint publishing initiative that produced this set as part of the Schomburg's major fund-raising campaign. Without Dodson's foresight and generosity of spirit, the set would not have materialized. Without William P. Sisler's masterful editorship at Oxford and his staff's careful attention to detail, the set would have remained just another grand idea that tends to languish in a scholar's file cabinet.

I would also like to thank Dr. Michael Winston and Dr. Thomas C. Battle, Vice-President of Academic Affairs and the Director of the Moorland-Spingarn Research Center (respectively) at Howard University, for their unending encouragement, support, and collaboration in this project, and Esme E. Bhan at Howard for her meticulous research and bibliographical skills. In addition, I would like to acknowledge the aid of the staff at the libraries of Duke University, Cornell University (especially Tom Weissinger and Donald Eddy), the Boston Public Library, the Western Reserve Historical Society, the Library of Congress, and Yale University. Linda Robbins, Marion Osmun, Sarah Flanagan, and Gerard Case, all members of the staff at Oxford, were extraordinarily effective at coordinating, editing, and producing the various segments of each text in the set. Candy Ruck, Nina de Tar, and Phillis Molock expertly typed reams of correspondence and manuscripts connected to the project.

I would also like to express my gratitude to my colleagues who edited and introduced the individual titles in the set. Without their attention to detail, their willingness to meet strict deadlines, and their sheer enthusiasm for this project, the set could not have been published. But finally and ultimately, I would hope that the publication of the set would help to generate even more scholarly interest in the black women authors whose work is presented here. Struggling against the seemingly insurmountable barriers of racism *and* sexism, while often raising families and fulfilling full-time professional obligations, these women managed nevertheless to record their thoughts and feelings and to *testify* to all who dare read them that the will to harness the power of collective endurance and survival is the will to write.

The Schomburg Library of Nineteenth-Century Black Women Writers is dedicated in memory of Pauline Augusta Coleman Gates, who died in the spring of 1987. It was she who inspired in me the love of learning and the love of literature. I have encountered in the books of this set no will more determined, no courage more noble, no mind more sublime, no self more celebratory of the achievements of all African-American women, and indeed of life itself, than her own.

A NOTE FROM
THE SCHOMBURG CENTER

Howard Dodson

The Schomburg Center for Research in Black Culture, The
New York Public Library, is pleased to join with Dr. Henry
Louis Gates and Oxford University Press in presenting The
Schomburg Library of Nineteenth-Century Black Women
Writers. This thirty-volume set includes the work of a generation of black women whose writing has only been available previously in rare book collections. The materials reprinted in twenty-four of the thirty volumes are drawn from
the unique holdings of the Schomburg Center.

A research unit of The New York Public Library, the
Schomburg Center has been in the forefront of those institutions dedicated to collecting, preserving, and providing access to the records of the black past. In the course of its two
generations of acquisition and conservation activity, the Center has amassed collections totaling more than 5 million items.
They include over 100,000 bound volumes, 85,000 reels
and sets of microforms, 300 manuscript collections containing some 3.5 million items, 300,000 photographs and extensive holdings of prints, sound recordings, film and video-
tape, newspapers, artworks, artifacts, and other book and
nonbook materials. Together they vividly document the history
and cultural heritages of people of African descent worldwide.

Though established some sixty-two years ago, the Center's
book collections date from the sixteenth century. Its oldest
item, an Ethiopian Coptic Tunic, dates from the eighth or
ninth century. Rare materials, however, are most available
for the nineteenth-century African-American experience. It

is from these holdings that the majority of the titles selected
for inclusion in this set are drawn.

The nineteenth century was a formative period in African-
American literary and cultural history. Prior to the Civil
War, the majority of black Americans living in the United
States were held in bondage. Law and practice forbade teaching them to read or write. Even after the war, many of the
impediments to learning and literary productivity remained.
Nevertheless, black men and women of the nineteenth century persevered in both areas. Moreover, more African
Americans than we yet realize turned their observations, feelings, social viewpoints, and creative impulses into published
works. In time, this nineteenth-century printed record included poetry, short stories, histories, novels, autobiographies, social criticism, and theology, as well as economic and
philosophical treatises. Unfortunately, much of this body of
literature remained, until very recently, relatively inaccessi-
ble to twentieth-century scholars, teachers, creative artists,
and others interested in black life. Prior to the late 1960s,
most Americans (black as well as white) had never heard of
these nineteenth-century authors, much less read their works.

The civil rights and black power movements created un-
precedented interest in the thought, behavior, and achievements of black people. Publishers responded by revising traditional texts, introducing the American public to a new
generation of African-American writers, publishing a variety
of thematic anthologies, and reprinting a plethora of "classic
texts" in African-American history, literature, and art. The
reprints usually appeared as individual titles or in a series of
bound volumes or microform formats.

The Schomburg Center, which has a long history of sup-
porting publishing that deals with the history and culture of
Africans in diaspora, became an active participant in many

of the reprint revivals of the 1960s. Since hard copies of original printed works are the preferred formats for producing facsimile reproductions, publishers frequently turned to the Schomburg Center for copies of these original titles. In addition to providing such material, Schomburg Center staff members offered advice and consultation, wrote introductions, and occasionally entered into formal copublishing arrangements in some projects.

Most of the nineteenth-century titles reprinted during the 1960s, however, were by and about black men. A few black women were included in the longer series, but works by lesser known black women were generally overlooked. The Schomburg Library of Nineteenth-Century Black Women Writers is both a corrective to these previous omissions and an important contribution to African-American literary history in its own right. Through this collection of volumes, the thoughts, perspectives, and creative abilities of nineteenth-century African-American women, as captured in books and pamphlets published in large part before 1910, are again being made available to the general public. The Schomburg Center is pleased to be a part of this historic endeavor.

I would like to thank Professor Gates for initiating this project. Thanks are due both to him and Mr. William P. Sisler of Oxford University Press for giving the Schomburg Center an opportunity to play such a prominent role in the set. Thanks are also due to my colleagues at The New York Public Library and the Schomburg Center, especially Dr. Vartan Gregorian, Richard De Gennaro, Paul Fasana, Betsy Pinover, Richard Newman, Diana Lachatanere, Glenderlyn Johnson, and Harold Anderson for their assistance and support. I can think of no better way of demonstrating than in this set the role the Schomburg Center plays in assuring that the black heritage will be available for future generations.

CONTENTS

The Works of
Katherine
Davis Chapman
Tillman

INTRODUCTION

Claudia Tate

A race is but a total of families. The nation is the aggregate of its homes.
—ANNA JULIA COOPER, *A Voice From the South* (1892)

Home is undoubtedly the cornerstone of our beloved Republic . . . and marriage constitutes the basis for the home.
—GERTRUDE MOSSELL,
The Work of the Afro-American Woman (1894)

During the 1890s, when Katherine Davis Chapman Tillman was maturing as a writer, black intellectuals, known as "race men"—like William E. B. Du Bois, William Monroe Trotter, Booker T. Washington, and Kelly Miller—were increasingly concerned with the urgency of defining a new civil identity for black Americans that would enhance their opportunity to appropriate American cultural values, social attitudes, and political rights without sacrificing their unique cultural heritage. The new black American, known then in some circles as the Afro-American, would not only reinforce black peoples' frustrated claim to the rights and privileges of American citizenship but would also refute the charge that black people were reverting to savagery, as was alleged to be evident in the so-called epidemic of sexual assaults on white women, perpetrated by black men, many of whom were subsequently lynched. Black newspaperwoman and racial activist

3

Ida B. Wells-Barnett was especially vigilant in condemning lynching as racist economic and political repression. Despite her highly vocal campaign, most historical accounts of this period have marginalized Wells-Barnett (like other black women activists)[1] and instead have focused on Washington and Du Bois, inscribing them as the early advocates for the race. Certainly, they were paramount. However, while accurately citing their dominance, twentieth-century cultural historians have also been influenced by the tendency of these "Victorianized" black male intellectuals to exclude (or condone the marginality of) their black female counterparts from opportunities to share leadership roles. As a consequence, historians have largely excised the record of racial advocacy by black women.

Washington and Du Bois defined the new black American in terms of civil status and in the rhetoric of interracial politics, though they adopted what ostensibly appears to be mutually antagonistic strategies.[2] Washington proposed that black people should refrain from agitating for immediate political or civil equality and concentrate instead on obtaining property, vocational education, and economic self-sufficiency. Du Bois conversely proposed that black people should demand their full constitutional rights and intellectual freedom as well as assert their civil parity with white Americans. After Washington's address at the 1895 Cotton States Exposition in Atlanta, later known as the "Atlanta Compromise," in which he publicly condoned segregation and deferred black voting rights, the dominant political establishment sanctioned him as the leader of his people. Yet despite Washington's and Du Bois' divergent political strategies, rhetoric, and modes of challenging discrimination, affirming racial pride, promoting social reform, and countering racist slander, Victorian social decorum conditioned both men, along with their con-

temporaries. According to Victorian prescriptives, men had
socially endorsed access to the political sphere and attendant
hegemonic activities, while respectable women—ladies—were
to accept their domestic roles at home as wives and mothers.
Gender governed the value formation and subsequent behavior not only of the white population but of the black population as well. Thus Washington and Du Bois, like the other
black male intellectuals of their time, would have understood
social activism as principally a masculine prerogative and would
have felt that it was their right as men to dominate the work
of racial uplift.[3]

Still, though Washington's Tuskegee Machine and the
Du Bois-dominated American Negro Academy (ANA) and
Niagara Movement were traditionally male in membership,
their activities did not always exclude women. Anna Julia
Haywood Cooper spoke at the rostrum with Washington at
the 1893 Hampton Negro Conference, which reexamined the
Hampton Institute's program of vocational education.
Cooper—along with another black woman, Anna H. Jones—
also participated in the 1900 Pan-African Conference (partly
organized by Du Bois), and she may have been the only
black woman invited to join the ANA, which included forty
of the "Talented Tenth"—educators, clergymen, journalists,
bibliophiles, and poets (among the ANA's founding members were Du Bois, Alexander Crummell, Francis Grimké,
William S. Scarborough, and Kelly Miller).[4] Cooper's participation in these prestigious organizations does not suggest
that gender codes were less restrictive than generally believed. To the contrary, her life and writings emphatically
indicate that gender conventions severely restricted all black
women's public ambitions. Yet the fact remains that Cooper
did take part in activities that were believed to have been
exclusively male. That contemporary scholars of African-

American cultural history are frequently unaware of her role
in these organizations may be more a product of the continued inscription of rigid gender conventions in twentieth-century
black historiography and the routine deletion of women from
history than the actual result of an archival investigation of
her participation.

The rigidity of gender codes notwithstanding, many black
women felt the urgency of social activism and appropriated
the name "race women" for themselves.[5] As an abolitionist,
Frances Watkins Harper was the most prominent among the
first generation of such women, and by the end of the nineteenth century she was joined by Cooper, Gertrude Bustill
Mossell, Mary Church Terrell, Fannie Jackson Coppin,
Josephine St. Pierre Ruffin, and of course Ida B. Wells-
Barnett, among others. During the 1890s these race women
organized a number of women's associations with racial
progress as the agenda: the National Colored Women's League
in 1892; the National Federation of Afro-American Women
in 1895; and the National Association of Colored Women's
Clubs (NACW) in 1896. This latter organization was the
largest and most powerful, providing an important platform
for black women activists throughout most of the twentieth
century. But despite the significant contributions that these
organizations and individuals made to racial progress, they
were routinely sidelined in African-American intellectual discourse. Consequently, the cultural history of black women,
indeed women in general, is generally not well known.

Anna Cooper (1858–1964) and Gertrude Mossell (1855–
1948), the authors of this introduction's epigraphs, were
proponents of higher education and enlarged opportunity not
only for black men but also for black women. Cooper was a
scholar (the fourth black woman to receive a doctorate) and

principal of Washington, D. C.'s M Street High School, which later became the famous Dunbar High School. Mossell was an educator who spent most of her life engaged in social activism. By evoking domestic rather than civil tropes, both women self-consciously feminized social activism in ways that permitted black women access to activist discourse. Thus by relying on the rhetoric of domesticity, Cooper and Mossell redefined the collective advancement of black people as the progress not of outstanding individuals but instead of black families. In addition, Cooper and Mossell measured the accomplishments of the race in terms of the social status of black womanhood. Cooper gave this viewpoint emphatic expression in what is probably the most famous passage from her book, *A Voice From the South:*

> Only the BLACK WOMAN can say "when and where I enter, in the quiet, undisputed dignity of my womanhood, without violence and without suing or special patronage, then and there the whole *Negro race enters with me.*" (p. 31)

Throughout their works, then, Cooper and Mossell feminized the discourse of interracial politics by recasting it within an intraracial domestic context, as the two epigraphs illustrate, thereby insisting that the work of racial uplift was indeed very appropriate for African-American women. By celebrating the maternal virtues of an educated black womanhood and by placing this idealized persona in the service of racial advancement, Cooper and Mossell simultaneously argued for social justice for both black men and women.

But just as Mossell and Cooper used the essay as a medium for arguing that black women had a special mission in the elevation of the race, so other post-Reconstruction black women writers—Frances E. W. Harper, Pauline E. Hopkins, Amelia E. Johnson, and Emma Dunham Kelley (-Hawkins), for instance—appropriated the novel for similar purposes.[6] Both types of writing repeatedly feminized the discourse of racial politics to the degree that each type now seems a standardized and self-consciously gendered, strategic response to black people's desire for racial affirmation. Like Mossell and Cooper, post-Reconstruction black women writers of fiction and non-fiction domesticated the political discourse and redefined the new black American identity not in civil or interracial rhetoric but in domestic tropes: the moral perfectability, economic prosperity, and political autonomy of the black family. Hence black women writers placed social arguments, which otherwise exceeded the boundaries of Victorian feminine propriety, within an enlarged sphere of decided domesticity.

Late nineteenth-century readers were especially adept at discerning the political implications of domestic tropes. By contrast, late twentieth-century readers have not been so well schooled in that culturally conditioned reading strategy. Twentieth-century protest literature has taught us to identify racial discourse as polemics that overtly contest the dominant hegemonic order. Consequently, nineteenth-century domestic tropes often appear opaque to us, prompting our contention that sentimental fiction about family life is intellectually and politically naive, restrictive, indeed, overly simplistic. Late nineteenth-century black people, however, did not perceive marriage and family life as mere objects of female desire; these social and civil institutions were seen as central prerequisites for racial progress, as the basis of civilization itself.

Katherine Tillman, like her black female contemporaries, repeatedly relied on domestic tropes in her writing for expressing the desire of African Americans for civil liberty. Her novellas, plays, poetry, and essays were published almost exclusively in *The A. M. E. Church Review,* a quarterly journal (hereafter referred to as *The Review*), in the *Christian*

Recorder, or by the A. M. E. Book Concern, all publishing entities of the African Methodist Episcopal Church. Despite the volume of her publications and sound evidence of literary competence, as judged by conventional literary criteria, she remains a minor writer. This label is by no means used to demean her talent, though it has served to obscure many writers whose careers constitute large and important parts of literary history, parts without which we can achieve only a limited understanding of the undisputed major writers and of specific periods in literary history. The label "minor writer" assists me in placing Tillman's literary career into historical and canonical contexts. Her work approximates that of many early, minor, black writers, heretofore obscure, who similarly asserted their authority to interpret black culture, question its values, and preserve its integrity through the dissemination of the written word. In addition, by examining Tillman's career, we can see how she (and "minor" writers like her) helped to establish supportive publishing networks, transformed (in this case) a black congregation into a literary audience, and stimulated a black intellectual climate for engendering literary productivity.

Most significantly, Tillman's works provide clear opportunities for us to observe the strategies that late nineteenth-century black women writers used to gain legitimate access to the professionalization of the work of racial uplift. Like Mossell and Cooper, Tillman insisted that "the work of the Afro-American woman" was not apportioned for self-aggrandizement. In fact, Tillman repeatedly and deliberately effaced black, female professionalism not only behind approbations of advancing the race but also behind religious inspiration, pious selflessness, moral duty, and feminine diminutives. For example, feminine diminution and moral piety are the principal tactics in her essay "Some Girls That I Know."

Here Tillman referred to real life subjects as "pen-pictures
. . . to stimulate other girls in their efforts for good." Addressing her readers as "Dear girls," she continued,

> may these lines invite you to deeds that shall win the fairest
> laurels that ever decked the brow of woman. Have a purpose
> in life, and live for its achievement. Let nothing low or in-
> ferior to your aim keep you from that fair haven where you
> would be. . . . There is not an obstacle in your path but
> what by perseverance you may overcome. (p. 69)*

Also like her black contemporaries, male and female, Tillman catalogued the accomplishments of black women as evidence of racial advancement, prosperity, and ultimately
equality. In the essay "Afro-American Women and Their
Work," she contended that the propensity for intelligent industry was a duty-bound "gift . . . from Christianity" (p.
71), further arguing,

> We have been charged with mental inferiority; now if we
> can prove that with cultivated hearts and brains, we can ac-
> complish the same that is accomplished by our fairer sisters
> of the Caucasian race, why then, we have refuted the false-
> hood. . . . We owe it to God and to the Negro race, to be
> as perfect specimens of Christian womanhood as we are ca-
> pable of being. (p. 86)

As if the above assertion of racial equality were not emphatic
enough, Tillman explicitly exhorted, "All men are created
free and equal and women ditto" (p. 89). However, having
affirmed sexual equality as well, she resorted to a discursive
posture that her black female contemporaries frequently used
to efface that affirmation, especially at the conclusion of a
work; she closed her essay by evoking the prescribed gender

---

*All quotations from Tillman's works are cited by the page numbers in this
volume.

code, insisting that women's most important work lay in the home: "Since home-making is of such great importance, every woman who expects to have one should learn how to make it the happiest place on earth. We should remember that there is nothing more serious than a marriage, save it be a birth or death" (p. 92). In Tillman's words, "The home is an institution for which we are indebted to Christianity. It is of equal importance with the school and the church" (p. 90). Writers like Tillman who were black, female, and accorded minor status therefore left behind a tradition of black social advocacy, although their works slipped into the margins of African-American intellectual discourse.

Born to Laura and Charles Chapman on February 19, 1870, in Mound City, Illinois, Katherine Davis Chapman Tillman began writing as a child. In 1888 her first published poem, "Memory," appeared in the *Christian Recorder,* in which Tillman published individual poems during the early years of her career. While still in high school in Yanktown, South Dakota, Tillman became a regular short story contributor to *Our Women and Children* (which is no longer extant), while occasionally publishing articles and poems in the *Indianapolis Freeman.* (None of these early pieces is available to include in this volume.) Upon the completion of high school, she attended the State University of Louisville in Kentucky and Wilberforce University in Ohio. In a commemorative poem, "The Pastor," published both in the *Christian Recorder* (18 Oct. 1894) and in her collection of poetry, *Recitations* (1902), she alludes to a Reverend G. M. Tillman who I assume was her husband. After 1902, the biographical details of Tillman's life disappear from available records; thus I cannot date her death.

What is clear, however, is that Tillman published a sub-

stantial number of works of fiction, nonfiction, drama, and
poetry. At the time that Lewis A. Scruggs was completing
*Women of Distinction: Remarkable in Works and Invincible in
Character,* published in 1893, he noted that Tillman was
preparing a volume of short stories for girls. I have been
unable to locate that volume or any further reference to it,
but much of what Tillman did publish is still extant. In addition to her poetry, she published two novellas—*Beryl Weston's Ambition: The Story of an Afro-American Girl's Life* (1893)
and *Clancy Street* (1898–1899)—in *The Review.* In 1894 she
produced the sketch "Miles the Conquerer" in *American Citizen Magazine.* She also published three articles in *The Review* that were of particular interest to black females: "Some
Girls That I Know" (1893), "Afro-American Women and
Their Work" (1895), and "The National Association of Colored Women's Clubs" (which has not been included in this
volume because it is essentially a record of the minutes of the
association's national conference held on 4–10 August 1914
at Wilberforce University). Her two literary essays—"Afro-
American Poets and Their Verse" (1898) and "The Negro
Among Anglo-Saxon Poets" (1898)—and her two literary
biographies of European writers who would have been clas-
sified as Negroes had they lived in the United States—"Alexander Dumas, Père" (1907) and "Alexander Sergeivich
Pushkin" (1909)—appeared in *The Review* as well, as did
her short story "The Preacher at Hill Station" (1903).
Moreover, she arranged for the A. M. E. Book Concern,
based in Philadephia, to publish a number of individual works:
the plays *Aunt Betsy's Thanksgiving* (n.d.), *Thirty Years of
Freedom* (1902), and *Fifty Years of Freedom, or From Cabin
to Congress* (1910), and her eighty-five-page collection of poetry, *Recitations* (1902). The original title page of *Recitations*
lists three additional publications by Tillman: *Lincoln's*

Proclamation, The Men Makers Club, and *Heirs of Slavery.*
Lincoln's Proclamation bears a 1902 copyright date, but there
is no known copy. *The Men Makers Club* and the 1909 A.
M. E. Publishing House edition of *Heirs of Slavery* seem
not to have been copyrighted or to exist any longer, although
another version of *Heirs of Slavery: A Little Drama of To-
day* appeared in the January 1901 *A. M. E. Church Review.*
In 1907 Tillman published "Paying Professions for Colored
Girls" in the *Voice of the Negro.* I suspect that she self-published
Quotations from Negro Authors (1921) and the drama *The Spirit
of Allen: A Pageant of African Methodism* (1922). The January
31, 1895 issue of the *Christian Recorder* refers to "an interesting and instructive little book by Mrs. Katherine Davis
Tillman," entitled *How To Live Well on a Small Salary* ("Notes
and Comments, p. 2), and the Library of Congress Copyright Registry attributes Tillman as the author of *Poems and
Drama* (1908), but unfortunately, neither of these works has
been found.

The fact that almost all of Tillman's known works were
published in *The Review* and *Christian Recorder* or by the
A. M. E. Book Concern signals a nurturing author–publisher relationship, which she characterized in her essay "Afro-
American Poets and Their Verse" as largely responsible for
the proliferation of race literature. "For poets thrive rapidly," she wrote, "in a congenial atmosphere, and if we wish
the best of which our poets are capable, we must inspire them
to greater efforts by our appreciation of what they have already accomplished" (p. 94). Evidently, Tillman was one
such writer whom *The Review* nurtured in its congenial climate, especially as she wrote stories and essays for a readership that for most part shared her racial identity, values, and
point of view.

First established in 1841 as a quarterly, and reappearing

in 1884, *The A. M. E. Church Review* published articles that
covered the breadth of black cultural development (Logan,
p. 321). In 1884 the circulation was approximately 1,000,
and in 1889 it was 2,800 (Logan, p. 321). According to one
editor, "Every phase of the race problem, the political, economic, social, ethical, and religious aspects of it, has been
exhaustively discussed in *[The Review]*" (Hagins, p. 603).
The articles ranged in interest "from the commonplace to
those of scholarly breadth, depth of thought, and beauty of
expression," with the general consensus, among the journal's
editorial staff, that its articles were not to be surpassed by
those in the *North American Review* (Hagins, p. 603). National in scope, *The Review* dedicated itself to dual purposes:
"giv[ing] an opportunity to the scholarly men and women of
our race to express themselves upon leading topics of the day,
in which we have, with all men, a common interest" ("Editorial," p. 79); and providing a forum to display the "progress . . . being made among [African Americans] in religious, literary, financial and industrial pursuits" (p. 80).

   The Review, then, was a particularly vocal medium in re-
futing the allegations of such prominent eighteenth-century
Enlightenment theorists as David Hume, Immanuel Kant,
Georg Hegel, and Thomas Jefferson, all of whom based the
inferiority of Africans on their presumed lack of achievement
in the arts and sciences (Gates, pp. 66, 94, 113–14, 129,
141). *The Review* appropriated the major Enlightenment tenet
that literature is the mark of civilization, and then dedicated
its pages to presenting the ongoing tradition of race literature
and other evidence of African-American civilization. For example, Daniel H. Murray, a congressional black bibliophile, wrote in *The Review* that "literature is the highest form
of culture and the real test of the standing of a people in the
ranks of civilization" ("A Bibliography," pp. 25–26). Mur-

ray repeated this viewpoint in his essay "Bibliographia-Africania," a work documenting African-American literary culture, by citing Voltaire: "It was Voltaire who said, 'All the world, except savage nations, is governed by books' . . . the true test of the progress of a people is to be found in their literature" (p. 187). Tillman also appropriated the tenet in "Afro-American Poets and Their Verse." In the form of a rhetorical question, she emphasized black people's legitimate claim to civil justice by referencing their artistic productivity:

> For what ostracism shall be able to continue when directed against a people in whom dwell the divine trio—Poetry, Music and Art? . . . Let no man who loves the Negro race then decry poetry, for it is by this and other proofs of genius that our race will be enabled to take its place among the nations of the earth. (p. 94)

Black intellectuals turned to their literature as tangible proof of progress. Indeed, writing race literature, tabulating and cataloguing it, thereby producing numerous book-length works of encyclopedic proportions, became a major preoccupation among black intellectuals—physicians, scholars, teachers, writers, and ministers—at the turn of the century. For example, the educator Irvin Garland Penn edited *The Negro Press and Its Editors* in 1891; physicians Monroe A. Majors, Daniel W. Culp, and Lewis A. Scruggs respectively edited *Noted Negro Women: Their Triumphs and Activities* in 1893, *Twentieth Century Negro Literature: Or, a Cyclopedia of Thought on the Vital Topics Relating to the American Negro* in 1902, and *Women of Distinction: Remarkable in Works and Invincible in Character* in 1893; the Rev. William J. Simmons edited *Men of Mark* in 1887; and the bibliophile Murray edited *Murray's Historical and Biographical Encyclopedia of the Colored Race throughout the World* (n.d.).

In addition, *The Review*—like the *Voice of the Negro*, the *Colored American Magazine, Southern Workman, Southland,* and the *A. M. E. Zion Church Quarterly,* to name just a few popular black periodicals of that epoch—was a vehicle for both fostering and celebrating the development of African-American literature, religious and secular biases notwithstanding. These and other serial publications nourished late nineteenth-century black literary culture by widening its access to those with varying degrees of talent and ambition. By providing their contributors with receptive black readerships who shared their social values, moral codes, and educational pursuits, black periodicals encouraged the development of writers like Tillman and celebrated their desire for individual achievement by recasting it as evidence of collective racial progress. As Tillman insisted, all black literary production, no matter how humble or lofty, deserved serious attention. "Then, let the poem of the rudest construction not pass unnoticed," she wrote, "lest we throw away a diamond of precious thought; while to those whose many commendable poems entitle them to the rank of poets let us give our hearty encouragement, bidding them God-speed in singing their songs" "Afro-American Poets, p. 94).

In this same essay, Tillman publicly acknowledged the support that *The Review* had given to writers like herself in a note of appreciation: "To the editors of Afro-American journals who have encouraged us to sing our trembling lays by giving them a place in their columns, we owe a debt of gratitude" (p. 100). Thus Tillman and her readers seemed unified on matters of race, to the extent that she could address even controversial racial issues with little fear of alienating her audience. The high degree of compatibility between Tillman and her audience seems to have remained steady throughout her career, producing an enduring authorial credibility that would allow her to use especially her poetry to criticize her readers' and her own intraracial prejudices. Yet she, like the other contributors to *The Review,* knew that outside the congenial, insular, and encouraging intraracial literary context of *The Review*—and outside segregated black communities—was a hostile white society that had by the 1890s effectively disenfranchised black people, negating their desire for freedom and equality with second-class citizenship.

Practically all of the historical and sociological studies about black people written by white people at the turn of the century are explicitly racist and routinely depict blacks as inhuman. In addition, the popular culture of that period was outright hostile to them. Intoxicated with their so-called "Manifest Destiny," as historian Rayford W. Logan chronicles in *The Betrayal of the Negro* (1965), white people generally felt that it was their duty to exploit all inferiors, and black people were number one on the list. Given this racist climate, we can appreciate the motivation that compelled post-Reconstruction black writers—men and women alike—to celebrate idealized black characters in their writing as a counterargument. On the one hand, black writers confronted the viewpoint that black people were childlike and required paternal discipline, as depicted in the literature of the Plantation School by such writers as Joel Chandler Harris, Thomas Nelson Page, and James Lane Allen. On the other hand, black writers confronted the allegation that black people were inveterate criminals who had to be separated from civilized society at all costs, as depicted in the violently racist novels of Thomas Dixon, Jr.—*The Leopard's Spots* (1902) and *The Clansman* (1905). Thus the black people who wrote for *The Review,* to name just one black periodical, did not encounter simply a generally racist climate; they also felt its sharp specificity and encountered its danger. A few examples of these "academic" studies and their racist contentions are sufficient to illustrate the interracial hostility of the period.

Phillip Alexander Bruce, a Virginia aristocrat, was one of the many proponents of the social theory that came into cultural currency in the 1880s and that alleged the regression or retrogression of the Negro. Throughout his career, Bruce described what he contended were black people's inherent savage tendencies. In 1889 he published *The Plantation Negro as Freeman* in which he argued that adult blacks with no recollection of slavery more closely resembled original Africans than did their immediate forebears who had been slaves (Williamson, p. 121). He cited as evidence the belief in black male licentiousness with white women:

> There is something strangely alluring and seductive to them in the appearance of a white woman; they are aroused and stimulated by its foreignness to their experience of sexual pleasure, and it moves them to gratify their lust at any cost and in spite of every obstacle. This proneness of the negro is so well understood that the white women of every class, from the highest to the lowest are afraid to venture to any distance alone, or even to wander unprotected in the immediate vicinity to their homes; their appreciation of the danger being keen, and the apprehension of corporal injury as vivid, as if the country were in arms. (Williamson, p. 121)

Governor Benjamin Ryan Tillman of South Carolina, an extremely outspoken proponent of the re(tro)gression theory, used it to deal the fatal blow to post-Reconstruction enfranchisement of black people in that state. When he was elected to the United States Senate in 1895, he took the inflammatory theory with him and helped to spread its tenets across the country.[7] The immediate results were that segregation codes became even more stringent, and racial violence dramatically increased as black people fought a losing battle to hold onto their constitutional rights.

Another spokesman for the re(tro)gression theory was Nathaniel Southgate Shaler, a Harvard University professor (Williamson, p. 119). In 1904 he wrote in *The Neighbor: The Natural History of Human Contacts:*

> Here, as in the Old World the Negroes have not only failed to exhibit a capacity for indigenous development, but when uplifted from without have shown an obvious tendency to fall back into their primitive estate as soon as the internal support was withdrawn. (Williamson, p. 120)

Although Shaler corroborated the racist consensus and cited as evidence of re(tro)gression the increased number of "assaults of Negroes on white women in the South . . . since the emanicipation," he was not in favor of lynching (Williamson, p. 120). But while his brand of re(tro)gression was not as violent as others', his intellectual prestige served to sanction the more radical versions of re(tro)gressionism that were to follow.

My last example of the re(tro)gression theory serves to illustrate how deeply this racist principle insinuated itself into early twentieth-century American culture. In 1910 a Columbia University graduate student, Howard Odum, set out to prove a domesticated version of re(tro)gression. Odum's Ph.D. dissertation contained little that was original inasmuch as his basic thesis had been already been in the racist domain for decades. He argued,

> The negro has little home conscience or love of home, no local attachments of the better sort. . . . He has little conception of the meaning of virtue, truth, honor, manhood, integrity. . . . (Gutman, pp. 458–59)

"No people," he continued, "can live above their home life," and "in his home life the negro is filthy, careless and indecent. He is as destitute of morals as any of the lower animals" (Gutman, p. 459). Odum contended that an absence of moral restraint or an underdeveloped social self "ha[d resulted in the negro's] not develop[ing the] love of home and family [and] the desire to accumulate property," and he concluded that it was slavery that had "kept the home of the negro in a more organized state" (Gutman, p. 459). Five years later, when D. W. Griffith made motion-picture history with *The Birth of a Nation,* a cinematic adaption of Thomas Dixon's racist novel *The Clansman,* negrophobia reached new heights. The decades of saturating white Americans with the virulent racism of re(tro)gressionism combined with the apparent realism of film to excite a mania similar to that resulting from Orson Welles's 1938 broadcast, *War of the Worlds,* which convinced thousands of Americans that they were under attack by extraterrestial monsters.

The outrage that the proponents of Negro re(tro)gression incite in late twentieth-century readers of Tillman's works is no doubt similar in varying degrees to that which post-Reconstruction black people experienced daily. But rather than respond with the combative rhetoric of racial protest that has become popular in recent years, Katherine Tillman, like many black women writers of her era, addressed her constituency in race literature, using a domestic rhetoric of racial affirmation—familial love, labor, and loyalty among black people. These writers deliberately set out both to refute the intense negrophobia of the period and to underscore the hypocrisy of the genteel tradition that mocked black people's desire for education, social rituals, and material comfort. Tillman herself dramatized affirming domestic values in her fiction, Sunday school drama, and verse, and she appropriated Victorian

sensibility about the sanctity of the home to enhance her por-
trayals of homebound black heroines who, by exemplifying
courage, self-sacrifice, moral purity, and spiritual piety, served
as models for black people. Her reliance on techniques that
did not directly contest racism does not suggest, however,
that she (as well as most black women writers of that period)
skirted over it polemicism; she simply tended not to focus on
it in her writing. Instead, she (like they) used imaginative
literature—fiction, poetry, and drama—to fortify black people's resolve to secure pious, prosperous, and nurturing
households for themselves, despite the oppression that they
routinely encountered. Her works suggest that such a strategy may have been a most potent subversion of racist allegations.[8]

During the late nineteenth and early twentieth centuries (especially 1890–1910), most black Americans were poor;
nevertheless, there were pockets of middle-class black communities throughout the country. But irrespective of their
economic means, all African-Americans saw their dreams of
freedom turn into the nightmare of Negro re(tro)gressionism
that Rayford W. Logan described as the "nadir" of the Negro's status in American society.[9] Reconstruction had ended
without securing either Negro suffrage or equal protection
under the law for black people, as the Fourteenth and Fifteenth Amendments to the Constitution fell victim to a resur-
gence of state's rights, prompted by government officials
like Ben Tillman. Prejudicial educational and property-
ownership requirements, grandfather clauses, and sheer ter-
rorism had by the late 1890s effectively disenfranchised black
people throughout the South. Opportunity for economic development among black people had likewise languished as
large numbers of the recently emancipated became enslaved

to the new institutionalized tyranny of peonage farming, commonly known as sharecropping. Jim Crow segregation laws (fortified by *Plessy v. Ferguson*, 1896) and racial violence closed off practically all avenues of social, economic, educational, and political advancement, making black people's desire to be full-fledged American citizens more than a contest of will. "But poverty," as historian Herbert Gutman explains in *The Black Family in Slavery and Freedom* (1976), "did not entail household disorganization" (p. 432). Gutman cites state and federal census records of 1880, 1900, and 1905 to support his claim, finding that the male-headed household typified those of both ordinary and privileged means among late nineteenth- and early twentieth-century African-Americans (p. 433). Such evidence, however, does not allow us to describe, in vivid detail, what the first free, adult generation of black people, especially those who had secured middle-class status, would have regarded as an ideal home life. And even more important, this evidence does not suggest how black ideologues of that period embraced both the concept and the reality of the black family to keep their dream of freedom alive during those most oppressive times.

In order to reconstruct that generation's idealized domestic ambitions and its frustrated aspiration for racial justice, indeed, to theorize how that generation intertwined as well as bolstered the dual desires for freedom and family security, I suggest that we turn our attention to black post-Reconstruction fiction. Although black writers, as Dickson D. Bruce, Jr., remarks, "were hardly representative of the black population as a whole during this period" (pp. 4–5), and were better educated and possessed greater economic security than the black population at large, they nevertheless voiced their people's collective abhorrence of racial oppression and their desire to live happy and productive lives. Whereas black writers in general appropriated the then-popular forms of the dominant literature to undermine racist attitudes, black women writers like Katherine Tillman also focused on the unique ways in which women could mobilize as wives and mothers to advance the struggle against racism. Tillman's novellas—*Beryl Weston's Ambition: The Story of an Afro-American Girl's Life* and *Clancy Street* (like Harper's *Iola Leroy*, Kelley's *Megda* and *Four Girls at Cottage City*, Johnson's *Clarence and Corinne* and *The Hazeley Family*, and Hopkins's *Contending Forces*)—provide interesting and, I suggest, representative views of nineteenth-century black domestic and racial ideation.

In *Beryl Weston's Ambition*, the heroine, Beryl Weston, is "the eldest child . . . of a successful farmer, who ha[s] a snug bank account and many acres of rich land, which he ha[s] accumulated by sheer force of pluck and thrift since the day of his emancipation" (pp. 212–213). Part of Tillman's mission in such stories was to dramatize black people's appropriation of the American dream of prosperity and their devotion to the ethic of hard work, frugality, and property ownership, projected against what seems like the Washingtonian ideology of self-sufficiency. The story's opening scene describes Beryl as "a very pleasant picture." Cast in a conventional sentimental stance—in mourning—she is "robed in a black gown, that fitted her slender form perfectly, her long, black hair coiled in a classical knot at the back of her head, her great black eyes . . . were somewhat red, and her pale face swollen from weeping" (p. 209). Beryl's dilemma does not arise from the typical financial hardship that routinely set nineteenth-century women's sentimental fiction in motion

(Bayn, pp. 11–21), but rather from her mother's dying request that she leave college and manage the family household. In Tillman's words,

> Beryl must take her mother's place as far as possible. See that the meals were served promptly; look after the dairy and garden produce; patch, darn, have the entire charge of the children. (p. 226)

Thus Beryl's ambition to be an "instructress in the modern languages and higher mathematics" (p. 217) must be exchanged, at least temporarily, for a modest life of domestic self-sacrifice. By tentatively substituting the Victorian model of feminine selflessness of domestic nurturance for professional esteem, the text not only underscores the importance of self-sacrifice but demonstrates that it is ironically the necessary prerequisite for attaining public esteem.

What separates this heroine from Harper's Iola Leroy or Hopkins's Sappho Clark is Tillman's realistic delineation of the wide range of domestic chores to which Beryl devotes each day. No doubt Harper's Iola Leroy would have also had a series of domestic duties to perform, but Harper chose not to represent them in the text. Instead, she used Iola to express, though abstractly, the moral, social, and educational ambitions of newly freed black people. In contrast to Iola's frequent lofty declamations about loyalty to the race and its willingness to toil for economic prosperity, and her prophecies of a prosperous future, Beryl's manner of expression is rather ordinary. Iola asserts,

> "My heart . . . is full of hope for the future. Pain and suffering are the crucibles out of which come gold more fine than the pavements of heaven, and gems more precious than the foundations of the Holy City." (Harper, p. 256)

Beryl simply says,

"I like churchwork. I am so glad that there is a prospect of a new church for Westland!" (p. 240)

Not only is Beryl clearly less emphatic, but she also talks a lot less throughout her story than Iola. What occupies Beryl's day is industry—domestic and intellectual:

> She arose at 4 in the morning, exercised for a few moments with a pair of Indian clubs, . . . assisted Binie [a day worker] in preparing an early breakfast for the farm hands, dressed Joey [her brother], read a chapter in her Bible, and did the housework. In addition to all this, she heard the children's lessons from 9 to 10 o'clock in the morning, and recited lessons in geometry and Greek . . . between the hours of 10 and 12. In the afternoons she ironed, sewed or read, as the occasion demanded. At night she read aloud from some interesting book, helped Binie with her English studies, and practiced her music. (p. 230)

This "daily routine of labor" (p. 230) outlines both Tillman's contention of what was appropriate education for black women and her refusal to polarize two distinct theories about Negro education. Like Pauline Hopkins, who in *Contending Forces* linked Booker T. Washington's industrial education to W. E. B. Du Bois' academic education by making their respective fictive proponents inlaws, Tillman characterized Beryl's education as a combination of industrial training and academic scholarship, and set both within a Christian framework.

Through Beryl, Tillman characterized domesticity as a practical application of industry and intellect. Indeed, Beryl is the very product of the educational program for black women that Iola Leroy referenced with exuberance and by the title "Education of Mothers" (Harper, p. 253) alone. Beryl's life personifies Iola's call "to higher service and nobler life"

(Harper, p. 257). As Tillman explains, Beryl "is bound up
in her books, children and church," and the influence that
she exerts on the young women in her community is indica-
tive of the "important part [that she is to play] in the work
of uplifting the race" (p. 238). Such references elevate domestic management to the rank of a scholarly discipline, underscore a direct relationship between the presence of an exemplary role model and the reproduction of that model's
behavior throughout her community, and qualify black women
as especially well suited for the activity of racial reform. But
what is unique about Tillman's revision of the black woman's
idealized ambition is that its fulfillment ultimately does not
exclude professional accomplishment. Beryl does in fact become an "instructress" at the story's close. Rather than merely
duplicate Iola's role of "quietly [taking] her place in the
Sunday-school as a teacher, and in the church as a helper"
(Harper, p. 278), Beryl achieves her original ambition,
thereby emphasizing an extension of the female sphere beyond the home to embrace opportunities routinely associated
with upper-class black men. She crosses the boundary between fiction and life as well by providing black women readers
of Tillman's epoch with an exemplary, prefeminist heroine
to imitate.

Thus, unlike the so-called "new woman" [10] of the turn of
the century, the new black heroine, embodied in characters
like Beryl Weston, did not reject domesticity for a life that
exceeded traditional Victorian sex roles. To the contrary, this
new heroine used her domestic role to achieve that life. Her
ideal state was to be married to an admirable, ambitious, and
sympathetic man. Together they empowered their children to
move closer to realizing social equality than their parents had.
Unlike the new woman who explicitly argued for sexual
equality, the new black heroine mediated Christian piety and

the Victorian social conventions that qualified marriage, re-
defining it as a mutually compassionate institution that fostered greater opportunity for equality of authority between
husbands and wives. By the end of the story, after Beryl
marries Norman Warren, she is defined not solely as her
husband's helpmate but as a leader in her own right: "Dr.
Warren and his wife are everywhere recognized as leaders in
every movement for the advancement of their own oppressed
race." Not only has Beryl become a "teacher of the modern
languages," but she also has two children who "have come to
bless [her] married life" (p. 246). Her multiple roles—professional woman, social activist, loving wife, and nurturing
mother—correspond not to the prescribed lifestyle of a late
Victorian woman (and certainly not of even an elite black
woman of that epoch) but to that of a late twentieth-century
working professional woman, wife, and mother who has had
the benefit of education, economic privilege, social groom-
ing, and a compassionate husband.

The novella's self-assured closure—"and knowing that Beryl
is useful, honored and happy, let us leave her, for her highest ambition now is to serve the Lord" (p. 246)—serves to
reinforce the reader's awareness that the fullness of Beryl's
life is her highest, sacred ambition and not an issue or social
contention. To emphasize this point further, I suggest that
the text subtly and effectively censures a turn-of-the-century
requirement of the Board of Education for virtually all school
districts, mandating that "no married woman—black or
white—could continue to teach."[11] The novella simply disregards that regulation and makes Beryl's full service to the
Lord include an outlawed occupation for a married woman.
Moreover, Beryl is not an ordinary schoolteacher; she is a
college "instructress." *Beryl Weston's Ambition,* then, drama-
tizes the expansion of a woman's sphere to the limit of her

own competency, in this case male professionalism, and does not constrict her life within Victorian prescriptives.

What distinguishes Tillman's *Clancy Street,* published several years later in 1898–1899, from *Beryl Weston's Ambition* is its sweeping local color, its analysis of urban, intraracial, and multiethnic social settings, as well as its focus on dramatizing the economic consequences of emergent capitalism on an ordinary, working-class black family. Influenced by the advent of realism in the works of writers like Samuel Clemens, Sarah Orne Jewett, Bret Harte, and George Washington Cable, Tillman (like her black female contemporaries, Victoria Earle Matthews and Octavia Albert) [12] placed the heroine of her novella—Caroline Waters—in a more realistic setting.

Named for the street on which this family resides, *Clancy Street* is a serialized, conduct novella set in a poor section of Louisville, Kentucky. A variety of black residents whose speech, appearance, and daily activities resonate with concrete ethnographic details characterize the local black, working poor, as the beginning of Chapter 2 illustrates:

> Clancy street was narrow and ill paved, but fairly clean and fairly filled with rickety tenements and mouldy cottages for which the white agents demanded the most exorbitant rents, which rents, I regret to chronicle, for this very reason in many instances went unpaid. . . .
> The inhabitants of Clancy street were mainly tobacco "hands," in a large red brick factory near by, where the plant was dried, stemmed and packed for shipping. . . . High up in the first block and farthest removed from the smoke and smell of the factory, in the most inviting of the cottages, a tiny frame building fairly covered with morning-glory vines now all abloom, lived [the Waters family]. (p. 254)

Through the hope and despair of her characters, Tillman explained what she contended were cultural reasons for their vices—stealing, infidelity, drinking, and wastefulness—thus distinguishing criminal behavior from intemperance and capriciousness. Concerning stealing, for example, she wrote,

> For two hundred and fifty years . . . [ex-slaves] had been deprived of the fruits of their toilsome labor. . . . A proverb was current among them, that a man who had belonged to a white man, could steal anything from white people—he only took what rightfully belonged to him. From this you will readily see that their ideas concerning the tenth commandment were badly warped. (p. 252)

Tillman insisted that these and other vices were "bad feature[s] of slavery's training period" (p. 252).[13] Although interracial confrontation does not come into view of Tillman's selective focus, the characters are well aware that interracial hostility is a routine occurrence and that, to evoke her own words, " 'Down South' was a very undesirable place for Negro men in those days" (p. 268).

Intertwined with discussions about Negro superstitions— "cungerin', fixin', trickin', poisonin' and hoodooin' "—and with the then-popular ethnic remarks about European immigrants, like "if that don't beat the Jews" (p. 260), is the story of Caroline Waters, a virtuous Negro girl. But unlike the idealized heroines of black sentimental fiction, Caroline is representative of the masses of black urban youth; she does not transcend but is subject to the real consequences of urban poverty: inadequate education, employment discrimination, ravaging epidemics, and urban vices. We can taste and smell the varying quality of her life by observing a meal at the Waters's "pine table scrubbed to almost immaculate whiteness," where the family eats either a "choice bit of boiled shoulder, yellow corn-cakes, tea and a pitcher of Orleans molasses" (p. 256) in good times or "army coffee [brown meal and water]. . . . corn cakes and boiled potatoes" in

bad times (p. 265). Unlike Beryl Weston, Caroline is not
nestled in a snug farm house but lives in a small, rented
tenement. In addition, she does not expect to complete high
school, let alone college. Caroline's ordinariness and vulnerability are further emphasized when her mother explicitly
initiates her in "the facts of life" of many a poor girl: "You're
only a colored girl, Ca'line, and poor; but I'd rather see you
going barefooted in your little sunbonnet and calico slip, and
know you're all right, than to see you in silks and satins and
know you didn't come by them honest" (p. 273). The dic-
tates of nineteenth-century polite society, of which we are
well aware, forbade respectable women to mention the word
prostitution, despite the fact that it was virtually impossible to
be ignorant of its practice in urban centers. However, Tillman's social commentary transcends this genteel prescriptive,
though she addressed the urban blight of prostitution by referring to it obliquely with the well-known, coded, polar
opposite—"an honest woman"—in which case honesty means
preserving not truth but sexual purity.

Tillman departed from the simple conduct code of repeatedly depicting virtue as a means of enhancing its reproduction in society, a code largely endorsed by mid-nineteenth-
century moral reformers like Lydia Maria Child.[14] Instead,
Tillman seems to have used *Clancy Street* as a medium for
explicitly addressing the sexual vulnerability of poor "colored
girls." This intention is reinforced when the novella drama-
tizes an alternative consequence to a life of prostitution by
referring to Caroline's best friend, Hettie, who initially suc-
cumbs to its financial lure. Again, the word *prostitution* is not
mentioned; the text employs another familiar code—a "life
of sin" (p. 282)—that not only provides a religious context
for prostitution but more importantly suggests the possibility
of redemption. Although the Bible acknowledges that prom-

ise for the fallen woman, late nineteenth-century social conventions did not readily sanction this viewpoint. Female sexual inconstancy, insofar as Victorian society was concerned, was irreparable. *Clancy Street,* however, is subject to a black woman-centered morality. As a result, the ultimate sincerity of Hettie's character erases the sin of her former life and transforms her into "a worthy woman" (p. 287). As in Pauline Hopkins's *Contending Forces,* the moral framework of *Clancy Street* mitigates the potency of the father's law for premarital virginity by insisting that reformation of a woman's moral character is finally more important than prior unsanctioned sexual experience. A virtuous character, then, is the only prerequisite for spiritual redemption for men and women alike in a female-centered fictive frame.

When Tillman shifts her focus to depicting ideal black male characters, she moves the story outside the household setting so as to embrace more completely the institutions of community, church, and school. Such a move demands that these male characters confront what Tillman effaces in her black female-centered stories—white people and their racial discrimination and prejudice. One such story is the sketch "Miles the Conquerer" (1894). It is a somewhat simplistic tale of moral reward, depicting a brief period in the life of an extremely virtuous black youth whose self-sacrifice is the vehicle for reforming a racist schoolmate. Social complexity reappears in Tillman's writing with the short story "The Preacher at Hill Station" (1903) and the plays about social history, *Aunt Betsy's Thanksgiving* (n.d.), *Thirty years of Freedom* (1902), and *Fifty Years of Freedom, or From Cabin to Congress* (1910). Unlike her conduct novellas, which place domestic ideality in the foreground, these latter works are not black female *Bildungsromans;* they do not depict either individuated, exemplary, feminine character development for

African-American women or idealized households. Instead,
these works render the cultural significance of the slave heritage for black people and its consequences on common situ-
ations and events in African-American life. Rather than simply formulate virtuous black models for emulation and
appropriate the ethic of hard work, these works also turn to
black cultural history for inspiration. Although they probably do not appease our demands for artistic sophistication, we
must remember that these are early representations of black
discursive authority. They reflect what Gertrude Mossell called
"the mighty river of our race literature" and her widely shared
belief that "any achievement of man embodied in literary
expression becomes in large degree fixed and settled, and is
a point of departure for new achievements." Unapologetic
about the quality or subject of early literary efforts, Mossell
insisted that

> utterance is now our birthright; we shall from now on, if we
> desire, drink of the deepest draughts of literature. We shall
> walk, gropingly, it is true as little children along this great
> highway of the world's literature, but what inspiration must
> we find! . . . Let us see that we despise nothing—the croon-
> ings of our aged nurses, the weird monotone of the slave
> song, the folk-lore. . . . Let us not undervalue their worth,
> but gather and string them like pearls of great price upon
> the chain of memory. No race today has a greater inspiration
> to noble literary work. ("Life and Literature," p. 325)

Apparently sharing Mossell's literary views, Tillman relied on the language, perspective, and values of the characters in "The Preacher at Hill Station." Rev. Clark is the
preacher; he is a college-educated black Methodist newly
charged to administer to the spiritual and secular needs of a
congregation led by former slaves who are, at the time of the
story, old men and women. Cast against a backdrop of frus-

trated black enfranchisement, Rev. Clark faces a commonplace situation in one arena in which black people could exercise full control—church politics. The story portrays the
anxiety of the older, uneducated members of this rural, religious community over the possibility of their displacement
in matters of church policy. Aunt Jennie is one member who
recants her prejudice against the new minister: "An' ter think
how I worked against dat blessed man 'case ole Lias done
tole me dat our minister was one ob dem edjercated fools,
an' when he come to de chapel we ole folks gwine be put
back in de corner" (p. 288). Under Rev. Clark's leadership,
the church becomes the "recognized center for all good en-
terprises," housing a "six months term of school" and "a
circulating library," promoting "something more than a parrot form of knowledge of the Ten Commandments," and
teaching frugality (p. 295). Significantly, this story characterizes a preacher not as a passive man focused only on the
life hereafter but as a hero for black political rights.

Near the conclusion of the story, Rev. Clark encourages
the men of his congregation to stand up for their rights even
if they must die:

> "Don't leave the polls, if we die, let's die like men. Out
> of one blood hath God created all the nations of the earth. If
> you are fired upon while doing you duty as American citi-
> zens, you must protect yourselves," and placing himself in
> the lead, Clark led the way to the polls and the Negro men
> followed him and cast their votes amid derisive yells and a
> perfect shower of stones. (p. 296)

After leading black voters to and from the polls, Rev. Clark
is injured by a racist assault, and a race riot breaks out. Yet
he is able to convince "the better class of Hill Station's white
citizens, those who had become intimately acquainted with

Clark's work, and knew that he was no politician trying to use his own struggling people as a mere stepping-stone to his ambition" (p. 297) to believe his version of the event.

Through Rev. Clark, Tillman subtly effaces the real political threat of black enfranchisement. Rather than depict voting as active social volition, the text characterizes it as a duty that black people are obliged to honor. Not to do so, then, would mean shirking a trusted responsibility: "Who would not despise any man, black or white, who held this great privilege and would not try to use it?" (p. 297). In other words, the black citizens of Hill Station are not demanding their rights but are merely honoring the laws that white legislators have seen fit to create. As if Tillman could not abide by her own subtlety of circuitous effacement of political power, she compels Rev. Clark to evoke the name of a radical abolitionist to fortify his congregation's resolve as they confront the impending riot: "Friends, John Brown is dead, but his truth is marching on" (p. 297). After this evocation, the story once again resorts to deliberate, political self-effacement as Rev. Clark embraces two symbolic rewards: "He brought two trophies that were worthy of the occasion—Ora, the sweetest bride Hill Station ever saw, and 'Lias [his young assistant], as a new messenger of the gospel" (p. 297). Hence, at the story's closure the text evokes a domesticated sign for political autonomy. The privatized symbol for political hegemony—marriage—moves to the story's forefront as the public symbol—voting—recedes.

While Tillman's fiction and drama address black people's ambitions in the external world, her poetry both celebrates Christian piety as the source of her people's abiding strength and affirms African-American identity by critiquing ambivalent racial attitudes. Her verse often follows the two basic traditions in early black poetry that literary scholar Joan R. Sherman has identified as integrationist or dialect (p. xxix). Integrationist poetry, Sherman explains, arises from an inability to fight racism directly; thus

> black poets sought to "whitewash" their art while educating and uplifting their people. Their integrationist poetry also justifies the race to white society by propagandizing for America's cherished habits of hard work, self-reliance, and Christian idealism. Black poets emulate the white literary establishment's inspirational, romantic, and sentimental poetry on orthodox subjects: love, nature, death, religion, and family, couched in conventional forms and language. (p. xxix)

Dialect poetry, Sherman further explains, depicts blacks as harmless, happy "darkies" as "a defensive response to the images of blacks as demonic, murderous savages" (p. xxx) found in white popular culture of the period.

Tillman's early career as a writer began with her submission of individual poems to the *Christian Recorder* and *Indianapolis Freeman*. As we would expect, those poems that are extant are devoted to spiritual and inspirational subjects, adhering to the conventions that Sherman outlines above. Titles like "Lift Me Higher Master," "Allen's Army," "A Psalm of the Soul," "The Highest Life," and "A Rest Beyond" (the latter of which appeared in Mossell's *Work of the Afro-American Woman*) are representative. In addition, the *Christian Recorder* published her tribute poems to exemplary individuals. For example, in "My Queen," Tillman expounded on the virtues of Miss A. H. Jones, the "lady Principal of Wilberforce University" (and probably the Anna H. Jones who was the other black woman with Anna Cooper at the 1900 Pan-African Conference). Tillman also celebrated Wells-Barnett in "Lines to Ida B. Wells" and presumably

her own husband in "The Pastor." She wrote general tribute
poetry as well, like "Afro-American Boy," "A Tribute to
Negro Regiments," and "The Superannuate."

Variants of several of the *Christian Recorder* poems appear
in Tillman's 1902 collection *Recitations,* but this latter work
has a different tenor. Traditional integrationist poetry does
not dominate it; instead, it resounds with themes of racial
affirmation and protest. Interestingly enough, the dialect verse
in *Recitations* portrays complaining "darkies" rather than happy
ones. Many poems depict subjects of racial oppression and
directly challenge both black and white people to abide by
moral consciousness instead of by racist practices. Several poems
deal with the conventional subjects found in integrationist
poetry; however, they are usually set in explicitly black cultural contexts and evolve largely as narratives in variations of
the ballad stanza. In addition, the poems seldom employ the
elevated diction, classical or romantic imagery, or erudition
of integrationist verse, but use the spoken idiom of black
people—the working poor and the middle class—and address
ordinary issues of their daily concern. Thus many of the racial poems are predictable. "That Ye Be One" is a visionary,
religious poem about the brotherhood of all men. "Our Cause"
praises white abolitionists for condemning slavery, but censures the absence of post-Reconstruction white advocates for
racial justice. This poem concludes by demanding that African
Americans be their own heroes and fight for their constitutional rights:

> Brave Sumner! Whittier! are ye gone!
> Thou hast no like to call upon.
> Garrison! Lincoln! We call in vain,
>
> We shall not see thy like again.
> Then be the Black his own defense,

And though his struggles be intense,
Fight hard, fight e'er for every right
That's granted by our Charter's might!

"Uncle Ned's Story" is a dialect poem about a stock subject—the devotion of Ned's slave wife to her aged white mistress. "Sen' Me Back to de Souf" is another dialect poem about an old black man who implores his daughter to return him to his Southern home. Although he realizes that the North is ostensibly less oppressive to black people, he is aware of its subtle racism:

I kno's dat our fo'ks am wronged in de Souf,
But den de Norf hab a spite at dem too,
An I'se too ole to be changin' my views,
I laks ole ways better'n new.

"The Black Boys in Blue" recalls the bravery of black soldiers who fought for their country throughout American history and instructs the country to extend what should be its unwaning respect to them as heroes. And "A Hymn of Praise" expresses gratitude to God "For all the great prosperity/Enjoyed by our race to-day."

Others poems are not so predictable; indeed, their originality alone merits inclusion in anthologies of early African-American poetry. "A Southern Incident" is a dramatic poem in which a Southern lady is redefined as one who has the moral courage to act consistently with compassion. By giving up her car seat to an old black woman, the lady chooses to act according to her own convictions rather than to codes of decorum that conceal troublesome issues behind a superficial facade of pious gentility. The old woman's expressed gratitude calls into question the conventional usage of the term "Southern lady" and the customary virtues associated with one:

"Well, you is a rale lady,"
She sighed from her pleasant retreat.

"De Lawd bless you fo' yo' kindness;
You has he'p me mo' dan you kno',
But folks can see you's a lady
Dat nebber hab seen you befo'.' "

In this poem a real lady is not qualified by family status or codes of feminine propriety; a real lady is conditioned by the integrity to act morally and compassionately.

"When Mandy Combs Her Head" is the most startling poem in the collection. Particularly interesting are its indeterminacy of speaker and complex attitude about Negroid characteristics.

If there's one thing more than t'other
'Bout which something might be said,
And a subject that's important,
It's a colored person's head.

My Mandy's been to high school,
And she's got her books down fine;
She can figure like a lawyer,
And read Latin, line for line.

But there's one thing that tries her spirit,
And an hour when tears are shed,
Oh, I hear the storm approaching
When my Mandy combs her head.

She starts at it Sunday morning,
Soon as ever she's done her work.
And begins to comb and pull
And to fume and sigh and jerk.

"'Taint no use to try to fix it.
Lord, I wish that I was dead!
Here I've worked hard for an hour
Trying to do something with my head."

Or it may be that at bedtime,
Just before her prayers are said,
Mandy gets the comb an' starts up
Working on her tired head.

How she'll fuss an' pull an' jerk it,
Working on that stubborn fleece,
'Till I hear her mother say,
"Mandy, stop an' get the grease!"

Like the oil upon the waters,
Things get better for a while.
The big comb it quits its jerking,
An' then Mandy tries to smile.

"Lord, I wish I'd been around here
When the Lord was giving hair;
While the white folks was a-getting,
I'd been sure to get my share."

Pap, if Gabriel blows for Judgement,
An' my name you don't hear read,
Don't you'n mammy get exited,
I'll be fixing of my head!

"When Mandy Combs Her Head" is a poem of ironic ado-
ration in which Tillman has the black male speaker appropriate the act of hair combing, a Victorian ritual celebrating
white feminine beauty, and apply it to a black woman. Nappy
hair has traditionally been a taboo subject among black people, and making it the ostensible topic of a poem foreshadows
Nappy Edges (1978) by Ntozake Shange, though Shange's
persona, unlike Tillman's, is clearly more assertive of a non-
European standard of feminine beauty and independent of
the racist color symbolism inherent in Western Christianity.

At first glance, the speaker appears to be Mandy's father;
however, the absence of quotation marks around the last stanza
indicates that the speaker is actually addressing his own father

and is a peer of Mandy's. This suggests the traditional persona of the ritualized lover: The speaker is Mandy's lover/admirer, and he too is literally entangled in problematic hair. Given their shared condition, the poem implies that, like Mandy, the speaker too will be late for Judgment.

The poem also includes an intertextual allusion to "When Malindy Sings" from Paul Laurence Dunbar's *Lyrics of Lowly Life*. Published in 1896, this work yielded Dunbar a national literary reputation and, along with other collections of dialect poetry, became very well known among black people, many of whom grew up reciting particular poems. In fact, in her essay "Afro-American Poets and Their Verse," Tillman writes about finding a copy of *Lyrics of Lowly Life* in the public library of Keokuk, Iowa (p. 98). In "When Mandy Combs Her Head," she invokes similarities with both the title and the title character of Dunbar's poem and juxtaposes Mandy's "stubborn fleece" with Malindy's stupendous voice. In so doing, she sets up a complex intertextual and parodic frame for examining both Mandy's desire to have straight hair and, I suggest, the persona's circuitous and sympathetic criticism of that desire. Although some of Tillman's readers may not have approved of the poem's subject, she could risk giving nappy hair poetic attention because she and her audience probably shared a basic ambivalence about the aesthetic value of light skin color and straight hair in the black community. Thus she could censure their and her own ambivalence by elevating nappy hair to a poetic subject. Moreover, she could risk underscoring satiric commentary by juxtaposing hair texture with Christian salvation precisely because she and her readers shared common religious beliefs about Judgment Day.

Moral and spiritual piety, mental and physical good deeds qualify the lives of Mandy and the persona, earning them the right to have their names inscribed in the book of salvation. However, the last stanza implies that they both will miss reading their names at the divinely designated time because they take excessive time to smooth down their hair. The reference to Judgment demands that the reader evaluate the attributes of Mandy's (and her admirer's) character. When compared to her intellectual talent, scholastic attainment, and finally her spiritual piety, Mandy's desire for straight hair becomes so insignificant as to be absurd. The poem therefore becomes a celebration of the unimportance of hair texture, a celebration that ultimately questions the applicability of Western aesthetic standards to black people.

When this poem is compared to "Bashy," Tillman's condemnation of black society for self-abnegation becomes even sharper. The object of the latter poem is Bashy, a dark-skinned black girl who finds out the hard way that her beloved "Thought her too black to make a wife,/ So she drifted on to a dreadful life." She is condemned not only by intraracial color prejudice but also by a Western cultural framework that ascribes valuelessness (and by implication immorality) to anyone, anything dark. It is precisely the pervasive, racist iconography of color, inherent in Christianity's depiction of sin, that helps to trap pious black people in a dilemma, undermining their efforts to assert racial pride. Thus by means of a rhetorical question the poems implores black people to rise above racial disaffirmation:

> Oh, women and men of the Negro Race,
> Can we not rise above color of face?
> Teach our girls that the worst disgrace
> Is blackness of life, not blackness of face!

The concluding imperative ironically encodes Bashy's inability to transcend the insidiously demeaning power of the language she uses and the religion she professes.

"She Who Never Had a Chance" is a prefeminist protest poem that aligns poverty with prostitution. Two lines poignantly intertwine the moral and social burden of crime in general and prostitution in particular through the specifically graphic image of female subordination:

> Rich women may leave wine rooms in fine homes to dwell,
> But poor girls leave them on journeys to hell.
> That's where I went, and these scars on my face
> And my red, swollen eyes tell my frequent disgrace.
> *It seems that I have been through the whole catalogue of crime,*
> *Under each new lover I have served out my time.* (Emphasis
>   mine)

Like all of Tillman's works, *Recitations* seeks a black readership for the purpose of enhancing its racial pride and desire for racial progress through collective self-criticism.

By the time that Tillman's early plays—*Aunt Betsy's Thanksgiving, Heirs of Slavery,* and *Thirty Years of Freedom*—were published, Negro minstrel shows, that is, white men with blackened faces acting out nostalgic darky antics about plantation life, had already evolved into full-scale variety shows. Minstrel shows had been successful from the 1820s through the early post-Reconstruction period, codifying darky roles to the extent that they are still so familiar as not to require cataloguing here. With emancipation, black people usurped these roles, claiming that they were " 'natural' and 'spontaneous' representatives of plantation Negroes" (Toll, p. 202). Unfortunately, their contention of authenticity locked them even more rigidly into the stereotyped roles of plantation darkies, despite the evolution of minstrel parody in the subdominant culture. Both types of "authentic darky" minstrel shows were very popular throughout the Northeast, Midwest, and South. However, many black people, particularly members of the bourgeoisie, "complained that when black minstrels presented these caricatured images, they legitimized white stereotypes" (Toll, p. 256). Black minstrelsy's double cutting edge of parody notwithstanding, the minstrel stage seldom fostered black people's willingness to work hard, save money, acquire property, and live the moral life. Instead, it took religious and normal school drama to disseminate the work ethic throughout the general black population and to affirm that ethic as a means of achieving prosperity.

The virtues of the Protestant work ethic and·racial pride are precisely what Tillman's plays affirm, but they place that affirmation in the context of Northern employment discrimination and Southern racial antagonism that arose from growing economic competition between black and white laborers and businesses. This competitive atmosphere requires some background information for explaining the economic basis underlying racial strife.

Despite the fact that most black people in the South were very poor, their large numbers alone made them an integral economic factor. They supplied the labor for producing cash crops, and their purchasing power created a significant demand in consumer industries. When large numbers of black people left sharecropping for the North or when they boycotted white business establishments, white communities recognized the seriousness of those actions and retaliated with outrageous sexual allegations. As Ida B. Wells-Barnett repeatedly insisted, Southern black people were lynched for contesting economic, not sexual, hegemony. In the North, hard-working and frugal black people were rewarded both with employment discrimination that mocked their struggle to obtain education and with housing segregation that extorted their hard-earned savings. Hence, the South used lynching to oppress upwardly mobile black people, and the North used starvation.

These economic realities comprise the social backdrop for Tillman's plays, which examine ordinary black people's efforts to improve their lives. Of the three extant—excluding the pageants, *Heirs of Slavery* and *The Spirit of Allen*—one play is set in the South, and two are set largely in the North. Like George Bernard Shaw, who used his plays to highlight the social hypocrisies of turn-off-the-century England,[15] Tillman exhorted virtue in her black characters while confronting her white characters with their duplicity. Filled with bits of black folklore, dialect, and song; series of contrived entrances and departures to move the action forward; and allusions to a wide assortment of late nineteenth- and early twentieth-century social issues, Tillman's three dialogic plays literally talk the black characters out of frustration and into hopefulness.

Set in the South, *Aunt Betsy's Thanksgiving* depicts Aunt Betsy and her young granddaughter, Ca'line, living in respectable poverty until Nellie (Aunt Betsy's daughter and Ca'line's mother), who was presumed dead, returns with her new husband and makes a comfortable home for them all. The happy ending does not conceal instances of subtle racism. For example, in an exuberant moment Ca'line exclaims to her grandmother, "You is as good as dey [white folks] is. All of us is if we behave ourselves! Teacher said so" (p. 307). Aunt Betsy responds pragmatically, "Dat teacher better be careful what he says 'bout white folks. Never mind whether we's as good as dey is or not. Git all de learning an' de sense dat you kin git, an' you'll be all right" (p. 307). This scene reveals that, like the proponents of Washingtonian intraracial politics, Aunt Betsy has learned to avoid inciting racial hostility by remaining reticent on the issue of racial equality.

The moral of the scene is further reinforced when Ca'line's new stepfather explains that the old woman will suffer her neighbors' jealousy when they see her new cottage: "Our white friends did not object to Aunt Betsy's cabin, but many of them will object to Aunt Betsy's cottage furnished, as it will be, with all modern improvements" (p. 308). As long as Aunt Betsy lives in poorer circumstances than the local white people and behaves as if she were inferior, they treat her hospitably. However, when she and her family work hard to advance themselves, their "white friends" seem unable to accept the change in circumstances.

Set in both the South and the North, *Thirty Years of Freedom* gives us Aunt Savannah, an old black woman much like Aunt Betsy. Her realistic recollection of the plight of slaves contradicts the nostalgic, paternalistic settings of the then-popular novels of the Plantation School. As Aunt Savannah recalls:

> Oh, how many nites has I laid 'wake an' wept case day done sole my baby gal away. Po' cullud folks, dey's had a hard time! All dese years dey's been forced to toil fo' dere masters in de cane-breakers, in de c'on fields an' on de cotton plantashun, an' what hab been dere reward? Sometimes dey's bin treated lik' human' an' sometimes lik' brutes! (p. 315)

After this brief characterization of slavery, the remainder of the play concentrates on affirming hard work, frugality, and Christian piety as the means of achieving black family cohension and resulting prosperity. Aunt Savannah gives explicit expression to each virtue. First, she recalls how she has worked hard and saved her money in order to support her family: "I's sabed up de money dat I urned nussin' since de war fo' dis berry hour. I bo't dis cabin home, thinkin' ef eber I foun' my chile, she'd had a home." Second, she practices strict sexual propriety: "I 'lowed no man to look at me sence Gawge Wash'nton Linkum Peabody died. . . ." And third, she has discarded primitive superstitions: "I dun tole yo' dat I don' b'liebe in dat Voodoo no mo' " (p. 317).

Aunt Savannah is also Tillman's vehicle for exposing Northern racial prejudice and discrimination. Before moving to the North to live with her daughter, Aunt Savannah characterizes it as a veritable promised land for black people:

> Dat may hab bin de case in de pas', but my darter am a dress-maker, en bof ob my gran'chillen dun bin graduated 'long side ob de riches' white chillen in de Norf . . . my niece, Cinthy Ann Jones, dat went Norf wid de white fo'ks, tells me dat de cullud people puts on lots ob style. . . . Yes, en my darter Ella says dat sum ob de cullud fo'ks has 'vanced so far dat dey hires white hep to do de work. Ain't dat scrumptous? (p. 320)

Her glorified description of the North is countered by a young black man who insists that, despite its hostility, the South holds real possibility for racial progress:

> Tell your friends in the North that as they boast of their greater freedom and larger opportunities, we of the South-land expect to hear of greater advancement than we are able to make. Tell them we are planting churches and school houses on every hilltop, and that we are filling the valleys with banks, groceries and other places of business. In spite of our ostracism, we are gaining ground and look forward to a bright future. (p. 322)

After Aunt Savannah moves, she confronts the two dominant signs of Northern racism: segregated housing and job discrimination. Just before she arrives to live in her daughter's cramped, overpriced tenement, her grandchildren and their friends tell a series of stories about employment discrimination that resound with one message: "Over the doorway of every honorable profession [the white man] has written in letters of fire 'No Negroes Need Apply' " (p. 324). For example, a young black woman renders the following racist scenario:

> When I graduated from the High School I tried to get a school, just as my white classmates did, but the authorities informed that if I wanted to teach school I would have to go South; then I applied for a clerkship, but the proprietors said that all the girls would leave if the firm employed a colored girl, so I gave up the struggle and concluded to enjoy life as best I could in the depths of which my color had consigned me. (p. 325)

Another young black woman adds,

> When I finished school, several of my girl friends entered the business college and learned to be bookkeepers and stenographers; well, I saved up and took both courses, but just as Winona says, I found no one brave enough to employ a colored girl. Some have given me job work, but no one would take me into an office on account of this hateful American prejudice. . . . (p. 325)

The play reaches its climax when Aunt Savannah translates a great debt owed to her into an opportunity for her grandson to practice law. Despite this small gain, most of the play argues the advantages that the South offers to industrious black people, complete with closing remarks that endorse Washingtonian self-sufficiency and reticence on racial and political equality:

> Grandmother, you. . . . have made the best possible use of your Thirty Years of Freedom. May we profit by your example and prove alike to enemies and friends that we are as worthy of freedom as any race of people on God's green globe,

and that, though surrounded by ostracism, we will continue
to educate, to accumulate wealth, to cultivate the principles
of morality and to worship the God who has delivered us
from bondage. . . . (pp. 339–340)

Like *Thirty Years of Freedom*, Tillman's next play, *Fifty
Years of Freedom*, also emphasizes hard work and tenacious
resolve as strategies for acquiring prosperity, despite racist
obstacles. This later dramatic narrative appropriates many stock
incidents of the slave narrative to depict the rise of a poor
orphaned black boy—Benjamin Banneker Houston—from a
lowly field hand to a celebrated lawyer and congressman. At
the beginning of the play, Ben decides to run away to the
North to escape a cruel white boss and to emulate a young
black man who "went from the South and worked his way
through one of the biggest white colleges" (p. 345). This is
the first of several decisions made by black people that assert
their right to direct the course of their own lives. On one
occasion, Ben's Aunt Rhoda explains to him that "you don't
have to stay no where you don't want to unless you're bound
out by the law. We're free now, thank God" (p. 346). On
another occasion, Aunt Rhoda's husband asks, "What dey
gwine ask de white fo'ks fo'? Ain't we cullud fo'ks free? Is
de 'Mancipation Proclamation passed in Congress or not? Ain't
we free same as de white fo'ks?" (p. 349). Indeed, confirm-
ing the fact of emancipation, of freedom of choice and movement, is the very issue that *Fifty Years of Freedom* addresses.
Early on, Aunt Rhoda exhorts: "Me and m'os' all my fo'ks
used to belong to the Whites, and I was the chillen's nurse
after mammy died and I never could make up my min' to
leave the old place" (p. 350). It takes Ben, the agent of a
confirmed emancipation, to use his freedom, courageously and
thereby to realize his personal ambitions. Untimately, his
actions enable Aunt Rhoda to sever her ties with a past life

of slavery and to relocate in the North where she and her children lead prosperous lives.

In addition, the play affirms that the desire for higher education is an appropriate ambition for black men to have and interrogates conventional beliefs about limiting education for women. Early in the play, when Ben first tells Lindy (his future wife) that he's "going to the North and find the college that colored lawyer graduated from," he implores her to "stay here with Aunt Rhoda and learn all you can. . . . Girls don't have to know as much as boys and when I get through school I'll come back and take you away with me" (p. 353). Lindy does not follow his instruction. During the six years of his absence, she educates herself in order to be "a fit companion for him" (p. 381). Deliberately silent about the amount or quality of her education, the text is nevertheless emphatic in its insistence that black women require more than elementary schooling.

The play further affirms a woman's exercise of independent will through the character of Miss Lou White, the daughter of Colonel White, Aunt Rhoda's employer. Whereas Colonel White believes that "Negroes don't need any school, they're not worth the powder and lead it would take to blow them up with" (p. 355), Miss Lou believes "that education is good for everybody" (p. 356). Throughout the play she disregards social conventions sanctioning deference to males and argues for social equality for black people. Her father tolerates her behavior by blaming her education for what he terms "strange notions about Negroes and the way they should be treated" (p. 365). Hence, the play attributes to education the growth of independent thought and liberal racial attitudes, and the courage to exhibit both. Given Miss Lou's influence on her father, the play also demonstrates the direct relationship between a liberal education and social progress.

Miss Lou not only has independent views on racial issues,
but she also refuses to respect her father's choice of a suitor
for her. Telling her betrothed that she has "a mind and will
of [her] own" (p. 365), Miss Lou cancels the engagement.
Thus she characterizes the increased female autonomy of the
"new woman"; she governs her own personal life and pre-
sumes the authority to express her own ideas and enact her
own decisions. The play endorses her independence from male
domination by granting her an inheritance from her liberally
minded British relations and by allowing her to select her
own spouse, a man who shares her racial views.

This play, like its predecessors—*Thirty Years of Freedom*
and Tillman's domestic fiction—asserts an independent will,
education, and virtuous character as the proper prerequisites
for a wife and mother, black and white. Whereas *Thirty Years
of Freedom* ends by focusing on the idealized black family,
Fifty Years of Freedom extends the story beyond the traditional closure for sentimental texts. In the latter drama two
marriages occur near the end, but neither is depicted on stage:
Lindy marries Ben, and Miss Lou marries Arthur Norton.
Nor are honeymoons and early years of marriage present in
the dramatic action. Unlike Tillman's "Preacher at Hill Station," which literally weds the marriage and racial-political
discourses at the story's closure, the ending of *Fifty Years of
Freedom* underscores its own overt political focus by subor-
dinating the fact of Ben's marriage, as his tenth wedding
anniversary becomes the occasion for celebrating the fulfillment of his earlier promise:

> Friends, some seventeen years ago, when our distinguished
> orator and fellow townsman arrived at Bayview, fresh from
> a Kentucky cabin I had to plead to get him admitted to our
> University. Step by step he has made his way, until he is
> acknowledged to be one of the most polished orators of the

day. Not only does he excel in oratory, but his services in municipal and state affairs have proven him to be a man of deeds as well. He has thrown himself into every work of reform and shown himself a leader of men, it is therefore a very great pleasure to me to say to you that Mr. Benjamin Banneker Houston will represent us in Congress. (p. 387)

The careful reporting of the internal history of the drama invites us to place Ben's election in an external historical context. The play informs us that Ben "has crowded eight years' work into his six years' chance" (p. 384) and that professor, Arthur Norton, has known Ben for seventeen years. When we recall *Thirty Years of Freedom,* published in 1902, we find a logical correspondence between the thirty years that are reconstructed in that drama and the thirty-seven-year period bound by the ratification of the Thirteenth Amendment. However, *Fifty Years of Freedom* suggests illogical or non-sequential historical alignment. The play's copyright date of 1910 precedes the fiftieth anniversary of freedom, whether dated from the Emancipation Proclamation of January 1, 1863, or from the ratification of the Thirteenth Amendment of December 18, 1865. Either way, the play's time frame is too short: three to five years, respectively.

Given this temporal disruption, I suggest that the play closes by looking backward to the future. It re-envisions the future election of black legislators like those who served during the Reconstruction era and places that event both within the play's textual, temporal boundaries and into indefinite (though not too distant) external history. Hence, the drama conflates past and future black political activity into a temporally indefinite heroic event to which Ben's closing remarks refer:

I would say to the young men of my race that there is hope for them. No matter how discouraging things may look at

times, honesty of purpose and hard work will win out. The
Providence which takes me from the cabin to Congress will
smile on all who put their trust in God and do the Right.
(p. 388)

Ben's remarks extend beyond the dramatic frame of the play
and petition black people to emulate his resolve with the as-
surance that they too will realize the just rewards of their
emancipation.

Aunt Betsy's Thanksgiving, Thirty Years of Freedom, and
Fifty Years of Freedom reflect the harsh reality of segregation
at the turn of the century, a time when the promises of Reconstruction proved false. More important, Tillman wrote
these plays specifically for normal and Sunday school perfor-
mance; thus they disseminated among black people pragmatic
tactics for holding fast to their deferred dream of freedom.

Tillman's last known dramatic work is *The Spirit of Allen:
A Pageant of African Methodism* (1922). As its title suggests,
it is a celebrative work, commemorating African-American
spiritual and secular history. The pageant begins as a classi-
cally robed Mistress of Pageant directs a long line of characters clad in stylized classical, Renaissance, plantation, and
current street dress across the stage of history. The first part
of the pageant is set against slavery and depicts both the
founding in 1794 of the African Methodist Episcopal Church
in Philadelphia and the installation in 1816 of Richard Allen
as its first bishop. The Civil War and Emancipation Proclamation are curiously absent from the pageant, as the symbol-
ically reconstructed history moves forward to 1922 to highlight the church's foreign missionary and national activities.
For scholars of literary history, Scene 12 of the play—"At
the Court of Literature, 1922"—is particularly interesting.
Here the church's publications—*Christian Recorder, Southern
Recorder, Western Recorder, Voice of Missions, A.M.E. Church*

Review, Women's Missionary Recorder, Allenite, and *Allen C. E. Star*—appear as successful plaintiffs "against the A. M. E. Church, for non-support" (p. 409). The pageant resumes its jubilant tone as the triumphant march brings the presentation to a finale: "On a pedestal the spirit of Allen looks down. Music of: 'Onward, Christian Soldier' is heard as procession of all characters in Pageant, except King Cotton passes" (p. 425). Significantly, King Cotton, the Southern monarch of a past economy, does not march into a symbolic future.

Given the rigidity of late nineteenth-century gender coding, we ought not be surprised that marriage is prominent at the conclusions of much of Tillman's fiction and drama. Like other late nineteenth- and early twentieth-century black women writers, she not only appropriated Victorian gender prescriptives and their symbolic configurations, but she also seemed to have consciously represented, in her fictive and dramatic domestic allegories of prosperity for black Americans, her political desire for racial and sexual equality. However, by contemporary literary standards Tillman's domestic fiction and Sunday school drama seem artificial and too devoted to the demands of the happy ending, and we are bored with her heroes and heroines, just as we are bored with those of Harriet Beecher Stowe, Louisa May Alcott, and Susan Warner, to name a few very popular nineteenth-century white American women writers.[16] When we compare Tillman's fiction and drama to nineteenth-century racial protest literature (say, by Charles Chesnutt and Sutton Griggs),[17] or to better known twentieth-century protest literature, we find that complex issues of race (such as alienation, the extensiveness of institutionalized racism, and intraracial discrimination) are either unrealistically depicted or missing altogether. For example,

in *Beryl Weston's Ambition,* the description of Beryl's long
train ride from her Northern college to Tennessee makes no
reference to the legislated and federally sanctioned segregation of railway transportation and public accommodation.
Absent also are probing studies of complex character, anal-
yses of interracial politics, and subtleties of plot. Present,
though, is the sentimental marriage story, which has become
so familiar as to be clichéd with familiar (and sexist) critical
derision. Looking at the novellas, short stories, and dramas
even from Tillman's temporal perspective, we see the tight-
ened focus on family as a somewhat reactionary response to
the increasing pervasiveness of Jim Crow segregation laws.
Because we have inherited the literary values engendered by
social protest writing, we expect the fictive word to fight racial oppression directly like a weapon, to evoke Richard
Wright's famous analogy, and not to circumvent racial hostility altogether. However, Tillman's era was extremely hostile to explicit racial contests. The means that she and many
of her black contemporaries found to fight racism were subtle
by necessity. Rather than attack an unjust social system, from
an extremely disadvantaged position, Tillman's essays, novellas, short stories, and plays endorse personal development
through apparently one-dimensional, transparent, prettified
discourses of untarnished faith in the American dream, while
her poetry relies mostly on Christian piety to sustain a cri-
tique of inter- and intraracial prejudice.

Her novellas, in particular, are fashioned as female narratives of domestic ideality. They outline ideal patterns of
male and female ego formation as well as racial individuation
and socialization through the configuration of a black female
protagonist.[18] That heroine is also the discursive element for
setting the fictive, domestic enterprise into motion. Eventu-
ally, these stories of black female development move toward

fruition as the heroine either selects an admirable mate for forming an exemplary household or dies believing in that idealized objective. The ardor of marriage is represented not as romantic passion but as magnanimous compassion for others and dedication to the advancement of the race. Moreover, by tightly circumscribing these black female *Bildungsromans* within an intraracial (e.g., segregated) domestic context, the novellas also avoid depicting interracial hostility. The principal characters seem liberated from severe racist consensus and are ironically free to define themselves. Their superlative gentility underscores the racist hypocrisy inherent in the white genteel tradition. Yet without the punitive intrusion of white society in their lives, they either rise or fall to the level of their own abilities and are rewarded (or punished) on the basis of their individual worth. Although Caroline Waters and especially Beryl Weston seem ensconced in the narrative artifice of Victorian sentimentality, they—along with the heroes and heroines of Tillman's plays—nevertheless are vehicles for engendering the new ethos of bourgeois individualism among late nineteenth-century African Americans. No longer bound to the laws of genealogy of the plantation aristocracy, the nobility of Tillman's characters defines their lives, qualifies their ambitions, and metes their reward.[19] The social values that guide her novellas also govern her plays.

Tillman appropriated particular genres for exploring different social issues. Her fiction and plays dramatize the formation of a black middle-class cultural ethos. Largely set in an intraracial context and cast within a domestic milieu, these works depict the development of personal identity, racial pride, and ambition as an individuated model for the collective advancement of black people in general. The plays especially present black characters who recall, interpret, and evaluate their own personal histories, marking the transition from an enslaved past to a future of freedom and prosperity. From a late twentieth-century vantage point, these accomplishments seem simple, but for black writers to assume interpretative authority over the cultural representation of slavery and its aftermath during this intensely oppressive period marks considerable political sophistication. Tillman's verse in *Recitations* is predominantly racial in character, authorial tone, and intended audience. It deserves attention precisely because it so clearly falls outside the integrationist tradition that dominated late nineteenth- and early twentieth-century poetry.

At the turn of the century, Tillman's works assisted a new social law, based on virtue and not heredity, to move into the domain of common sense and, thereby, contested prior codes of racial supremacy. Thus the very texts that we have considered to be somewhat lacking in literary and social value were among those responsible for teaching late nineteenth- and early twentieth-century African Americans new truths about their social, moral, and physical perfectability.[20] What is important for us to see is that Tillman's works, like those of her black contemporaries, helped to displace the social system of privilege arising from plantation aristocracy by valorizing individual worth in ways that were independent of race, class, color, and sex.

NOTES

This introduction to Tillman's works is an excursion from my forthcoming book—*Domestic Allegories of Political Desire: Or, The Politics of the Domestic Discourse in Nineteenth-Century African-American Women's Writing*. Both were supported, in part, by the Faculty Research Program in the Social Sciences, Humanities, and Education at Howard University; by the Ford Foundation; by the D.C. Commission on the Arts; and most recently by the George

Washington University. I would like to thank my sister-critics—Vicki Arana, Carolyn Brown, Eve Hawthorne, and Marilyn Mobley—for criticizing my manuscripts with compassionate candor. I also express my appreciation to my research assistants Michael Wahholtz, Hazel Ervin, and Klaus Braun. In addition, I would like to thank Cynthia D. Bond, Director of Research for the Black Periodical Literature Project at Cornell University, for providing me with copies of many of Tillman's poems, stories, and essays. I am also grateful to the staffs of the Moorland-Spingarn Research Center at Howard University; Yale University's Sterling Memorial Library; The New York Public Library; the Boston Public Library; Rembert E. Stokes Learning Resources Center Library of Wilberforce University; the John Hay Library of Brown University; and the Library of Congress for their dedication to the preservation of African-American cultural documents and for their patient assistance in making these documents available to me.

1. See Hazel V. Carby, " 'On the Threshold of Woman's Era' "; and *Reconstructing Womanhood*, pp. 3–19, 95–120.

2. See William E. B. Du Bois, *The Souls of Black Folk*, pp. 207–390, esp. "Of Booker T. Washington and Others," pp. 241–52. Also see Booker T. Washington, *Up from Slavery*, pp. 23–206, esp. the chapter entitled "The Atlanta Exposition Address," pp. 145–57.

3. Black women largely respected the late nineteenth-century gender codes that separated male and female ambition in the work of social uplift. As a result black women formed a number of their own organizations. See Cynthia Neverdon-Morton, *Afro-American Women of the South*, pp. 1–3, for a general discussion of black people's appropriation of Victorian gender codes. Also see Mrs. N[athan]. F. [Gertrude Bustill] Mossell, "The Opposite Point of View," in *The Work of the Afro-American Woman*, pp. 115–25, for Mossell's summary of prevalent gender attitudes among her black contemporaries.

4. For discussion on the presumption of exclusively male membership of the American Negro Academy, see Mary Helen Wash-

ington's *Invented Lives,* pp. xviii, xxix; also see Neverdon-Morton, 1–3. For discussion on Cooper's invited membership in the ANA and her and Anna H. Jones's participation in the 1900 Pan-African Conference, see Louise Hutchinson, *Anna J. Cooper,* pp. 107–10. For Cooper's participation in the Hampton Negro Conference in 1893, see Hutchinson, p. 60.

5. See note 3.

6. See The Schomburg Library of Nineteenth-Century Black Women Writers (New York: Oxford University Press, 1988) for Frances Harper, *Iola Leroy* (1892); Pauline Hopkins, *Contending Forces* (1900); Amelia Johnson, *Clarence and Corinne* (1890) and *The Hazeley Family* (1894); and Emma Dunham Kelley (-Hawkins), *Megda* (1891) and *Four Girls at Cottage City* (1898).

7. See Rayford W. Logan, *The Betrayal of the Negro,* pp. 82–85, for a detailed account of Benjamin Tillman's strategy for black disenfranchisement.

8. See Nancy Armstrong, *Desire and Domestic Fiction,* particularly her introduction, "The Politics of Domesticating Culture, Then and Now."

9. Logan coined this expression for this particular period of African-American history; see his *Betrayal of the Negro,* p. 62.

10. See Anne Firor Scott, "What, Then, Is the American: This New Woman?"; Carroll Smith-Rosenberg, "The New Woman and the New History"; and Peter G. Filene, *Him/Her Self,* pp. 19–43.

11. The quote is from Mary Helen Washington's introduction to Anna Julia Cooper, *A Voice From the South,* p. xxxii. May Miller Sullivan, who graduated from Howard University in 1920, corroborates Washington's statement. According to Miller Sullivan, female instructors were to notify the Board of Education of impending marriage plans. If they did not voluntarily retire from teaching immediately after marriage, they were compelled to do so. (Interview, 29 January 1989, at Miller Sullivan's home in Washington, D.C.) Also see Hutchinson, p. 49, who writes that until 1923 married women were required by law to retire from teaching. As a result a large "spinster" teacher population arose. In 1890–1891,

for example, the District of Columbia employed 265 black teachers, 225 of whom were female.

12. *Aunt Lindy* (1889) by Victoria Earle Matthews and *The House of Bondage* (1890) by Octavia Albert. The latter has been reissued in The Schomburg Library of Nineteenth-Century Black Women Writers (New York: Oxford University Press, 1988).

13. The phrase "slavery's training period" is particularly reminiscent of "the school of American slavery," in Booker T. Washington's *Up from Slavery*, p. 37.

14. See Lydia Maria Child, *The Mother's Book*, pp. 86–168; and *The Freedman's Book*.

15. Shaw's most controversial plays include *Mrs. Warren's Profession* (1894), *Man and Superman* (1903), and *Major Barbara* (1905). See Robert F. Whitman, *Shaw and the Play of Ideas*.

16. See Joanne Dobson, "The Hidden Hand"; Judith Fetterly's introduction to her edited volume *Provisions: A Reader from 19th-Century American Women*, pp. 1–40; and Ann D. Wood, "The 'Scribbling Women' and Fanny Fern."

17. Sutton Griggs, *Imperium in Imperio* (1899) and *The Hindered Hand* (1905); and Charles Chesnutt, *The House Behind the Cedars* (1900), *The Marrow of Tradition* (1901), and *The Colonel's Dream* (1905).

18. I have applied Nancy Armstrong's argument about the political content in nineteenth-century white women's domestic fiction to post-Reconstruction black women's domestic fiction.

19. Ibid.

20. Ibid.

WORKS CITED

Armstrong, Nancy. *Desire and Domestic Fiction: A Political History of the Novel*. New York: Oxford University Press, 1987.

Baym, Nina. *Women's Fiction*. Ithaca: Cornell University Press, 1978.

Bruce, Dickson D., Jr. *Black American Writing from the Nadir: The*

Evolution of a Literary Tradition. Baton Rouge: Louisiana State University Press, 1989.

Carby, Hazel V. " 'On the Threshold of Woman's Era': Lynching, Empire, and Sexuality in Black Feminist Theory." *Critical Inquiry* 12 (Autumn 1985): 262–77.

———. *Reconstructing Womanhood: The Emergence of the Afro-American Woman Novelist*. New York: Oxford University Press, 1987.

Child, Lydia Maria. *The Freedman's Book*. Boston: Tichnor and Fields, 1865.

———. *The Mother's Book*. Boston: Carter and Hendee, 1831.

Cooper, Anna Julia. *A Voice From the South*. Introduction by Mary Helen Washington. Xenia, Ohio: Aldine Printing House, 1892; rpt. New York: Oxford University Press, 1988.

Culp, Daniel W., ed. *Twentieth Century Negro Literature: Or, a Cyclopedia of Thought on the Vital Topics Relating to the American Negro*. Atlanta: J. L. Nichols & Co., 1902.

Dobson, Joanne. "The Hidden Hand: Subversion of Cultural Ideology in Three Mid-Nineteenth-Century American Women's Novels." *American Quarterly* 38 (Summer 1986): 223–43.

Du Bois, William E. B. *The Souls of Black Folk*. In *Three Negro Classics*. Introduction by John Hope Franklin. Rpt. New York: Avon, 1965.

"Editorial." *A.M.E. Church Review* 9 (July 1892): 79–81.

Fetterly, Judith, ed. "Introduction." In *Provisions: A Reader from 19th-Century American Women*. Bloomington: University of Indiana Press, 1985.

Filene, Peter G. *Him/Her Self: Sex Roles in Modern America*. Baltimore: Johns Hopkins University Press, 1986.

Gates, Henry Louis, Jr. *Signifying Monkey: A Theory of Afro-American Literary Criticism*. New York: Oxford University Press, 1988.

Gutman, Herbert. *The Black Family in Slavery and Freedom, 1750–1925*. New York: Pantheon Books, 1976.

Hagins, Rev. John E. "Publications and Literature of the African

Methodist Episcopal Church." *A.M.E. Church Review* 19 (Jan. 1903): 596–604.

Harper, Frances E. W. *Iola Leroy, or Shadows Uplifted*. Philadelphia: Garrigues Brothers, 1892; rpt. New York: Oxford University Press, 1988.

Hopkins, Pauline E. *Contending Forces: A Romance Illustrative of Negro Life North and South*. Boston: Colored Co-operative Publishing Co., 1900; rpt. New York: Oxford University Press, 1988.

Hutchinson, Louise Daniel. *Anna J. Cooper, A Voice From the South*. Washington, D.C.: Smithsonian Institution, 1981.

Logan, Rayford W. *The Betrayal of the Negro*. New York: Collier, 1965.

Majors, Monroe A., ed. *Noted Negro Women: Their Triumphs and Activities*. Chicago: Donohue and Henneberry, 1893.

Mossell, Mrs. N.[athan] F. "Life and Literature." *A.M.E. Church Review* 14 (Jan. 1898): 318–26.

———. *The Work of the Afro-Amreican Woman*. Philadelphia: Geo. S. Ferguson, 1894; rpt. New York: Oxford University Press, 1988.

Murray, Daniel. "Bibliographia-Africania." *Voice of the Negro* 3–4 (1906–1907): 186–91.

———. "A Bibliography of Negro Literature." *A.M.E. Church Review* 16 (July 1900): 19–27.

———. ed. *Murray's Historical and Biographical Encyclopedia of the Colored Race throughout the World*. N.p.: Self-published, n.d. Copy at the Moorland-Spingarn Research Center, Howard University, Washington, D.C.

Neverdon-Morton, Cynthia. *Afro-American Women of the South and the Advancement of the Race, 1895–1925*. Knoxville: University of Tennessee Press, 1989.

"Notes and Comments." *Christian Recorder* (31 Jan. 1895): 2.

Penn, I.[rvin] Garland, ed. *The Negro Press and Its Editors*. Springfield, MA: N.p., 1891.

Scott, Anne Firor. "What, Then, Is the American: This New

Woman?" *Journal of American History* 115 (Dec. 1978): 679–703.

Scruggs, Lewis A.[rthur], ed. *Women of Distinction: Remarkable in Works and Invincible in Character*. Raleigh, NC: Self-published, 1893.

Shange, Ntozake. *Nappy Edges*. New York: St. Martin's Press, 1978.

Sherman, Joan R., ed. "Introduction." In *Collected Black Women's Poetry*, vol. 2. New York: Oxford University Press, 1988.

Simmons, W.[illiam] J., ed. *Men of Mark*. Cleveland, OH: Geo. M. Rewell & Co., 1887.

Smith-Rosenberg, Carol. "The New Woman and the New History." *Feminist Studies* 3 (Fall 1975): 185–98.

Toll, Robert C. *Blacking Up: The Minstrel Show in Nineteenth-Century America*. New York: Oxford University Press, 1974.

Washington, Booker T. *Up from Slavery*. In *Three Negro Classics*. Introduction by John Hope Franklin. Rpt. New York: Avon, 1965.

Washington, Mary Helen. "Introduction." In Anna Julia Cooper, *A Voice From the South*.

————. *Invented Lives*. New York: Anchor, 1987.

Whitman, Robert F. *Shaw and the Play of Ideas*. Ithaca: Cornell University Press, 1977.

Williamson, Joel. *The Crucible of Race: Black–White Relations in the American South Since Emancipation*. New York: Oxford University Press, 1984.

Wood, Ann D. "The 'Scribbling Women' and Fanny Fern: Why Women Wrote." *American Quarterly* 23 (Spring 1971): 3–24.

ESSAYS

~ ~ ~

SOME GIRLS THAT I KNOW

A perfect woman nobly planned,
To warn, to comfort and command;
And yet a spirit still and bright,
With something of an angel light.
                    —WORDSWORTH.

There is one phase of my literary career that I thoroughly enjoy, and that is the privilege of writing to the young women of my race. Sometimes I address myself to them in stories, as in "Our Ruth,"* sometimes in poetry, but always I have an earnest desire to reach them and help them, even as I have been helped by the pen of some gifted woman. And if I shall succeed in accomplishing the one-tenth part of the good to the girls of my people that Miss Alden and Louisa M. Alcott have for the girls all over the globe, I shall be content. These girls of whom I shall write you are real flesh-and-blood heroines.

To one of these girls there came, some years ago, a terrible misfortune that threatened to blight her whole life. By a sad accident one of her arms had to be amputated. Painting, mu-

A.M.E. Church Review 9 (Jan. 1893): 288–92.
*"Our Ruth" is apparently a story written by Tillman, but it is no longer extant.

sic, books, all had to be laid aside. What a terrible blow for
one so young, so full of life! Verily, there seemed no compensation under the sun equal to her great loss. What did
she do? Did she, as do many of our girls when confronted
with a great sorrow, sit down and bemoan her fate? Ah, no,
my heroine is made of better stuff than that. She looked up
to Him who letteth not a sparrow fall to the ground without
His notice, and she was comforted.

When her health would permit she again entered the arena
of life. The anguish she endured upon first encountering a
battery of curious and pitying eyes when she entered college
with one empty sleeve pinned down at her side, only she and
the angels know.

Two talents were left to her, a fine intellect and a sweet
voice; although she might never be an artist or a musician,
she could write out the beautiful thoughts that came to her
for the happiness of others, and she could use her voice for
the glory of God.

These were the noble resolutions made on the funeral pyre
of her youthful dreams, and these resolutions were the foundation stones of the useful life my heroine is leading to-day.
Of such a character, we say with the poet:

> "But to know her was to love her."

.   .   .   .   .   .

Another dear girl has had, all her life, to fight her enemy—
ill-health. She, too, is ambitious. Time after time she has
been compelled to give up her studies on account of her health.
Although thus thwarted in her life's aim, instead of devel-
oping an irritable disposition, she is the most amiable girl I
know.

The only daughter of a widowed mother, no means were

spared to surround her with the little luxuries that make life pleasant to the average college girl in our not too-well furnished buildings. It was always this girl's delight to share her pleasures with some one less fortunate than herself. To illustrate: she owned, among other novelties, a tiny oil-stove and a rocking-chair; these two luxuries found their way into every sick-room in the building. To make others happy was, and is yet, the keynote of her life. Conscientious, pure-minded, like a fair Calla lily, she grows more beautiful in thought and firmer in execution each year.

In the Young Women's Christian Association, of which she was the honored president, she did untold good, always exerting a rare influence for good. Undemonstrative, sometimes painfully shy, she has blessed many lives by living her own so well, and we look for greater things now that God has granted her desire, and she has graduated with honor from her Alma Mater.

> "Sowing the precious seed,
>   Onward and on we go;
> Sowing it here, sowing it there,
>   Knowing not which will grow."

. . . . .

Among the fragrant flowers of a varied past is the life of a girl who has just reached happy womanhood. The eldest in a large family; the care of all the younger children devolved upon our heroine, for her father was a traveling clergyman and her mother's occupation kept her away from home from morning until eve. The cooking, mending and ironing, as well as the nursing, fell to the young girl's lot. Loving, patient, forgetful of self, she glorified her humble duties. "For mother," was the magic word with which she performed all her tasks, and amused the younger ones with innocent games and home-made toys. Over the oldest boy, a lad two years her junior, she wielded a mighty influence for good; and now, a bright young lawyer, rejoicing in a stainless manhood, this brother thinks with pride of the sister who was always, after his mother, his best friend. "She was always an odd child," her friends said, and I, too, think that she is an old-fashioned girl; for, strange to say, her mother's pleasure has always been the girl's first consideration, and in the whole twenty-five years of her life she has never given her mother a single cross word. What a record in this generation of disobedient offspring! I know that the angels have written over her name in great letters of gold studded with stars, "An obedient daughter," one who, like the boy Jesus, was subject unto her parents. She never had a lover until she was twenty, and no silly flirtations were allowed to occupy her heart and hands. Verily, a daughter of daughters, an accomplished young woman, one who can "bake and brew" as well as play the piano and sing. It is hardly necessary to add that she is an earnest Christian. It was but a long-expected pleasure when the other day I received from the Capital, where she resides, an invitation to her wedding.

> "Heaven is not reached at a single bound;
> But we build the ladder by which we rise
> From the lowly earth to the vaulted skies,
> And we climb the ladder round by round."

.   .   .   .   .

Number four is a little house-fairy of my acquaintance, over whose head eighteen summers have lightly passed, leaving her but a child in innocence and truth. Nature has been very lavish in her gifts to this young maiden, for she possesses beauty, an attractive voice and a sunny disposition that win for her many friends. The youngest member of a very large family, and if she were easily spoiled she would have become so long ago. On the contrary, by her many acts of love and thoughtfulness for others, she is laying up for herself treasure "where moth and rust do not corrupt, nor thieves break through and steal." She is of an ardent, impulsive nature, but her actions are tempered with zeal for Christ; and when I recall her glad voice and joyous young face, and her love for all things beautiful and true, I have no fears for her future. "My love is like a red, red rose."

These pen-pictures were written in order to stimulate other girls in their efforts for good. They are taken from real life and without the knowledge of the subjects.

Dear girls, may these lines invite you to deeds that shall win the fairest laurels that ever decked the brow of woman. Have a purpose in life, and live for its achievement. Let nothing low or inferior to your aim keep you from that fair haven where you would be. I could tell you of a great number of young women who have climbed to positions of eminence through their own exertions.

There is not an obstacle in your path but what by perseverance you may overcome. "To thyself be true, and it must follow, as the night the day, thou canst not then prove false to any man."

AFRO-AMERICAN WOMEN
AND THEIR WORK

Woman has always had a mission in the world. Since God made Eve in the fair gardens of pardise as a helpmate unto Adam, it has been woman's task to aid man in all of his stupendous undertakings. And though by her woman's curiosity, sin was born and ushered in upon the fair young earth, so all through the precious boon of motherhood, came life divine, life everlasting unto all.

Since Christ was once cradled upon a woman's breast, there is no crown too royal for woman's brow and no task so great, but that her hands can assist in its accomplishment.

But woman has not always occupied the honorable position that she now does. For centuries she lived in a state of degradation unappreciated, misunderstood and scorned as a being as inferior to man as the rays of the candle are to the beams of the noonday sun.

There are indeed women upon the pages of history like Cleopatra, the queen of Paganism, who lured Mark Antony from his post of duty, like Heloise the devoted wife of the Monk Abelard, who suffered the blighting touch of calumny for the sake of her husband; like Joan of Arc who suffered martydom but succeeded in her inspired mission, of crowning the young dauphin. Brilliant women like the friend of Pericles, the gifted Aspasia, Hannah Moore the friend of female education, and like George Elliot the famous novelist. But their names are few until Christianity made its advent

The A.M.E. Church Review 11 (Apr. 1895): 477–99.

into the world and taught man the true worth and ability of women. We find Miriam prophesying in gladsome song before the Israelitish hosts after they had triumphantly crossed the Red Sea, and we find Deborah a judge over God's chosen people for a number of years and we are not surprised, for Christianity is emphatically the friend of women and wherever its blessed influences are felt woman occupies her true station in life.

Woman was once regarded either as a toy created for man's gratification, or as a slave doomed to an endless servitude unto his Majesty. Immoral women fared better than those who were virtuous, and the few women who were educated became so within the gloomy walls of the convents. To have told a woman of Paganism or even of Medieaval days of the busy honored lives of the mothers and daughters of the Nineteenth Century, would have been regarded as fanaticism.

All of the privileges that woman enjoys to-day are gifts from Christianity, and above all else she should prize this boon, this heaven-bequeathed heritage, and spread the gospel of Christ from shore to shore, from island to island, and from nation to nation!

The woman who throws her influence against the teachings of Christianity is fighting her own best interests and undermining the earth beneath her own feet.

But it is not my purpose in this article to speak of woman in general, although the subject has a peculiar fascination for me, but of Afro-American women in particular. Of their trials, their triumphs and their possibilities. My motive is to show to the public the part that our women have played in the great drama of Negro progress, and in order to do this it is only necessary to point out the leading ladies and the "hits" that they have made, and allow you the privilege of weaving about them any bit of romance that you chose.

Quite recently an Afro-American editor assumed a look of grave importance, and dipping his goose quill into the printer's ink, threw out the following challenge: "What have the women of the race done for its elevation anyway?" I shall answer that question with interesting facts which cannot be disproved.

For the period of two and a half centuries Afro-American women were slaves to the white people of this country. As laborers they were divided into two great classes—field hands and house servants. The field hands toiled in the fields, picked cotton, howed corn and ploughed side by side with the men. Those who had children too young to be left alone took them near their place of work and put them on the ground where, with often a bit of bacon rind in their hands, they were expected to be quiet. Each of the female cotton pickers was required to pick a certain number of pounds each day, and in case of failure for any reason, received a severe lashing. This task was usually performed by white or black overseers, who were, if possible, a thousand times more brutal than their masters. I was once told by an ex-slave, that during slavery, while serving in the capacity of overseer, he was required to whip his sweetheart, a delicate young woman of 18, because she failed to pick the required amount of cotton. Her body was lacerated in a terrible manner by the stinging blows of the overseer's whip. "How could you?" I asked indignantly. "O, I jess' had to; ef I had'n' they'd a killed me," was the response.

The house hands comprised the housekeepers, cooks, chambermaids, ladies' maids, sewing women, laundresses and nurses. In fact before the war it took six or eight women to do what is now required of one. The housekeepers were often the mistresses of their masters and exercised over them many of the privileges of a wife. Sometimes this intimacy existed for years, and children were born who received kindness or blows, according to the disposition of the master. As Charles Carleton Coffin says: "Men and women of Caucasian blood, departing from morality, found the door of society shut against them; but slavery being patriarchial it was not a crime, not even an offence against morality for a planter to choose a Hagar from his slaves. Society placed no bar in his way, the church no ban upon his actions. Hagar could be taken into the master's household, appear in silks and satins with Ishmael for the pet of the family, or both be knocked off to the highest bidder in the mart, separated and sent, one to the rice swamps of Georgia and the other to the cane brakes of Louisiana, Hagar weeping and mourning for her child and the planter with the price of blood in his pocket, be received in any parlor in Charleston, or made Governor of the State."

The owners who might have educated these illegitimate children were in many cases suddenly snatched off by the relentless hand of death, and mother and children were left at the mercy of the dead man's relatives. In a book entitled, "Half a Century," Jane Swissholm relates the story of a man who had two beautiful boys by a female slave and then whipped her to death for grieving because they were sold. The owner in those days had only to look over the slaves and select one that suited his taste. All were subject to his uncurbed will and inclinations. Dreadful, indeed, was the condition of our women in those days, for beside being unable to protect themselves against the advances of their masters, they were compelled to surrender husband, lover and children to the pitiless auction block, knowing that in all probability they were taking then their last farewell.

Like the male slaves, the Afro-American woman had no

rights that any one was bound to respect. They were often compelled to witness the whipping of their children for the most trivial offences.

Again, on certain plantations, they were kept like other stock, for breeding purposes, to breed boys and girls for the horrors of the slave pen. In view of this fact it is not astonishing that many of these suffering women resolved to die rather than to bear children, and took means to destroy their unborn babes.

But life was more endurable for them beneath the rule of kind masters, for there the whip was rarely used, the slaves were well fed and allowed to earn money for themselves by working at night. Where this was the case an affectionate feeling sprang up between owners and owned that was only broken by death. Sometimes their clothing was provided by their mistresses. A large supply of yellow cotton for under-clothing and linsey cloth for dresses was purchased at regular intervals. And this was fashioned into garments by the skill-ful fingers of the Negro needlewoman. These articles were given out according to the discretion of the mistress or housekeeper. By doing work at night, when they should have been taking their rest, some of the slave women were enabled to purchase their own clothing, and they got what suited them. Others hired their own time, that is they obtained permission from their owners to work for others, and paid a high percentage for the privilege.

But it was against the law for them to learn to read or write and thus we find to-day many splendid women who cannot tell one letter from another. They had no homes as we understand the term. They lived in quarters often a row of one-roomed cabins. A large family occupying in some instances a single room.

By some masters they were allowed to hold religious services and by others they were not. Nevertheless many a poor slave sought Jesus in those dark days and found in Him consolation for all of their woes.

An incident related by Mrs. Stowe, in "Uncle Tom's Cabin," seems appropriate just here. It was after Tom had been sold to Legree. The women were baking Tom's cake of corn meal, and Tom drew out his Bible. "Whats that?" asked one of the women.

"A Bible," said Tom.

"Good Lord haint seen one since I was in Kaintuck."

"Whats dat ar book anyway?" asked another woman.

"Why the Bible!"

"Laws a me whats dat?" said the woman.

"Do tell! You never hearn tell on't. I used to hear Missus read on it in Kaintuck."

"Read a piece any ways," said the first woman curiously.

Tom read—"Come unto Me all ye that labor and are heavy laden and I will give you rest."

"Them's good words enuf," said the woman; "who says them anyway?"

"The Lord," said Tom.

"I jes' wish I know whar to find Him," said the woman. "I would go; pears like I never should get rested again. My flesh is fairly sore and I tremble all over every day and Sambo's allus jawin' at me, 'cause I doesn't pick faster and nights it's most midnight fore I get my supper and den pears like I don' turn over and shut my eyes fore I hear the horn blow to git up and at agin in the mornin'. Ef I knew whar the Lord was I'd tell Him."

These women were owned by a nation, whose government is based on God's word and who contributes thousands of dollars annually for the support of missionaries in foreign lands.

Although descendants of heathen parents, the Negro women readily adapted themselves to the requirements of civilized life, and the majority of them developed into excellent work-women. They cooked, they sewed, they spun and wove, in fact did all manner of drudgery without compensation. Many were the hardships that they endured and many were the prayers that went up to God for deliverance. Was God asleep? Or had He forgotten His dark hued sons and daughters in America? Oh no, God is omnipotent and He is also omni-present. Jehovah sleeps not. When the time had fully come, He answered their prayers. Woman began to interest herself in the dreadful conditions of her sister. A spark of womanly sympathy flashed up into the hearts of Lucretia Mott, Lydia Child and Harriet Beecher Stowe, and they began with the zeal of ancient crusaders for the abolition of the slave-trade. Those who were themselves too timid to speak in public, inspired their male friends with their own heaven-born en-thusiasm, and the good work spread.

It took years of earnest work and prayer and it took a gigantic loss of life to procure our freedom, yet when "Uncle Tom's Cabin" had been cried over by gray-haired men, blooming matrons, young folks and children, the battle was half won. It was completed by the great Civil War of 1861–64, and the war was over, the Afro-American was free. Free!

> "The land was free! 'Twas free from end to
> End, from cliff to lake 'twas free! Free as
> Our torrents are that leap our rocks or
> Plow our valleys, without asking leave! Or as
> Our peaks that wear the caps of snow in the very
> Presence of the regal sun!"

From the bitter night of bondage the soil of Ph[i]llis Wheatley, a native African poetess of great merit, who was received with honor in England, and Frances Ellen Watkins, also a poetess had blossomed, like the fragile violets that greet us first of all the flowers in early spring. Ph[i]llis has performed her mission and gone to rest, while Frances in the person of Mrs. Harper the gifted authoress and lecturer is still living and actively engaged in the work of elevating her people.

Although uneducated and poor, Afro-American women have been large-hearted and ambitious. The first five dollars that was given to the Lincoln Monument, was given by Charlotte Cushman, an ex-slave. The spirit of kindness and self-denial that animated the bosom of our women, when during the war they divided their crusts and clothes with the Union soldiers, and caused them to hide the soldiers at the risk of their own lives seemed a part of their natures.

Generosity is a characteristic of our women. Rarely indeed does an appeal for help, coming from any source fall unheeded upon their ears. Out of their poverty, they give largely, and no class of women on the globe excel them in benevolence.

Left penniless at the close of the war, many of them with large families dependent upon them, instead of wringing their hands in despair, they went cheerfully forward to build homes, to educate their children and if possible to lay by a bit for a rainy day. Like the mother of the late Dr. Simmons, many of our women toiled both early and late at the washtub in order that their children might have the intellectual training of which they themselves had been so unjustly deprived. And how proud of these mothers should these children be, and how grateful for the many sacrifices that have been made for them. Every wrinkle in the dear old face should be regarded as a thing of beauty, and it should be the aim of their after lives to make life pleasant for their parents. But to return, by their frugality and labors, their husbands were able to purchase homes, those who desired to do so and to contribute largely to the cause of the gospel and of education. Many of these noble women are dead now, but their memory is yet green and their children rise up and call them blessed. Such, in brief, was the life of our women from their coming as slaves to America to the issuing of the Proclamation of Emancipation.

What can we say of their progress to convince skeptical friends, black and white, that they are deserving of credit? We will touch briefly upon their relation with

The Religious World.

What would be the condition of the churches of all races and denominations, if the women were to withdraw their moral and financial support? The result is frightful to contemplate! Our women I am happy to say seem peculiarly adapted to church work, in fact for benevolent work of any nature. Signs of human distress always evoke their sympathies and the more consecrated their lives become to Christ, the more energetic become their efforts to push forward His Kingdom on the earth. It is the women in our churches who assist the perplexed pastor in devising plans for the annihilation of state and church debts, and who assume the charge of clothing the pastor and his needy family in a little purple and fine linen occasionally; who prepare at home, little feasts and invite this everyday hero, that he may fare sumptuously at least one day out of the seven, and who often seem to their pastor angels in disguise. By organizing themselves into aid societies, known as King's Daughters, Gleaners Women's Christian Temperance Union, Epworth League, Baptist Union and Christian Endeavors, they have been able to do much good for God. It is often seen in the columns of our race journals, that in various places our women have raised immense sums for the erection or renovating of churches or for some Christian enterprise. One women's organization known as the "Women's Mite Missionary Society of the A. M. E. Church" raised $1,525.46 during the year ending November 1, 1893. Also we have a female Evangelist, Mrs. Amanda Smith who has traveled extensively and who has recently published a book, relating her experiences in the Old and New World. There are missionaries dead and missionaries living, who have immortalized their names by their zeal in carrying the gospel to heathen Africa. Women brave and true, like Mrs Ridgel who accompanied her husband to Africa and succeeded in opening up a girl's school and who has written such interesting letters home to us. But do not think the work has been exhausted. There is plenty of work for women to do in religious circles and work that should not be neglected. As long as there is a struggling enterprise on the globe, as long as there are girls wandering from virtue in lives of infamy or a boy feeding on husks of sin, and the coming of Christ is delayed by the triumphs of Satan, just so long must they labor. There will be no rest for women in the religious sphere, until the Book of Life has been closed and they hear the Master's approving sentence, "She hath done what she could." Let us now take a bird's eye view of Afro-American Women in

EDUCATIONAL LINES.

Religion and Education are closely allied. Under this head we will for the sake of brevity consider education in its broadest sense—that is the mental development of all the faculties. We will first speak of that class of women who are known as business women.

It has been asserted by the enemies of the Afro-American

race, that their women have no business capacity. But what are the facts of the case? In almost every avenue of business, our women are rapidly becoming engaged and where they are not, is due to prejudice rather than incompetence.

The Dinahs and Chloes of ante-bellum days, who were then justly noted for their exquisite cookery, have bequeathed to their descendants a talent for cooking, which when cultivated is hard, to be excelled by the most accomplished English or French Chefs. Besides those who command good salaries as cooks in public and private establishments, there are those who are engaged in managing hotels, boarding houses, restaurants and catering establishments upon their own accounts. Mrs. C. V. Parris, of Chicago and Mrs. V. Smith, of Clinton, are women who have succeeded with first-class boarding houses, and Mrs. Lee, now of Los Angeles, California, but formerly of Sioux City, Iowa, and Mrs. Williamson, of Des Moines, are well-known caterers. In New Orleans, there are Afro-American women, who earn a fair living by selling through the streets, bread, fruits, cakes and pies. It is impossible to enumerate the vast number who have purchased homes, yes have become owners of snug fortunes by doing laundry work, this never failing resource and almost universal occupation of the laboring class of our women. Instead of scorning this useful occupation, they have embraced it as a friend and through its aid have realized many cherished dreams.

> They made the foaming washtub
>   With honest labor ring,
> And in its soapy contents,
>   Saw many a precious thing.

Among the women who have succeeded in this line is Mrs. Eliza Warren, of Oskaloosa, who owns a thriving laundry and some valuable property.

Another profitable employment for our women is that of sewing. The women who as slaves so artistically fashioned and draped the silken garments of their mistresses, now have the pleasure of seeing their daughters succeeding in life as dressmakers. Owning elegantly appointed shops, and receiving the best of prices for their work. Miss Rosa Lindsay, of Dakota, who employs several experienced white seamstresses, and who has more apprentices than she can use, and Miss Ida V. Penland, a Louisville dressmaker, are the only ones that I shall mention here. Having been personally acquainted with Miss Lindsay, I know that she has few superiors as an artist in her line of business. She is a most excellent dressmaker.

Besides dressmakers there are hundreds who sew by the day, earning from 50 cents to $2.00 per day, according to the quality of their work. There are others who earn considerable by doing artistic needle work, or fancy work, as some call it. As in every other trade, we find that the most competent receive the best pay, for there is always "room at the top." There was never a period in Negro history when our dressmakers were not patronized by the women of the race as liberally as they deserved to be, but I am thankful to say that this ungenerous spirit is being displaced by one of sweet helpfulness, and our dressmakers are better appreciated by both Afro-American and white women.

One of the wealthiest of our business women is Mrs. T. H. Lyles, a hair dresser of St. Paul, Minn., who owns or controls two hair stores in that city. Mrs. T. J. Houston, of Washington, D. C., pursues the same vocation with much success. With these appears the name of Mrs. Rebecca Elliott, inventor of the "French hair system," who is well known through her widely circulated advertisements.

In Louisiana we find Mrs. Allain owner of a prosperous dairy farm, and in one of the Canadian provinces another

Afro-American woman, a Mrs. St. Johns, is engaged in the ice trade. Mrs. St. John employs several men and teams, and reaps yearly a handsome profit. Others are engaged successfully canvassing, as Miss James, of Washington, D. C., who is canvassing now for the *Ladies Home Journal* in the hope of winning a musical scholarship, and a Mrs. McCutchen, who owns and works a farm of eighty acres a few miles from Oskaloosa. Besides there are women who are clerks, barbers, dealers in second-hand clothing and in various kinds of merchandise. In the face of these facts who shall dare assert that our women have no business capacity? Verily it doth appear that their ability exceeds their opportunity. In my opinion, what our business women need most is our cordial support in every way and when they obtain it they will create a place for themselves in the business world that shall win the admiration of all. In addition to that which they have done already, it is encouraging to note that they are taking the lead in forming co-operative associations for the establishment of banks, stores, and industrial training schools. God bless our business women; and may their number increase daily. The next to which I beg leave to direct your attention is

THE WORLD OF ART.

Beneath the divine inspiration termed art, we will group the artists and musicians of the race. Under the first division we note Miss Mattie Hicks, instructor in drawing and painting at the State University of Kentucky, who is spoken of as an excellent artist, and Miss Mattie Roberts, of Michigan, who is instructor of the same branches at Wilberforce University. Also Miss Ella Dudley, of Kansas, who is, as far as I know, the only woman of the race who is a professional photographer. But the most noted artist among Afro-American women is Edmonia Lewis, the sculptress, who resides in Rome.

Miss Lewis creates men and women of marble. Her work sells at handsome prices, and her society is courted by all lovers of art who have an opportunity to meet her. Her best productions are "Hiawatha's Wooing," "Forever Free," and "Hagar in the Wilderness." In addition to these we have many amateurs who only need training in order to become a credit to the profession. Considering the Afro-American's past environments and her present achievements in the world of art, we cannot help but feel that there is a bright future for her in this field.

When we come to musicians we are compelled to look here and there and select out of the great number of really meritorious musicians whom we know.

As a singer and as a teacher of both vocal and instrumental, Miss Nellie Brown Mitchell, a graduate of the New England Conservatory of Music, ranks very high. Mrs. Mitchell was for two years at the head of the department of vocal music at Hedding Academy, New Hampshire, where all of the pupils were white. Madame Sisseretta Jones, the black Patti, whose voice in some elements is said to rival that of Adeline Patti, is undoubtedly, if all press comments are true, the greatest female singer of the race. When Madame Jones appears in public, she wears upon her breast medals that have been bestowed upon her by foreign countries. This gifted creature of song travels under the management of Major Pond, who also contracts engagements for such notables as Lyman Abbott, the pulpit orator, George W. Cable, the Southern Novelist, who wrote "Madame Delphino," Will Carleton, the prince of American poets, the African explorer, Stanley, T. Dewitt Talmage, the foremost preacher in America, and James Whitcomb Riley, the "Hossier Poet," all of them white. Following Mme. Jones closely are Flora Batson Bergen, Madame Selika and Madame Plato, all famous singers, who have won honorable reputation in their chosen fields.

Besides these who have reached such high planes of greatness is a class of rising prima donnas, singers who are not so well known, as Neale Hawkins, of Chicago, Rachel Walker, of Ohio, and Mrs. Mary Coalson, of Des Moines.

Another branch of art in which Afro-American women have distinguished themselves is elocution. Three of our women—Hallie Q. Brown, Henrietta Vinton Davis and Ednorah Nahar, are especially proficient in this art, and find no difficulty in entertaining the most cultured and fastidious audiences. It is thought by some who have heard the two ladies, that Miss Brown is as difficult to excel in the rendition of humorous and pathetic pieces as is Miss Davis in those that are tragic. Miss Nahar is the best female concert manager of which we know, and is a fine elocutionist beside. But we cannot linger longer upon this pleasant scene, for we must take a peep at our women in the lecture field. Madame Lois, of whom we do not hear so much as we used to, and who is an eloquent woman, Mrs. Fannie Coppin, who has spoken in London, Mrs. Rodgers Webb, preacher of purity, Mrs. Frances Harper, a temperance lecturer, Ida B. Wells, who was in England lecturing against lynch law, are the best known of the Afro-American women who now occupy the platform in America. But in the future I believe that there will be many of our women who will enter this field. Lecturers are or should be educators. Their aim should be to instruct rather than to tickle the wit, to *be* rather than to *seem*. Such a one, who goes forth with an earnest heart to disseminate truth among the people, should be regarded as a benefactor of mankind. Would to God we had now fifty educated Christian women who would devote their lives to this work. Women who would travel from East to West and from North to

South, and speak to our people upon subjects that lie near to
our hearts, and that retard or improve our progress as a people. The important subjects of economy, of temperance, of
social purity and of our duty to God and to ourselves. What
a grand field for women, and how necessary that we should
have them as lecturers. One of the best speakers that the race
ever had was Sojourner Truth, an escaped slave, who occupied the platform with such great men as Garrison and Phillips, and of whose utterances it is said that with the same
culture, they would have been as undying as those of the
African Saint Augustine. Sojourner lives in modern art. She
is the original Libyan Sibyl, a statue carved by the celebrated
Mrs. Story and exhibited at the World's Exhibition in London in 1862.

Another field, in which our women find remunerative employment, is that of medicine. A people numbering eight
millions as we do, ought to have at least one thousand female
physicians, which would average one for every eight thousand persons. This field is a new one for white women too,
and we like them, should pay attention to this honorable calling. Instead of educating all of the girls for teachers, let
some of them study medicine or denistry. We have a few
Negro women physicians already. Dr. Susan McKinney, of
New York City; Dr. Brown of Virginia, who by the way is
the first woman ever admitted to practice in the state; Dr.
Artishia Gilbert of Kentucky and Drs. Consuello Clark and
Carrie Golden. Ida Gray of Cincinnati, is the only dentist
that we have as yet, but there is a young Afro-American
woman in Des Moines, a Miss Lizzie Weaver, who is engaged in the study of dentistry. Those who would like to
adopt either of these professions, must make a way for themselves. Say with the courage of one of old "I'll find a way or
make it." Do not be afraid to venture into untried paths.

You will find many loyal friends among the men and women of the race and you will find some good white friends also. As some one has said: "The best way to succeed is to succeed"—Remember that

> "Laugh and the world laughs with you,
> Weep and you weep alone."

If we are poor and have to live out at service, and if we have an ambition to become something more than we are, why then let us make the life of service a stepping stone to that grander and nobler existence for which we crave. Be assured that the function of our hopes will more than repay us for our trials. May none of us be disposed to hide our talents. A terrible charge has been made against us as a race. We have been charged with mental inferiority; now if we can prove that with cultivated hearts and brains, we can accomplish the same that is accomplished by our fairer sisters of the Caucasian race, why then, we have refuted the falsehood. Many of us give up too easily. Because we are Negroes and are poor, we feel that it is our duty to crush our aspirations and be contented to dwell in the valley of humiliation, when we might be upon the mountains, heralding some joyous message to the hungry multitudes at our feet. We owe it to God and to the Negro race, to be as perfect specimens of Christian womanhood as we are capable of being. In the profession of law only one Afro-American has dared as yet to venture and that is Ida Pratt. Others will no doubt follow in the course of time and become as celebrated as Belva Lockwood.

Another important class of educators, are the women of the race who teach in our public schools and colleges. We will, as in other lines, mention those who are the most prominent. Mrs. Frances Harper and Mrs. Fannie Coppin, besides their rank as lecturers, are widely known as educators. Mrs. Coppin is a graduate of Oberlin College and is at present principal of the "Institute for Colored Youth," which is located in Philadelphia. Mrs. Sarah Garnet, who has taught in the state of New York for twenty-six years and who is a member of the Teacher's National Association and Mrs. Anna Julia Cooper, Instructor in Latin and English Literature at Washington, D.C., are among our best teachers. Miss A. H. Jones, another Oberlin graduate, who teaches in the High School of Kansas City, and the Misses Cordelia and Florence Ray and Miss Cato, who have received from the University of New York, the degree of Master of Pedagogy, also deserve honorable mention. Besides those mentioned are thousands who are engaged in the work and are successfully teaching both Afro-American and Anglo-Saxon children how to become intelligent factors in this great universe.

Another pleasant feature is the fact that a number of our women are engaged in journalism. It seems almost incredible that after so short a period of freedom, there are Afro-American women serving on the staff of prominent white journals, as Miss Lillian Lewis of Massachusetts, and writing stories for magazines like *Harper's* and *Frank Leslie's Magazines*, but true nevertheless, and in Mrs. Matthews better known as "Victoria Earle," we have a writer who writes for the *Family Story Paper* and other fiction papers. The number of women who contribute poems, essays and stories to race magazines is already large, and it is being constantly increased. Three of our best poetesses are wives of clergymen, Mrs. M. E. Lee is the wife of an A. M. E. Bishop. She is a writer of cultured verse that is eagerly read. A number of her poems have appeared in the *Christian Recorder*. Mrs. Charlotte F. Grimké the author of a number of beautiful poems, which are universally admired, is the wife of a Presbyterian cler-

gyman. It is to be lamented that Mrs. Grimké does not place
her poems in book form upon the market, so that all might
know how gifted she is. Mrs. Frances Harper writes both
poetry and prose of the best type and has published two books
of poems, "Forest Leaves" and "Southern Sketches." Mrs.
Josie Heard, also the wife of a clergyman of the A. M. E.
connection, is a poetess of great merit. She has sold all of the
first edition of her published poems and is now preparing a
second edition. Miss Cordelia Ray is the author of a volume
of poems entitled "Sonnets," that are highly spoken of by the
press and Miss Virgie Whitsett, of Iowa, and Miss Mamie
Fox, of Ohio, are rapidly winning their way to fame as writers of good and original poetry. Mrs. Lambert is a graceful
writer, and for keen, satirical articles, Miss Ida B. Wells
cannot be excelled by any woman.

Then we have women who have published original stories.
Mrs. Matthews has written a charming Southern story entitled, "Aunt Linda," and Mrs. Harper has given to the world
"Iola Leroy, or Shadows Uplifted," a story treating of the
Race Problem. Mrs. A. E. Johnson has published two of
her stories in book form, and Mrs. Cooper author of "A
Voice from the South," is said to have produced the best
book ever written by a Negro on the Negro. In this field the
work of our women is barely begun. With their vivid imag-
inations and quickness of perception, they are destined to fill
an important place in the ranks of the literati of this land.
But we will have to prepare for the work even as others have
had to prepare for it. Literature has its attendant drudgery
just as is found in other professions. "Non palma sine pul-
vere," no palms, without dust, no crowns without crosses is
as true of literature as of other things. In coming days Afro-
American women who faithfully portray the lights and shadows of Negro life will receive better compensation, for then

their work will be appreciated. Let us now turn to that large class of women who live in service.

It is becoming fashionable among our younger women to scorn a life of service. Some girls would rather marry a man that they did not care for especially, than earn their own living by hiring out. They are beginning to feel that somehow it is a disadvantage to live out. But it never has nor ever will it be, a disgrace to earn one's living honestly. There is no aristocracy in this country. All men are created free and equal and women ditto. Some women look upon a life of service with such contempt that they fail to perform their duties in a satisfactory manner, and are constantly being discharged. Such women should remember that living in service is far happier than being yoked in an unhappy marriage, and a million times preferable to a life of shame! The laboring classes of our women have done a great work for the race. It is owing to their liberality that we have many of the privileges that we now enjoy. Let no one, then, scorn the vast army of domestics who dwell in the land, for in God's sight there is as much honor in doing one's best in that sphere as in any other. But we cannot linger longer here. Two more scenes and the curtain will drop for the last time. The first picture is that of our society women.

The pessimists of the race, those who are continually on the outlook for the darkest side of life, tell us that we have no society worthy of the name, but such ignorant critics have failed to obtain a passport into the circle of refined Negro men and women, who are to be found in every city of the United States.

Our society women are lively, charming and usually wellbred. They observe the same laws or etiquette, that are observed by devotees of fashion the world over. They call, receive and dress according to their means and often beyond

their means, just as other women do. She requires dainty
morning gowns, elaborate dinner dresses and stylish street
costumes, with hat, gloves and wraps to match, just like the
rest of the feminine world. The fashionable Afro-American,
like her Caucasian sisters spends her time in novel reading,
card playing and in whirling through the intricate mazes of
the dance. Others who have consecrated their lives to God
find their time taken up with various religious and intellectual organizations, such as the King's Daughters and many
secret benevolent societies. Two of the best known of their
clubs are the "Woman's Tourgee Club" of Chicago, and the
"Harriet Beecher Stowe Circle" of Des Moines. A later organization is the "Women's Industrial League" of Washington, D.C., which is doing creditable work.

We now come to the consideration of the last thought and
the one that is of the most importance.

AFRO-AMERICAN WOMEN IN THE HOME.

When Howard Payne, wrote:

> " 'Mid pleasures and palaces though I may roam,
> Be it ever so humble there's no place [like] home,"

he voiced the sentiments of millions.

The home is an institution for which we are indebted to
Christianity. It is of equal importance with the school and
the church. Our earliest impressions of the outside world are
received in the home and though we may wander many miles
from the place we call home, yet it will ever occupy a sacred
spot in our memories.

If, as some writer has said, the hand that rocks the cradle
rules the world, how important that that hand shall be trained
to guide wisely the children beneath her rule!

It is in the home that our women, and indeed all women, are seen either at their best or at their worst. It is here that they are either home-makers or home-breakers. Look at these two scenes. Two young couples embarked out on the sea of life. One takes for their motto, the Golden Rule: "Do unto others as you would have them do unto you." The other one: "I am going to rule my house." One woman tries to be a helpmate indeed unto her husband, and the other spends her money faster than he can earn it. One meets her husband when his day's work is over with a pleasant smile, while the other keeps on hand a goodly supply of frowns and cross words. Number one is easily contented, for she knows that she has her husband's love and that brighter days are just ahead for them, but nothing satisfies number two, for she is a home-breaker, as surely as the other is a home-maker.

I am sorry that I cannot say that the majority of our homes are what they should be. It would be a miracle if they were after so many centuries of heathenish influences have surrounded our ancestors, and of course, left their marks upon us. But we are not discouraged, for we find here and there Afro-American homes, that are models of Christian culture and happiness, and we know that education and religion will create many more.

A great improvement is being noticed everywhere in our homes. Plaster is appearing upon the dingy walls of the Southern cabin, books and pictures are finding their way within these homes; and life is becoming broader and more beautiful to the inmates. In the West our homes vie with the cultured abodes of Afro-Americans of the North, East and South, and thus all are learning the value of home.

Since home-making is of such great importance, every woman who expects to have one should learn how to make it the happiest place on earth. We should remember that there is nothing more serious than a marriage, save it be a birth or death.

Some women of to-day marry with the idea of a separation if the new life does not suit them, but this is not the spirit in which the sacred vows should be taken. "Until death do us part," should be the thought, "as the maiden reverently stands with her husband before the man of God who officiates."

Not only for our own happiness should we build ideal homes, but for the sake of the little one that God gives many of us to train for Him. How can we have noble boys and pure minded girls, if they are not reared in Christian homes amid good influences? What our race will be in the future depends greatly upon the kind of men and women that we are training now.

Let us as Afro-American women pledge ourselves to the elevation of our home. Let us war against intemperance, against infidelity, against gambling in saloons or parlors, against bad literature and immorality of all kind, for these are the demons that destroy our homes. Let us enlist under the banner of Christ and help to subdue these evils. The world needs our efforts and let us go forth in His name to conquer.

> "We have not wings, we cannot soar,
>   But we have feet to scale and climb,
> By slow degrees, by more and more
>   The cloudy summits of our time."

AFRO-AMERICAN POETS
AND THEIR VERSE

"Oh many the poets that are sown by nature, men endowed
with highest gifts, the vision and the faculty Divine; yet
wanting the accomplishment of verse, which in the docile
season of their youth, it was denied them to acquire through
lack of culture and the inspiring aid of books."

—WORDSWORTH.

Had the great English poet addressed these lines particularly
to the Negro race, they could not be more fitting than they
are, for it is, in my opinion, one of the encouraging features
of our much criticized race that they are largely poets and
musicians composing in their night of bondage hymns of
plaintive sweetness, to which the crowned heads of Europe
have bent a charmed ear, and in these later days writing
verses that find grace in the eyes of the distinguished author
and critic, William Dean Howells.

Any one who has been a close reader of the columns of
our various race journals, has doubtless observed the poetical
effusions which have so frequently adorned them. Verses good;
verses bad; verses indifferent. Written in all styles of metre;
and, in many instances, without the remotest idea of versifi-
cation. Occasionally, a bit of genuine poetry has greeted our
eyes and received a hearty welcome, because if was a produc-

A.M.E. Church Review 14 (April 1898): 421–28.

tion of our own, and, therefore, a herald of better days ahead. For what ostracism shall be able to continue when directed against a race of people in whom dwell the divine trio—Poetry, Music and Art? Of what avail to close our doors, our companionship, yea, our souls, to those high spirits who dwell in thought with Moses, Milton, Shakespeare; above all, with the master mind of the universe, Jesus Christ?

Let no man who loves the Negro race then decry poetry, for it is by this and other proofs of genius that our race will be enabled to take its place among the nations of the earth. Then, let the poem of rudest construction not pass unnoticed, lest we throw away a diamond of precious thought; while to those whose many commendable poems entitle them to the rank of poets let us give our hearty encouragement, bidding them God-speed in singing their songs. For poets thrive rapidly in a congenial atmosphere, and if we wish the best of which our poets are capable, we must inspire them to greater efforts by our appreciation of what they have already accomplished.

It is, perhaps, a part of human nature to praise that which is old, and to underrate the good in the new, but it is poor policy, after all. Ralph Waldo Emerson taught American literature to stand on its feet, when, in his essay on the American scholar, delivered at Harvard, 1837, he said, "We will walk on our own feet; we will work with our own hands; we will speak our own minds. A nation of men can exist only when each man believes himself inspired by the divine soul which also inspires all other men." Let us have done with servile admiration of other men's work, and dare to think that genius dwells with us as well as with other nations. Let us discover our own poets instead of waiting for other men to recognize them.

Again, by encouraging the muse of poetry we shall confer

an inestimable blessing upon the rising generation, for the life of any nation is moulded largely by its literature. Thus the Israelites were inspired by the song of Miriam to give gladsome praise to Jehovah, and the ancient Greeks by Homer, to those deeds of valor that have won them fame that will never die. Thus was Scotland thrilled by the passionate lays of Burns, "The Ploughman Poet," England by Shakespeare and Tennyson, Italy by Dante, and America by that brave galaxy known and revered wherever civilized man is found— Whittier, Longfellow, Lowell, Bryant and Holmes. It is my purpose to notice briefly the Afro-American men and women who have written verses that may truthfully be designated as poetry.

The first to break the silence of African bondage was the gifted slave poetess, Ph[i]llis Wheatley, who was, contrary to the custom of the times, well educated by her mistress, receiving more training in the classics than did Whittier, New England's bard. Ph[i]llis wrote a book of poems that attracted attention both in the Old World and the New. One of her poems addressed to General George Washington elicited that great man's warm approval. A specimen of this poet's style may be seen in a poem entitled "A Hymn to Morning."

> "Attend my lays, ye ever honored nine,
> Assist my labors and my strains refine;
> In smoothest numbers pour the notes along,
> For bright Aurora now demands my song.
> Aurora, hail! And all the thousand dyes
> Which deck thy progress through the vaulted skies!
> The morn awakes and wide extends her rays;
> On every leaf the gentle zephyr plays,
> Harmonic lays the feathered race resume,
> Dart the bright eye and shake the painted plume,
> Ye shady groves, your verdant glooms display

To shield your poet from the burning day.
Calliope, awake the sacred lyre,
While the fair sisters fan the pleasing fire.
The bowers, the gales, the variegated skies,
In all their pleasures in my bosom rise,
Seen is the illustrious King of day!
His rising radiance drives the shades away;
But oh, I feel his fevered beams too strong,
And scarce begun, concludes the abortive song."

Unfortunate in her marriage, Phillis died while in the bloom of life, and now lies at rest in some unknown New England grave.

But ah! thy memory still is green,
    And poets will rejoice because of thee;
And thou wilt help them tune their harps
    To sweeter strains of minstrelsy.

After a long interval, a Maryland poet, Frances Ellen Watkins, now F. E. W. Harper, comes upon the scene. Mrs. Harper has written many beautiful poems, some of which have been purchased by reputable Anglo-Saxon magazines. One of Mrs. Harper's best poems, "The Black Hero," appeared in the *A. M. E. Review* a few years ago. As might be expected, a number of this poet's verses have been inspired by slavery and the peculiar environments of her people since their emancipation. An instance is one of her earliest poems, "Ellen [Eliza] Harris," containing the lines:

Like a fawn from the arrow, startled and wild,
A woman swept by me, bearing a child:
In her eye was the night of a settled despair,
And her brow was overshadowed with anguish and care,
But she's free—yes, free from the land where the slave
From the hand of oppression must rest in the grave,

Where bondage and torture, where scourges and chains,
Have placed on our banner indelible stains.

Mrs. Harper has also rendered valuable aid to the temperance cause by verses written upon that subject.

Altogether, we have great reason to be proud of our oldest living poet, and her declining years should be sweetened by our great appreciation of her work.

Had Albery A. Whitman written nothing save that remarkable poem entitled "The Freedman's Triumphant Song," a World's Fair poem, read in Memorial Art Palace, September 22, 1893, he would be established in the minds of thinking people as a poet. No man with Negro blood coursing through his veins can read this poem without a feeling of pride, both in the author and the composition. After describing the night of slavery, he sings in exultant notes:

But freedom came, thank God, at last,
And broke the gates of iron caste!
Then at his task the bondman heard
The call that equal rights conferred,
And rushed to where the cannon's boom
In broken ranks had made him room,
And there in his uncovered might,
On liberty's eternal height,
With glory's sunshine on his head,
He trod where none but heroes tread,
And flying the old flag full and fair,
He held it high and waved it there.

Through all the city's streets there poured a flood,
A flood of human souls eager, intent;
One thought, one purpose, stirred the people's minds,
And through their veins its quickening current sent;
And when at last our country's saviours came
In proud procession down the crowded street,

Still brighter burned the patriotic flame
And loud acclaims reached forth their steps to greet.

This is only a small portion of the whole poem which
abounds in graceful metaphors, and contains an easy flow of
words. This poem I consider one of the best short poems in
the English language.

Mrs. Grimké comes nearer the ideal of a universal poet
than any the race has produced. Her verses appeal to all
classes and races. It is to be hoped that in the near future she
will give to the world a volume of the poems that have endeared her to lovers of verse all over the world.

Paul La[u]rence Dunbar made his *debut* into the literary
world a few years ago with his modest little volume of verse
styled "The Ivy Leaf." His poems touched a responsive chord
in the hearts of his Afro-American readers, and were read in
various lyceums, the writer having upon one occasion made
use of that gem of Negro dialect, "When de co'n po'n's hot."
It was not lack of appreciation on the part of his race, but
rather a lack of means, that kept them from giving the poet
the encouragement that was due him.

Mr. Howells, did a commendable thing in introducing
Dunbar to the literary world. "Full many a gem of purest
ray serene," may be found hidden in the race Dunbar represents if some great man will but bring them to light.

I was well pleased to find Dunbar's latest volume of
poems, "Lyrics of Lowly Life," in the public library of Koe-
kuk. The dialect poem entitled "De Pahty," where the hungry parson, "one eye shet an' one eye open," after a hasty
blessing, "Lawd, we tank you fo' sich generous hearts as
dese; make us truly thankful, Amen!" Says, "Pass dat possum
ef yo' please;" and the "Ode to Ethiopia," are among the best
of the collection. Hitherto, Mr. Dunbar has done his best

work in his humorous dialect verse, but, in the future, to use the words of Prof. H. T. Kealing in a critical review of Dunbar's poetry: "we shall await in hopeful expectation, the maturing of Mr. Dunbar's great genius and the sustained trial of his power, till he stand crowned by the serious of the world as 'black, but comely' in the proportion of all his poetic parts."

Mrs. Josie D. Heard became known to the public some time ago by the publication of a little volume of verse appropriately styled "Morning Glories." Out of this volume, the assistant superintendent of Wanamaker's great Sunday school in Philadelphia selected verses to illustrate the golden text of the current Sunday School lesson. These verses were printed on cards and distributed by hundreds. Mrs. Heard's poems are worthy of a careful perusal, and are sure to give pleasure to the reader. As in the case of Mr. Dunbar, we feel that Mrs. Heard has yet to do her best work in this direction.

Robert Clayton, who has written any number of beautiful poems for the *Christian Recorder,* among them, "The Greatest Gift" and "The Death of Summer," writes with grace and dignity. Miss Cordelia Ray has given to the public a volume of sonnets that has been favorably commented upon by the Anglo-Saxon press. Some time ago Miss Ray contributed a little gem of poetry entitled "Niobe," to the columns of the *A. M. E. Review.* February 1894, a poem dedicated to Richard Allen fell under my notice in the columns of the *Christian Recorder.* Since then, from the pages of a scrap book, it has been read again and again with increased pleasure. It is a strong poem, well written, and exceedingly rhythmical. Added to this, it possesses sufficient dramatic power to render it suitable for recitation. The author is Dr. H. T. Johnson, editor of the *Christian Recorder.* Listen:

> Fond freedom's bells peal forth in merry chimes,
> And ye loud anvil strokes, ring out your notes
> In gladsome echoes from departed times.
> Thy tale to listening millions now unfold;
> With brazen tongues or iron-volumed throats,
> Proclaim our hero's deeds a century old,
> Our hero's arms the gyves and shackles broke,
> That first his own form held, alike his mind,
> Then, Samson-like, from spell bound slumber woke,
> Employed his strength to liberate his kind.

Those who have not read the whole of this poem can judge by this fragmentary part of its excellence.

Others whose verse has refreshed us on our way, are Bishop Tanner, Mrs. B. F. Lee, T. T. Fortune, Alice Ruth Moore, Virgie Whitsett and Mamie Eloise Fox.

If so much has been accomplished within forty years of arduous struggle with poverty and prejudice, what may we not expect under more favorable circumstances? To the editors of Afro-American journals who have encouraged us to sing our trembling lays by giving them a place in their columns, we owe a debt of gratitude.

A great poet like Milton or Shakespeare we have not produced, nor even one to rank with Tennyson or Longfellow, but we have accomplished enough to warrant us in believing that, with riper scholarship, in the course of time, the Afro-American poet will contribute to the world's literature, poetry, beautiful, unique and strong.

THE NEGRO AMONG ANGLO-SAXON POETS

The type of Negro oftenest depicted by modern fiction writers, is a genuine Southern production, a race of ante-bellum days—the simple-hearted, affectionate Negro, who has no higher ambition than to serve faithfully the children of his former master. Isabel A. Mallon's story entitled, "The Colonel and Me," in the recent issue of the *Ladies' Home Journal,* is an example of this class of literature of which thinking Negroes are becoming heartily tired.

While these stories occasionally interest, they never inspire the Negro reader, and besides, give the Anglo-Saxon reader false ideas concerning the race. It is praiseworthy to be a good servant, but all Negroes are not content to be merely hewers of wood and drawers of water. Out of the Negro race must come soldiers, statesmen, poets, authors, financiers and reformers, and fiction that is written with Negro men and women as heroes and heroines must keep these facts in mind.

In sharp contrast with the narrowness of the majority of prose writers, especially those of American descent, are the lines which have been written of the Negro by some of the world's greatest poets.

"The poet," says Ralph Waldo Emerson, "is the sayer, the namer. He is a sovereign and stands on the centre. . . . the end of expression. . . . The signs and credentials are that he announces that which no man foretold."

Viewing the poet through the eyes of America's foremost

A. M. E. Church Review 14 (July 1898): 106–12.

essayist, it is extremely interesting to note the place occupied by the Negro in Anglo-Saxon poetry.

Beginning with the poet who declared "Ethiopia shall soon stretch forth her hands unto God," we find a more inspiring ideal of Negro manhood.

If we go to Shakespeare, the king of poets, and the acknowledged master of English prose, we shall find among his marvelous delineations of character a type of Negro manhood both generous and brave.

Othello, a brave Moorish general of undeniably black complexion, by the bewitching tales of his exploits on the "tented field," woos and wins Desdemona, the only daughter of Brabantio, a Venetian. To use Othello's words:

> "She loved me for the danger I had passed,
> And I loved her that she did pity them." (Act I, Scene 2.)

> "I fetch my life and being
> From men of royal siege and my demerits
> May speak unbonneted to as fair a fortune
> As this that I have reached." (Act I, Scene 2)

Following the reading of this interesting tragedy, we see how a noble, unsuspicious nature is gradually poisoned and disturbed by the crafty Iago, until the gentle Desdemona is believed by Othello to be untrue to her marriage vows and dies a victim to the Moor's unfounded jealousy.

There seems little doubt to unprejudiced minds that Othello had Negro blood flowing through his veins. Shakespeare refers to this fact several times in the play, and of all the writers who have lived none knew better than Shakespeare how to say exactly what he wished. Iago, alluding to Othello's color, calls him an "old black ram," and Brabantio says that Desdemona

"Runs from her guardage to the sooty
Bosom of such a thing as thou."* (Act I, Scene 2.)

*The labored effort to prove that Shakespeare did not intend Othello as a
Negro must in time give way to fairness, common-sense and the Shakes-
pearean text itself. In speaking of the passage in Act I, Scene 1, where
Shakespeare makes Roderigo, the Venetian gentleman, call Othello "the thick-
lips," Edward Knight, the editor of Collier's edition of Shakespeare, exercises a plethora of ingenuity upon a paucity of material to disprove this
intention. He says the popular notion of the difference between a Moor and
an uncivilized African was in Shakespeare's day somewhat confused. Mr.
Knight confesses that "it is by no means impossible that Othello was represented as a Negro" on the stage of that time, but thinks it impossible that
Shakespeare conformed to that idea. He cites Coleridge as coinciding with
his views, though not denying that there would have been nothing unusual
in the presentation of a Negro character in such a role.

The answer to all this is that by their own admission such a thing would
have been no innovation and that no antagonism would have interfered; that
Shakespeare, "the myriad-minded," was not fettered by latter-day prejudices
against the Negro; that whatever may have been the motive of Roderigo in
calling Othello "thick-lipped," the designation could only have point by
specifying a physical peculiarity actually existing, and one, too, considered
characteristic of the Negro; that to this day Negroes are called in Europe
black-a-moors; and by the historical fact that in Venice all colors and nation-
alities mingled, including Negroes, on terms of perfect equality; that it was
a regular policy of the Venetian Republic to employ foreign officers in places
of command in order to lessen the danger of intrigues at home. These last
two points are fully and strongly brought out by a writer as follows:

Rymer, certainly no friend to the Negro, in his "Short View of Tragedy,"
admits this custom in Venice and also, with censure, accepts the view that
Shakespeare certainly did intend to make Othello a Negro. Here are his
exact words (p. 91): "With us [the English] a black-a-moor might rise to
be a trumpeter; but Shakespeare would not have him less than a lieutenant-
general. With us a Moor might mean some little drab, or small-coal wench:
Shakespeare would provide him the daughter and heir of some great lord or
privy councilor; and all the town shall reckon it a very suitable match."

Literary honesty requires that the truth be told.

While not a part of the argument, it is an interesting "aside" to say that
a negro, Ira F. Aldridge, was long considered in Europe as the best imper-
sonator of the character Othello on the stage. [EDITOR.] of *The Review*
—C. T.

Desdemona says in extenuation of her love for the Moor:
"I saw Othello's visage in his mind" (Act I, Scene 3).

For another spirited tale, let us read "The Runaway Slave
at Pilgrim's Point," written by Elizabeth Barrett Browning.
A slave girl loved a fellow slave. Her affection was returned,
and they pledged themselves to be true to each other, but
alas, as the slave girl says;

> "We were black, we were black,
> We had no claim to love and bliss;
> What marvel if each went to wrack?
> They wrung my cold hands out of his,
> They dragged him where I crawled
> To touch his blood's mark in the dust.
>
> A wrong followed by a deeper wrong,
> Mere grief's too good for such as I,
> So the white man brought the shame ere long,
> To strangle the sob of my agony,
> They would not leave me with dull wet eye,
> It was too merciful to let me weep pure tears and die."

Time passed, and an unwelcome child with the master's like-
ness stamped upon its little face, looked up into its slave
mother's face and demanded nourishment.

> "For hark! I will tell you low, low
>   I am black you see,
> And the babe who lay on my bosom so
> Was far too white for me;
> As white as the ladies who scorned to pray
> Beside me at church but yesterday,
> Though my tears had washed a place for my knee."

Crazed by her wrongs, the poor girl took her baby's life,
and afterward buried it in the quiet woods that surrounded
the plantation. To her pursuers she cried;

"I am not mad; I am black,
I see you staring in my face,
Ye are born of the Washington race,
And this land is the free America;
And this mark on my wrist (I prove what I say)
Ropes tied me up here to the flogging place."

"You think I shrieked then? Not a sound!
I hung as a gourd hangs in the sun,
I only cursed them all around
As softly as I might have done
My very own child! From these sands
Up to the mountains, lift up your hands,
O slaves, and end what I begun."

The next poem to which the reader's attention is invited, is
Whittier's Toussaint l'Ouverture, founded upon an incident
of real life. Toussaint l'Ouverture, the black chieftain of Hayti,
formerly a slave on the plantation "de Libertas," belonging
to M. Bayou, successfully led an insurrection against the
slaveholders and won freedom for his enslaved countrymen.
Remembering the kindness of his former owner, Toussaint
generously assisted the family to escape to Baltimore. The
Island of Hayti, under the rule of Toussaint was happy and
prosperous, until, in 1801, the brave leader was treacher-
ously betrayed by order of Napoleon and conveyed to France,
where he died, April, 1803, about eight months after his
arrival.

Says Godwin, "The West Indies since their first discovery
by Columbus cannot boast of a single name which deserves
comparison with that of Toussaint l'Ouverture."

"Brief was the silence, once again
Pealed to the skies that frantic yell;
Glowed on the Heavens a fiery strain,
And flashes rose and fell;

And painted on the blood red sky
Dark naked arms were tossed on high
And round the white man's lordly hall
Trode fierce and free the brute he made,
And those who crept along the wall,
And answered to his lightest call
              With more than spaniel dread—
The creatures of his lawless beck
Were trampling on his very neck!
Then, injured Afric—for the shame
Of thy own daughters, vengeance came
Full on the scornful hearts of those
Who mocked thee in thy nameless woes,
And to thy hapless children gave
One choice—pollution or the grave!
Dark-browed Toussaint!—the storm had risen,
Obedient to his master-call,
The Negro's mind had burst its prison,
              His hand its iron thrall."

In concluding this grand tribute, Whittier feelingly says:

"Sleep calmly in thy dungeon tomb
Beneath Bensancon's alien sky,
Dark Haytien! for the time shall come,
Yea, even now is nigh,
When everywhere thy name shall be,
Redeemed from color's infamy,
And men shall learn to speak of thee,
As one of earth's great spirits, born
In servitude and nursed in scorn,
Casting aside the weary weight
And fetters of its low estate,
In that strong majesty which knows
No color, tongue or clime."

Another poem that appeals to all bold, courageous souls in
"The Warning," by Henry Wadsworth Longfellow, who,

some critics aver, won more English hearts over to the anti-
slavery cause than did the "Quaker Poet."

> "Beware! The Israelite of old who tore
> The lion in his path, when poor and blind,
> He saw the blessed light of heaven no more,
> Shorn of his noble strength and forced to grind
> In prison and at last led forth to be
> A panderer to Philistine revelry!
> Upon the pillars of the temple laid
> His desperate hands, and in its overthrow
> Destroyed himself, and with him, those who made
> A cruel mockery of his sightless woe
> The poor blind slave, the scoff, the pest of all,
> Expired and thousands perished in the fall.
> There is a poor blind Samson in this land
> Shorn of his strength and bound with chains of steel,
> Who may in some grim revel raise his hand,
> And shake the pillars of this Commonwealth,
> Till the vast temples of our liberties,
> A shapeless mass of wreck and rubbish lies."

Once more and I am done. Some time ago in the columns of
the *Judge,* appeared the thoughtful face of a Negro woman.
Underneath the portrait was a poem by A. T. Worden, entitled, "An American type."

> Behold in their calm face,
> The modern Sphinx with such a thoughtful mien
> As bids us pause, when like a Frankenstein
> A nation dares create another race.
>
> No longer here the crude
> And unformed features of a savage face;
> But in those pleading eyes a kindred race,
> Asks for the highway out of servitude.

Like as the Amazon
With mighty currents marks the ocean hue
Until her leagues of tide blend with the blue,
So do these patient millions still press on.

Such at the cradle side
Have crooned as foster-mothers, sung and wept,
Across the chamber doors of pain have slept,
And for their sisters pale have gladly died.

Two hundred weary years
Of burden-bearing in a shadowed path,
And yet no hand is raised in cruel wrath,
And all their wrongs evoke as yet but tears.

Study the problem well
For in this sphinx a message somewhere lies;
A nation's glory or its shame may rise
From out the reading what these features tell.

It is from perusing poems like these that our sorely tried
spirits arise refreshed, and we are enabled to go on from
"strength to strength."

ALEXANDER DUMAS, PÈRE

In these days, when it is the fashion for many of our white writers to make a great bugaboo of the fact that sometime in the future there is a probability of so serious a calamity as the amalgamation of the white and black races of this country, and everything in science, history and literature than can be found in disparagement of Negro blood is brought to light and served to us in various books and magazine articles, it is a good tonic to review the life of the man styled as the greatest French romantic novelist and the most universally read storyteller of the world, and to be informed that this great man's grandmother was a Negro woman, Louise Cessette Dumas.

Alexander Dumas was born July 24, 1802, at Villero-Cotterets, a little town on the way from Paris to Laon. His grandfather was the Marquis Antoine Alexander Davy de la Poilleterie, a French nobleman, who for some reason exiled himself to San Domingo and there married the Negro woman of whom we have spoken.

The son of this union took his mother's name, enlisted in the French army, and rose to the rank of general. In 1792 he married an inn-keeper's daughter. Ten years later Alexander, the future man of letters, was born. One of his biographers says of this event: "He was a quadroon and dowered at birth with many of the characteristics, good and bad, of the African race—the ardent imaginative temperament, the levity

A. M. E. Church Review 24 (Jan. 1907): 257–63.

of nature, the impulsive soul—a host of qualities which were strange to the comprehension of both friends and enemies in [and] after life; because side by side with them were all the native characteristics of the Frenchman, existent in full vigor."

When Dumas was barely more than a baby the General died, leaving his wife and child in poverty. His mother moved to her father's house, and little Alexander's education began. When five or six years old he could read and write. Among his first books were the Bible and Robinson Crusoe. Dumas writes of himself at this period: "I can still see myself about the height of a jack-boot, and in a little cotton jacket, taking part with the utmost precocity in the conversation of grown-up people, and contributing thereto my store of knowledge, profane and sacred."

When he was old enough to decide, his mother gave him his choice of being a Davy de la Poilleterie, a Marquis, and an aristocrat, like his grandfather, or a simple "Dumas," like his Republican father. Without hesitating, he chose to be a "Dumas," and by his genius immortalized the name of his Negro grandmother in preference to hanging on to an aristocratic title.

The beginnings of Dumas literary life date from the visit of Auguste Lafarge, a Parisian clerk, to the little town of Villers-Cotterets. When Lafarge left he had composed a verse against some haughty inamorata, and Dumas reading it became ambitious to write verse also. In a pen picture of himself at this time he speaks of himself as rather a good-looking young monkey, with long curling hair which fell over his shoulders and did not crispen until he was fifteen.

He was a spirited young fellow and exceedingly fond of outdoor life.

While serving as junior clerk of Mr. Mennesson, the Notary, the young Vicomte Adolphe Ribbing de Leuven came to Villers-Cotterets, and completely captivated the heart and mind of Dumas. Leuven had written love verses and plays and had read one of them at the Gymnase Theatre, at Paris. This was the turning point in Dumas' life, for it resulted in his going to Paris to seek his fortune. They had very little money, for his mother's capital only amounted to 253 francs, but her son took some letters written to his father by Marshals Jourdan, Victor Sebastiana as letters of introduction, and having knelt in prayer with his mother set out for the great city of Paris.

At Paris he received a distinct disappointment. General Dumas' friends would do nothing for his son. However, through General Foy, he received a clerkship in the Secretary's department of the Duke of Orleans, with the salary of fifty pounds a year.

Dumas now settled down to hard study. The days, from seven to ten at night, belonged to his employer, but the other part of the night he read Juvenal, Tacitus, Suetonius; studied geography and physiology and the theatrical productions of the period.

The first fruits of this study was a little play, "La Chasse et l'Amour," collaborated by Dumas, Leuven and a new friend, Roussean. This was accepted at the Ambign Theatre in 1825 and presented with great success. Now came a volume of short stories from our young writer's pen "Nouvelles Contemporaines" (1826). He also contributed without pay to a magazine called Le Psyche. Complaint was made to Dumas' chiefs about so much time being given to literary pursuits and he endured much annoyance for a while. A new drift was given to his thoughts by the arrival of Kean and a company of English actors, who presented "Hamlet," a play Dumas had already studied, and determined him to become a dramatist. He says of this event, "From that moment my

career was decided; I felt that the special call which is sent to
every man had come to me then. I felt a confidence which
has never since failed me. Nevertheless, I did not disguise
from myself the difficulties which such a life work would
involve. I knew that above all other professions this one demanded deep and special study, and that to operate with success I should first need to study dead nature, long and earnestly. Shakespeare, Corneille, Moliere, Calderon, Goethe
and Schiller, I laid their works before me like bodies on the
surgeon's table, and with scalpel in hand, I probed them to
the heart to discover the secret of their life."

"Christine" was the first drama written after this period,
and the author obtained permission to read it before the staff
of the Francaise. It received loud applause and was accepted,
subject to revision. It is said that on his way home to his
mother he lost his manuscript and rewrote it that very night.
His next drama was Henry III. He was then twenty-five.
This play was an immense success, and like Byron, Dumas
awoke the next morning and found himself famous. His room
was crowded with bouquets, which he placed on the bed of
his mother, then ill, and he sold the manuscript of his play
for 6,000 francs.

At the Salon of Nodier, to which Dumas, through Nodier's daughter, Marie Mennessier Nodier, had the great good
fortune to be admitted. He met Hugo, De Vigny, Sainte
Beuve, De Musset and other famous French writers. Afterwards a place was always kept for Dumas at the famous Sunday dinner of the Arsenal.

Dumas began to taste the sweets of fame in a yet higher
degree. He was made assistant librarian to the Duke of Orleans at £100 a year. As author of "Henri Trois" (Henry
III), he was the lion of Paris during the winter of 1829.
During his first years in Paris, Dumas fell in love with Ma-

dame Marie-Catherine Lebay, a pretty young seamstress. His affections was returned, and an intimacy ensued, resulting in the birth of Alexandre Dumas fils, 1824.

In 1830 occurred the downfall of Charles X and the accession of Louis Phillipe, Duke of Orleans, Dumas' former master. The dramas, "Napoleon" and "Antony," were written, "Napoleon" being doomed to failure, and "Antony" a starling success. Charles VII and "Richard Darlington" were his next dramatic efforts.

In 1832 Paris was swept by cholera and Dumas was a victim to it, but his strong, robust vitality brought him through safely. In July, 1832, being in disfavor with the King, Dumas made a tour of Switzerland. The next year he visited England and the South of France. In 1837 our hero, having been an intimate friend of the young Duke of Chartens, now Duke of Orleans, received from him a Knight's cross of the Legion of Honor.

In 1838 Dumas's mother died of an apoplectic stroke. Dumas now wrote the three comedies that critics say will outlive his dramas, "Mademoiselle de Belle-Isle," "Unmanage Sons, Louis Quinze," and "Les Demoiselles de St. Cyr."

In 1840 occurred Dumas' marriage to Mlle. Ida Ferrier. She is described as a beautiful woman of mediocre abilities.

In 1844 appeared Dumas' greatest romances, "Count Monte-Cristo" and the "Three Musketeers." Dazzled by the new fame and fortune that had come to him, Dumas made the mistake of erecting a beautiful theatre costing thirty thousand francs (£30,000), called the Historique, and building himself a palace which he named Monte-Christo. As a housewarming for his palace, he gave a splendid reception to six hundred guests.

Being of an exceedingly hospitable nature, Dumas lived surrounded by parasites. In 1847 the downfall of the House of Orleans took place, and in 1851 Louis Napoleon became Emperor. From this time Dumas, who was a man of great independence of character, began to decline in fame and fortune. He fled to Brussels and joined Victor Hugo, where he wrote fifty volumes. Dumas, who could earn a fortune almost with a stroke of his pen, never knew how to save, and old age found him penniless. When he was quite ill he allowed his son, Alexander Dumas, to take him to his house at Puys near Dieppe, where he remained loved and tenderly cared for until December 5, 1870, when his great creative brain became mute. Two years later his son took him back to Villers-Cotteret, to rest besides his father and mother, as he had wished.

Says Harry A. Spur in his Life and Writings of Alexandre Dumas: "If like Defre we were about to offer fiction in the guise of biography, we should be tempted to preface the story of Dumas thus:

"The life and adventures of Alexandre Dumas of the world, who was both a black and a white man; a Royalist and a Republican; an aristocrat, and a Sans-Culotte; who took part in three revolutions, and made three different reputations; who wrote more books than any other man living or dead, who erected two 'Monte-Cristos,' one of which made his fortune and the other of which unmade it; who enriched the world and was poor all his life; together with an account of his exploits as dramatist, romancer, traveller, politician, wit, journalist, diplomatist, soldier, lecturer, cook, historian, poet, etc."

"He was not France's, he was not Europe's—he was the world's," was the verdict of Hugo.

A poem written by Alexandre Dumas, fils, entitled "To My Father," contains this stanza:

"Work then for the coming ages,
That shall hold thy days so dear;
Strive and testify and suffer,
Like some ancient prophet-seer.
Though thy onward course shall keep
Calm and peaceful like the Rhine,
That grand old river, to thy brink let all nations
Come, and grateful of thy flowing current drink,
'Twill be still as clear and deep."

PAYING PROFESSIONS
FOR COLORED GIRLS

Debarred as our girls are from many avenues of lucrative employment, it is wise for them to consider what work is open to them and what their chances of success are in their chosen field.

Teaching is a paying profession and one that is being followed by thousands of our young women in the separate schools of the south and in the mixed schools of the north, east and west. The profession of teaching has, aside from other difficulties, this objection: if there is a tendency toward a tuberculosis condition, the confinement of the school room seems to aggravate this tendency, and a permanent breakdown is liable to ensue. A well-trained mind, a strong character and a vigorous pair of lungs, are essential to the highest success in the school-room. The salary of a teacher is from $25 upward, some earning $1,200 a year and more. In teaching, as in other professions, in the long run merit goes up and mediocrity down. Miss Elizabeth Carter, a young colored woman teaching in the mixed schools of New Bedford, with almost all of her pupils belonging to the white race, and Mrs. Belle Patton teaching in the mixed schools of Chicago, are two of the many colored women who are efficient, well-paid teachers. Often we hear the complaint from high school girls that after graduating they cannot teach unless they leave home and go South, or to some place where separate schools are in existence. They come to this conclusion before making an

Voice of the Negro (Jan.–Feb. 1907): 54–56.

application for a position at home and, of course, get nothing. I do not at present recall an instance where a colored girl of moral worth and standing, who took the normal course after completing her high school course, failed to get a place if she made her examination. We miss many good things in this life for lack of earnest effort.

Nursing is a paying profession. This profession requires first of all a sound body, a fair education and much self-control. Our girls take to nursing so easily that it almost seems an inheritance from the soft-voiced southern "Mammies" of the southland who in ante-bellum days and even now are indispensable in the sick-rooms of the south. The apprenticeship in the training schools lasts from two to four years and is not very expensive. Any colored girl who feels herself adapted to this kind of work can secure the training by a persistent effort. Hampton Institute, Tuskegee, Meharry Medical College, Howard University, Washington, D. C., Douglass Hospital, Kansas City and the well-known Provident Hospital at Chicago, are the largest and best equipped schools of the race. And there are some white institutions whose doors are open to colored girls also. The trained colored nurse who enters white homes on deeds of mercy is a sure wedge in the walls of racial prejudice. Her patience and skill often cause an entire revulsion of feeling in regard to the colored race. Another way in which the colored nurse can help to solve the problems of race is to assist the colored physician in decreasing the mortality among our people. She can give wholesome advice on "cleanliness," "Ventilation," "Sanitation" and "Social Purity" that will mean the salvation of thousands of the poor and neglected homes of our people. The trained nurse receives from $15 to $25 and $40 a week, and more according to the wealth of her patients.

Dress-making and tailoring are good paying professions for colored girls. The colored girl who can do first class work in either or both of these trades can get all the work she wishes from both white and black patrons. It is the dress-maker who botches and can neither fit or finish off her work well that has to sew cheaply and seldom gets the second trial from the same customer. As willing as most colored women are to patronize their "own color," they cannot afford to have their goods spoiled. The girl aspiring to be a dressmaker or ladies' tailor should learn from a good school or shop and practice on her own school clothes first. Dress-makers earn—some of them—five dollars a week, others hundreds, according to the amount of work accomplished and the class of people for whom they sew. Colored girls sewing by the day earn from fifty cents a day to three dollars a day and their lunch.

Millinery is proving a paying profession for colored women. Our women often buy expensive hats when they have nothing to wear with them. The progressive colored milliner studies the features, complexion and prospective gowns of her customers and makes her hat to harmonize with these. In Chicago and other large cities some of our women are running successful stores, while an ever-increasing number of women are doing parlor millinery. Other milliners earn fair salaries by going from place to place teaching classes in millinery. One parlor milliner who devotes only a part of her time to hat-making, earned for some time $18 a week.

Hair-dressing, hair manufacturing, manicuring and chiropody afford paying employment to many colored girls. Hair-work seems to be pleasant and profitable and those running first-class shops and those doing "satchel trade" from house to house earn good salaries and wages and form valuable acquaintances among the wealthy class of white people. Colored girls can often get into white shops as apprentices and receive their trade in this way without any cash expense to them. Some colored hair-dressers earn a good living by giving scalp treatments to colored women's heads. Splendid results often come from these treatments and a nice growth of soft healthy hair replaces the short, harsh hair of former days. Then there is the much criticised "Hair Straightener" for whom, when she thoroughly understands her business as some of them do, I have the greatest respect. Colored women have a very natural and womanly desire to have "good hair," and if this can be obtained by healthy artificial methods, they are wise to take advantage of them.

Domestic science is and will continue to be one of the best paying of all of the professions open to our girls. The skilled cook is in constant demand and at excellent wages. There are not many who earn a thousand a year, as does the French chef of an American millionaire, whose name I do not recall; still cooking pays well.

> "We may live without friends;
> We may live without books,
> But civilized man
> Cannot live without cooks."

In St. Louis, at the world's Fair, I met a young colored woman who was employed as *a demonstrator* of white cottolene by the N. K. Fairbanks Co., at a salary of $40 a week! In Chicago in Siegel & Cooper's mammoth department store a colored girl is employed to demonstrate the finest brand of goods carried by the house. At the famous Paris exposition a colored woman went from the United States to Paris to demonstrate the uses of corn. Aside from positions as teachers of cooking in schools and private classes, as cooks in cafes and boarding houses, good wages and comfortable homes may be obtained as cooks in wealthy private families. In Colorado Springs women cooks earn from $20 to $35 a month. Indeed, cooking may well be classed among the fine arts and it is a profession that one can always be improving in. Every colored girl, whether compelled to earn her own living or not, should pride herself upon being able to serve an appetizing meal. If the girls need a stimulus in that direction, perhaps it will be well to remind them of the old adage: "The shortest road to a man's heart is through his stomach."

Courses in domestic science may be taken in almost any city now through the women's clubs.

Catering is an excellent profession, but requires more executive ability than is required of a mere cook. I knew a colored woman in Chicago who went to the homes of her white patrons and charged each one $5 for preparing and serving a party luncheon or dinner and clearing up everything. This woman sometimes earned $60 a month, and had part of her time to herself. This woman was pleasant-mannered, very neat in her dress, and a perfect cook—items that are never overlooked by employers.

All branches of house work pay well to those who take the pains to give satisfaction in their work and make it a rule never to slight a single task. The demand for competent girls in this field of work is always greater than the supply. Colored girls are apt to shrink from domestic service, while the German, Irish and Swede girls crowd into them, learn quickly and begin to start a bank account, looking toward an independent old age.

Canvassing for first class papers, magazines or useful articles pays well to the stout-hearted girl who starts out with the determination to sell her goods.

In conclusion, home-making is perhaps the best paying profession of all and this is the goal toward which every girl's heart naturally turns. To be the presiding genius over some good man's heart and home, ah! this is a profession worth while; for here may be found a place for all of the best that is in us. This profession also requires skill and it, too, is one of those in which one can be constantly learning; and there is none that brings sweeter reward.

"For home-keeping hearts are happiest."

To this profession the girl should bring love, courage, strength and patience and from these she will receive wisdom, love, reverence and happiness.

ALEXANDER SERGEIVICH PUSHKIN

African Russian Author
First National Poet of Russia

If it be true that all the world loves a lover, it is equally true of the poet. We feel a kinship with him, because he interprets life's meaning for us, lightens life's gray skies, and expresses that which we feel within our own dumb selves but have not the gift to impart. Beneath the magic touch of the true poet, earth, air, sea and sky, become places of enchantment, and we look upon them, not as we would, but as the poet wills that we should look.

Thus the poet, regardless of his nationality, becomes the common property of mankind. The Greek poet, Homer, finds himself upon the library of the student and book-lover, in company with the Roman poet, Virgil, the Persian poet, Omar Khayyam, the German Goeth[e], the French poets Racine and Hugo, the Scotch bard, Burns, the English poets, Chaucer, Shakespeare, Milton, Browning, Byron and Shelley, the Russian poet, Pushkin, and the array of American poets, among whom are Poe, Longfellow, Bryant, Lowell, Holmes, Field, Riley and our own lamented bards of humbler note, Alber[y] Whitman and Paul La[u]rence Dunbar.

Who while listening to the melody and rhythm of Dunbar's verse cares that he was a Negro, save his own people who rejoice in the fact because of the discriminations in this country against persons of Dunbar's race. The Mexicans bought copies of his poems eagerly during a recent trip made in Mexico by a colored agent.

A. M. E. Church Review 25 (July 1909): 27–32.

Who is it that does not owe a debt to these poets whom I have mentioned and to others of their ilk of whom time forbids us to speak? They have spoken to us from different parts of the earth and at different periods, but we have always been better for the messages they have brought and they have given us hours of happiness that no other source could give.

I have chosen to say a few words about the Russian poet, Alexander Sergeivich Pushkin, because little has been known of him hitherto, here in America at least; and for one or two other reasons. One of these reasons is that on the [m]aternal side of the poet's ancestral line, he is of Negro descent and in our country would be classed a Negro.

I confess to a deep interest in the study of heredity. I have a friend, an American Negro woman, who is the descendant of a German physician and a native Guinea African woman on the maternal side, and of a blue-blooded Kentuckian and an Indian woman on the paternal side. Having the opportunity to study this friend I have tried to account for her various characteristics on this wise: her love of language and poetry and philosophy and impatience under restraint I have attributed to the irascible old German doctor who was also a slave-holder in the state of Missouri. Her low stature, complexion, which is a clear brown, her love of nature, and ambition, her intense sympathy with her own people I put down to the credit of the African ancestors. From the Kentuckian she probably gets her love of braggadocio and hero-worship, her clannishness, and from the Indian woman that loyalty to friends which makes her so dear to me and others. In studying the life of Pushkin, I like to think that the African blood flowing into his veins gave to the cold sluggish Russian temperament just the warmth that was needed, to make him a great poet, as it made a great composer of Samuel Coleridge Taylor, son of a native African father and En-

glish mother, a man who ranks among the foremost compos-
ers of England.

If Pushkin's African blood was not an actual help to him
in supplying the color, warmth and imaginative qualities that
are indispensable to the poet, it did not prevent his taking
his place in Russian history, as Russia's first national poet.

Alexander Sergeivich Pushkin was born in Moscow, May
26, 1799, of well-to-do Russian parents. On his mother's
side he was descended from Ibraham Hannibal, a Negro who
was sent to Russia as a present to Peter the Great, and afterwards reared at court. Ibraham was educated at Paris, and
when he died had risen to the rank of general and was the
owner of considerable landed property.

It is said by his biographers, that he inherited the broad
nose, thick lips and curly hair that are characteristic of Negroid types.

His father and uncle were both men of considerable literary accomplishments, and Pushkin was from birth surrounded by books and people who were possessed of culture
and intellect.

Pushkin as a child was very stupid and his parents took
little interest in him, but his nurse, Arina Rodiovna, a true
Russian type of the faithful old house servant, gave the lad
the tenderest care. It was from Arina that Pushkin learned
the legends and folk lore that he turned to such good account
in his poems of national life.

When the boy was about seven, he seemed to awake from
his state of stupidity and showed such a taste for learning that
his father at once engaged tutors for him. Before he was
twelve he had written some verses and little plays. The verses
it is said were written in the style of La Fontaine and the
plays in that of Moliere.

August 1811, he entered the Lycee at Tsarsky Selo, where

he neglected the curriculum of the college for the school library and the editing of the college paper.

As early as 1814, he was a contributor to the Europy Vestnik.

The turning point in Pushkin's literary life dates from January 1815, when Derhavin a writer of the day attended a public examination at the Lycee and heard Pushkin recite his own verses "Reminiscences of Tsarsky Selo." Derhavin was so impressed with the young poet, that he took a copy of the poem back to Petersburg with him, and showed it to his literary acquaintances. Pushkin was no longer unknown, and among his friends and ardent admirers Joukovsky, a popular poet of the day, proved to be the most devoted and helpful. Kramzin, the Russian historian, also admired the young poet's genius and read to Pushkin the manuscript of his afterward famous history.

Inspired by his literary atmosphere the young man set himself seriously to writing verses and wrote two hundred Lyrics and Epigrams and the long poems, "Russian and Lioudmilla."

When Pushkin left school he entered a regiment. His splendid physique and excellence in all kinds of sports made him a favorite in the regiment and he plunged with the rest into a fast life.

There was at this time in Russia a secret organization formed in support of what was known as the liberal movement as opposed to the established form of government. Pushkin's sympathies were with the rebels and he contributed a number of poems to their cause. These verses caused complaint of Pushkin to come to the ears of Alexander who thought seriously of sending the poet to Siberia but through the intervention of Pushkin's friends changed the sentence to exile in Southern Russia. Here he was taken ill with a fever. General

Raevsky, an old friend of his father's obtained leave to take
the young man home with him and at Raevsky's charming
home the poet spent some of the happiest hours of his whole
life.

The Raevsky girls are said to be the originals of the heroines of Pushkin's masterpiece, "Eugene Onegin." It was
here that he fell under the spell of Byron's poetry which he
admired so greatly at first that he tried to imitate it.

From the Raevsky's he was ordered to Kishniev but because of reckless conduct was ordered to Ismail and from
there he was transferred to Odessa. Pushkin now abandoned
Byron for Shelley and tried to imagine himself an atheist.
The Government, that all important factor in Russia, hearing
of this new departure, exiled the poet to his father's estate at
Mikhailovsky, August, 1824. He had plenty of time for re-
flection after he got home for his father was very much in-
censed toward him at first and left him to himself for a good
while. Pushkin devoted his time to reading the Bible and
composing "Eugene Onegin," a novel in verse.

A new plot being formed against the government and it
being discovered that the poet's sympathies, if not his aid,
had been given to the revolters, he had a narrow escape from
the gallows.

The Emperor Nicholas I. sent for Pushkin shortly after
and at the royal palace in Moscow the emperor and poet
agreed to be friends; Pushkin to remain in court.

The literary circles of Moscow welcomed the poet with
open arms and he was given an ovation everywhere he went.
He was quite happy until he found that he was like a bird in
a gilded cage, for the Minister of Police had him under
constant surveillance.

Part of the condition of his friendship with the Emperor
was that Pushkin submit all he wrote to the Emperor for

criticism before publication. Through the influence of the Minister of Police some of the poet's poems were rejected as unsuitable for publication and he became discouraged.

In 1828 he met the girl who afterwards became his wife, a Miss Goucharev. Three years later they married and lived at Moscow, then at Tsarky Selo. At the latter place he wrote a series of national poems that won for him the place of first national poet of Russia. These poems aroused the admiration of the whole country and as a suitable reward for the glory shed upon the nation Pushkin was given a post in the Ministry of Foreign Affairs with a salary of 5,000 roubles a year. In order it is said to keep him out of political mischief, the poet was ordered to search for material for the life of Peter the Great. During this period he wrote the history of Pougachef's Rebellion, "The Captain's Daughter," a prose tale, and several poems.

Unfortunately Pushkin's gifts and popularity had made him bitter enemies who had resolved upon his ruin. A flirtation between Pushkin's young wife and a Baron de Heckeron Dantes created a scandal concerning which the poet's enemies taunted him until he challenged the Baron to a duel. It was fought with pistols, January 27, 1837, and Pushkin was mortally wounded. He was carried to Petersburg where he died after two days of great suffering.

All classes united to do the dead poet honor, mourning him as their national poet.

It is said of Pushkin, "He rises in each subsequent work, to greater artistic perfection, shows more mature originality and attains to that objective plasticity by which he approaches Goeth[e], and Shakespeare." And again, "He embodied all that had preceded him in Russian literature while he also inaugurated a new period. He was the most perfect master of his material that had yet appeared in Russia. He ennobled everything he touched. He possessed an impeccable sense of form and irresistible musical charm and a felicity of expression and picturesqueness of vision which remain to this day the legacy to many Russian poets and novelists who follow him."

Here is one of his poems called "An Eastern Song."

> I think thou wert born for this,
>   To set the poet's vision burning,
> To hold him in a trance of bliss,
>   And by sweet words to wake his yearning.
> To charm him by those eyes that shine,
> By that strange eastern speech of thine
> And by those feet those tiny treasures,
> Ah, thou wert born for languid pleasures
>   And glowing hours of bliss divine.

POETRY

❧ ❧ ❧

INDIVIDUAL POEMS PUBLISHED
BETWEEN 1888 AND 1902

MEMORY *

Of all the powers that be in earth,
That fill the soul with joy or mirth
To memory's care it has been given
To fit our souls for hell or heaven.
Sometimes upon the mountain side
With God, foul sin will glide
Into our most holy place
And challenge Jehovah to his face.
The sinful echoes of a doubtful past
Rush o'er the mind and hold it fast.

But why art troubled, O my soul,
Since Jesus' touch has made thee whole?
Bid Memory waft to thee the story
Of thy great Saviour's wond'rous glory,
Tell thee sweetly, calmly, well,
How He saved thy soul from hell—
How when friendless, poor, alone,
Thou couldst nothing do but moan,
He revealed Himself to thee
Made the joyful, set thee free.

Christian Recorder (12 July 1888).

131

ONLY A LETTER*

'Twas only a letter that came
    From a mother to her boy;
But it filled his heart with shame
    And chased his worldly joy.

For it said, "Dear son, I am getting old,
    My eyes are growing dim,
And I can scarcely hold
    The book to read the hymn—

So I thought I'd ask you to write
    Once a week the sermon and song,
When you're not too tired at night;
    'Twould powerfully help me along."

The boy's heart was strangely moved
    And something like a prayer
For the mother that he loved
    Was felt a stirring there,

"So mother thinks I'm living right,
    And go to hear the preacher,
And try to live as in His sight,
    The Great and Wond'rous Teacher.

It's never too late to mend,
    So I'll begin to-day—
All evil practice end—
    O, how do people pray?

* *Christian Recorder* (9 Aug. 1888).

Oh, mother's God, look down
  And bless an erring boy,
So far from thee I've grown—
  Come, fill my heart with joy."

The prayer was heard in heaven,
  And answered from the throne,
And all the clouds ere riven,
  Bright rays of glory shon[e].

'Twas only mother's letter,
  But a sinful soul was turned,
A heart changed for the better,
  Youth's lessons are re-learned.

MY QUEEN*
To Miss A. H. Jones, lady Principal
Wilberforce University

All honor to my dark-eyed Queen,
As you rule in your realm of love—
God keep you from danger dark unseen,
God guide you with His love.

Pure as a flake of fairest snow
Hast thy whole life e'er been—
Ah, never a nobler one I trow
Than thou, my stately queen.

Thou hast learned in sorrow's school
Some lessons, I know of pain
Hast let thy heart's deep lava cool
And found thy cross again.

Christian Recorder (10 Sept. 1891).

God bless thee as the years roll on,
Strengthen thy woman's hands,
Bring thee into the perfect dawn,
Where mystery expands,

Where dark things are all made clear,
And like a troubled dream
Life's woes shall disappear,
For love shall reign supreme!

THE GLAD NEW YEAR*

Swiftly cometh the glad New Year,
    Leaving in throes of pain,
The dying year, whose reign is o'er,
    And will never come again.

How shall we welcome the glad New Year,
    As it enters our erring life?
By banishing sin from the door of our hearts,
    And shutting out malice and strife.

If we have erred in the year that is dead,
    Let us live in the New Year aright:
Let us hasten to right the wrongs we have done.
    Ere our spirits shall take their flight.

Ah! There is many a heart that the glad New Year
    Findeth torn and bleeding with pain;
If thou hast aught to do with this woe,
    Go quickly and bring joy again.

* *Christian Recorder* (10 Jan. 1893). A different version of this poem appears in Tillman's *Recitations* (1902).

And let the coming of God's New Year
  Bring joy and peace to all.
And help us to bear the burdens of life,
  While we wait for the Master's call.

LIFT ME HIGHER MASTER *

Lift me up higher Master
  My sinful, yea, blinded eyes
Would fain, now behold they glory,
  So, higher, let me rise.

Lift me up higher, Master,
  Above the things of earth
Renew my soul this hour
  As at its Christly birth.

Help me to scale the mountains,
  Transfigured by thy love
And all that is unworthy
  Oh from my heart remove,

Help me to scale the mountains,
  Transfigured by thy love
And all that is unworthy
  Oh from my heart remove,

For naught oh, gracious Master,
  Is worthy thus to be
An awful stony barrier
  Betwixt my God and me.

* *Christian Recorder* (26 Apr. 1894).

Lift me up higher Master,
  Higher, higher every day
Fit and prepare my fickle soul
  For its immortal sway.

LINES TO IDA B. WELLS*

Charlotte Corday for the English,
  Joan of Arc for the French,
And Ida B. Wells for the Negro,
  His life from the lynchers to wrench.

Thank God, there are hearts in old England
  That feel for the Negro's distress,
And gladly give of their substance
  To obtain for his wrongs a redress.

Speed on the day when the lynchers
  No more shall reign in our land,
When even the poorest of Negroes
  Protected by Justice shall stand.

When no more shall cries of terror
  Break on the midnight air;
While poor and defenseless Negroes
  Surrender their lives in despair.

When the spirits of Phillips and Lincoln,
  Of Sumner and Garrison brave,
Shall hurl the murderous lynch-law
  Down to its dishonored grave.

Christian Recorder (5 July 1894). Another version of this poem is in
Recitations.

When loyal hearts in the Southland,
  And those of the North that are true
Shall give to the struggling Negro
  That which is by nature his due.

And the cloud that threatens our land
  Shall pale beneath Liberty's Sun,
And in the prosperous future
  Shall vanish the wrongs to us done.

Go on, thou brave woman leader,
  Spread our wrongs from shore unto shore;
Until clothed with his rights is the Negro,
  And lynchings are heard of no more.

And centuries hence little children,
  Sprung up from the Hamitic race,
On History's glowing pages
  Thy loving deeds shall trace.

And the wise Afro-American mother,
  Who her children of heroines tells,
Shall speak in tones of gratitude,
  The name of Ida B. Wells!

THE PASTOR*
Dedicated to Rev. G. M. Tillman

In a lonely little parish
  For a year, a man of God,
Taught in love the common people
  Of the pathway Christ has trod.

Christian Recorder (18 Oct. 1894). A different version of this poem is in
Recitations.

Told to them the old, old story
   Of the wondrous one who gave
His own life on Calvary's summit,
   Lost and ruined souls to save.

Sometimes it was told in gladness,
   Offender when filled with pain
That they followed not the Savior,
   Though besought o'er and again.

Oft he deemed his labor wasted,
   Many times discouraged grew,
But withal he had resolved that
   He would to the cross be true.

But no life that's truly given
   To the service of the Lord,
E'er is lost but in the seeming,
   So declares His precious word.

Time removed the patient preacher
   To another little place,
And again he taught the people
   Of the pleasant ways of grace.

Words that months ago he'd spoken
   One day quickened into life,
And a soul communed with Jesus
   That before had known but strife.

Many more were led to Jesus,
   Through the zealous loving one
And when life's conquests are over,
   And the victory is won.

Humbler worker hear thy sentence
  Rejoice e'er thou weary one,
Hear thy sovereign's gracious welcome,
  "Good and faithful soul, well done."

A REST BEYOND*

If this world were all, and no
Glorious thought of a Divine
Hereafter did comfort me, then
Life with too much pain were
  Fraught and misery.
I should not care to live another
Day, with burdened heart and naught
To cheer my soul upon its lonely way,
  From year to year.
So many cares beset me on my way;
So many griefs confront me in the
Road, how wretched I, no hope,
No faith to-day, in Heaven
  and God.
The friends I love, for whom my life
Is spent, do oft misjudge and rob
Me of their love. Ah, if I had
No hope in Jesus, sent down from above!
Why should I care to stay in such
A race? far rather give the
Bitter struggle o'er and die,
Caring not to face what the

*In Mrs. N. F. Mossell, *The Work of the Afro-American Woman* (Philadelphia: Geo. S. Ferguson Co., 1894; rpt. New York: Oxford University Press, 1988), pp. 92–93.

Future hath in store.
But just beyond is Heaven's
Eternal shore, a mansion
Waiteth for each sincere soul,
A blessed rest forever more
    Is at the goal.

ALLEN'S ARMY *

You have heard of Alexander,
    Who upon Asiatic plain,
On and on to victory
    Let his host of warrior-men.

You have read Napoleon's conquests
    Upon the fields of Europe, vast
And of Washington the hero,
    Whose fame will through the ages last.

You have heard the stirring story
    Of Sherman marching to the sea
Followed by a cloud of bondmen
    Shouting sweet songs of jubilee.

Of Grant and his brave black soldiers
    Storming strongholds of rebel-men,
You have heard these thrilling stories,
    For oft have they been told by pen.

But have you heard of Allen's army
    Who are now many thousands strong,
Who are struggling for the future,
    Working hard against the wrong?

* *Christian Recorder* (7 Feb. 1895).

Step by step these men are coming;
   Hear their cheers come over the plain,
"We belong to Allen's army;
   We are Richard Allen's men."

Here we stand a valiant army;
   Husbands, wives and children too,
Sworn to Christians doctrines,
   Proud that we are A. M. E.'s true.

Not with any carnal weapons
   Will we win in this great fight,
But with God and Truth and Justice,
   We will battle for the Right!

Many foes menace our forces;
   Rank Prejudice and Vice we find,
But we'll never cease the struggle
   Till the victor's wreath is twined

Round our heads and acclamations,
   As our arduous work is crowned,
Of welcome home to Allen's army,
   Through the heaven's shall resound.

A PSALM OF THE SOUL*

Oh, Father, my heart is heavy laden,
   And grief has settled o'er me like a pall;
And behold in earth or Heaven,
   My anguished soul on none but thee can call.

* *Christian Recorder* (9 Jan. 1896).

No, none but thee a word of cheer can give,
  In this the deepened gloom of a sad day;
Oh, come to my heart dear Father,
  And bid my bitter sorrow steal away.

Teach me to see how blessed good shall come
  From everything that seemeth to me ill;
If I but wait, but trust my all to thee
  And ever seek to do thy loving will.

And while I cannot see a ray of light,
  Yet lend me faith to love thee well;
And conquering grace for every trial,
  Till I beyond the pearly gates shall dwell.

Tonight I need thy rod and staff
  To comfort me, for I am travel-worn;
My hands are weary with much toil,
  My feet are badly bruised and torn.

Reach down and hide me in thy cleft,
  Where I may rest awhile my weary feet;
And there I pray that thine own voice
  In soothing tones my longing heart shall greet.

So shall I then be comforted,
  My soul shall then rejoice in thee;
The oil of joy thy presence sheds
  Shall fill my soul with ecstacy.

HEART-KEEPING*

Thoughts suggested by a sermon on
"Heart-Cultivation," delivered by Rev.
G. M. Tillman, at Davenport, Ia.

Thy heart so prone to waywardness,
  Thy heart so fond of sin,
Oh keep thy heart with diligence;
  Let every thought be clean.

Let evil books whose impure thoughts
  Would soil thy heart's fair page
Be resolutely thrust aside,
  By youth as well as age.

Ask God for strength when morn's
  First rays, across thy pathway shine;
At eve when stars shine overhead,
  Thy heart to God incline.

Let every impulse of thy soul
  Upward to God incline;
So shall from morn, till setting sun,
  A perfect heart be thine.

For, from thy heart in living streams,
  Life's issues ever flow,
A stream of evil or of good.
  Of blessing or of woe.

Christian Recorder (12 March 1896).

And when 'tis thine to exchange worlds;
  Time for eternity,
'Tis then the keeping of thy heart,
  Decides thy destiny.

AFRO-AMERICAN BOY *

Afro-American boy whose face
Africa's sun hath fondly kissed
Though by American prejudice hissed
With her proudest sons take thy rightful place.

Lift to the breeze thy thoughtful brow
Heir of America's lands and schools,
God, above men forever rules
He has a care for such as thou.

Thou art as dear to His great heart
Who cannot be mocked by outward show,
As any soul whom thou dost know
In the busy streets of the world's great mart.

Only be brave and do thy task
Purity of life mayst thou possess,
Thou canst not succeed in life with less
This alone doth thy Father ask.

FAITH'S VISION *

There is a place no mortal eye
  Hath ever seen,

* *Christian Recorder* (24 June 1897).

* *Christian Recorder* (29 July 1897). Another version of this poem is in *Recitations*.

Where spirits of the just may dwell
   In state serene.

Where pride and pomp are laid aside
   And no one cares
For glittering gems or coronets
   The earthly monarch wears.

The noble of the earth are there,
   The rich in truth,
And some who by the world were deemed
   Poor and uncouth.

The faithful widow there is comforted
   By psalms of joy
And many a mother clasps in ecstasy
   An angel boy.

These little orphaned hearts are glad
   Around the throne,
Who oft on earth wept bitter tears
   Poor and alone.

The sick, the sad, the sorrowing who loved
   The Savior well,
Laid crosses by for shining crowns, and
   Went, with him to dwell.

There too, shall we, when we have done
   Our task, gave up life's lease,
Begin a life whose wondrous joy
   Shall never cease.

A TRIBUTE TO NEGRO REGIMENTS*

Watch as they march from the West to the Sea,
Cavalry brave and armed infantry:
Men who have fought, so the records say,
Like lions, on the frontiers far away.

"Black Buffaloes," the Indians called them first,
But when in the fight they got the worst
Of the awful burst of shot and shell,
They turned and rushed away pell-mell.

There were Negroes fighting at Bunker Hill;
In 1812 they were at it still,
And when they were called in '61,
Thousands shouldered the government gun.

Loyal? I guess so—game till death;
Braver soldiers never drew breath.
Just treat them like men 'tis all they ask,
And then they are ripe for the sternest task.

They fight, not as Negroes, they fight like men;
As men with rights they gladly maintain.
They fight for a land that's theirs by birth,
And die for a cause, the grandest on earth.

THE SUPERANNUATE*

Watch him totter down the street,
Haste the dear old man to greet;

---

* *Christian Recorder* (9 June 1898). A different version of this poem appears
in *Recitations*, under the title "The Black Boys in Blue."
* *Christian Recorder* (16 March 1899). Another version is in *Recitations*.

From his steps so very slow
And his voice so weak and low
Nature doth to us relate
Leaveth our superannuate!

But yesterday quite in his frame
The foremost preacher of his time,
Warning in love old age and youth
To choose the blessed ways of truth.
How Time did all his powers abate
And left him—Superannuate.

But still he loves the Sacred Word,
And often shouts "Praise ye the Lord,"
And bids the younger men go on
And win the prize as he has won.
He is no railer 'gainst his fate,
Though he is superannuated!

Yet when fell first the dreaded word,
His inmost soul within him stirred
To lay his precious life work by,
And like all worn out things to die
He felt so old, so out of date
To be a superannuate!

And now he's ling'ring by death's stream
Across the wave comes silvery gleams
Of waters still, of pastures green
And forms arrayed in dazzled sheen,
Mansion and crown from his await,
Thrice blessed! Superannuate!

WHICH?*
"And whosoever will be chief among
you, let him be your servant." St. Matt. xx: 27.

Which of us shall be chief—
   Who have the softest seat?
For whom shall robes of power
   Be deemed most just and meet?
Who above his brethren
   Shall the most exalted be?
Who from toil and service
   Shall now be made most free?

Bring out the kingly crown,
   The one that fame adorns;
Not Jesus' crown—
   The painful one of thorns.
Bring out the royal robes,
   Not like the one He wore,
Not yet the heavy cross
   The suffering Saviour bore.

Who will bear His cross?
   Who will share its shame?
Who will humbly live
   To glorify His name?
Who will spread His kingdom?
   Who will preach His word?
Who will heed the Spirit's
   Faithful teachings heard?

* *Christian Recorder* (6 July 1899).

He who would be thy chief,
　　Shall humblest servant be;
The greatest life among ye all—
　　Uplifting most of Me.
Remembering above all,
　　My blessed spoken word:
That "never yet was servant
　　Greater than his Lord."

THE HIGHEST LIFE*

To will, to do, to work, to strive
　　To be supremely strong,
To highest things to be alive
　　And turn unscathed from wrong;
To love the good that God has made
　　In earth and air and sky,
To do while here our little part,
　　And after that to die.

Such death as comes to Mother Earth
　　By Winter's frost and snow,
And then in Heaven's eternal Spring
　　More beautiful to grow;
Such air to breathe, such days to live
　　Are for all souls most meet.
This, then, were highest life to live,
　　And life most full and sweet.

Christian Recorder (8 Nov. 1900).

SOUL VISIONS *

Have you ever seen a vision
   In the day or in the night
Of what you might, if you dared to be
   And you shrank back in affright?

And accepted a lower purpose
   Or lived by a weaker thought
And sacrificed your ideals
   For earth-things that you sought?

We call our visions madness
   And cast our ideals away
And are ever less than we should be
   Had we bade our visions stay.

For those who most helped the world
   In its onward march to roll
Have cherished day and night
   The visions of the soul.

THE WARRIOR'S LAY *

Sometimes like wee tired children
We wish for restful place
To cuddle and rest our worn selves
Ere duties new we face.

Christian Recorder (21 Aug. 1902). Another version is in *Recitations*.

Christian Recorder (22 Oct. 1902). A different version of this poem appears in *Recitations*, under the title "The Worker's Song."

But the need of the world is great
And Duty clamors strong
And off we are at work again,
Battling against the wrong.

And the hardest battle we wage
Is the war that's within
Where the soul must wield its armour
Against the hosts of sin.

For no true success in battle
Can come to warriors bold
Until our foes within,
The victor's place they hold.

RECITATIONS

THAT YE BE ONE

A dream I had of busy workers,
Followers of the Crucified,
Men and women of all races,
Laboring meekly side by side.

Prejudice and racial hatred
Had been buried 'neath God's love;
One great thought theirs souls united—
Men, to lead from Self, above.

Shone dark faces as if visions
Of God's glory beamed within,
Shone fair faces with like rapture
Over souls redeemed from sin.

Crumbled down the walls of darkness,
Perished Satan in his pride,
When the hosts of God united,
When they labored side by side.

"Ye are brethren," sweet the message
Until now an empty sound,
Now caught up by holy millions,
Echoed all the world around.

Recitations was originally published by the A. M. E. Book Concern (Philadelphia, 1902). Reproduced in this volume by courtesy of the Moorland-Spingarn Research Center, Howard University, Washington, D.C.

Saxon, Negro, Jew and Hindoo,
All had felt the quickening flame
That had made of every nation
One in Jesus' hallowed name.

Speed the time, oh, glorious Father,
When in all reality,
Christians out of every nation
May be truly one, in Thee.

IN OLE CA'LINY

'Twas in de merry month of May,
    When down in old Ca'liny
De winter to de springs gibs way,
    An' de woods smell sweet and piney,
Hi inhis nes' de bluebird sang
    Jas' lak he was in meetin',
All troo de woods de music rang
    De po' slaves' ears a-greetin'.

'Twas den I sed de words ob love
    O'er which I long had pondered,
An' kissed de fus de little dove
    To whom my heart had wandered.
She slipped her toil-worn hand in mine
    As dere we stood togedder,
While oberhead de bright sunshine
    Warmed up de sweet spring wedder.

But dat was May. December's bref
    Came sweepin' o'er Ca'liny
An' all de flowers yield' do def

An' so, too, did my Biny.
I laid her in de woods to res',
   De woods so sweet an' piney,
Where fus' I did my love confess,
   Way down in old Ca'liny.

OUR CAUSE

Time was when in the Black's defense,
In hours with awful perils dense,
Brave men stood up and plead his cause
And stormed against inhuman laws;
But now where clanked his heavy chain
His slavers would rebind again,
And from him freed but yesterday
Take every manly right away!

Brave Sumner! Whittier! are ye gone!
Thou hast no like to call upon.
Garrison! Lincoln! We call in vain,

We shall not see thy like again.
Then be the Black his own defense,
And though his struggles be intense,
Fight hard, fight e'er for every right
That's granted by our Charter's might!

A HYMN OF PRAISE

Oh, God, when days were dark indeed,
   When we were fast in Slavery's chain,
Thou then our parents' prayers did heed
   And helped us freedom to obtain.

And when adrift upon the world
    A child race 'mid the great and strong.
Thy banner o'er was unfurled
    And gently were we led along.

Help us to e'er remember Thee
    And e'er to endless homage pay
For all the great prosperity
    Enjoyed by our race to-day.

CLOTELLE—A TALE OF FLORIDA

Clotelle! Orange-blossoms, "A lover and a grave."
    "Sweets to the sweet," and laurels for the brave!
Can I tell the story as it was told to me
    Down in Florida by the deep murmuring sea?

Gentle muse, I now invoke thee,
    Lend thy power while I shall tell
Men the story of a slave-maid
    Of the bright-eyed slave Clotelle!

Light and tripping were her footsteps,
    Beauteous both her face and form,
Yet no power could protect her
    From the trader's golden charm.

Lived Clotelle on a plantation
    Near the Gulf Stream's turbid wave
Lived through childhood's years unheeding;
    She was but a helpless slave.

Sixteen years had lightly o'er her,
    Tenderly o'er the maid had sped,
When the time came to Clotelle
    That love's dreams her fancies led.

Cupid threw at her an arrow
   Aimed at fair Clotelle his dart,
And love entered the recesses
   Of her innocent young heart.

Dark her lover was and stately
   As a prince of olden days,
And among slaves both old and young
   Naught was heard of Pierre but praise.

Fate smiled on the poor slave lovers,
   Oft they met in woodland bowers,
Oft exchanged love-vows in rapture
   In those happy stolen hours.

Planned the two a little cabin,
   Orange blossoms overhead,
Mocking-birds to lend their music;
   An, those days too quickly sped!

But one day to the maiden
   Sorrow, agony and shame,
For with words of subtile meaning
   To her side her master came.

Said the planter to the maiden,
   "Thou art by far too fair to toil;
Hands like thine, so small and shapely,
   Were not meant to till the soil."

"Come and be my loved companion,
   Robed in silks and jewels rare;
'Tis no miser who entreats thee,
   Come and all my riches share."

Shrank poor Clotelle from her master
   With a countenance of shame,
While in low and tender accents
   She sobbed forth her lover's name.

"I love Pierre, O worthy master,
   And death with him beneath the sea
Would suit better far thy maiden
   Than a life of shame with thee!"

Then the planter's brow grew clouded
   And his voice both harsh and stern.
"If you thus my will defy, girl,
   That I am your master you shall learn.

"You love Pierre, you say—my servant;
   You prefer my slave to me,
Your love will but prove his ruin;
   Never thou his bride wilt be."

Sank Clotelle's young heart with boding,
   All her joy was turned to pain,
All the fond hopes she had cherished,
   Vanished, ne'er to come again.

From that hour Pierre was doomed
   By the planter's wish to die;
For he swore to see him hanging
   Lifeless 'neath the southern sky.

At last accused of awful crime
   Too hideous to breathe aloud,
Poor Pierre was hanged one fatal day,
   Surrounded by a pitying crowd.

Clotelle gazed on him in anguish.
  "Farewell, Pierre, my love," she cried.
"Farewell, sweet," to her he whispered,
  Ere the fatal noose was tied.

When 'twas o'er, Clotelle stood silent,
  Till her eyes the planter's met,
Then she ran like one demented,
  Shrieking, "Pierre, thine am I yet."

Rushing to the water's edge,
  Plunged she in its maddening foam,
And returned the planter, baffled,
  To his princely, slave-bought home.

Rest in peace, Clotelle, sweet maiden;
  Near the Gulf Stream's turbid wave,
Thou who for the love of virtue,
  All untimely filled thy grave!

A SOUTHERN INCIDENT
(Founded upon a true incident)

It was in a Southern city,
And the people from near and far
Clad in their august robes of wealth,
Crowded a passing car.
They quickly filled all the seats,
And then began to chat,
Of the weather, country, fashions—
From farms to the latest style hat.

An old colored woman
Came slowly struggling in,
And looked with hopeful glance
A pitying smile to win
On her arm an old worn basket
Hung awkwardly down in her way,
While to the strap she caught wildly.
Eighty years she'd seen if a day.

But men of vigorous manhood
And women young in years,
Kept their comfortable seats in silence
And found her a subject for jeers.
And then a young Southern woman,
And gladly the tale I repeat,
Rose in the car and said kindly,
"Here auntie, take my seat."

An electric shock thrilled the hearers,
She was an old colored woman, you know,
But they knew that the deed they had witnessed
Was as white as the falling snow.
The old woman comfortably nestled
In the depths of her cosy seat.
"Well, you is a rale lady,"
She sighed from her pleasant retreat.

"De Lawd bless you fo' yo' kindness;
You has he'p me mo' dan you kno',
But folks can see you's a lady
Dat nebber hab seen you befo'."
Three cheers for the Southern lady,
Who dared that act to do,
And speed the time when the Southland,
Shall be filled with such charity true.

WHEN MANDY COMBS HER HEAD

If there's one thing more than t'other
'Bout which something might be said,
And a subject that's important,
It's a colored person's head.

My Mandy's been to high school,
And she's got her books down fine;
She can figure like a lawyer,
And read Latin, line for line.

But there's one thing tries her spirit,
And an hour when tears are shed,
Oh, I hear the storm approaching
When my Mandy combs her head.

She starts at it Sunday morning,
Soon as ever she's done her work,
And begins to comb and pull
And to fume and sigh and jerk.

" 'Taint no use to try to fix it.
Lord, I wish that I was dead!
Here I've worked hard for an hour
Trying to do something with my head."

Or it may be that at bedtime
Just before her prayers are said,
Mandy gets the comb an' starts up
Working on her tired head.

How she'll fuss an' pull an' jerk it,
Working on that stubborn fleece,
'Till I hear her mother say,
"Mandy, stop an' get the grease!"

Like the oil upon the waters,
Things get better for a while.
The big comb it quits its jerking,
An' then Mandy tries to smile.

"Lord, I wish I'd been around there
When the Lord was giving hair;
While the white folks was a-getting,
I'd been sure to get my share."

Pap, if Gabriel blows for Judgement,
An' my name you don't hear read,
Don't you'n mammy get excited,
I'll be fixing of my head!

UNCLE NED'S STORY

Lay aside yo' books boys,
   An' listen to ole Ned
While I tell to you a story
   No man has eber read.

'Twas durin' ob de wah,
   De wah ob sixty-three,
When thousan's ob brave Union men
   Lef' home the slaves to free.

Way down on de ole plantashun
   Was my wife Chloe an' I,
A takin' keer ob po ole Miss,
   Who's den about to die.

De Union soldiers came one night,
   An' said we'd soon be free;
An' dat we could go 'long o' them,
   An' fight for liberty.

Now all had gone sabe us,
   De slaves an' massa, too,
An' lef' us home to 'tend ole Miss,
   Case dey'd allus foun' us true.

Now, I laks to be called hones',
   But I ain' nebber took much stock
In de white folks a-praisin' me,
   Dat used the auction block.

My Chloe she made a reg'lar feast
   An' watched dem wid delight;
Until dey eat an' den prepared
   To march out in de night.

I tied my few ole clo'es up quick,
   An' tole Chloe do de same,
But dere she stood jes' lak a block,
   An' me callin' her name.

"Come, Chloe, be quick, dey'll go away,
   An' we nebber will be free.
Ain't you had enuf ob massa's whip,
   An' 'nuf of slavery?

But Chloe she muttered 'bout ole Miss,
   Almos' in de grave,
An' said she couldn' leave her den,
   Ef 'twas her soul to save.

Chloe stayed, while I marched away
   On de battle-fiel';
An' thoughts ob her kept me in heart,
   My Chloe true as steel.

When all was done I hurried home,
But no Chloe a welcome gave;
By old mistress' side she's buried
In a lonely Southern grave!

SEEKING THE LOST

Many Negro newspapers have from time to time maintained
a "Lost" column, for the purpose of bringing together families that were sold apart during the period of American slavery.

Is you de blessed editor
    Dat brings de dead to life,
United sons an' darters,
    An' husban's wid dere wife?
You is! Well I'se ole Mose,
    I hails from Virginny,
I'se huntin' fer my long-los' folks,
    Ole ooman' an' little Winnie.

On de banks ob de Missippy,
    In ole Missouri State,
'Twas dar dey took my wife
    When we fus' separate.
My other two chillen was boys,
    Dey's livin' now wid me.
Ef I can fin' my wife an' gal,
    How happy we will be.

I don' min' de money,
    I wants my wife an' chile,
I want to see my folks

I'se mourned for dis long while.
You don't know de sorrow
    Dat's filled my heart for y'ars,
Nor de days an' nites da
    I's spent in bitter tears.

My wife's name was Mandy,
    An' sah, she was a cook,
An' one ob de fines',
    Do' she don' use no book.
Why, Kernel Butler sed her cakes,
    Was fit for any king,
An' comp'ny time she was de one
    Dat heaven's gates jes' opened wide

An' den she was a powah in prayer,
    Fer when she prayed it seem
Dat heaven's gates jes' opened wide,
    On all our souls to beam.
What made 'em sell her? Easy tole,
    Dey cleared up de estate
At master's death an' all was sole
    An' 'bliged to separate.

Li'l' Winnie was de baby then,
    'Twas thirty years or mo.'
Ef libin', she's a woman now,
    An' Mandy's head's lak sno'.
Tink you know' 'em? Winnie's yo wife,
    Mandy's libin' in dis yeah town!
Praise de Lawd, an' you, too, mister!
    Ole Mose' po' lams is foun'!

PHYLLIS WHEATELEY *[sic]*

O little maid from Afric's slave coasts brought
By traders cruel to be put up and sold
As other goods by scheming merchants are,
A human life exchanged for senseless gold.
Rude, helpless child, right glad am I
That then thy lot and tender years
A woman's generous sympathies awoke
And thou wert christened with a woman's tears.

Oh, little did she dream that genius rare
Slumbered within thy childish brain,
Or that the time would come when thou
Wouldst lasting fame obtain;
But nurtured by a Christian woman's care
In all the graces true and sweet thou grew,
And soon the wise, the famed and the great
To pay thy genius homage quickly drew.

Thy verses with their melancholy strain
Breathed from a soul so filled with poesy
Won my friends to thee, O Phyllis dear,
And made thy mistress more than proud of thee.
And Washington, our nation's chief,
Paid tribute to thee, gifted Afric maid,
Much pleasure found in lines thy dark hands penned
And thou with courtly praise did lade.

And England, too, applauded thee, dear one,
And read thy graceful verses, with all pride.
Alas, that thou while in the bloom of life

Thy earthly task gave o'er—and died!
But, ah, thy memory still is green,
And Afric poets still are inspired by thee,
And thou wilt help them tune their harps
To grander strains of minstrelsy!

IDLERS AND TOILERS

Heaven's great crowning day had come,
And all had gathered there,
And those who had no sheaves
Cried out in great despair.
"We ate and drank in thy presence
Whilst Thou passed through our street,
We knew Thee Lord, and now we pray
Thee give us welcome meet."

"Ye ate and drank in My presence,
While I passed through thy street,
And carelessly sat and feasted
With beggars unhelped at your feet.
For self ye wholly lived,
Despising Mine and Me.
Depart, ye ruined souls,
That worked iniquity.

"Far from earth's care and its sorrow
Ye lived your lives away.
Crowns are for the toilers,
Stand ye far back, I pray."
And abashed, the idlers vanished
Within a cloud of gloom,
While for weary toilers
The heavenly hosts made room.

THE HAPPY CHRISTMAS BELLS

The happy Christmas bells are ringing,
　The heavenly choir their anthems singing
The sweetest words of tongue or pen—
　Peace on earth, good will to men!

A Saviour born in poverty
　Brings to the world true liberty.
We sing the song angels sang then,
　Peace on earth, good will to men!

The song the angels sang of peace
　Its heavenly strains shall never cease,
Till discord from our earth shall flee
　And then shall feel soul harmony.

Till man his brother's care shall feel,
　And labor for his brother's weal,
And men of every tongue and race
　The truths of Christ's great life embrace.

With heavenly hosts Him we adore,
　Who all our sins and sorrows bore,
And upward still our songs ascend,
　Peace on earth, good will to men!

AT ANCHOR

My bark, so tempest-tossed in days of youth,
Hath anchored now in seas of heavenly truth,
And peace, ne'er found in Pleasure's wanton ways
Now gently hallows all my passing days.

The work unblest, because an idol made
Down at the Cross, my soul at last hath laid
One lingering look at awful Calvary,
One look at Calvary's Christ, hath
Wrought this peace for me.

My faith, before so weak, is suddenly made strong.
I toil but worry not; all doth to God belong.
Dark often is my way, but songs in night time come
As happy pilgrims sing in sight of home.

Henceforth I tread but in the path He trod,
Henceforth I joy but in the love of God.
My life, my all to Thee, O blessed Christ, I give,
To Thee who suffered death that sinful men might live.

Farewell, unrest, and all my worldly pride
The prince of Peace my soul hath satisfied.
My ship hath cast her anchor; all, all is well,
And mortal tongue can ne'er my soul's deep rapture tell.

OH, AFRICA!

Oh, Africa, dear Africa,
    Upon thy sun-kissed shore,
Shall the sable sons of Hamite sires
    Ne'er be masters more?
Or shall thy glowing splendors
    Of earth and air and sky,
Except for alien nations
    In dark oblivion lie?

Oh, canst thou not arise,
    Dear children of the sun,

As in thy primal strength,
   Before thy day is done?
Shall not thy old proud history,
   Thy pyramids of stone,
Thy mummied kings, thy riches,
   Arouse to crowns unwon?

The Sphinx, that wondrous marvel,
   Shames on us more than thou,
With all thy former glory,
   And naught but languor now.
The best king in the forest, the tiger
   In his lair,
Still throw their lordly challenge
   Upon the evening air.

But thou art torn and bleeding,
   And thou dost not arise,
And all thy fair, fair country
   Is searched by alien spies.
Throw down thy rude, dumb idols,
   Thy gods of wood and stone,
No help is there in idols,
   Help comes from God alone!

COLOR

There is a silent majesty which speaks
   From lives of noble men
Of every nation, tongue and clime,
   Beyond malicious ken.

And men with countenance as black
  As skies of midnight hue
May yet be men of highest type
  Of manhood strong and true.

And shall a thing of color be
  A certain mark of infamy,
And shall all merit be despised
  That's seen thro' color-blinded eyes?

Believe with sturdy Burns,
  Manhood depends on worth,
And scorn the prejudice that spurns
  The dark-faced men of earth.

THE SUPERANNUATE

Watch him totter down the street,
Haste the dear old man to greet.
From his steps so very slow,
And his voice so thin and low,
Nature doth to us relate
Leaves our superannuate!

But yesterday quite in his prime,
The foremost preacher of his time,
Warning in love old age and youth
To build their lives on Sacred Truth,
How Time did all his powers abate
And left him superannuate!

When first fell the dreaded word,
His inmost soul with pain was stirred
To lay his precious life-work by

And like all wornout things to die,
He felt so old, so out of date,
To be a superannuate!

But still he loves the Sacred Word,
And often shouts, "Praise ye the Lord!"
And bids the younger men go on
And win the prize that he has won.
He is no railer 'gainst his fate,
Our brave old superannuate!

And now he lingers by Death's stream,
Across the wave comes silvery gleam
Of waters still, of pastures green,
And forms arrayed in dazzling sheen,
Mansion and crown for him await,
Thrice blessed superannuate!

IF YOU ARE IN THE RIGHT

If you are in the right, why, say,
Don't look down in that hangdog way.
Lift up your head, your heart as well,
If you are in the right—why, time will tell.

If you don't think that God is dead,
If you believe the words He's said,
Lift up your head and go along,
Start up a verse of some good song.

When God shall settle His accounts
You'll get just what to you amounts.
If you are right, why, say,
Just lift up heart and voice, and pray!

THE NEGRO

We hold ourselves too cheaply;
   In God's sight
Manhood is simply manhood, nothing more,
   Nor worse nor better in His truth's clear light,
Then why should we our origin deplore?

If in time past a black man stood
   For naught; if ignorance was
Black Men's bequeathed store,
   It holds not true in days so grandly fraught
With Black Men's genius, spread
The wide world o'er.

We scorn ourselves, our past
Recalls the yoke.
   Are we than others better, once enslaved?
What nation but hath groaned till chains were broke?
Till they by some great Moses' hands were saved?

Erect we'll stand, as doth become a man
   "God's image cut in ebony," Fuller said.
Our revealed thoughts and aspirations can
   The world's thought in a juster channel lead.

SEN' ME BACK TO DE SOUF

What does I wan' fo' Christmus gib?
   Now, daughter, don' git mad,
Fo' I mus' say to one an' all,
   You is de bes' chile dat I'se had.

You've tried quite hard since I've been heah
   To mek me feel young lak an' gay,
But nothin' meks it seem lak home.
   I want to be home Christmus Day.

Don' think me ungrateful fo' what you've done;
   You have been kin' as kin' can be,
But I miss de sight ob my Southern home,
   An' dar's fren's I longs to see.
Dar is ole Marse Jack, dat is gray lak me,
   An' who lives jes' fo' blocks away.
He will not be here long, and I'd lak chile to see
   Him an' all de res' Christmus Day.

I kno's dat our fo'ks am wronged in de Souf,
   But den de Norf hab a spite at dem too,
And I'se too ole to be changin' my views,
   I laks ole ways better'n new.
Dar's good sister Lu an' ole Uncle Joe,
   Dat's missed me while I was away.
Dar's no one heah dat will miss me but you,
   I want to be home Christmus day.

Dar's no one dar kno's about de rain,
   Nor when it's gwine to sno', chile, lak me.
Why, de nabors dey allus been 'pendin' on Ned
   All ob de signs ob de wedder to see.
Den in the church, when de preacher gibs out
   De words dat he has fo' to say,
He needs me to he'p by shoutin' Amen!
   I's gwine to be dar dis Christmus Day.

I know dat I ain't stayed away berry long,
   An' dey'll laf to see me so soon;
But, chile, I mus' go back to de sweet sunny Souf,

De lan' ob de possum an' coon.
Dar's whar I'se raised an' has buried my dead,
  An' now I ain't got no mo' fo' to say,
'Cep' dis, ef yo' want yo' ole pap to live,
  Sen' him home fo' nex' Christmus Day.

BASHY

"A Negro girl killed in a house of shame."
In cities oft you may hear the same.
How the poor girls go down in the struggle of life,
And yield to dishonor, both maid and wife.

But Bashy, I'll swear, never had a chance;
A black face never does enhance
A woman's value in our land.
Black faces are, well—not just in demand.

Not only in proud Anglo-Saxon race,
But Negroes there are who hate a black face!
We have men who will pass a black girl by
Because she is black—that's the reason why.

You see, we look up to the Saxon race,
And prize above all a white man's face!
And our Bashy was black and ignorant, too,
And what was a poor black outcast to do?

She tried hard to work, but a green farm hand,
Is it strange she never could understand
How to please Miladi on the avenue,
Who could not teach her what to do.

Bashy loved, and she gave her all.
The man who caused her awful fall
Thought her too black to make a wife,
So she drifted on to a dreadful life.

Till one day, while filled with maddening drink,
Bashy was thrust o'er eternity's brink
Without a chance for a whispered prayer
That God would have mercy on her despair.

Her murderer was hung, but every day
Some poor girl goes down in the self-same way,
Some Bashy of our struggling race
Is made an outcast by her face!

Some black mother crooning her baby to sleep
Prays now that the Father of all may keep
Her girl away in the city to toil,
Pure from the deeds and thoughts that soil.

When she hears the news of her girl's dark shame,
And the strain she has brought on her soul and her name,
The house will be dark and the mother's heart
Ache till the life-threads break apart.

Oh, women and men of the Negro Race,
Can we not rise above color of face?
Teach our girls that the worst disgrace
Is blackness of life, not blackness of face!
That women are needed pure-souled and high,

Who sooner than fall will prefer to die!
That a black girl needing a helping hand
Will be helped by the blackmen of the land.
Lift the women up and the race ascends;
Let the women go down, and our progress ends.

SHE WHO NEVER HAD A CHANCE

No, I never had a chance, sir, to be good,
I want it to be plainly understood.
You see, it was this way: mother married again
After father died, and you know what then,
The new father wanted us all out of the way,
And he made us feel it every day.
A curse and a blow, a blow and a curse,
Every day somehow things would grow worse.
Till I got to be near seventeen,
And met with the handsome fellow I had seen.
He'd treated me squarely and things might have gone right
Had not my father on one fatal night
Locked me out of doors, sir, for late coming in,
And called me a name that drove me to sin.
Rich women may leave wine rooms in fine homes to dwell,
But poor girls leave them on journeys to hell.
That's where I went, and these scars on my face
And my red, swollen eyes tell my frequent disgrace.
It seems that I have been through the whole catalogue of
     crime,
Under each new lover I have served out my time.
I couldn't be lower if to be so I tried,
And I often wish when born I had died,
And when the doctor said to me to-day,
"Moll, you will never live to be gray
That heart of yours and that bad cough
Are certain to hurry you off,"
Why, I laughed, for, sir, I just long to die!
Why, ont beneath the cool green grass to lie,
Respected at last, for grim death elevates all,

I am willing at any time to fall.
Ready to go? No, not if you mean good,
For I know that good people should
Study their Bibles, be steady and pray;
And I, sir, was never brought up in that way.
The lessons I learned were to drink, swear and dance.
To be good, sir, I never had the chance.
I've looked in cottages as I passed at night,
Little children in mother's arms clasped tight,
Or wee little ones kneeling down to pray,
And I've choked and sobbed and hurried away,
For I am a woman past forty-three,
And no one has ever said prayers to me.
And I have seen happy well-treated wives,
And I've sighed for our own miserable criminal lives;
But I've dared oft to be thankful that no baby came
To share in it's mother's dark life of shame!
But, sir, you are the chaplain, the priest of men's souls;
Some strange question oft within my mind rolls.
These society women that they call swell,
What's going to keep them from hell?
I read the papers and I know their life,
The heartless coquette, the unfaithful wife,
The parlor carousal, the club room's dance,
Don't tell me these people haven't had a chance.
Their names won't take them to heaven, I've heard,
Then they all will be lost, if there's truth in God's word.
They'd never think of helping a woman like me,
Nor could they, for no better are they that I see,
A good deal more money, a fashionable name,
And one in debauchery and in their shame.
Somehow, I have never liked a low life,
And if I had e'er been a good man's wife,

It seems to me no man's jewels or gold
Would have tempted my feet to stray from the fold.
But regrets are in vain, soon all will end,
And down to the grave without smile or friend,
Without, perhaps, one tearful glance,
Exit Moll—she who never had a chance.

THE HEROES OF THE IOWA CONFERENCE

"Welcome the coming, speed the parting guest."
A great man goes, a great man comes,
And all hearts are at rest.
For the zeal of our Grant for the Lord God of hosts
Is one of our proudest loud-spoken boasts.
For Bishop, they say when you stand for the Lord
That sinners are saved by the power of the Word,
That revivals of blessing break out in your train,
And that forces long dormant awaken again.
We are glad this is true, and in hamlet and town
May the forces of sin through you be pulled down,
And in each of our churches, from end to end
The Holy Spirit in power descend.
A thousand welcomes to you, dear sir.
We have met to-day your heart to cheer,
For the woods are with Methodist preachers thick,
Heroes each one of them, tried men and true,
The makers of our Conference, I present them to you.
And on behalf of the preachers assembled to-day,
Permit me these words of introduction to say:
Here is our Presiding Elder, Dr. George W. Gaines,
A man who generally says what he means;

Stalwart and staunch, true to his race,
Who some day the bench of bishops may grace;
And Presiding Elder Bundy, absent most of the time,
Overseeing his great work in the Snowball clime.
Here is Dr. Ransom, our brilliant host,
Whose gifts are the Conference' pride and boast.
Dr. Carey, pastor of old Mother Quinn,
A man whose graces are sure to win.
And dear Father Thompson, whom we all love
And hope may be given a seat above.
There's Daniels, a strong and earnest man,
Who says he'll raise money if any man can;
And Tillman, the Joshua of St. John,
Leading the young flock bravely on.
There's Slater, full of gospel fire,
And Butler, looking to go higher.
Dr. Booth, among our scholars the best;
Father Malone, the great pioneer of the West;
Seymour and Shaw, who lately came;
Fenwick and Jones, of growing fame.
I wish I had time to speak of them all,
Theological Reeves and dear Father Hall,
Bass, McDowell, Joplin and Grant,
Holly and Taylor, but you see I can't.
There's Rhinehart, Thomas, Gordon and Boyd;
There's Williamson, Peterson, two Johnsons and Ford;
There's Phillips and Higgins, Dr. McGee,
G. W. Jones and John Ferribee,
Williams, Christy, Jackson and Fort,
Lewis, Porter and Searcy, your hands to support.
Basfield, Taylor, Dowden, you see;
Dr. Peterson, F. J., and his brother, J. D.;
Festimun, Speece, Wharton and Knight,

Anderson and Brooks, young men of great might;
C. Peterson, McNeal and Mr. N. Work,
And Graves, who never a duty will shirk.
From here to the snowy plains of the West
Our heroes go forth and each does his best.
They've toiled hard and built up the work that you see,
And each one is anxious promoted to be.
They follow their Master, they fear no foe;
With you as their Bishop forward they'll go,
Living for Jesus, whatever the cost;
Dying like heroes on guard at their post.

UNCLE NED'S RETURN

"Well, Mary, I'se home once again,
An' my heart am' brimmin' wid joy
To be at home wid my old fren's,
Why, hit makes me feel like a boy!

When de engine stopped at de place
Whar de fo'ks dey gits off an' on,
Don' you min' I waved hit a long farewell,
An' was glad to see hit was gone.

Why, de fo'ks dat was down to de train
Jes' to meet an ole fellow lak me,
Dey come in crowds, an' I felt proud
So many ole fren's thar to see.

I rode home in Massa Jack's chair,
Jo's boys was my hosses dat day,
An' when I got home de house was full,
Dey'd come frum eber which way.

Dey had built a fire on de h'arth,
An' de cabin was good an' warm.
De possum was roasting wid taters round,
An' de fo'ks lak bees 'gan to swarm.

I'se glad to be back home again,
An' my joy grows more wid each day.
Good by, chile, be good to yo'self,
I'se home, an' I'se heah fo' to stay."

UNCLE IKE'S TESTIMONY

De Lawd does save; His Son He gave
Fo' me do' I is po'.
Ise surely glad dat I is had
De Lawd my, fren' fo' sho.
De Lawd am mine, an' ebery line
He sen' me by His word
I'se hid away, as day by day
His gospel I hab heard.

I love de Lawd; His precious Word
Hab bro't me to de light.
I'll trus' His grace my foes to face
An' conquer in de fight.
He blesses me an' keeps me free'
Frum danger an' frum sin.
I praise de Lawd I'se heard His Word
An' He had took me in!

OH, DEAR SOUTHLAND

My heart for thee is longing,
And thoughts of thee keep thronging,

Oh, dear Southland!
My grief I cannot master,
My tears but flow the faster
When I would them command.

For thee my tears are flowing,
To thee I'd fain be going,
    My dear Southland!
I would that I could see thee,
I'd never, never leave thee,
    My own, my loved Southland!

THE GLAD NEW YEAR

Swiftly cometh the glad New Year,
Leaving in throes of pain
The dying year whose reign is o'er,
And who never will come again.
How shall we meet the glad New Year
As it enters our erring life?
By banishing sin from the door of our heart
And shutting out evil and strife.

If we have erred in the year that is past,
Let us live the New Year aright;
Let us atone for the wrongs we have done
Ere our spirits shall take their flight.
There may be a heart that the glad New Year
Findeth torn and bleeding with pain.
Oh, if thou hast aught to do with its woe,
Go quickly and bring joy again.

FAITH'S VISION

There is a place no mortal eye
   Hath ever seen,
Where spirits of the just may dwell
   In state serene,
Where pomp and pride are laid aside,
   And no one cares
For glittering gems or coronets
   The monarch wears.

The noble of the earth are there,
   The rich in truth,
And some who by the world were deemed
   Poor and uncouth,
The widow there is comforted
   By psalms of joy,
A mother clasps in ecstasy
   An angel boy.

There little orphaned hearts are glad
   Around the Throne,
Who oft on earth wept bitter tears,
   Despised alone!
The sick, the sad, who loved the
   Savior well,
Laid crosses by for crowns and went
   With Him to dwell;
There, too, shall we when we
   Have done our task,
   Gave up life's lease,
Begin a life whose wondrous joy
   Shall never cease.

WHEN EDIE'S IN THE KITCHEN

When Edie's in the kitchen
How my heart with rapture glows,
And when things begin a-smelling
How my zeal no longer knows,
For around I can't help poking
And remarking with a sigh,
I know that something good
Is a-coming by and by.

And I'm never disappointed,
Though, of course, it's hard to wait,
While the salad's fate hangs fire,
Or the pudding boileth late;
But all delays prove raptures
And my reward is sure,
For better cooks than Edie
Never opened oven door.

Biscuits always light and puffy,
Fish cooked a la Normandy,
Salads that will fill your spirits
With a sweet, calm ecstacy.
When Edie's in the kitchen
Give yourself no concern,
For everything she dishes up
Will be done just to a turn.

When Edie's in the kitchen and the fellows
Sparkle round,
A little nervous feeling
Kinder makes my head turn round,

For by and by, I know—
   It's just the way of life—
   Some likely chap will coax away
   My Edie as his wife.

THE WORKER'S SONG

Sometimes like tired children
We sigh for restful place,
To cuddle and soothe our weary selves,
Ere duties new we face.

But the need of the world is great,
And duty clamors strong;
And off we are at work again,
Battling against the wrong.

The hardest battle waged
Is the war that's on within,
Where the soul must wield its arms,
Against the hosts of sin.

For no true success in battle,
Can come to warriors bold
Until o'er foes within
The victor's place they hold.

SOUL VISION

Have you ever seen a vision
In the day or in the night
Of what you might if you dared to be
And you shrank back in affright?

And accepted a lower purpose
Or lived by a weaker thought,
And sacrificed your ideals
For earth things that you sought?

We call our visions madness
And cast our ideals away,
And are ever less than we should be,
Had we bid our visions stay.

For those who most help the world
In its onward march to roll
Cherish night and day
The Visions of the Soul.

TO-DAY

I had a song I would not sing
Because it seemed a simple thing.
I sang my song, and hearts in pain
Found heart to live and strive again.

I had a word I feared to say
A hope that lived with me always,
Nor breathed the hope, nor said the word,
And life for two fore'er was marred.

So sing the song you have to-day,
Though weak, yet cheering be thy lay;
Breathe love's fond hope and let be heard
In waiting ears love's tender word.

THE ANNUAL CELEBRATION

Away back in Missouri,
Where they do things up so fine,
When the melons and the pumpkins
Are a-ripening on the vine,
All the loyal Colored people
In that part of the nation
Begin to send their invites out
For their annual celebration.

Few of them take much interest
In affairs of church and state,
Or in the serious problems
That our statesmen agitate.
But among the Missourians,
Abe Lincoln's Proclamation
Is the occasion every year
For an annual celebration.

The colored folks are all on hand,
To hear again the precious news,
And white folks, too, galore.
They've heard so oft before,
How in the year of sixty-one
The Hero of the nation,
Abe Lincoln, Moses of our Race,
Signed that wondrous Proclamation.

The speech is long, the children tire,
But the old ones laugh and cry,
For they've been through the scorching fire,
And they sit and think and sigh.

The speech is o'er and the band strikes up,
And the well-dressed population,
Grandsires and striplings, all enjoy
Their annual celebration!

Some high strung college preachers,
Just out and up to date,
Said Missouri folks' annual
Was several months too late;
That on the first of January
Abe Lincoln's Proclamation
That freed the nation's host of slaves
Should have its celebration.

They ran those preachers out of town—
How could they celebrate
With Jack Frost on the ground?
'Twas the preachers out of date!
But when the watermelons,
That fruit of God's creation,
Are ripe and sweet, Missouri folks
Have their annual celebration.

THE BLACK BOYS IN BLUE

Watch as they march from the West to the sea,
Cavalry brave and armed infantry,
Men who have fought, so the records say,
Like lions on the frontiers far away.

"Black Buffaloes," the Indians called them first,
But when in the fight they got the worst

Of that awful burst of shot and shell,
They turned and rushed away pell-mell!

There were black boys fighting at Bunker's Hill;
In 1812 they were at it still,
And when they were called, in sixty-one,
Thousands shouldered a government gun!

Ne'er should the love of their country wane
For the black boys who sank in the gallant Maine
Nor the heroes who charged with such good will
And saved the Rough Riders at San Juan Hill.

THE PASTOR
Dedicated to Rev. G. M. Tillman

In a lonely little parish
For a year a man of God
Taught in love the common people
Of the pathway Christ has trod.

Told to them the old, old story
Of the wondrous One who gave
His own life on Calvary's summit
Lost and ruined souls to save.

Sometimes it was told in gladness,
But there, too, were hours of pain.
That they followed not the Savior,
Though besought o'er and again.

Oft he deemed his labor wasted,
Many times discouraged grew,
But, withal, he had resolved that
He would to the cross be true.

But no life that's truly given
To the service of the Lord
E'er is lost but in the seeming,
So declares the precious Word.

Words that months ago he'd spoken
One day quickened into life,
And a soul communed with Jesus
That before had known but strife.

Then the pastor's heart was gladdened
And his Godly faith renewed,
For he'd proved the precious promise.
He had waited on the Lord.

BLACK AND WHITE

Two little ones played by the roadside green,
And an artist smiled at the pretty scene,
Laugh they aloud in pure delight,
Two little boys, one black, one white.

Two little fishermen idle away
The precious hours of one school day,
Trying in vain to get a bite,
Two little boys, one black, one white.

Two little truants homeward bent,
But there, alas, supperless sent

Straight off to bed, in broad daylight,
Two little boys, one black, one white.

Two little heads over hard lessons bend,
Wishing the goblin king might send
Some elf to take teacher away,
While they ran off to have their play.

Two little friends very loyal to each other,
Give to their mothers no ends of bother,
Must be together, both day and night,
Two little boys, one black, one white.

Two little boys kneel by the bed,
And somewhat sleepily prayers are said.
Angels bear to the throne of light,
Two little boys, one black, one white.

But, alas, when these two are men,
Where will be their old friendship then?
Will the white man give to the black man his right?
And will they still be friends, one black, one white?

DON'T BE ASHAMED TO DO RIGHT

There are things of which we should be ashamed,
There are deeds that won't bear the light,
But a motto good for both young and old,
Is, don't be ashamed to do right.

Perchance you are on the unpopular side,
And you stand alone in the fight,
Just hold your ground, my struggling friend,
And don't be ashamed to do right.

Riches and fame are good in their way,
But they can't give half the delight
That comes to the soul that is anchored on truth.
And is not ashamed to do right.

Then a cheer for the famed and a cheer for the wise
As onward they soar in their flight,
But louder yet let us cheer for the souls
Who are not ashamed to do right!

CHRISTMAS TIME

The air is filled with hearty cheer,
For merry Christmas time is here,
And passing down the crowded street
Bright, joyous faces there we meet;
The shops are bursting o'er with toys
To please old Santa's girls and boys,
And stockings now are darned with care,
For Santa Claus will soon be here.
The children early seek their bed,
But filled is every little head
With thoughts of Santa Claus so kind
Who all the stockings soon will find.
Oh, happy Christmas time, I trow
That all will not they gladness know,
For hearts are filled with anxious care,
And some are hardened by despair,
And those whom distance bears apart
From loved ones dear unto their heart
Will grieve for those they may not see
Despite the merry Christmas glee;

But hopeful still should be each heart,
For though by distance borne apart,
To dearest ones and well-loved friend
A Yule-tide token we may send,
And in memory of the Christchild's birth,
May pray for men of every clime
The hallowed joy of Christmas time.

AN EASTER LILY

The church was ablaze with glory,
    The glory of Easter tide,
And a crowd of struggling Arabs
Eagerly pressed outside.

"Oh, ain't them flowers stunnin'!
    Wouldn't it just be fun
If one of them ladies in there
    Would give each of us fellers one?"

And one of the altar committee,
    With a little of wealth to spare,
Heard the voice of the blessed Master
    In the little Arab's prayer.

She was off and back in a minute,
    Her hands filled with lilies fair;
Each boy received his flower
    With a shout that rent the air.

"May your lives be as white," said the giver
    A sermon short but strong,
And one that went not unheeded,
    But helped to save them from wrong.

And in an hour of after life,
    Amid her future joys,
The giver found in a man of God
    One of her Arab boys!

AMERICA'S FIRST CARGO OF SLAVES

It was midnight in Africa,
    And on the western shore
Stood chained a huddled line of slaves,
    Full twenty souls or more,
    While darkness like Egyptian night
Reigned over all the land,
    The slaves were hurried on the ship,
And borne from Afric's strand.
    On board a man-of-war they go
To breathe the ship's foul air,
    To stifle in the ship's close hole
And shriek their wild despair.
    Ah, who could tell the awful woe
This fatal act would bring,
    Surely in that Dutch captain's ears
A million death cries ring!

Oh, charge not God with will to see
    His Afric sons enslaved
That doomed to dreary servitude
    Their lost souls might be saved.
Oh, no; for better in our land,
    The land possessed by Ham,
To dwell in perfect liberty
    Beneath the waving palm,

To have the gospel brought to us,
  As 'tis to Asia sent.
Than we like beasts should toil for years
  That Christian light be lent,
To labor like the patient ox,
  Like to him no more to know
Than endless toil for others' gain
  And take in peace his blow.

The ship sailed on o'er stormy seas
  Till this strange cargo came
  To Jamestown's mart, and thus began
  Our country's greatest shame.
Oh, what a fatal hour that bro't
  The slave to this free shore,
On history's page the fearful blot
  With time doth blacker grow.

Two hundred weary years,
  The Negro tilled the soil,
Until America was rich
  With fruits of Negro toil.
Two hundred weary years
  But freedom came at last,
And no other lowly people
  Have ever climbed so fast.
See how they struggle, see!
  Will no one lend a hand,
Will no one help a race oppressed
  Within this Christian land?
Give them an equal chance,
  Freedom of life and aim,
This only can atone
  For America's dark shame!

THE BLUE VEIN CLUB

Down in Darktown there is trouble
　Of a most peculiar kind,
And the next "hair-straight'ner" found there
　Will some angry women find.

A Blue Vein Club was started
　By a ginger-faced Miss Dare,
And she said that every member
　Must have straight or straightened hair,

Miss Dare she did the straightening
　For a neat five dollar bill.
There were all in all one hundred
　Swallowed Miss Dare's Blue Vein pill.

All went well until it rained,
　And the hair it all went back,
Then a hundred colored women
　Went the straightener to attack.

But the Dare mansion was silent,
　They had left, the neighbors said,
And the Blue Vein Club in Darktown
　Has been bursted in the head.

LINES TO BISHOP ARNETT

Awake to life, poetic muse, and sing
　The deeds of our great Churchman, Arnett, Great
Awake, and let the earth with echoes ring,
　And praise our hero, famed in Church and State.

Sing of a life from lowest planes upreared,
   Sing of a man self-made and truly great,
Of Bishop Arnett, to all hearts endeared,
   Of great Arnett, Napoleon of his fate!

Give me a man, Philistia's giant cried,
   Boastful and proud, in gleaming armour clad,
And groans of dismay rang down Israel's side,
   For they, God's host, no giant champion had.

But when this cause seemed lost, David, the future king,
   Then but an obscure warrior in the field,
He who could fight for God as well as sing,
   Golith slew, and caused the foe to yield.

"Give me a man," the scornful Saxon cried,
   "A man of Negro blood, I challenge you,
To stand in Senate chambers at my side."
   "Alas," we sighed, "this thing is hard to to do."

For we who feel warm Afric's blood
   Throbbing and coursing through our veins
Love our own race, and feel we should
   In spite of all revere its hallowed strains.

For they who worship God, the Father dear,
   Know that all men are loved of Him alike;
We are despised of men who often err,
   Such gave to Christ His cross, His crown of spike!

But God sent Arnett on to lead our host,
   He swift of speech and large of heart and brain;
No pigmy-souled creation, or we had been lost,
   But a man with whom the interests of a kingdom might
      have lain.

He stood in senate halls amid great men,
  And there for us his people loudly spoke,
Denounced injustice with his voice and pen,
  Till the last "Black Law" had vanished from Ohio's
    statute book.

He spoke for us, the women of the race,
  Helpless and dumb through slavery's years of pain.
He bade our men accord to us an honored place,
  As queens within their hearts and homes to reign.

Honor, to whom honor—bring forth the laurel wreath,
  And place it on our grand, brave leader's head.
We love him well, why wait for scenes of death,
  Why keep our flowers for the voiceless dead?

Three debts we owe that we can never pay,
  His service to his Church, his Race and Womankind,
While love's incense upon his shrine we lay,
  With heart's that throb, and tears that blind.

IDA B. WELLS

Thank God, there are hearts in England
  That feel for the Negro's distress,
And gladly give of their substance
  To seek for his wrongs a redress!

Speed on the day when the lynchers
  No more shall exist in our land,
When even the poorest Negro
  Protected by justice shall stand.

When no more the cries of terror
  Shall break on the midnight air,
While poor and defenseless Negroes
  Surrender their lives in despair.

When the spirit of our inspired Lincoln,
  Wendell Phillips and Summer brave
Shall enkindle a spirit of justice
  And our race from oppression save.

When loyal hearts of the Southland
  With those of the North, tried and true,
Shall give to the struggling Negro
  That which is by nature his due.

And the cloud that threatens our land
  Shall pale beneath Liberty's sun,
And in a prosperous future
  Be atoned the wrongs to us done.

Go on, thou brave woman leader,
  Spread our wrongs from shore to shore,
Until clothed with his rights is the Negro,
  And lynchings are heard of no more.

And centuries hence the children
  Sprung up from the Hamitic race
On history's unwritten pages
  Thy daring deeds shall trace.

And the Afro-American mother
  Who of Negro history tells
Shall speak in words of grateful praise
  Of the noble Ida B. Wells!

EPOCHS

Youth

I lie out in the meadow grass,
I lie out there and cry,
And the prairie dog and field mouse
Pass me unheeded by.

The grass blades sting my face,
Even the daisies annoy,
I am a Negro boy.
For I am the child of a hated race,

Different from all of the boys
That romp with me at the school,
I have felt it many a day,
In action and in rule.

My skin is dark, my hair is crisp,
But I didn't make it so;
I keep for it a menial's place,
But, O God, it is hard to do!

Why did you make a thing like me
For mankind to despise?
Why must I live to cower down
Before their scornful eyes?

I walk, I think, I act, I feel,
I wrestle, box and run;
I scorn to cheat, to lie, to steal,
Even in times of fun.

To-day, while leaving the old schoolhouse
Proud in a prize-won joy,
I heard it said in undertone,
"Too bad he is a Negro boy!"

"Why?" said the master's calm, grave voice.
"Why, ask you?" said the man.
Because he is of Negro blood,
And must live 'neath racial ban.

Tho' he has brain, he must keep back,
For this is the white man's land;
The Negro and all inferior folk
Must bow beneath the Saxon command.

They that were once our helpless slaves
Are safest at our feet
Would you grant Negro rule?
How then the problem meet?

"One is our Father, even God,"
The master made reply.
"All men are brothers, here I stand,
All pride of caste must die.

Let's give the black a white man's chance;
Nay, more, the chance of a man.
Take away all our caste-fixed bars,
And then outstrip him if we can."

Manhood

To-day, to-day I am twenty-one,
My days at the schools are done,
And out in the world in the dim unknown
Are its wars to be fought and won.

I'm happy today o'er a trifling thing,
A smile from the girl I love,
It means so much from a girl like her,
As pure as the stars above.

I've finished the schools with honors proud,
Good for the mother and I,
The little mother, who's toiled so hard,
I'll repay her before I die.

Out in the world I'll go and work
For her and the girl of my heart,
My brown-faced maid with her love-lit eyes
And hair of the silkiest sort!

Ha! ha! the same old foe,
The thing I met in youth,
The color of my face a bar,
The same old ugly truth.

But I'll conquer yet, I swear I will,
For God lives, and He's true,
And somewhere in American hearts
Are stains of justice, too.

I'll get a chance some way, somehow,
To earn bread like a man,
Despite the foes who every day
The fires of hatred fan!

Old Age

Old age! Thank God, I've fought and won
An honorable place in life,
I've made a home like I said I would
For the mother and the wife.

PIPINGS OF DAWN

When o'er the hills the rosy colored dawn
Steals on the nightwrapped world in fair array,
When thro' the air the heralds of the morn,
The pretty feathered tribe, begin to pipe their lay.

Pipings of dawn, weak, faint, perhaps, at first,
And sweet tho' faint, unto the love-tuned ear,
And when of melody, a glorious burst,
That calls the slumbering world to be astir.

Thus be these lines a prophecy of dawn,
Of larger hopes and deeds that are to be;
Of fruitage ripened in fair freedom's morn,
Such is my hope and such my gift to thee.

FICTION

~ ~ ~

BERYL WESTON'S AMBITION
The Story of an Afro-American Girl's Life

CHAPTER I.—A TELEGRAM

"The eternal stars shine out as soon as it is dark enough."

"Telegram for you, Beryl," called out Cora Grey, as she ran past Beryl's door; and Beryl, with a sensation of dread penetrating her slight frame, hastened to the Principal's room, for it was at one of the leading Afro-American Colleges in the United States that the above scene took place.

The Principal, a sweet-voiced woman, of perhaps forty years, gave Beryl a look of compassion, when she handed her the telegram, saying, as she did so, "Be brave, my child." Beryl gave one glance at the fatal paper, and then with a long, pitiful cry, "My mother's gone!" fell senseless at Miss Hand's feet. Kind hands bore Beryl to her room and placed her upon the bed.

"Oh, what is the matter with Beryl?" cried little Eva Ross, Beryl's room-mate, and her staunch admirer.

"Her mother is dead, and Beryl will have to start home on the first train in order to be at the funeral, for her mother died yesterday morning, and the weather is quite warm yet," said Cora Grey, who had followed the sad group into the room.

"Oh, Cora! It will break Beryl's heart, for she fairly idol-

A. M. E. Church Review 10, chs. 1–5 (July 1893): 173–91; 10, chs. 6–10 (Oct. 1893): 308–22.

ized her mother," cried Eva, with tears of sympathy in her sweet, brown eyes.

"It is awful bad for Beryl. She is the smartest girl in the whole school, too," said Cora, who paid little regard to the rules of English grammar, and rather prided herself upon the large amount of slang that she had at her command.

One by one, the girls tip-toed out of the room, in obedience to a message that came from Miss Hand, to let Beryl get all of the rest possible before she left on her sad journey.

Eva Ross was much attached to Beryl, who, although sixteen years of age, never snubbed the poor orphaned girl, two years her junior, as did many of the older girls; and when the girls had gone from the room, she began to cry. Her sobs seemed to arouse Beryl, for she opened her eyes wonderingly for a second, when she recalled her woe, and burst into a passionate weeping.

"Don't, please don't, cry so hard, dear Beryl, you make my own heart ache. It's like losing my own dear mamma all over again," cried Eva.

"What time is it? I must go at once," cried Beryl, springing wildly from the bed.

"Miss Hand sent word that you could not start until five in the morning. It is now six in the afternoon. She said that you must go to bed, and that I could attend to your packing."

"Shall I bring you your supper, or will you go down to the dining-room?" asked Cora, coming into the room.

"Neither, Cora; I do not care for a morsel of food," sobbed Beryl. "Take Eva down with you; don't let her starve herself for me."

Poor girl, she was nearly frantic with grief. She was just sixteen, and this was the first great sorrow that had ever darkened her life, and so, for a while, everything was a mass of gloom and confusion to her young soul; but away in the wee hours of the morning there came a still, small voice unto her heart, chiding her for her reckless grief; breathing to her of Gethsemane and its awful agony, of Calvary and its shame! Then, in quick succession, came the thought of the glorious Easter Morn, when, radiant with the glory of His blood-bought victory, Jesus arose from the tomb! "So, too, shall my darling mother arise from the cold, dark grave, and be forever in the sunlight of the Master's presence," murmured Beryl to herself—and the thought strengthened her as nothing else could have done. There were many sad hearts among those who witnessed Beryl's departure, but Eva, perhaps, felt the parting more acutely than all the rest, for Beryl had befriended her in many ways, and the warm-hearted, yet sensitive child would gladly have shared Beryl's sorrow had it been possible.

"You will be back inside of two weeks, will you not, Beryl?" asked Cora, for she and Beryl were very intimate friends, and Cora had no dainty scruples about questioning anyone.

"Why, yes, Cora, I expect to be back by to-day week, for there is nothing to keep me from returning," replied Beryl.

"Here is something for you to read when you become tired of your own thoughts, Beryl," said Miss Hand, handing Beryl a small volume of poems.

"Thank you, dear Miss Hand," cried Beryl, "you have done so much for me I shall never forget your kindness."

While Beryl was speaking, the train came steaming into the depot, and the good-byes were hastily exchanged. The good-natured porter found Beryl a pleasant seat and she soon became so absorbed in thought as to be utterly oblivious to her surroundings.

Robed in a black gown that fitted her slender form perfectly, her long, black hair coiled in a classical knot at the back of her head, her great black eyes gazing mournfully out of the window; despite the fact that her eyes were somewhat red, and her pale face swollen from weeping, Beryl made a very pleasant picture. At least a gentleman who sat on the opposite side of the car thought so, for he gazed at Beryl with a look of admiring interest. All unconscious of his scrutiny, Beryl amused herself for a while with an album containing the photographs of many of her friends. Tiring of that, she laid it aside, and took up the book that Miss Hand had given her at parting. She opened the book, and began listlessly to turn the leaves when she came across these lines, marked in Miss Hand's characteristic style.

> "Is it raining, little flower?
>   Be glad of rain!
> Too much sun would wither thee:
>   'Twill shine again.
> The sky is very black, 'tis true;
> But just behind it shines the blue.
>
> "Art thou weary, tender heart?
>   Be glad of pain!
> In sorrow sweetest things will grow,
>   As flowers in rain.
> God watches, and thou shalt have sun,
> When clouds their perfect work have done."

Beryl's sad face brightened. "What a pretty poem!" she thought. "How like dear Miss Hand, to mark this one of all the rest! If I can only be like her,—noble and beloved by every one, how happy I shall be!"

Presently the train stopped, and the gentleman who had been watching Beryl so closely, got up and left the couch, and Beryl noticed him for the first time.

He was a splendid type of Afro-American manhood. Of a princely form, broad-shouldered and handsome, he had a, winning expression upon his brown, bearded face, that caused one instinctively to place reliance in him.

"What a distinguished-looking man!" said Beryl to herself. "He looks like a foreign prince, whose portrait I have seen somewhere or other."

To Beryl's surprise, upon the stranger's return (for the train stopped about a quarter of an hour), he brought her some fresh rolls and a cup of tea. The girl tried to refuse, for the act seemed rather forward to her, but the stranger, in an authoritative tone, bade her drink the tea before it got cold, and she did so, meekly enough for her.

When Beryl had drank the tea, he again left the coach with the empty cup, and when he returned, contrary to Beryl's expectations, he resumed his former seat and took up a newspaper.

"I thought sure that he would presume upon his kindness and compel me to converse with him, but how courteously he acts!" was the thought that traversed Beryl's brain.

CHAPTER II.—A RETROSPECT

"Into each life some rain must fall: some days must be dark and dreary."

She began to watch him now. She looked with increased respect at his dark, handsome face, set off, as it was, by a fine pair of brown eyes, and a firm, sweet mouth. While she was thus occupied, the stranger looked up from his paper, and their eyes met in a long, lingering glance.

"Aren't you tired of travelling alone?" asked he.

"Yes, sir," said Beryl, honestly.

"How far do you go?"

"I am on my way to Westland, Tennessee," replied Beryl.

"Can it be possible? That is my own destination! I am going to see the original of that photograph," said he, handing Beryl a cabinet photograph.

"Oh! That is Nurse Warren; are you acquainted with her?" cried Beryl in a surprised tone.

"Well, I was once, but I haven't seen her for twenty years. I was born under slavery's cursed ban, and sold from my mother at the age of seven. I am the long-lost son, Norman Warren, of whom you have heard her speak, perhaps, at some time."

"Oh, it seems to be too good to be true! Poor Mrs. Warren has been trying to find you for ever so long—before I was born, even," cried Beryl, joyously, forgetting her own grief in anticipation of her old friend's joy in meeting her long-mourned-for boy.

"So you know my mother, do you?" said Norman Warren, pleasantly. "What is she like? Tell me about her!'

"Oh, she is the dearest woman! She nursed Ellie and me when we were quite small. She is my godmother, too."

"What relation am I to you, then?" asked he, teasingly; then, glancing at her black dress, he asked, in a reverent tone, "You have lost some dear friend, I presume, have you not?"

"Yes, my mother," said Beryl, and then burst into a shower of tears. There were only about a half dozen passengers in the same coach with Beryl, and they paid little or no attention to her, for which she felt thankful.

Warren regretted having asked her that unlucky question, but it was too late then, so he apologized gracefully and resumed his former seat.

While Beryl is sobbing out her grief for her dead mother, let us take a glance at her past life.

She was the eldest child of Jim Weston, a successful farmer, who had a snug bank account and many acres of rich land, which he had accumulated by sheer force of pluck and thrift since the day of his emancipation. He was unlettered, and rather uncouth in manner, but he was a true Christian gentleman at heart, and supported the village school generously. His wife had been a lady's maid in the days of slavery, and had by stealth learned to read and write. She had spent much time in study since her freedom, and was teaching in the log schoolhouse, at Westland, when Jim Weston first met and loved her. She was as dainty and refined as Jim was rude and uncouth, but there was something attractive in his rugged manhood, and she grew to love his dark and manly face, and to wait his coming with joy.

Three children were born to them—Beryl, Ellen, and Joseph—but Beryl, her first-born, was her mother's idol. From the time that Beryl's childish lips could form a request, it had been her mother's delight to gratify her. Of course, she grew up spoiled and willful. What else could be expected?

Beryl attended the village school until she had mastered the course of study demanded of her there. Afterward she took up algebra and French, under the guidance of a young white woman.

Beryl was regarded as a great prodigy among her untutored acquaintances, but Mrs. Weston knew that the girl had much to learn, so she sent her, at the age of fourteen, to the best known of the Afro-American colleges, where she had spent the last two years of her life, except the vacations. It was at College that Beryl first realized that there were other girls more brilliant in certain lines than herself, and that if she would be loved by her classmates she must lay aside her haughty manners and imperious speech. This was hard at first. For a long time, Cora Grey, a sprightly Afro-American

brunette, was her only friend. How these two girls ever became intimate friends is difficult to conjecture, for they were
totally unlike in every way.

Cora was indolent by nature and was never known to recite
a lesson perfectly, except occasionally one in French, while
Beryl rarely missed any lesson, no matter how difficult. So
studious was she that Miss Hand was often importuned for
permission to keep the light burning after hours. "My child,
you will break yourself down," said that worthy woman, over
and over again. But although Beryl was of a sensitive, nervous temperament, she enjoyed superb health, and kept at
the head of her classes.

Just after Thanksgiving, a revival started at the College,
and Beryl watched the proceedings with great interest, for a
revival at Westland and at school were evidently two different things, both in their arrangement and outcome.

There, at Westland, the minister yelled, roared, pounded
loudly upon the sacred desk, and in fact did all he could to
arouse the congregation to a perfect frenzy, whereupon
screams, broken benches and Pandemonium in general became the order of the day. Upon these performances Beryl
had always looked with an innate disgust, while she strongly
appreciated many of the Christian women and men who belonged to the Westland church.

Some time after the revival had begun, Eva Ross insisted
upon her room-mate's attendance at one of the meetings, which
were held by the Young Women's Christian Association one
night in each week.

Beryl drew back with a cold "No, thank you, I have my
Cæsar to learn," that chilled Eva's loving heart, for she was
a bright little Christian and very zealous in the Master's cause.
Beryl was very fond of Eva; like every one else, she could
not resist the sunny nature that shed its warm rays benignly

upon all with whom the girl came into contact. Knowing that she had wounded Eva's feelings caused Beryl to feel very uncomfortable, and Cæsar became wrapped in such intricate mystery that she threw the book down in despair, and took up a half-finished essay, which she was preparing to read before the Alcott Literary Club, of which she was a member, when Cora knocked at the door. "Aren't you coming down to the Y. W. C. A.?" she demanded. "No; are you?" asked Beryl in some surprise, for Cora cared nothing for spiritual things, preferring ever a novel, Ouida's usually, and a box of caramels, to the most eloquent sermon that could be preached.

"Yes, indeed, I am! That strange young man from the Bermudas has arrived and I want to get a peep at him; Leona Graves says he is quite good-looking."

"Do you know your geometry, Cora?"

"Of course not," replied the fair delinquent. "I rarely do, but that is of little consequence, for I mean to go on the stage, and I do not need mathematics at all, only to count my fortune." "Well if you won't go, tra-la-la," and the girl was gone. Beryl still endeavored to study, but Eva's reproachful eyes seemed to stare at her from every page. She thought of the many willing services that Eva had rendered her, and of her patience when she (Beryl) was in one of her trying moods.

"Dear little thing, I ought to have gone down with her," murmured Beryl to herself. "I wonder if I shall ever be as good as she is."

Just then there floated up the stairway, and through Beryl's open door, in full, rich tones, the following words of a hymn familiar to Beryl from childhood:

> "Dear Jesus, I long to be perfectly whole,
> I want Thee forever to live in my soul;

Break down every idol, cast out every foe,
Now wash me, and I shall be whiter than snow.'"

Somehow the words seemed to burn into Beryl's heart, so filled were they with pathos and truth.

"I believe I will go down after all and see what they are doing," said our heroine, and acting upon the impulse of the moment, she went down-stairs to the chapel, where the meeting was held.

CHAPTER III.—A PRODIGAL DAUGHTER

"And he said, Young man, I say unto thee arise."

"To each young man or young woman, who has not obeyed the divine call, comes this message this evening, 'Young man, I say unto thee, arise.' "

"Arise from what, do you ask? First of all, from Sin, to an active faith in the Lord Jesus; then from the castle of Indolence, the Slough of Despond and the pleasures of Vanity Fair, you must come forth to wage an eternal warfare with Ignorance and Vice."

"Do you know," continued the speaker, who was no other than Miss Hand, "that God is giving you these blessed opportunities of college life and good associations, that you may be better able to glorify His Name? How heedlessly you take His gifts! Many of you deem it a nuisance to repeat at even the prayer taught you at your mother's knees. Who will have the moral courage to arise this evening and take a decided stand for Christ? I see before me an army of young Afro-American men and women, filled with ambition, who are

preparing to fill various positions in the world. Ah! let me
entreat you not to start forth on your life-work with Christ-
less lives! Your ancestors and mine had a gigantic enemy in
the form of Slavery, to prevent their progress in civilization
and happiness, but we have three foes to contend with—Sin,
Ignorance and Prejudice; let us arm us for the fight!"

While Miss Hand was speaking, like Saul on his way to
Damascus, Beryl heard a voice, saying "Beryl, Beryl, why
do you resist my love? Come, for I have need of thee"; and
a light broke into the darkened recesses of her soul, that
compelled her to own Christ as her Saviour.

> "When the storms of life are raging,
>   Tempests wild on sea and land,
> I will seek a place of refuge,
>   In the shadow of His hand,"

sang the choir, and to every one's surprise, when the song
was ended, Beryl Weston arose and asked for help to begin
a life for Christ.

"Thank God!" said Miss Hand, in her heart, "she has
chosen the good part."

Several others arose for prayer, and the meeting was adjourned.

Beryl found the joy and peace that comes to every forgiven
soul ere the morning dawned in at her window. No one ever
doubted her conversion, for there was a radical change in her
whole life. If before, her motto had been "For Self," truly
it was now, "For Christ," and Beryl grew strong in her
Christian life.

Beryl's ambition was to become an instructress in the modern languages and higher mathematics. It is, perhaps, need-
less to say that Miss Hand was her model. Indeed, this excellent woman deserved to be imitated, for she was another

Mary Lyon, of Mt. Holyoke fame, albeit her skin was a
shade darker.

Beryl worked hard, and when her year's labor was ended
she was ready to enjoy her vacation. When she arrived at
Westland, it was, of course, summer, and from the country
roadside the yellow buttercups, sweet wood-violets, and modest spring beauties tossed their crowned heads gaily. From
the old apple tree, at the farm-yard gate, came Robin's cheery
"Bob o'link, bob o'link!" Bossy—Beryl's own Jersey cow—
and Lionel, her dog, came joyfully forward to welcome her
approach as the old-fashioned buggy neared the house, and
Beryl's voice rang out upon the air. Ellie and Joey, aged
respectively eleven and three, came running out to meet her,
but the form that she longed most to see was absent.

"Father, where is mother?" she cried, anxiously.

"I s'pose she's lying down. She's been ailing considerable
with them heart spells of hern, agin. She gits roun' too much,
I think. She's been fixin' up the house a sight, gittin' ready
for you."

Hardly tarrying long enough to kiss the children, Beryl
hastened to her mother's room. She found her lying down,
but she arose when Beryl came in, and held her in her arms
for a long time without speaking. She seemed quite well for
the first few days after Beryl came home, and the girl's heart,
which had been saddened by her mother's illness, grew buoy-
ant again, and she roamed the beautiful woods, with Ellie
and Joey, until she got as brown as a berry. She also got up
several excursions, and persuaded her mother to bring her
sewing and join them in the orchard. When they were comfortably seated, Beryl would real aloud passages from her
favorite authors. Afterwards a dainty luncheon would disappear as if by magic, and the little party would return to the
house.

To Ellie and Joey, "Sister Beryl" was a perpetual revelation. She knew everything that children liked. She laughed with them over the trials and ultimate triumph of that wondrous maiden, known in Fairyland as Cinderella; sighed with them over the fate of Little Red Riding Hood, and gayly applauded the heroic Jack and his adventures with the Bean Stalk.

Not only did she make herself interesting to the little folks, her father found her a ready listener to the smallest details concerning the farm. She advised him about the drainage, talked him into putting a bath-room into the new house that he was building, and discussed the probabilities of the crops with an originality of thought, surprising to say the least.

But of all the family, Mrs. Weston got the greatest comfort out of Beryl. She was very proud of Beryl, and never grew weary of hearing "At the College," Beryl's constant refrain. She was deeply impressed by Beryl's gentleness toward her, and thought the change due to Beryl's college training; but one memorable night the girl followed her mother into the latter's bed-room, and drawing up a low stool, sat at her mother's feet and told the story of her new birth. There, in the stillness of that room, they mingled their happy tears, for Mrs. Weston had come to Christ during the lonely hours of Beryl's absence.

Eva Ross, who lived with a kind aunt in Ohio, wrote weekly to Beryl, and her letters helped our heroine. In a cheerful strain, Eva would dash off a sketch of her trials and triumphs in the Christian warfare, as easily as Cora wrote of her numerous parties and beaux.

"Why not have your friend Eva with you during this the last month of your vacation?" suggested her kind mother; and in a few days after her suggestion Eva made her advent into the Weston family, and captivated all hearts with her lovable ways.

What capital times they did have! Village, farm, woods

and flowers afforded enjoyment to their sweet girlhood, and people stopped at sight of their glad young faces, and gazed at them with pleasure. Upon the Lord's day, with reverent hearts, they visited His temple, and lifted their joyous voices unto Him who hath redeemed us by His blood!

CHAPTER IV.—DEEP WATERS

"The loved and lost! Why do we call them lost?
  Because we miss them on our onward road?
God's unseen angel o'er our pathway crossed,
Looked on us all, and, loving them the most,
  Straightway relieved them of life's weary load."

When the pleasant vacation was ended, Beryl returned to her college life with fresh zeal and enthusiasm for the work.

She was now so great a favorite with her school friends, that honors of all kinds were heaped upon her. Offices in all of the College societies were given her, until she was kept quite busy. But she liked it. It was only what she intended doing in her joyous future, now being enacted on a small scale.

Swiftly the year flew by as if on winged steeds, and the College Commencement was at hand, when Beryl received the fatal telegram, telling of her mother's death.

But we have lingered long enough, let us now return to our heroine, for we left her weeping.

Beryl wept on until her over-wrought nerves found rest in sleep. She was entirely lost to the outer world, until some one touched her, bidding her arise, for she was now at her journey's end. That some one was Norman Warren. He got Beryl's things together, helped her off the cars, and left her sobbing in her father's arms, then hastened on in search of his mother, where we will leave him for awhile.

"Don't take on so, Beryl; your mother is happy in Heaven to-night," said Jim Weston huskily. "She would not like to see you grieving so. There is a sealed letter for you on her bureau, written by her and placed there by her own request for you."

Beryl listened tearfully. "How are the children, father?" she asked.

"Oh, they keep well as common," replied her father. "They wanted to come and meet you at the depot powerful bad, but I hated to take Charlie and Bill both from the field while we are so busy; so I just hitched Bill to the little cart and come along."

In Jim Weston's speech there was abundant proof that seventeen years of association with a woman of refined speech, like Beryl's mother was, had not been wholly lost upon her uneducated husband. She had not only taught him to read, write and cipher, but had persuaded him to take *The Yankee Blade* and a popular magazine known as *The Arena*, so that he might become well informed concerning the vital topics of the hour.

"Binie's staying with us now, right along. Your poor mother begged me to give her a home here on the farm, and said as how she'd be a sight of help to you in doing the roughest part of the work. You see there's a sight to be attended to— the milking, the churning, washing, cooking for four hands, besides the family and the housework, to say nothing of the poultry," continued he.

"How long has she been at the farm?" asked Beryl absently.

"You mean Binie? Why, she's been there ever since you left, mighty nigh. She is a good worker, but she's got a purty cross tongue in her head," said Jim Weston, reining Bill in at the same time. "Hello, there, Joey! Let the bars down! Here we are at home!"

After Ellie and Joey had been caressed to their heart's content, and Binie had been shaken hands with, Beryl ran up to her mother's room and obtained her letter, when she returned to her room and locked the door to guard against intrusion. Her heart was very sore, because her mother had been buried before she arrived home, and she read the letter eagerly, for it seemed a message from the skies. It read thus:

> MY DARLING BERYL:—When you read this letter your mother will be gone from the earth, and you will see her no more, until you meet her upon the other shore. God bless you, daughter, and keep you from sin.
>
> And now, my child, I am going to ask a hard thing of you. I want you to give up College, and study at home, where you can look after the comfort of your father and the children. Joey will give you but little trouble, while Ellie is willful and will require great care.
>
> I know your great ambition, darling, but you will not regret your sacrifice for mother in the years that are to come. If I could but see you once more.
>
> Farewell, my child, my first-born.
>
> Your dying mother,   FRANCES WESTON

Poor Beryl sat stunned. Not go back to College, when she was getting along so nicely, and every one loved her? Not have Miss Hand's hearty counsel to guide her in her search for knowledge? Never to be a graduate? Oh, it was too hard! Beryl fell on her knees and prayed to die. She felt this blow all the more because of her terrible bereavement, and lay for hours upon her bed, wrestling with self and her dead mother's wishes.

"Oh, I cannot, I cannot give up College!" she moaned over and over again.

Ellie knocked several times at Beryl's door; but as Beryl did not answer, she concluded that her sister was asleep and left her. But little Joey had no notion of being thus deprived of Beryl's society, for when she failed to answer his call, he yelled, at the top of his voice, "Sister Beryl, let me in; I want to hear you sing 'bout de free little cats, and tell me 'bout de pictures." There was no answer. "Please let me come in," pleaded the dear baby voice, and Beryl had not the heart to refuse his pitiful pleading. "What makes your eyes so red? Are you crying 'bout mamma? She's gone to a beautiful city and has lots of pretty sings to look at. Papa said so, and me and Ellie's going to be good so we can go to see her," said Joe, with the trusting faith of infancy, and Beryl felt that her little brother had given her a just rebuke for her want of faith. She clasped one of Joey's chubby brown hands in hers, slowly descended the stairs, while these words haunted her brain, "Give up College."

"Where is Binie?" asked Beryl when she saw the supper-table spread; "isn't she coming in to supper?"

"She's 'shamed to, 'cause she's so crippled, and says she'd rather eat by herself," said Ellie.

"Yes, 'cause Ellie makes fun of her all the time and calls her old crooked back!" cried Joey indignantly.

"Well she is a 'crooked-back,' " said Ellie sullenly.

"Oh Ellie, how could you?" cried Beryl. She went to the kitchen door. "Binie, oh Binie," she called.

"What do you want?" harshly demanded the deformed girl, issuing from the dairy with a crock of yellow cream in her hands.

"I want you to come to your supper. The idea of your running off and this my first evening at home!"

"Very well, Miss Beryl, I'll come in for your sake; but a poor crippled creature, like I am, ought to be dead and out of the way!"

"Oh Binie!" was all that Beryl could say.

"Sister Beryl, come and make Joey behave himself," came in Ellie's shrill voice from the kitchen, and Beryl, followed by the reluctant Binie, re-entered the house.

Her father and the farm laborers came in, and Binie's inviting repast was eaten with a relish by all save Beryl, who felt no inclination for food.

"Well, well, it does beat all, how Mrs. Warren's prayers have been answered after so many years of waiting," said Beryl's father. "That young man that got off when you did was Norman Warren," looking at Beryl.

"Yes, I know; I meant to have told you, but I forgot it."

"It's just like a story in a book," continued Jim Weston. "He's been to a great college in Europe and is a fine doctor now. I went to take some peaches over to the old lady and there was as fine a looking man as I ever saw in my life standing in the kitchen door, and calling to Mrs. Warren to come in and see something or other that he had brought her."

When the tea-table had been cleared, and the dishes washed and put away, the farm hands retired to their respective homes, and the family adjourned to the sitting-room, where Jim Weston soon became lost in the columns of his favorite newspaper.

CHAPTER V.—LIGHT AHEAD

"Over and over again, no matter which way I turn, I always find in the Book of Life some lesson that I must learn."

Binie's sad state gave Beryl something to think of beside her own troubles. Here at her very doors was a creature passing through life burdened and disfigured, discontented and full

of despair, and no one doing anything to brighten her life.
Could she not lighten Binie's weary soul?

"Binie, here is the *Ladie's Home Journal,* perhaps you will
find something interesting to you in it," said our heroine in
her most winning manner. Binie took the magazine in a re-
sentful sort of manner. "I ain't much on stories," she said
crossly.

When she became absorbed in the paper, as she did in a
few moments, Beryl studied her face at her leisure. The girl
had fairly good features, when they were not contracted by
the habitual scowl that was seen upon her face. She owned a
pair of piercing black eyes, and a sharp voice that made her
more enemies than friends. She was left an orphan at an early
age. A fall from a house-roof was the cause of her deformity.
Her life hitherto had been a stern, loveless one, with few
gleams of sunshine to lighten its gloom.

That evening was an important epoch in Beryl's life. Seated
in the low rocker that used to belong to her mother, with
Joey on her lap, and Ellie on a stool at her feet, she saw her
lifework before her, and she heard the Master's voice saying
"Beryl, will you not follow Me? I know the path is thorny,
but it leadeth unto Me. Will you not follow?"

Beryl bowed her head on Joey's curly one, and from the
depths of her soul took up her heavy cross.

"Well, daughter, let's have a song and a word of prayer,
and then retire, for it is growing late," said her father; and
the girl arose obediently and went to the organ.

> "I need Thee every hour,
>   Most gracious Lord;
> No tender voice like Thine
>   Can peace afford.
> I need Thee, oh I need Thee,
>   Every hour I need Thee;

Oh bless me now, my Saviour,
I come to Thee."

Ellie's shrill treble and Joey's baby voice joined in the touching refrain, and a flood of melody rang through the room.

Tears shone in Binie's black eyes when the song was ended. In a few words, filled with longing and pathos, Beryl's father addressed the Throne of Grace, and the family separated for the night.

Beryl spent the following morning in writing letters to Miss Hand, Cora Grey, Eva Ross and other friends, and listening to her father's instructions concerning the management of the household affairs. Beryl must take her mother's place as far as possible. See that the meals were served promptly; look after the dairy and garden produce; patch, darn, have the entire charge of the children. In fact, she was required to do the very things that she disliked most, but she had decided and she would stay at her post, no matter how disagreeable it was.

It as a splendid Fall day. The orchard trees were loaded with peaches, pears, and delicious apples, and their odor was wafted through the open kitchen window, by the light autumn breeze. In front of the window by which Beryl stood, a climbing rose bush, fairly alive with great red roses, blushed at its own brilliancy. Over her head sat Bob, Ellie's mocking bird, perched within his gayly-painted cage, and trilling his wildest notes. Beryl stood lost in thought until she caught sight of a white sunbonnet coming through the orchard.

"Oh, Nurse Warren, I'm so glad you've come! Everything has gone wrong with me since I saw you last. I didn't get to see poor mother at all, and to crown it all I must give up my college work," and Beryl began to cry upon the motherly breast that often in childhood had sheltered her thus.

"There now, dearie, don't cry anymore; it will come out all right in the end," said Mrs. Warren soothingly. "God is watching over my bonny lass and when you can say with David—'What time I am afraid, I will trust in thee. I will hide in the shadow of thy wing'—life will be far happier. But Norman sent you a message!"

"What, Nurse Warren?"

"It is found in this book," said Norman's mother, handing the girl an elegantly bound copy of "Ben Hur."

"Thank you for bringing it to me. Oh, Nurse, were you not glad to see your son after so many years of cruel separation?" cried Beryl, suddenly remembering that she had failed to mention Norman Warren's home-coming.

"Glad? Child, it was an answer to prayer! Let me tell you something of my life: I was born a slave in the State of Virginia. Of five children, my only surviving one, Norman, was taken from me at the age of seven, and sold to a lady going North. It well-nigh killed me, but the hand of the Lord upheld me somehow. Then my husband died, and still I lived, though often, when I thought of Norman, my baby, living somewhere in this wide world without a mother's love, I did not care to live. I worked on, and as I grew to know more of God, I was ashamed of my rebellious spirit, and began to look for the sunny side of life. After the war, I moved here, and when I met your mother I felt that I had something to live for. I had plenty of work, and purchased the little home that I now own. Then I began to lay aside part of my wages, so in case my boy ever came back to me, he would have money with which to procure an education, or to start himself in business. Those were my plans. Listen, now. God worked in my behalf. Mrs. Hayes, the lady who purchased Norman, had a son of about the same age, whose name was Leon, and a little girl of four, called Una. Nor-

man risked his own life upon one occasion, and snatched both
of the children from a watery grave. From that hour Mrs.
Hayes treated him as her own. When he was eleven years of
age, she started him to school with Leon. Finding that the
other pupils resented Norman's presence in the school, Mrs.
Hayes, being possessed of an independent fortune, moved to
England where Norman and Leon had the very best educational advantages. Leon took to law, and Norman to medicine. Mrs. Hayes lived to see them both finish their courses
with credit, and the little Una wedded to a young Englishman of good family. She died very suddenly, and left no
will, so Norman was left unprovided for, and he would not
accept Leon's beggarly generosity or Una's proffered aid. He
had two hundred pounds that he had saved, and he resolved
to return to America in search of his mother. You know the
rest."

"How romantic!" cried Beryl, her red lips smiling her
pleasure. "Why, Nurse, you had a beautiful page in your
life that you never let me see."

"Yes, my child. But where are the children?"

"Out in the garden, picking strawberries for Binie's short-
cake."

"Is Binie at home?"

"Yes, Nurse, she just went into her room a short while
before you came."

"May we come in, Binie?" asked Mrs. Warren, tapping
at the door of the girl's room.

"Yes, ma'am," said Binie's voice, and they entered a small
bedroom, scrupulously clean, with pots of mignonette and
heliotrope in the window sill. Binie was seated at a table,
working away at something that looked like a drawing.

"Are you busy, Binie?" asked Beryl, with some curiosity
in her voice.

"I am drawing," said Binie, quietly.

"May I see your drawing? I did not know that you could draw. Oh, look, Nurse! Here is my picture! Oh, Binie, how pretty it is! Who taught you?"

"I taught myself," said Binie, with a touch of gratified pride in her voice. "I've lots of pictures in my trunk."

"Do let us see them," said Mrs. Warren.

Binie produced from a small box that did duty as a trunk, a roll of papers. When she unrolled them, a sketch of the one Afro-American Church at Westland came to view; then a pretty meadow scene. The Weston farm-house—Joey and Ellie standing on the porch—followed in quick succession.

"Binie, you excel me in drawing, and I have taken lessons for three terms!" cried Beryl. "What will you take for that farm-house sketch? I want to have it framed as a present to Miss Hand," said Beryl, producing her purse.

"I'd be glad to have you take it for a present from me," said Binie, somewhat awkwardly.

CHAPTER VI.—BINIE WELLS

"No, you will need money for paper, pencils and lessons for you must take lessons from some artist," cried Beryl, handing Binie a bright silver dollar.

"And I will pay you the same price for that sketch of the children," said Mrs. Warren. "And Binie," she added, "Norman draws and paints from nature; he will be glad to assist you, I know. Maybe you will be able to buy a dear little nest of your own some day—who knows?"

Binie's sharp eyes glistened. The world had undergone a great revolution for her during the last twenty-four hours.

"So your son has come home at last," she said to Mrs. Warren.

"Yes, thank God, he is with me once more. Well I must see the children, and then hasten home. Good-by."

The bright summer days waned, and winter found Beryl pursuing her daily routine of labor. She arose at 4 in the morning, exercised for a few moments with a pair of Indian clubs, a present from Doctor Warren, assisted Binie in preparing an early breakfast for the farm hands, dressed Joey, read a chapter in her Bible, and did the housework. In addition to all this, she heard the children's lessons from 9 to 10 o'clock in the morning, and recited lessons in geometry and Greek to Norman Warren between the hours of 10 and 12. In the afternoons she ironed, sewed or read, as the occasion demanded. At night she read aloud from some interesting book, helped Binie with her English studies, and practiced her music. So you see, my dear readers, that Beryl's life was a very busy one, and life was brightening for our heroine. Dr. Warren, who had begun to practice medicine and had a neat little office on the principal street of Westland, proved a valuable friend. His warm friendship, Miss Hand's helpful letters, together with the weekly journals edited by Cora and Eva, that came to her, kept Beryl in excellent spirits. But in order to do her full justice, I must add that she read her little Bible daily with ever-increasing interest, and tried harder than ever to walk in the footsteps of Jesus. The months grew into years, and two of them had passed away, when a new pastor came to the little church at Westland.

His coming occasioned considerable stir in the small village, for it became generally known that the new minister was a graduate from the Oberlin College, and was both handsome and eloquent.

The name of the young divine was Harold Griswold, and

he came to the church highly recommended for learning and piety.

There were at least three hundred Afro-Americans in Westland and the neighboring farming districts. They were mostly illiterate people, in moderate circumstances, and about fifty of them were members of Griswold's church. Norman Warren, aided by Beryl's counsel and her father's ready purse, had done much to elevate the narrow-minded villagers. He had given a series of earnest talks on practical subjects, taught a night-school until relieved by Caleb Dunn, an intelligent young man, who had labored on the Weston farm for four years, and now was in business for himself, being the proud possessor of a little grocery store and a buxom young wife.

The villagers fairly idolized the genial doctor, and his skill as a physician went far and wide. He had many Anglo-Saxon patients as well as Afro-American ones, and he was frequently called in to consult with the other leading physicians of the place. Mrs. Warren, in her capacity of nurse, lent her son valuable aid.

At the farm, Beryl, grown into striking beauty, stood on the lawn, attired in a pretty gown of spotted lawn, playing croquet with Norman Warren. "When did Mr. Griswold arrive?" Beryl asked, as she dexterously sent her opponent's ball far from the field of action.

"Last evening," was the brief reply.

"What is he like? Do tell me," cried Beryl pleadingly.

"Well," said Dr. Warren, "Harold Griswold is a very fine young man, I judge by his appearance and conversation, and about five years my junior. But I must go, Miss Weston, for I promised to call in at Mrs. Oates's this afternoon. Her little Fred is quite ill with what I fear is scarlet fever. Be careful with the children and do not let them go where there are any sick children. Good-by."

Beryl looked after his tall form, with a world of tenderness in her dark eyes. This was never fully acknowledged even to herself. Through two years' constant affection, Dr. Warren had evinced toward her a kind, brotherly regard—nothing more. He conducted his talented pupil safely through the most difficult theorems found in her geometry, and taught her to wrestle successfully with Greek and German verbs. Together they read all of the best modern poets; sighed over the hapless Elaine and her hopeless passion for Sir Launcelot; held up to scorn his friendship with the beautiful Queen Guinevere; admired to the highest extent that exquisite poem known as "Aurora Leigh," and still never a word of love was breathed into the young girl's ears. Norman Warren's code of honor was too high for that. He honestly admired Beryl; appreciated her sweet, unselfish life; her interest in education, religion, and all things of an ennobling nature; but it was rather in the light of a sister that he held her.

If any one had told him that Beryl loved him, he would have laughed at the bare idea, for the brave girl hid her secret so deep in the recesses of her heart that only God knew. True, Nurse Warren suspected the state of affairs, but she was a discreet woman, and she kept silent. She sometimes smiled softly when alone and rubbed her wrinkled hands together when she thought of a possible union between Norman and Beryl, for it was an event that she prayed for with the simple, trusting faith that was habitual to her.

Dr. Warren found little Fred Oates in a critical state, and it was late in the evening when he reached home. His mother met him at the door. "Norman, I have agreed to board the new minister. Do you care? Poor boy, he looks homesick already, and no wonder; Westland is a miserable contrast to Nashville, his former home. He is in the sitting-room; go in and entertain him while I prepare you a lunch."

Dr. Warren assured his mother that Griswold would no doubt prove an agreeable addition to their little family, and

Mrs. Warren looked decidedly relieved. Norman Warren walked into his mother's pretty best room, with a clouded brow. He did not like the idea of sharing his room with a stranger, but he felt sorry for the young man, and knew that there were few congenial homes in Westland besides his own and Caleb Dunn's.

Griswold was playing softly on the tiny cabinet organ that Dr. Warren had brought from England. He was a man of slender build, dark-brown complexion, with black eyes and thick curly hair that he wore rather long and brushed back from a broad, intellectual brow. He was rather handsome, though in a different style from that of Dr. Warren; for the greatest charm of the latter was the rugged strength that characterized his handsome features, while Griswold's features were almost womanish.

The two men discussed various topics in a general way until they hit upon the race problem, *i.e.*, the presence of the Afro-American race in America and their peculiar environments. Dr. Warren was inclined to the opinion that the Afro-Americans should emigrate to places where prejudice does not exist.

He said, "There is little or no show for the colored people in this country, and they ought to leave. During the whole fifteen years of my residence in England, I never saw as much rank prejudice shown toward persons of color as I witnessed during one day spent in the city of New Orleans. They are not allowed to eat in any of the hotels or restaurants, or to occupy the best seats in the theatre; in short, they are completely ostracised because of their color!"

CHAPTER VII.—THE RACE PROBLEM

Adversity's cold frosts will soon be o'er,
It heralds brighter days: The joyous spring

Is cradled on the winter's icy breast,
And yet comes flushed in beauty.
—MRS. HEMANS

"I am compelled to admit the truth of your remarks," replied
Harold Griswold, "and yet our people are making great
progress even in that place. Some of our wealthiest colored
men reside in the State of Louisiana. The Honorable Theo-
phile Allain, State Senator, and one of the wealthiest levee-
contractors in the State, is a fair sample of pluck, and Governor Pinchback, of the same State, who has an income of
$10,000 a year, is another. I know that we have fearful odds
against which to contend, and that the race between the two
races is an unequal one, but I believe that we ought to remain
in America, and 'push the battle to the gates.' If the colored
people go anywhere, let them go to the new States, where
they can find employment and better educational facilities than
they have in the South. But never let them dream of leaving
the land for which they have shed their blood upon a thousand battlefields!"

"You interest me!" exclaimed Dr. Warren. "Are the colored people indeed making progress in the former slave States?
You see I have not been reared in the United States, as you
have, and I am no doubt ignorant of many important facts
relative to my race."

Griswold indulged in a hearty laugh. "Why, Doctor," he
cried, "we are outstripping the dominant race in both education and wealth in several of the Southern States! In every
Southern State we have Afro-American colleges, taught and
controlled usually by competent colored men and women.
We have magnificent churches, banks, stores, several publishing houses, and over two hundred newspapers! If we have

accomplished this under the hand of God, and in the face of bitter persecution and foul calumny, what may we not expect when our foes shall cease to molest us, and we can dwell in peace under 'our own vine and fig-tree'?"

"I should like to examine some of the race literature," said Dr. Warren. The minister drew from his coat-pocket two papers and a magazine. "Here are some representative papers—the *Indianapolis Freeman*, the *Detroit Plaindealer*, and the *A. M. E. Review*," he said. Dr. Warren examined them carefully. "It is marvelous," he cried. "Less than fifty years have elapsed since we were forbidden to learn to read, and now behold the command that we have of the English language!"

They were now interrupted by Mrs. Warren, who bade them come out into the dining-room and partake of the lunch that she had prepared. They complied, and did full justice to the tempting viands. When they again retired to the sitting-room they resumed their former conversation, and the marble clock, another of Dr. Warren's European mementos, chimed out the mystic hour of twelve before they retired for the night.

As a result of their conversation Dr. Warren immediately sent in his subscriptions to several race papers, and ordered copies of Simmon's "Men of Mark" and Williams's "History of the Negro Race."

The following Sabbath dawned fair and clear. It was the time of Indian Summer. In the fields the yellow corn waved its plumed head, and looked upon the slender morning-glories clinging to its stalks in proud scorn.

At the farm, three of the inmates were in a state of glad confusion; Cora and Eva had come on a visit to Beryl, and all three of the girls were preparing for church.

Cora was as handsome as ever, and had lost none of her

former gay insolence. Eva was the same quiet soul that she had always been. She was preparing herself to go as a missionary to Africa, and came to the farm to recruit her strength.

"Who was that handsome man we met at the gate as we drove in?" asked Cora, turning toward Beryl with her mouth filled with hair-pins.

"Dr. Norman Warren," replied Beryl, with a slight reserve in her tones that did not escape Cora's keen ears.

"A doctor, too, and you never breathed a word about him in your letters, you little schemer! Fie on you, Beryl Weston! To punish such unpardonable negligence I shall have this village Adonis at my feet. Have you any objections, *ma chere?*"

"None whatever," answered Beryl, a trifle coldly.

"You girls had better stop discussing Doctor Warren, and get dressed for church," chimed in Eva's soft voice, as she arranged her pretty bonnet over her light brown hair, and shook out the folds of her best dress, a gray henrietta cloth. "See what my admirer has given me," she continued gayly, pointing to a gorgeous red rose that nestled against her bosom.

"Who, Joey?" cried Beryl, laughingly.

"None other is half so dear to me," sang Cora, and the happy trio marched out of the house, and, followed by Ellie and Joey, clambered into Farmer Weston's immense, old-fashioned carryall.

As Eva's wardrobe was so limited, Beryl suggested to Cora that they also wear their plainest gown, and, with a tender glance at a certain dainty blue silk, Cora consented. As the weather was still quite warm, they decided to wear white. Beryl looked very fair in her gown of simple white, with a knot of cherry ribbons at her throat, while Cora, in her elaborate gown of white embroidery and satin trimmings, looked what she was—a gay Afro-American woman of fashion.

They arrived at the church in excellent time, and sat in Farmer Weston's pew, which was quite near the pulpit.

The church was soon filled, for the people were anxious to hear the new minister.

The theme for his morning sermon was "Self-sacrifice." His remarks were based upon the statement of the Great Teacher, found in "He that taketh not up his cross and followeth after Me is not worthy of Me." In a simple manner, Harold Griswold told the old, old story of the Cross of Christ, and yet his hearers were deeply impressed by his words. His eloquent, earnest plea for the devoted lives that Christ demands of His own touched the heart of the most careless. "Do you find it hard to give up your own rebellious wills, and is the will of your Heavenly Father hard for you to follow? Hear the words of the blessed Saviour: 'He that taketh not up his cross and followeth after Me is not worthy of Me.' "

"Wasn't he fine?" enthusiastically cried Cora, at the end of the service; "I never heard a more eloquent sermon in my life!" But Eva and Beryl clasped hands in silence, with feelings too deep for words.

Cora's careless words concerning Doctor Warren revealed to Beryl the true state of her own heart. She saw that it would be almost intolerable to see Norman's love given to another, even though it might never be hers. She felt thoroughly ashamed that her love had been given unsought, but it was, alas, true. Burdened and oppressed, she fled to her Refuge. "Cast thy burden upon the Lord, and He shall sustain thee," she read in her well-worn Bible; and, again, "As thy days, so shall be thy strength."

Not even to Eva did Beryl confide the story of her love, and her friends deemed her indifferent to Cupid's arrows.

"Beryl's life is bound up in her books, children and church," said Doctor Warren one morning at the breakfast table.

"She is one of the noblest young women I ever met!" cried Mr. Griswold, warmly. "Why, it is astonishing to note the influence that she exerts over the young women in her Sunday-school class, married and single. There's Etta Jones, one of the wildest girls in the village. To my surprise, that girl rose for prayer at our last prayer-meeting. I attribute this change in her character directly to Miss Weston's influence. Again, in the humblest family, if there is a case of sickness or destitution, I am sure to learn of Miss Beryl's kindness from some of her admirers."

"She is an unusual girl, and I believe that God intends her to plan an important part in the work of uplifting the race," said Mrs. Warren.

Doctor Warren frowned slightly. He somehow considered Beryl as his own protégé, and he did not relish the idea of Beryl caring for any one except in the same friendly light that he imagined she thought of him.

CHAPTER IX.—THE LAWN FETE*

"Ah, me! the world is full of meetings
Such as this, a thrill, a voiceless
Challenge, and sudden partings
After."

And now began a season of gay festivities in honor of the new-comers—dinners, moonlight picnics, concerts and boating expeditions—until, as Ellie said, they never got to eat at home any more.

*Original text is complete, though it skips from Chapter 7 to Chapter 9.

Life for our heroine was not composed wholly of roses. The children tried her temper sorely at times. Ellie sometimes went into sullen fits of ill-temper, and no one could manage her save Beryl. She was a very pretty child, and received more notice than was good for her.

But little Joey was the idol of the neighborhood. His sweet childish ways and placid temperament won all hearts. Beryl found it very hard to be firm with him, for he was a merry little soul, and always explained his wrong-doing away in the most innocent manner.

Both of the little ones were pictures of health and happiness. Assisted by Binie, for whom Ellie now entertained the greatest respect, because she could make pictures, Beryl was enabled to keep both of them neatly clad. Despite the gayety of the season, she devoted much of her time to them, keeping ever before her her dead mother's letter.

It was the occasion of a lawn *fete* at the farm. Chinese lanterns hung in all of the trees. Booths were artistically arranged all over the smooth lawn, and the village Afro-American band, led by the energetic Caleb Dunn, furnished excellent music. Cora Grey, attired in the costume of a Jewish maiden, personated Rebecca at the well. She dispensed lemonade from an imaginary well, and she was liberally patronized. Eva, as Queen Esther, sat on a throne built for the occasion, a crown of roses upon her head, selling bouquets. Joey dressed as a page, and Ellie as a maid of honor, waited upon the older ones, for the *fete* was given for the benefit of a new church, and Beryl found work for all who desired it. Beryl looked unusually fair and sweet in a black lace gown and a small string of pearls about her throat. She acted as mistress of ceremonies. Cora was, as usual, surrounded by a circle of admirers. Dr. Warren was in the midst of an earnest chat with Eva, and Griswold sat apart with Beryl, discussing the plans for the erection of the new church. "What would we do without you, Miss Weston?" he murmured softly, charmed by her timely suggestions.

"Oh, very well, indeed," cried Beryl, gayly. "I like churchwork. I am so glad that there is a prospect of a new church for Westland! Dear Miss Hand has sent me five dollars of the fifty that I pledged myself to raise, and Cora gave me five dollars that she had laid away for a new bonnet. She has a warm, generous heart, in spite of her indifference to spiritual things. Poor girl, she had had little or no religious training at home, and she and Miss Hand never liked each other somehow. Cora graduates next June, and then she will teach music. She has sufficient means to support herself in idleness if the chose to do so. Only last night she said with tears in her brilliant dark eyes, 'I wish I had something to live for like you and Eva'; and our Eva quoted softly, 'Live for some good, be it ever so lowly.' "

"Yes, I admire Miss Grey's beauty, also her voice," replied the young minister, "but I admire, yea love, some one else a great deal more. Do you wish to know whom?"

Beryl did not answer, for she felt instinctively that he referred to her.

"It is your dear self, Beryl. I have loved you since first I saw your sweet face at our little church. I feel that you are the one woman in the whole wide world whom I desire for a wife. What does your heart say, Beryl?"

"I am so sorry, Mr. Griswold," faltered Beryl. "I never dreamed of your loving me; indeed, I didn't. I was never intended to be a minister's wife; I am too ambitious. It is now my pet dream to enter the literary arena. I am sorry to deny you, but I can never be your wife. I esteem you as a friend, and revere you as a laborer in the great vineyard of the Master, but that is all."

Beryl spoke gently, yet each word sank into the young man's heart like the thrust of a rapier-blade. He saw in Beryl everything essential to his earthly happiness, and his disappointment seemed greater than he could bear for a while. He sat with bowed head for a few moments, then he turned toward Beryl, and she saw tears in his eyes. He took her hand. "Promise me, for the sake of the great love that I bear you, that you will give yourself to no other man while I am on this work," he pleaded, and Beryl, in her sorrow for his wasted affection, agreed that it should be as he desired.

In the meanwhile Norman Warren, having finished his chat with Eva, sauntered over to Cora's booth. "Oh, fair Rebecca, I pray thee give unto a tired traveler a drink," he asked in a pleading tone.

"I ought to say no, for you have neglected me shamefully," said the gay coquette, as she poured him a glass of lemonade. He spent a pleasant half hour with Cora, then found Beryl and talked with her. And thus in gay converse the guests at Beryl's lawn *fete* whiled away the happy moonlight hours, until the hour of parting came, and they dispersed, delighted with their fair hostess and her gay festival.

The morning light found Beryl, pale and anxious, at Joey's bedside. He had taken ill in the night, and Dr. Warren being summoned pronounced it a case of diphtheria. He saw Beryl shrink as if she had received a blow when he gave his decision, and his own heart was filled with sympathy for her. He knew that Joey was Beryl's favorite, even as he was the favorite of all.

When, through skillful treatment, Norman got Joey's throat in a favorable condition, the child relapsed into a severe attack of scarlet fever.

During the weary weeks of watching by little Joey's bedside, a great tenderness of Beryl sprang up in Dr. Warren's heart. Like Jonah's gourd, in the night-time of sorrow and despair, his love grew and flourished. Neither by word nor look did he betray himself to the girl whom he had learned to love, but contested valiantly with the Death Angel from morning until eve.

Eva and Cora would fain have shared Beryl's vigil, but she would allow no one to take her place at Joey's bedside.

Anxious they watched, but in spite of love's vigilance one night the angel came and laid his hand upon the little child's brow! They were all in the room when he came. Jim Weston sat with streaming eyes at the foot of the bed, praying for grace to give back to God his little boy. Beryl had the little head cradled on her breast. Joey's face was radiant with joy. "Sister, [P]apa and all of you, listen; I dreamed last night that my dear [M]amma came for me—she looked so pretty in her white robe and crown. I love you all, but I am glad to go to [M]amma. Sing, sister, 'bout the precious jewels." But Beryl was too overcome with grief, and to the surprise of all, Cora looked at the little sufferer, and with tear-dimmed eyes sang "When He Cometh."

"Thank you, Miss Cora, Jesus has sent for me, and I am going to be one of His precious jewels sister has told me about so much. Miss Cora, are you one of His jewels?"

"No, little darling, but I mean to be," cried Cora, letting two pearly tears fall upon the sweet upturned face.

"Amen!" said Harold Griswold. "And Ellie," continued Joey, "you must love Jesus, and be good like papa and sister Beryl, then we'll all be together in heaven with dear [M]amma." He shook hands with Mrs. Warren, the doctor and his pastor, for he was a little soldier, and then he asked his father to come nearer so he could touch him. A few moments of prayer and the little form was motionless.

CHAPTER X.–CONCLUSION

"Sweet are the uses of adversity, which, like the toad, ugly
and venomous, wears yet a precious jewel in its head."

It was a long time before Beryl could rally from this blow,
for she had cared for her baby brother with a boundless devotion. Verily she thought she was the handmaiden of sorrow; she saw, too, that her father's heart was well-nigh broken, and she tried to arouse herself for his sake.

Cora Grey's conversion and union with the Church was
the first event that aroused her from her grief. From the
hour of Cora's conversion she made a complete consecration
of her young life to God, and was accepted by a Church
Society as a candidate for the mission field. Verily the hand
of God moves in a mysterious way. The next thing that happened was Dr. Warren's proposal, which happened in this
wise: They were coming home from church one Sabbath evening; Cora and Eva, with the pastor, were in the lead, while
Beryl and the doctor followed more leisurely. Norman Warren bade Beryl take his arm. "Do you remember our first
meeting, Beryl?" he asked tenderly.

"Yes, sir, quite well," Beryl answered demurely.

"I had not thought then that the time would ever come
when you would become dearer to me than my own life, little
one, but it is even so."

Beryl's heart leaped with a wild, tumultuous joy, as she
listened to the voice that was so dear to her, but she was
silent.

Norman bent his handsome head until his lips brushed
Beryl's cheek. "Tell me," whispered he, "can you return my

love? Do not keep me in suspense, darling; say 'Norman, I love you.' "

"Norman, I love you," repeated Beryl shyly, and Norman sealed their betrothal with a long caress. Then followed a few sweet moments such as true lovers experience the world over.

"And now, darling, how long before·I can claim my bonny bride? I have already spoken to your father."

At that moment there came into Beryl's mind the recollection of her promise to Griswold.

"I cannot become your wife for two years," she said faintly.

"Two years! Beryl, dear, are you dreaming?"

Finding that all of his persuasions were in vain, Norman desisted from his entreaties, and contented himself for the present as Beryl's accepted lover.

Filled with heart-great happiness, life assumed a roseate hue for Beryl, and in the privacy of her own room she began to arrange the beautiful thoughts that came into her mind, now like well-ordered sentinels, again like the sweep of a tempestuous sea. Some of her poetry found its way into one or two popular magazines. One poem entitled "Flowers of Memory" found its way into the great heart of the public.

A year later, when Griswold led Cora Grey to the altar, to the astonishment of many, Beryl was tacitly released from her vow. It was then that she explained matters to Dr. Warren. He was surprised, but soon rallied and began to plead for a speedy marriage.

"Why can we not be married in this month?" he demanded.

"Let me see, this is the 1st of June, isn't it?" said Beryl, meditatively.

"Yes, sweetheart."

"Well, I will try to be ready by the 30th," was her unexpected answer.

"Oh, Beryl, you have made me very happy. You will never regret giving your life into my care, if a lifetime devotion can repay your love."

The day of Beryl's wedding dawned fair and clear. The little village was alive with excitement, for Beryl Weston's wedding was a grand affair. Miss Hand, Cora, Eva, and several old friends were present at the ceremony. The path that led to the Afro-American Church was strewn with flowers, and the church was beautifully decorated with pond-lilies, roses and other flowers.

Ellie and five other children, attired in pretty costumes, were maids of honor. Beryl never looked fairer than upon her wedding-day. She wore a costume of rich white satin, with a cluster of magnificent roses fastened in her corsage, and a beautiful diamond cross, the gift of Norman's English friends to his bride, glittered upon her bosom. Upon her hand shone a costly ring set with pearl and sapphires, Norman's gift to his bride, and from her ears swung two glittering diamond pendants, the gift of Mrs. Warren. A deed to the new queen Anne house, which had just been completed, was Jim Weston's gift to his daughter, and a handsome writing-desk came from Miss Hand. Indeed, Beryl was the recipient of many useful gifts, for she had many friends. Binie's gift was a magnificent life-size painting of Beryl's mother, and of all her gifts I think Beryl thought the most of Binie's.

After the wedding Norman and Beryl visited all of the principal cities of the United States, after which they returned and resumed their lifework at Westland.

* * * * *

Some years have elapsed, bringing with them various changes.

Farmer Weston is dead.

Eva has given up her missionary career for the sake of a prosperous young farmer, who has rented the old farm, and adores his gentle bride. In her pretty home, with her baby, another little Joey, clinging to her skirts, Eva is as happy as a lark.

Griswold and Cora are in far-way Africa, laboring for the redemption of those who sit in great darkness.

Binie is growing more popular in the art-world each year, and she enjoys her beautiful life of the present all the more because of her wretched beginning. She has a little studio and cottage of her own now, and her pictures are greatly admired.

Ellie is breaking the hearts of the young men at the very college where Beryl received her impulse toward a new life, and Beryl, as teacher of the modern languages in the same institution, watches her grow into womanhood with affectionate pride, for Ellie has been adopted into the service of the King, and is really trying to be good.

Mrs. Warren has accepted the office of matron in an Afro-American Orphan Asylum, and is deeply absorbed in her work.

Dr. Warren and his wife are everywhere recognized as leaders in every movement for the advancement of their own oppressed race. Two children, Rene and Hugh, have come to bless their married life; and knowing that Beryl is useful, honored and happy, let us leave her, for her highest ambition now is to serve her Lord.

MILES THE CONQUEROR

Fifteen years ago, an Afro-American lad of twenty, stood at the doors of an eastern College, and craved admission. He was poor, and black and the stately professor regarded him with puzzled brows.

"Who are you?" he asked of the shabbily dressed youth.

"My name is Miles Brown, and I have walked from my home in Virginia here, in order to attend this school," was the reply that was given in a firm yet respectful tone.

"Walked from Virginia here!" echoed the professor in amazement, "who told you to come here?"

"No one, sir. While walking along the streets of Richmond, one day, I picked up a scrap of paper that contained an account of your commencement exercises, and I determined to graduate from this school."

"Do you realize what it will cost you to stay here long enough to graduate from one of the departments?" asked the professor.

"I know that it will cost a great deal, but I am young and can work."

"What can you do?"

"Almost anything about the house or barn. I have been attending to Colonel Gladwin's horses for over two years."

"Colonel Gladwin of Richmond; I know him. I will write to him at once. In the mean while I will take you on trust as under gardner. A boy that desires an education as strong as you do, ought to be helped to it. Shake hands with me, Miles."

American Citizen Magazine (20 Apr. 1894).

A strong emotion swept over the boy's soul. His eyes grew dim with tears. Poor lad, he had found so few friends in the world since his old mother had passed into eternity.

"Thank you professor for trusting me. I'll try not to disappoint you," he said huskily.

"Why do you want a college education Miles? I see from your language that you have somehow acquired a knowledge of the elementary branches of knowledge."

"I don't know sir, how to explain it, but I just feel hungry and thirsty inside to know all about the world and then the men and events that have moved it. [I know] that I am black, and that black people are considered an inferior people in every way, but I am determined to conquer every obstacle that lies between me and an education."

"Good for you!"exclaimed the professor. "Let us now go to my home, where you can get some dinner and a few hours of rest, before entering upon your school duties."

There was considerable indignation manifested by some of the pupils of the college, when Miles Brown was enrolled as a student, and a few aristocratic young southerners threatened to leave. However they remained and so did Miles.

The Afro-American lad did not find his school life clear sailing by any means. He was frequently hailed by the opprobious epithets of "Nigger," "Blackie" and "Coon," yet his courage never wavered and his aim stood ever before him clear and bright with hope.

He was slighted and rudely thrust out from the games and recreations in which the other young men indulged, and he took it all with Christ-like patience, until one day, God sent him a friend. The more completely he was ostracised the more intense became his application to his beloved books. But I will tell you how Miles won a friend.

Among the students who openly expressed their dislike

toward Miles was one Claude Howard, a native of Louisiana, a born aristocrat and one who thought that his birth and wealth made him as far above Miles as the sun is above the earth. Howard never lost an opportunity to taunt Miles about his black skin, and as he was wealthy, he found others who eagerly followed his example. Miles never replied to any of Howard's insults but upon all occasions treated him with scrupulous politeness.

It was Miles' second year at the college. By his unflagging industry and courteous manners, he had won the respect of both faculty and students. Howard and his clique still amused themselves at his expense.

One day Howard so far forgot himself as to strike Miles in the face.

For an instant there was a light in Miles' eyes that frightened Howard, bully as he was, then the dark face resumed its wanted calm.

"For God's sake don't do that again," said Miles in low suppressed tones, and Howard walked off with an assumed laugh. A few nights afterward Howard and two of his friends went out for a "lark" of course without permission. They all became intoxicated and being caught in a severe rain storm, all three contracted colds and fever. Howard's friends who were sturdy Englishmen, rapidly recovered, but Howard sank into typhoid fever of a very malignant type, and at Miles' own request, he was sent to nurse him.

Six long weeks Miles cared for his enemy, and at last he had the joy of seeing him sitting up and clothed in his right mind. It was a spring morning. The apple-blossoms sent their fragrance into the stick room and a robin perched on the window-sill sang of God's love, and the blessing of returning health.

"Miles," said Howard softly. Miles looked steadily out of

the window. "Miles, come here." Miles went to the bed. Howard grasped his hand. "Miles," he faltered, "I want to tell you before my devilish pride gets the best of me, how sorry I am for the way that I have treated you. I saw your noble qualities, yet I treated you worse than a dog because of your color. Since I have been paying the penalty of my recklessness, you have been as kind as a brother to me. I may be scornful and true to my raising Miles, but somewhere I have a heart, and you have won it. From henceforth let me be your friend."

Thus Miles won a friend.

Six years he stayed at the college toiling incessantly, and always striving to model his life after the great teacher, who spake as never man spoke.

When he graduated with the honor [no one] rejoiced more sincerely in his success than Claude Howard.

Miles is the honored president of an Afro-American College now. He's also an orator of ability.

Thinking over his life, I think of no better title than "Miles the Conqueror."

CLANCY STREET

CHAPTER I.   THE NEWLY-FREED

Clancy Street in Louisville, Kentucky's populous metropolis, some thirty years ago was held in great disrepute by the inhabitants of the adjoining streets—for this street for several blocks was the home of a large settlement of Negroes.

The recent masters and dealers in human flesh were still sore over the loss of their human chattel, and the newly-freed were striving painfully to adjust themselves to the changed order of things. Not that freedom had come unheralded. The majority of the American slaves who were emancipated by President Lincoln's proclamation, had been taught from their infancy to look forward to the year of jubilee—the day of freedom that was surely in the distance. In Israel's God they had strong confidence and their hope was expressed in many fervent, if ofttimes, ludicrous prayers and plaintive songs.

Just now they were intoxicated with their new possession, and too often acted like so many children in the face of the grave responsibilities that confronted them. From the outside world they received scant sympathy. Turned adrift without money or education, often without friends, they who had been reared as ignorant children, were clothed with the badge of citizenship, and told that they were expected to acquit themselves well in the various walks of life.

A.M.E. Church Review 15, chs. 1–2 (Oct. 1898): 643–50; 15, chs. 3–4 (Jan. 1899): 748–53; 15, chs. 5–6 (July 1899): 152–59; 15, chs. 7–9 (Oct. 1899): 241–51.

To the majority of the ex-slaves the conception of life was low. For two hundred and fifty years, or thereabouts, they had been deprived of the fruits of their toilsome labor, receiving as their share, only that which was necessary to sustain life, with the exceptions of the gifts that were given them on some plantation where they were owned by humane men. A proverb was current among them, that a man who had belonged to a white man, could steal anything from white people—he only took what rightfully belonged to him. From this you will readily see that their ideas concerning the tenth commandment were badly warped.

In regard to the sacredness of the marriage tie, matters were worse. Allowed by many masters to form this relation at will, well used to the separation of wives and husbands at the convenience of their owners, to say nothing of the constant amalgamation that went on during the whole dark period of bondage, now, that they were free men and women, saw no good reason why they should burden themselves with the vows of the marriage contract, or having done so why they should not break them *ad libitum*.

Then, too, with freedom came the opportunity to satisfy the craving for strong drink which had been fostered on the plantations by overseers and owners. Drink will in time brutalize the most refined nature. Drink transformed the ignorant Negro workman into a brute. He who had cowed beneath the overseer's stinging lash under the influence of liquor, became the terror of his wife and children.

Another bad feature of slavery's training period was the habit of wastefulness. The idea of laying aside a pittance of their wages for the exigencies of the future occurred to but few. "Eat, drink, and be merry" was the cry of the masses. They who had been so long oppressed, tried to look upon life as one continuous holiday.

Such was the status of this newly-emancipated people. The ideas they had absorbed were bad—dangerous in fact; but who led them into safe paths? Not the South, for she was still gazing at the desolation wrought for her by the Civil War, and unjustly hating her former slaves for her loss; not the North, although they were sending large sums of money for the education of the freedmen, and giving some of their bravest and truest women as teachers, because they were too widely separated from their pupils by racial prejudices, but the Negro churches standing here and there over the Southland, these were the training schools entered by the freemen. Here must be traced the influences which slowly but surely fitted this people for the duties of citizenship in our fair Republic. The men who preached to them were only partially educated at best, and some of them were illiterate indeed; but, like the humble fishermen of Galilee, who had been with the Master and had learned of Him the wisdom that cometh from above and the word they preached was with power. Through their influence the bonds of marriage were held more sacred, chastity and temperance were taught and the moral law in all its sublime beauty held up before the people as Jehovah's covenant with His chosen.

Too much credit cannot be given to the Negro ministers of this period. They were everything to their people—teachers, family counselors and spiritual advisers as well. Painfully aware of their own deficiency in the knowledge of books, it was no uncommon thing for a minister to preach at all of his regular services, carry on a large night school for the benefit of his adult members and then sit up the remainder of the night pouring over his own lessons.

In many of the country districts their labors were attended with grave physical dangers. Authentic accounts are given of Negro ministers being killed by vicious-minded whites who could not bear to see the Negro manhood which had lain dormant for centuries, now begin to assert itself the minute the awful pressure of slavery was removed. Some of the Louisville churches had been established long before the war by the free Negroes who had drifted there, and at the time that our story opens, were large and influential.

CHAPTER II.   ANNE.

Clancy street was narrow and ill paved, but fairly clean and fairly filled with rickety tenements and mouldy cottages for which the white agents demanded the most exorbitant rents, which rents, I regret to chronicle, for this very reason in many instances went unpaid. The tenants were inclined to be philosophical concerning their poverty adopting the adage:

> "For every ill beneath the sun
> There is a remedy or there is none.
> If there be one, try and find it,
> If there be none, why never mind it."

The inhabitants of Clancy street were mainly tobacco "hands," in a large red brick factory near by, where the plant was dried, stemmed and packed for shipping. The wages received by the workmen were small and inadequate to the demands of life in a large city, so their wives supplemented their efforts by washing, an employment in which Negro women are as hard to excel as in their cooking, and occasionally a Clancy street women went out in service. High up in the first block and farthest removed from the smoke and smell of the factory, in the most inviting of the cottages, a tiny frame building fairly covered with morning-glory vines now all abloom, lived Anne Waters, the foreman's wife, the sage of Clancy street, and the pride of its multi-colored inhabitants.

Anne was a fair-complexioned woman, a little below the average height, of mixed African and Anglo-Saxon descent with one or two Cherokee ancestors looming in the background. Anne's father had been a minister, and she had received more book learning than usually fell to the lot of the Negro women of her day. In consequence Anne held her head just a little higher than the rest of the neighbors. She took both of the leading Sunday papers and always read the news aloud for the benefit of Zeke and any of the neighbors who could not read for themselves. Zeke could read for she had taught him since they were married, but he read very slowly and stumbled awkwardly over the hard words. Anne also owned a handsome Bible—a family Bible—the glib-tongued agent had called it. Anne had paid for this fifteen dollars in weekly installments of twenty-five cents. It was truly a handsome book with its large bright print, and gorgeous illustrations which were only seen on Sunday afternoons when the little Waterses would crowd around Anne's knees and examine it in detail.

This Bible, a copy of "Peep O' Day," "Arabian Nights," a translation of "William Tell," and a miscellaneous assortment of "St. Nicholases," "Wide-awakes," and Family Story Papers comprised Anne's library, though not the range of her reading; for Anne was an omnivorous reader, and had access at this time to the library of an old employer. It was now nearly six o'clock, time for the men to quit work. Anne, neatly gowned in a dress of purple calico stood in the doorway, shading her eyes from the warm rays of the August sun.

"Ca'line, Ca'line!" she called. An instant later, a child, with a sweet, sensitive face, with a book in her hand, and a look of triumph in her large, dreamy eyes, came in view.

She was barely ten and small for her age, with little brown feet, guiltless of shoes, and was dressed in a blue calico slip of Anne's own manufacture.

"I've got it at last," she announced joyfully, holding up the book for Anne's inspection.

"Got what?" said Anne, a little crossly. "You've always got a book in your hand! I thought I told you to watch that meat that I put on to boil for your father's supper?"

"You did," very meekly, "I wasn't thinking, when I went to Hettie's. I'm sorry, but Hettie promised to borrow this for me from the lady her grandma washes for, and oh, mamma, what do you s'pose it is?"

"Cameron Pride?" asked Anne, interested in spite of herself.

"Better'n that. It's the book you said you cried over when I was a baby and Abe was little. It's Uncle Tom's Cabin!"

Anne's eyes sparkled. "Hand it here," she said, "I never cried harder over a whipping than I did the first time that I read this book."

Caroline was anxious to steal off in some quiet corner with the book by herself, but she knew that her mother was letting her off lightly for her disobedience, for Anne belonged to the old school of mothers, who believed with Solomon, that to spare the rod was to spoil the child. She quietly surrendered the book and went into the house.

In the center of the kitchen, the pine table scrubbed to almost immaculate whiteness, stood waiting for Zeke's arrival. A choice bit of boiled shoulder, yellow corn-cakes, tea and a pitcher of Orleans molasses was the simple bill of fare to which even now Caroline's brothers, Abram Lincoln and Ulysses Grant were looking forward with restless expectation.

To their intimate acquaintances the boys were known as

Abe and Lis, much to Anne's disgust, for she could never endure nicknames of any kind. She had named her boys after the two men who, in her judgment, were the best friends of her people. Grant, she had seen often in Memphis, when he was there with his troops, and the great general had taken the little slave girl upon his lap and spoken kindly to her. Caroline shared her mother's admiration for the heroes, and often pouted because she had not been named after one of her mother's celebrities.

"I would have named you after Harriet Beacher Stowe, the woman that wrote 'Uncle Tom's Cabin,' the book that helped to free us, but you see I was staying home with my father when you was born, and you Grandma Ca'line was so good to me, I couldn't do no less than name you after her. You wouldn't had those gold hoops in your ears, or that silk log-cabin quilt if it hadn't been you was named for your grandma," said Anne, and with this Caroline had to make herself content.

Steps were now heard around the house, and Lis, aged six, ran out to meet his father, while Caroline got ready the basin of warm water and towel for his ablution.

Zeke came in a little wearily. He was a stoutly built man of very dark complexion, honest and industrious. He had lived on a farm in the famous blue grass region of his native state until the outbreak of the Civil War, when he had enlisted on the Union side, served out his time, and received an honorable discharge. He had been wounded in one of his limbs, and walked a trifle lame. He hoped some day to receive a pension, then he would not have to work so hard. It had been hard for him. His leg had pained dreadfully while he stood cramped up in a huge tobacco hogshead packing pound after pound of tobacco within its limits. His dark face brightened at Anne's approach.

"It's a shame for old Barnes to work you so hard for nine dollars a week, and you the head packer and foreman of your set. I don't know where he expects to go to when he dies."

"The other factories aint no better. There's so many of us colored folks here, the bosses can get all of the hands they need at their own prices. If I was to step out to-morrow there'd be fifty men'd step up to take my place."

"Oh, I don't mean for you to give up the job you've had for the last ten years, and us paying ten dollars for these three rooms every month of our lives; but I do think it's as little as Barnes could do to give you ten dollars a week during the hot weather," concluded Anne a little lamely.

Zeke laughed. "The only trouble is, Anne, you and the boss don't see alike that's all."

"They had a big fuss up to Aunt Maria's to-day. Aunt Maria took a hatchet and went down to old Granny Ball's and purty near scared her to death," volunteered Abe, Anne's first-borne, a mischievous, fair-complexioned boy of twelve, the image of his mother.

"Yes, Zeke, I was going to tell you soon's you got home and you looked so tired that it skipped my mind. You know some of these Clancy street women's been trying to separate Bill and Maria for two or three years, because Bill works steady and makes good wages. It seems that Fannie Johnson's been running to Granny Ball's to get her to fix up something that would separate them. Well, Bill had been drinking heavy the other night, and came in as mad as a hornet. He beat Maria like a dog and told her he was tired of her. Maria knew she couldn't done anything to deserve such treatment, and it almost killed her. She couldn't think what had got into Bill. She'd almost made up her mind to take her things and go back to the white people that had raised her. You know she lived with the Bells ever since she was small, and they said she shouldn't suffer for anything while they lived, if they knew it. Well, the next morning, while Maria was sweeping off the front door step, she caught sight of something shining that was lying under the steps. She pulled out a bottle with some funny* looking stuff in it and a red flannel 'cunjer' bag with some queer looking roots sewed up inside of it. Maria took them in the house and didn't say a word to nobody till Bill came home to dinner looking for all the world like a sheep-killing dog. He was sober and seemed ashamed of the way he had acted. Maria said she boiled cabbage for his dinner and set out a jar of fine peach preserves that her white folks sent her last Christmas. Bill ate his dinner and when he had settled himself back for a good smoke she brought the things she had found under the steps and showed them to him. She says you could have knocked Bill down with a feather. You know Bill's more'n half white anyhow. Well, he just sat there, getting redder'n redder all the time. Finally, Maria says, he brought out an oath and said if he knew who did it he'd break their heads. Maria says she said, 'I know who did it and I'm going to tend to it myself. I don't know who it is that's trying to separate us, and it's well I don't, for I've been raised well and I don't want to disgrace my raising, but, Bill, as long as you live, don't strike me again, for I ain't one of the kind that will take it.'

"Maria says Bill looked at her steady like when she said that and she never flinched. She told him she meant what she said, and he could either make up his mind to do right or she'd leave him then: Bill never said nothing but he gave her a five dollar bill, and went out. Then Maria went down to Granny Balls and made her own she fixed up the 'cunjer', though Granny wouldn't tell who she sold it to. You know

---

*Funny was used almost always in the sense of curious. [Tillman's note.]

they say if it's thrown in the river it don't take any effect on the one it's intended for? Well, Maria marched Granny all through the hot scorching sun clear down to the Ohio river and made her throw the things in. Granny tried to scare Maria but Maria's bad blood was up and she told Granny if she fixed any more 'cunjer' for her and Bill she'd never live to fix any for anybody else."

"Well, if that don't beat the Jews!" said Zeke reflectively, pushing his chair back preparatory to his usual smoke.

"Come into the front room, Zeke, it is so much cooler. You children hurry up with the dishes and then you sit up and read 'Uncle Tom's Cabin.' "

"Abe, do you believe in cunjures?" said Caroline, when her elders were out of earshot.

"I have seen lots of folks that said they were conjured," said Abe evasively.

"Well I don't," said Caroline, "I believe it's all lies."

"Why Ca'line, uncle Liab was cunjered. Papa said somebody put a snake in him."

"I'm going to tell mamma on you," said Lis.

"I don't care, little tattle-tale," said Caroline.

CHAPTER III.   NEGRO SUPERSTITION

All nations have their superstitions and all individuals as well. Dr. Ridpath in his history of the United States, says that the darkest page in the history of New England is that which records the Salem witchcraft, a delusion which was widespread among the white people of this section in 1692, and was the cause of hundreds of innocent people being put to death. The celebrated Cotton Mather, a minister of Boston, a firm believer in witchcraft and the cause of many of the

deaths, wrote a pamphlet in which he expressed his thank-
fulness that so many witches had met their just doom, and
the pamphlet adds Ridpath "received the approbation of the
president of Harvard college."

The uneducated Negro of thirty years ago was supersti-
tious too. He firmly believed in signs—had them for everything imaginable. If a sparrow flew into the house it was a
sign of approaching death to one of the inhabitants. If a cow
was heard to low or a dog to bark during the night, to the
sick of the neighborhood, it was a sure omen of death. It was
a bad sign, they said, to see children walking backwards as
it foretold they would curse their parents, or to clasp their
hands above their heads, as it was a sign they would die by
hanging. Some of their signs were borrowed from their white
owners while others may be traced back to the tribal customs
and beliefs of native African tribes.

Cunjerin', fixin', trickin', poisonin' and hoodooin' were
the terms used in various localities to designate the labors of
Voodooism called by Sir Spencer St. John, an English author
and ex resident of Hayti, Vaudouxism, a diabolical form of
worship brought from Africa by Negro slaves and practiced
extensively throughout the Southern portion of the United
States and the Republic of Hayti. Voodoo or Vaudoux when
properly carried on means a well-organized band of men and
women who worship the devil under the form of serpents
and who lend themselves to all sorts of evil schemes in order
to be revenged upon their enemies. Each man had his priest
and priestess who, upon stated occasions, offered up animals,
usually a white goat or a fowl, to the evil one. Sir John says
that in Hayti these priests and priestesses known as the Pa-
paloi, are more dreaded than the police, so powerful is their
organization.

With the downfall of slavery and the opening of the school

rooms, Voodooism quickly declined among the Negroes of this country until at the time of which I write, only a few representatives of this wicked delusion could be found in any of the cities or villages, although the ignorant masses still believed in it, and held their belief with the tenacity which is so characteristic of uneducated minds.

But in nearly every community there was a much feared individual, male or female, who had the reputation of being able to settle all differences between lovers or discordant married couples and to furnish charms and other forms of conjuration for the wreaking of revenge upon the head of some unlucky individual.

Was a man suddenly seized with a pain, rheumatic or otherwise, the verdict was rendered forthwith that he was "tricked," and every one of his kind believed it, the victim strongest of all. Was a woman suddenly taken with a fever, she had been "fixed," her neighbors said, and there were not wanting individuals who were able to testify to the presence of snakes or lizards, which they had seen crawling beneath the patient's skin: and there are cases on record where people died from the effects of the mental terror engendered by the belief that they were being tortured by some some diabolical means.

Granny Ball was the Voodoo priestess of Clancy street. She lived in a room of one of the worst looking of the shabby tenements and carried on a flourishing business. Into this room God's sunshine never came save when a few rays stole in as the door was opened to admit some victim of granny's evil doings, for true to Scripture, the old woman preferred darkness to light.

She was a tall, gaunt, yellow complexioned woman now considerably bent with age, possessing a pair of piercing dark eyes and a countenance on which iniquity had long since set its seal. Granny had no relatives that the Clancy street folks had ever heard of, and as far as they knew she subsisted wholly upon the sale of her love-powders, her powers of conjuration and her ability to tell fortunes.

On the afternoon succeeding the events related in the previous chapter, Granny sat shuffling the cards for a neatly dressed Negro woman who wore a sullen look on her dark, comely face.

"You'd better let Bill alone, Miss Fannie," said Granny, impressed by the threats Bill's wife had made the day before. "I see lots of trouble ahead for you ef you keep on after him."

"You tole me you could gimme somepin that would make him foller me clar across de worl'; how cum you can't do it?"

"I kin, I kin, but Fannie, I'm workin' for your own good. Bill ain't easy to git, an' dese roots and 'yards cos' like everything, an' it'll take time, maybe a year to bring things round like you want em—sides—let me shuffle dese cards again. Look here; here's a yaller man with coal black mollyglasker (Madagascar) hair, jes' crazy 'bout you—a man wid money an' a single man at that. Here is a bundle an' two letters comin' to your house. I 'clar I never seen sich luck as you've got."

Fannie's dark face brightened. It would have been less than useless to argue with her against the sin of loving another woman's husband. On her plantation, it had been a common thing for a man to drop one woman and take up with another, but what if Granny's words were true? It was, of course, Jim, Colonel Butler's yaller-faced coachman, who lived just across from where she cooked. She had long admired Jim, when resplendent in a livery-befitting the coachman of a wealthy Kentucky Colonel. He would gracefully assist the ladies in the carriage and then drive down the fashionable thoroughfare with the air of a monarch. It seemed almost too good to be true, but strange things were always happening, and to be married to a nice looking man and have a regular escort to "meeting" was the dream of this poor woman's narrow existence.

"I must be gettin' back," she said as she arose, "an' git my white folks supper. What you charge me for dem big windy tales?"

"Fifty cents" mumbled Granny, and drawing an old-fashioned, beaded purse from her pocket, her guest paid the money and departed.

CHAPTER IV.   HARD TIMES

The winter of '82 was long and pitiless and very severe on the poor of Louisville, especially the Negro workmen, many of whom were unable to find employment. Not one in a hundred would apply to the city for aid, for the American Negro is an aristocrat by nature and holds in abhorrence city rations, city hospitals and city burials. Whoever will take the pains to examine the pauper lists of our cities will find out the truth of the above statement.

None felt financial strain more than the Clancy street folks. The big tobacco factory closed down in mid winter and some of the families were in actual want. Money was scarce, every one said, and it must have been, for the Clancy streeter who searched the streets and river wharves in search of work were but illy paid when they were fortunate enough to get a job.

The panic could not have occurred in a worse time for Zeke Waters. Anne who had worked at different times for a wealthy broom manufacturer ever since she had lived in

Louisville, was now at home with a feeble, thin-looking infant at her breast. Zeke had not had any work for over a month, and the last month's rent had about exhausted her savings. Abe, now a well-developed boy of 14, shoveled snow, and did all kinds of chores for whatever he could get, while Caroline divided her time between her mother and an Irish neighbor who frequently imbibed so much beer that she was unable to prepare her husband's dinner, and dreading a beating from her liege lord paid Caroline a few pence for her services in this direction.

On this particular day of which I write, it had been snowing for several hours and even now the snaky particles fell thick and fast upon the window pane. The wind blew fierce and cold and little Lis drew near the stove, where Anne, pale and careworn stood browning some meal on a gridiron.

"What you making, marmar?" he asked, with a hungry look on his little face.

"We're going to have some army coffee for supper, son. When rations are scarce in the army the soldiers brown meal and make coffee just like what we're going to have."

"We ain't had no dinner yet," wailed Lis.

"We have both together, son, when the factory is closed and papa and big brother are both out of work," said Anne, taking the little fellow in her arms.

"Is that all we're going to have for supper?" pointing with disgust at the coffee pot.

"No, indeed, we're going to have some nice corn cakes and boiled potatoes."

"I don't like taters. Ain't we going to have no meat nor butter, tall?"

"Lis ain't you 'shamed to tease your mother so, when she's sick," said Zeke, coming in suddenly. "The doctor said the

reason your mother was sick so long, she'd just starved herself all along for you children." Zeke brought with him a
covered basket.

"Not meat?" said his wife as she took the basket. They had
not tasted meat for almost three days.

"Yes, I got a job at the poor house this morning. There's
meat enough to last us three or four days—livers, hearts,
melts and a few ribs."

"Can you wait an hour longer, for supper?" asked Anne,
visions of a stew rich and savory, floating before her eyes. If
you can I'll have some dumplings for supper."

"You ain't got no flour," piped Lis, "how're you going to
make dumplings without flour?"

"Never mind, young man; you go and take up the baby.
I hear her fretting."

"She's allus a fretting," grumbled Lis. "Can't I have a
'piece' first?"

His mother handed him a piece of corn bread.

"Give the baby to me," said Zeke. "You little mite, when
I get to work at the factory again you must take milk for the
child. She's the tiniest baby we ever had."

Just then the door opened and Caroline entered; her dark
face flushed to a dusky red by the keen wind. "Where's Abe?"
she asked.

"He went to Mis' Rue's for me." Mis' Rue was Mrs. Rue
Davis, the wife of the broom manufacturer for whom Anne
had been working. "Miss Rue drove down to-day to see how
I was getting along, and told me to send up for some things
for the baby."

"The reason I asked was Mrs. Flaherty gave me a big pail
of coal for carrying Mr. Flaherty's dinner down to the shop,
and I wanted Abe to fetch it. I brought my supper home,
too," displaying a plate upon which were a sweet potato, a

lump of butter and two slices of rye bread. It's for you, mamma. I know how you miss your white bread and butter."

Anne smiled. It was true that she abhorred coarse food and in times of prosperity, did not use it often for herself or Caroline who also possessed a delicate appetite.

"We're going to have a feast to-night, but we must eat before it is dark as our oil is out. Why does not Abe hurry when he sees how blustery it is?"

"Never mind about the dark. I've got a dime. Mrs. Flaherty paid me to-day and I'll run over to Hudson's and get some oil," said Caroline proudly. She was twelve now, and felt that she should help share the support of the family.

"I'll go," said Zeke. "Keep your dime, Ca'line. I'll get the oil." When he came back a few minutes later Abe was with him, and the delicious odor of Anne's rib stew imparted the agreeable information that supper was ready. Very soon the family gathered around the table, and the little Waterses went to work with a will. Anne looked happier than she had looked for a long time. She fairly idolized her children, and it was like wormwood and gall to a proud nature like hers to see her children suffer for food and she ill and unable to supply their wants. Clancy street folks had always accused her of spoiling her children any way. It was true that they were better fed and better clothed and had more toys than other children of their street.

"Mrs. Rue sent down some of the children's flannel dresses for you to do up. She says that girl she's got done ruined I don't know how many now."

"Some of them Irish so stupid," said Anne contemptuously and with more of her old spirit than she had shown for many days. "Did she send the tea?"

"Yes ma'am, tea, a glass of jelly and two loaves of bread, 'sides a bundle for the baby and—oh, yes, she sent a note."

Anne opened the note and a crisp five dollar bill fell out. To be repaid in doing flannels said the note, and tears of gratitude came into Anne's eyes.

"And you all thought hard of your mother when she stayed away from you four weeks and nursed Mis' Rue's children through the diphtheria. No one ever loses anything by being kind. This will keep Mrs. Bills from worrying your father about the rent until we can get some more."

"Mrs. Rue's a good woman. She made me come in and warm good and gave me a lunch before I started home."

"I could'nt tell that it made any difference in your supper," said his mother, laughing, as they left the table.

That night Zeke told Anne that he promised to go to New Orleans in the morning as a deck hand. He hated to leave her so weakly he said, but nothing else was open. Anne gave a reluctant consent and passed the night in uneasy dreams. "Down South" was a very undesirable place for Negro men in those days, and she knew not whether Zeke would come home again or not. She was not a religious woman, but that night the prayer taught her by her young slave mother in Tennessee seemed to hover on her lips.

CHAPTER V. NEGRO SUPERSTITION

For the first time in three years, Caroline had been compelled to stay home and she regarded it as a great trial, Abe had not gone for a year save at night. He worked in the factory with his father.

Today Anne was washing Miss Rue's flannels and Caroline having put the house in order and sang the baby to sleep, was enjoying a visit from her "partner," as the Clancy street children called their friends. Hettie Ross was her friend's name, a beautiful, fair-skinned girl, two years Caroline's senior, who lived with her grandmother in the same block that Caroline lived. Though wholly dissimilar in disposition, the girls were very devoted in their friendship.

"We'll both be teachers after we graduate," said Caroline, who was even an enthusiast in the art of castle-building, "and we'll go together all the time, just like Miss Roberts and Miss Price"; "and wear the sweetest dresses and hats just alike," added Hettie, unconsciously betraying her weak point.

"And then on Sunday mornings they'll see us walking into church, looking so nice, and people will say, 'just see what fine girls Hettie Ross and Caroline Waters have turned out to be,' and when the preacher calls for money for mortgages or anything, we can each walk up and lay down a dollar, and my won't some of the colored people open their eyes."

"And we'll have beaus with us dressed just like Mr. Adkins and Mr. White, with gold specs on and swinging gold headed canes," said Hettie.

Caroline blushed, "I don't like either one of those men teachers," she said, "they're too cross, and anyway I'm not going to marry a school teacher, I'm going to marry a preacher."

Hettie was dumbfounded at such presumption.

"Oh Ca'line," she said, "the idea of you marrying a preacher when you aint got a spec of religion any more than I have, and none of your folks aint either, well I guess you won't!"

Well I don't care, I could get religion by that time, I guess," said Caroline meditatively, "and its so nice to be married to a good man like a preacher. You see you're all the time hearing about being good and saying prayers and its easy to be good." "Oh, I don't know, I don't think its ever easy being good, and getting religion's the hardest thing in the world. Don't you remember how hard we tried to get it last winter when Elder Biddle had his revival? You remember how we went up to the mourner's bench and how we cried?"

"Yes I cried myself to sleep and some old sister woke me up shouting and pounding me in the back, I don't think I could get it that way, but I am going to try again some day, because you know Hettie, it's the only way to be saved from hell-fire."

"The devil just sets there and punches people through and through with a red hot pitchfork, while they're roasting, don't he," said Hettie with a shudder.

"Yes indeed, and when he once gets you in there, you can't never come back as long as you live," said Caroline impressively. "Hettie, let's you and me get religion and be as good as we can all of our lives, so that we can go to heaven when we die. Mamma says it just flows with milk and honey." "Sure enough milk and honey, I wonder? I'd like to be there. I never had as much milk and honey as I could hold in my life!" "I s'pose so," said Caroline, "I'll ask mamma again."

"Ca'line," said Hettie in a whisper, "if I tell you something, will you cross your heart to God you won't tell anybody in the whole world?"

"Not mamma?"

"No, not your mother or anyone, its a secret Ca'line and you're the only girl I know I can trust it with."

"Yes," said Caroline, awed by her friend's manner, "I cross myself to God, I won't tell" (at the same time crossing her bosom as she spoke. "Crossing the heart to God," was a custom greatly in vogue among Clancy Street children, and was probably learned from some Negro children of an adjoining street whose parents were Catholics.

"Do you remember the nice-looking young white man that

passed by last fall when we were sitting on the doorsteps and said, 'Howdy do pretty girls?' "

"Yes," said Caroline, "That's Mr. Howard, the boss of the chair factory. I've heard papa speak about him being so overbearing toward the hands."

"I don't think he's overbearing one bit. I think he's nice as can be. He waited for me yesterday when I'se going past the factory and told me that I was the prettiest colored girl in town; and, oh, Ca'line, he has the sweetest smile, and he asked if I liked candy, and I said yes, and he gave me the loveliest box of candy you ever saw, and I took it home and hid it where grandma can't find it, and I'm going to give you some of it."

"Oh, Hettie, Hettie," said Caroline, half crying, "I wish you hadn't made me promise not to tell mother, because I know it's wrong for you to let him talk that way to you and give you candy. Last fall when I told mamma what he said, she looked awful mad at first, then she took me on her lap and told me that when a young white man talked that way to a colored girl, and tried to get her to like him, it almost always meant disgrace; and disgrace was worse than death."

"Well, we are pretty girls, the prettiest girls on Clancy Street, everybody says so and Mr. Howard's got eyes as well as other people, and you like Otto Lewis, if you do try to be better than anybody else. I s'pose you told your ma 'bout Otto writing notes to you in school, and how the teacher had you crying about it. You have your love affairs and I have mine."

"Otto's a colored boy and mamma thinks he's a nice boy, and she reads his notes and helps me to answer them," said Caroline, her sensitive nature thoroughly aroused by the peril which she concluded Hettie was in. Suddenly Hettie screamed and springing up from her chair started out, for there before her stood Anne, her sleeves rolled up and her face flushed with excitement.

"Yes I heard it—or enough to justify me in what I am going to say," she said in answer to the questioning look in Hettie's eyes. "Your mother is dead Hettie, your mother, so your grandmother told me, was her master's daughter. Your grandmother is too old to follow you around all the time. Mr. Howard means no good to you. Let him alone. You are a beautiful girl and if you will be a good girl, some nice young colored man will come along in a few years and marry you and take you to a good home." "Where's any of 'em got good homes," said the girl sullenly, "none of 'em on Clancy Street's got 'em." "They'd deal square by you anyhow," said Anne, "and that's more'n Mr. Howard or any other white man's going to do in this country. I think lots of you Hettie, and Ca'line can't go a day without seeing you. Let me persuade you to keep out of Mr. Howard's way, because you've got nobody in the world to protect you and when your good name's gone, you've lost all that you've got."

Hettie burst into angry tears. "I ain't done anything wrong. I just took the candy. I can give that back."

"Don't take it back; send it back, Hettie, by Abe, and then you and Ca'line take Miss Rue's flannels home, and when you come back you can make a big skillet full of molasses taffy, and pull it."

Hettie said she would and went home to ask her grandmother's permission.

Anne sat down by Caroline, who by this time was weeping violently over the reproof her mother had given Hettie.

"Do you know how I got this white face and straight hair and features like white folks?"

"Your grandpa was a white man," said Caroline, timidly.

"Yes, he was white, and belonged to one of the proudest families in Virginia. My grandmother on my father's side was born in Africa, a Guinea woman small in stature and black as a coal. Her master had been disappointed in love, early in life, and had never married. He liked the slave girl and took her as his wife. They had three children and they all looked exactly like their father. When they grew up, he tried to break them to the field, but not one of them would ever allow a whip to come on his back. One of them, my father, passed off for a white trader, and slipped a lot of colored people over into the free states. The old man sold the other two boys away down in Louisiana, and my grand-mother just grieved herself to death. In slavery times these things couldn't be helped, but they can be helped now, and every colored girl that wants the respect of black folks, and white folks as well, must stay in her place and keep white men folks in theirs. You're only a colored girl, Ca'line, and poor; but I'd rather see you going barefooted in your little sunbonnet and calico slip, and know you're all right, than to see you in silks and satins and know you didn't come by them honest!"

I think you will agree with me that there was a streak of poetry in Anne's nature when she was greatly moved, as she was now: her words flowed in a torrent of eloquence that seldom failed to establish the argued point. But she failed to save Hettie. Abe told them, that evening, that he saw Hettie and the young boss standing near the shop, apparently en-gaged in conversation.

In the light of this occurrence, it seemed a splendid piece of good luck that a door was opened for Caroline in one of the most exclusive white homes in Louisville.

CHAPTER VI.—AN EXPERIMENT

It happened on this wise. Mrs. Langdon, a beautiful Southern woman, a daughter of a Confederate colonel and a woman
whose good deeds among God's poor made her welcome
wherever she was known, was in search of a young house-
maid, one she could "bring up by hand," to use a familiar
phrase. Having tried two of the many girls that had been
recommended to her, and neither of them proving suitable,
she was on her way home when her attention was attracted
toward Caroline, who was just then coming across the street
from Mrs. Flaherty's. Caroline returned the lady's glance
with one of admiration at the beautiful face with the violet
eyes, and the lines of sadness, caused by suffering, that lingered about her lips.

"Are you looking for some one, ma'am?" she asked in the
musical voice which Frances Willard said is one of God's
many gifts to the Negro race.

"Yes; for a girl who wants to work and to go to school,"
said Mrs. Langdon.

The girl's dark face shone with eager excitement. "Would
I do? I want to go to school so bad!"

"You'd be kept pretty busy. There are three of us, and we
only keep two servants."

"I don't mind being busy, and I can do lots of work. I
would work all the time, if I could only get to go to school."

The Confederate colonel's daughter thought of the Negro
mammy who had cared for her through the first sixteen years
of her motherless existence, and of the little Negro playfellow
and maid, now a teacher in the far South, whom she had
taught by stealth the rudiments of knowledge. Her eyes grew

dim. What would be the distant of this lowly, ambitious people?

"Where is your mother? I would like to see her."

"In here. Walk in, please," and Caroline threw open the
door of their best room with considerable pride. The floor
was bare and white, with a few strips of carpet spread at
intervals; a bed, high, sweet and clean, occupied one corner;
a table filled with books, and papers, another; white portraits
of Lincoln surrounded by his family, Grant in his general's
uniform, Garfield, and a copy of the Emancipation Proclamation, elaborately framed and purchased at exorbitant prices
from silver-tongued agents, on the same plan as the family
Bible, hung in gloomy grandeur upon the humble walls. At
the windows, white muslin curtains hung in starchy prim-
ness. Mrs. Langdon made a mental survey of the apartment
and concluded that the girl would do.

Anne came in, neatly dressed, as usual, with the baby in
her arms. I forgot to mention that she had named her
Evangeline, in honor of Longfellow's hapless heroine. Lis
dragged along, holding to his mother's skirt: he feared that
the lady had come after his mother. Mrs. Langdon explained
the situation.

"I'm sure I'd be glad for her to have the chance, if her
father's willing; but he aint here, and won't be for two or
three days. I'd miss her help like everything, but I wouldn't
keep her out of a chance to go to school when she's just on
her head to go."

Mrs. Langdon drew out her tiny jewelled time-piece, "I'm
sorry your husband isn't here. Send your girl up when he
comes and let me know what he thinks about it. I will not
engage anyone else, until I hear from you again." "Here,
little bright eyes," calling Lis, "take this," handing him a

silver dollar, "and get some shoes for those little bare feet. Your baby looks thin. Is it sickly?" "It's just its teeth ma'am," replied Anne, and then the beautiful childless woman and the poor mother exchanged their thoughts on the care of children.

"And you have no children ma'am," said Anne in her kindly way. "I lost my little boy when he was a year old," she said quietly and Anne changed the subject. "Is your husband one of the Langdon & Horne's big tea firm on Main Street," she asked.

"He was until a few months ago, when he sold out to Mr. Horne and retired from business. Well I must go," and she was gone.

When Zeke came home from his trip to New Orleans with bright yellow oranges and delicious red-skinned bananas for the children and money enough to pay the back rent and grocery bill, the cottage re-echoed with happy laughter, and when the matter of Caroline's going from home was discussed, Zeke said that he could not decide a question like that with so much noise in his ears, he'd have to sleep over it. In the morning he awoke Anne and told her that the child could go, he had seen the whole thing in his sleep and the place was all right. Zeke relied much on these night visions and so did his friends, for strange to say, things usually happened as Zeke predicted.

CHAPTER VII.—AMID NEW SCENES

Caroline was up early the next morning. Fifty cents a week, her board and schooling seemed quite a munificent offer, and Caroline resolved to prove to her employers that she could do a great deal of work. She found the house quite easily from the card Mrs. Langdon had given her. It stood on Fourth Avenue, a street occupied almost entirely half way its length by wealthy white people, many of them ex-slaveholders. The house was a large red brick with broad stone steps leading up to the front entrance and surrounded by sweet magnolia trees and calycanthus shrubs that in summer days perfumed the whole place.

The family were at breakfast when the girl arrived, and Eliza, the good-natured goddess of the culinary department, ushered her into the dining room. Mrs. Langdon, more beautiful than Caroline ever thought in her morning gown of pale blue, smiled encouragingly behind the tall old-fashioned silver tea service in front of her. Her husband, a gruff old Englishman of sixty looked at Caroline as if he was trying to read her inmost thoughts.

"What is your name?" he demanded.

"If you please, sir, its Caroline," very timidly.

"Caroline—well, that's a good name, sensible English name. It's a wonder, though, you hadn't said Carrie. Think you can stay here and do what you're told?"

"Yes, sir."

"I think she'll do, Mrs. Langdon. At any rate she couldn't possibly do worse than those other two heathen you had here."

"A likely young girl," said his spinster sister, Miss Louise, somewhat to Mrs. Langdon's surprise and with visions of a course of lessons in English methods of house keeping in which she figured as instructress and this slip of a girl as pupil.

The rest of the morning was spent in initiating the girl in her duties which were numerous. Caroline listened attentively; her mind was set upon going to school and she resolved upon making the most of the opportunity that she had offered her.

"You can go to school every day and to church Sunday
mornings, but in the afternoons you must stay home to answer the bell while Eliza is out; also you can go home Sat-
urdays after the dinner dishes are washed," said Mrs. Langdon, and Caroline gave a glad assent to all. She did not see
how anyone could live in such a beautiful home with soft
velvet carpets beneath their tread, beautiful statuary and costly
pictures on the walls, and the choicest viands of the market
upon the table for their delectation, to say nothing of the
splendid library of famous books, without being perfectly
happy. But child as she was, she found that material things
failed to bring happiness. Her beautiful mistress was a semi-
invalid whose lovely Christian character alone kept her from
being irritable. Miss Louise, who had kept house for her
bachelor brother ever since their English home had been
broken up, and who, despite the fact that she was a devout
Episcopalian did not like American women never ceased to
regret the day her brother met the Confederate colonel's
daughter in London, while she and aunt were traveling over
the Old World. The two women never understood each other
and each day found them drifting farther apart.

Caroline's advent into the family drew them closer together than they had been during the previous years of their
acquaintance. For Miss Langdon took a fancy to the child
and brought forth garments both wonderfully and fearfully
made, to be made over for Caroline. "This I wore when I
was teaching in France," she said; "that hat I wore at a fete
in London," pointing to various ancient articles of dress.
Through their efforts Caroline was soon neatly equipped for
school, and thanks to Mrs. Langdon's artistic eyes in colors
that enhanced the beauty of the sweet brown face and caused
the little maiden to hold her head very erect indeed as she
proudly marched to school, her new lace shoes squeaking

loudly and to her ears musically at every step she took. Mr.
Langdon had provided the shoes and his wife had smiled to
herself when she saw they were of the best make the store
afforded. "They will last a good while," he had said, half
apologetically. The school Caroline attended was the Jackson
Street School, where a genial Negro principal and a corps of
lady-like teachers instructed several hundred Negro children.
Caroline liked her teacher at once. She was a fairfaced woman
under thirty, of even temperament and decided ability, who
seldom resorted to punishment. She gave Caroline a seat with
the brightest girl in the class, an action that greatly stimulated our little heroine's efforts.

Caroline found out that Otto Lewis, the boy about whom
Hettie had plagued her attended school in the same building
and the news filled her with girlish excitement. Otto was a
tall, ungainly, black boy with the brightest intellect of any
pupil in the building and withal of such excellent behaviour
as to have justly won the favor of all the teachers. He was
two grades above Caroline and she thought him a very su-
perior personage. The girl thought Otto not unlike the heroes of whom she read in books and she worshipped him
accordingly. When she learned that he was attending the same
building she attended, she resolved always to have her lessons
so well that no evil report of her stupidity should ever reach
her hero's ears.

Who looking at the little brown-faced maiden just turning
thirteen in a blue dress trimmed with bright buttons and
with a blue ribbon on her much prized lengthy braid of hair,
her large eyes sparkling with thought now fastened demurely
upon her book, would have been able to fathom the depth of
the feeling Otto had aroused in Caroline's young heart.

And Otto, there was something in Caroline's timid, sensitive nature that awakened all of his better nature and made

him glad that he was large enough to protect her. In vain did the other school girls endeavor to attract his attention from his little divinity. Otto's allegiance never wavered. When building castles in the air, as we all do in youth, he saw himself a principal with Caroline the mistress of a mansion on Fourth Avenue.

He was an only child whose mother Anne had known for years, and who had lived ever since the war, which widowed her, with a white family as cook. Anne encouraged Otto's friendship for Caroline and often asked him to her home, having wisely concluded since children will go to sweethearting as soon as they are old enough to know what it is, it was just as well for her to superintend matters.

CHAPTER VIII.—ALL THINGS ARE NEW

Caroline had never attended any church or Sunday School as regularly as she might have done had Zeke or Anne been members of any of the numerous Negro churches of the city. Now that she had permission to go, Caroline set out in search of a school. With the insatiable thirst after knowledge, which was even at this early period of her life, a prominent characteristic of the girl's disposition, the girl went from school to school until at last, in a little mission chapel, she found a Gamaliel at whose feet she could sit and partake of his treasured wisdom. This was Rev. Hall, the young pastor, a graduate of a noted Negro college, and of a New England theological school as well. The pastor was a little above the average in height, of light-brown complexion, goodly features and a gracious manner that drew the young to him as the music of the piper drew the children of Hamelin. He taught the Bible class, and his wife, his equal in every way, taught the little people.

Caroline joined the pastor's Bible class, and soon became absorbed in the study of that wonderful life to which the men of all ages must turn for help. She attended the school regularly, and persuaded Anne to come and bring the children. Anne came at first out of mere curiosity, but later because she liked the way the minister taught the lesson; and the children liked the songs. Mrs. Hall taught the school.

The whole family, including Zeke, had been attending the mission for some months, when one morning Anne was startled to see Caroline stand up in the school now numbering eighty pupils, and to hear her say as Andrew said to his brother, "I have found the Christ." It was the old, old story, ever new, another soul had found the shining way and started out like Christian to see the King in his beauty.

It had long been a custom among Negro worshippers to give an account both lengthy and visionary of their conversion, many of them exceeding that of the Apostle Paul, and far be it from your humble chronicler to say that the Lord who appeared to the two disciples on their way to Emmaus did not reveal himself to many unlearned souls in dreams and visions, but to Caroline had come no vision, only an inward abhorrence of that which He abhorred and a yearning desire to be like Him and to help in the spreading of his kingdom. "I thought of his goodness and purity; I thought of his kindness to sick and sad, I thought of his death on the cross and then I thought of my sins and I wanted so much to get rid of them and be near him, that I just gave myself to him fully and my burden left me and since then I have been so happy."

The effect of this testimony which was given unsolicited, was to quicken the spiritual life of the school, and soon one corner of the chapel became an inquiry room, where men, women and children asked the way of life eternal. Among them were Zeke, Anne and Otto. Burning with a zeal to bring others to Christ, Caroline and Anne went after Hettie who had now embarked upon a life of sin. Through their pleadings and prayers Hettie repented of her sins and, like Mary Magdalene, with her face bathed in repentant tears, set her face resolutely toward the city Beautiful. She, with the Waterses and a large number of others, joined the chapel and started out to spread the helpful message among others. Anne, with the energy that was characteristic of her, took upon herself the training of a class of girls just turning into womanhood and saved many of them from ruin by her timely counsel and care, while dear old Zeke kept on growing in grace until the Lord chose him as a mouthpiece and he became a local preacher and Rev. Hall's efficient helper. Abe, Lis and little Eva were out of the fold, but while they were in the school, Anne felt that it was only a question of time when the word would quicken into life in their hearts and she waited patiently.

In the meanwhile she was not only a hearer but an energetic doer. Within the precincts of her home she waged a constant warfare against the superstitions in which she had formerly professed so strong a belief. Fortune telling, beer drinking, lottery playing became objects of special abhorrence and were denounced unsparingly. Added to her cleanly habits and kindly disposition the tidal wave of Godliness which had overwhelmed Anne's life, made her doubly respected. "Anne Waters is certainly a changed woman," was the comment of Clancy street folks; "she was goodhearted before, but now it seems she can't do enough for other folks, and Zeke is most as bad."

While Anne was working in her humble sphere the young

pastor was wrestling with a problem which sooner or later confronts all pastors. "How can I reach the young men of the city?" he asked aloud as he and his wife and Caroline sat at the supper table one evening.

"How many young men are there in the church now?"

"Two, Otto Lewis and Ed Stuart," [said] Mrs. Hall.

"How would it do to hold a council with them, they are both young and might suggest something helpful?" said Caroline, timidly.

"I think that would be a good idea," said Mrs. Hall.

"So do I," said her husband; "I'll try it."

The result of the council was a series of meetings for men only where vice was handled boldly and the way of righteousness made plain. Succeeding these meetings were a series of revival meetings and ere long the good pastor had the joy of welcoming a score of young men into the church visible.

CHAPTER IX—GREATER LOVE HATH NO MAN

Caroline had been with the Langdon's seven years and the family thought almost as much of her as if she had been their own child. She had grown into a very attractive young woman and was now upon the eve of graduating from the high school as valedictorian of her class, an event which she had long anticipated with the most pleasurable emotions. She was standing at the window of her pretty bedroom looking idly at the people passing; on the bed lay her graduating dress a marvel of white silk and lace, a gift from Mrs. Langdon; a bracelet and watch testified to the regard of Mr. Langdon and sister and a locket from Otto together with books from her parents and pastor, and flowers from her teachers and students, showed how universally the young girl was beloved.

Caroline looked at her presents lovingly. "How good every one is to me," she murmured. "To-morrow night I shall receive my diploma. And my oration—what if I should forget it? How disappointed mamma and the Langdons and Otto and every one would be. I'll repeat it again." The subject of Caroline's oration was "Wilberforce, the champion of Negro Liberty." Not in vain had Caroline received the culture of books and schools. Her oration exhibited a breadth of thought and persuasive eloquence that surpassed the efforts of all former valedictorians, and had won the admiration of her principal. Caroline began to repeat her oration but was stopped in the midst of an eloquent passage by a scream and the hurrying of feet. "Mrs. Langdon is very ill, come quickly, Caroline," she heard Mr. Langdon say and in an instant she was at her benefactor's side.

Typhoid fever of the worst type was the doctor's verdict and the household was plunged in the deepest gloom. Caroline quietly assumed the position of nurse and would not abandon her post. She loved this woman next to Anne, she said to herself, and she would nurse her back to health.

"I cannot leave her like this, Mr. Langdon," she said with tearful glances at the hot face, "I love her, and I'm going to help take care of her."

It chanced at this time that Anne had just recovered from a severe illness, or Caroline might have surrendered her post to her mother. She had nursed Anne now she would nurse her second mother. Mrs. Langdon would prefer this, if she was conscious, she knew.

"You don't mean to say you aren't going to graduate Caroline after all the preparations that have been made?" said the

Englishman huskily. "Child, you have taught me a lesson. I can no longer doubt the capabilities of your race."

Many weary weeks elapsed before Mrs. Langdon was convalescent, and when she was, it was only to hear that there was an epidemic of the fever and Caroline was a victim.

"She's mighty low, too, Mrs. Langdon. I know they want to keep it from you, but she's bad off," said Eliza.

"Where is the child? Take me to her," said Mrs. Langdon, bursting into tears.

"Greater love hath no man than this, that a man lay down his life for his friends."

"She is at home. Anne would have it so. Our own doctor is attending her, and I hired a woman to stay with Anne night and day, and relieve Anne all she could. Everything has been done that could be done."

Mrs. Langdon smiled through her grateful tears.

"Caroline is very low," she continued, sadly, "she has not taken any food, save a little milk, for weeks. She is delirious part of the time just as you were, and asks incessantly for Miss Rett, as she always persisted in calling you."

"You must take me to her at once. I will be risking no more than she did."

Down in Anne's best room poor Caroline tossed restlessly upon the white bed. Three weeks of the raging fever had left her worn and emaciated, until her friends had lost all hope. Even the doctor shook his head when he looked at her.

Anne, pale and tearless, waited on her with tender solicitude. Caroline was her idol.

The pastor came. He took one of the wasted brown hands in his cool clasp and laid his other hand on her head. "The Lord is my shepherd," he began and to his surprise, Caroline began to repeat with him the sublime words of David's immortal psalm, "I shall not want. He maketh me to lie down in green pastures; he leadeth me beside the still waters. He restoreth my soul; he leadeth me in the paths of righteousness for His name's sake. Yea, though through the valley of the shadow of death I will fear no evil for thou art with me; thy rod and thy staff they comfort me."

Just then a carriage was heard to stop at the door. There was the rustle of a woman's silken garments, and then a beautiful woman was raining kisses on Caroline's wasted face, and everybody in the room was weeping silently, while Caroline smiled sweetly at the sight of the much loved face.

"It's all right, Miss Rett, don't worry so," she whispered.

"You've given your life for me, and I have vowed to give mine for the uplifting of your race," she said. "Your family shall never suffer want while I live Caroline."

Caroline smiled again.

"Everything is so pleasant," she said. I had a lovely dream just now. Mother, father, are you all here?" she asked, faintly. Anne sat on the bed and let Caroline rest against her bosom.

"Kiss me good-by," she said, and they tearfully complied. "Be good, Abe. Let not your heart be troubled," and with this she fell asleep. A careless observer might have thought the young life wasted because its ministry was so short, but it is true that "we live in deeds, not years." But not so one who followed the fortunes of the family and friends of the young girl. Not one who saw Abe's bitter tears and the beginning of the new life that was quickened in him by Caroline's triumphant exit from this world to the city of the King; not one who saw how zealous Zeke and Anne became, in helping the good pastor to sow seeds of life in the dark alleys of the large city—least of all those who saw Mr. Langdon and his wife consecrating the bulk of their fortune to the education of Negro youth and making Otto and Abe the first beneficiaries of the fund sending them to the very colleges where Rev. Hall received his training, also so touched were they with Hettie's grief at Caroline's death that they took her into their home and gave her the aid that she needed to make her a worthy woman. And years after when Otto and Abe were stalwart minister of the gospel and Abe had married a young teacher and held a little Caroline in his arms Anne felt compensated for her great loss.

If you should visit Clancy street, you would not be able to recognize it, for all of the old buildings have been torn down and replaced by handsome new ones.

Anne and Zeke were spending the sunset hour of their lives in great peace, in a handsome cottage of their own. Abe is preaching the gospel in the far West and is winning many souls for Christ. Lis, true to his early traits of character is a flourishing grocer and also an active Sunday School worker. Little Eva now a young woman of eighteen, Caroline's exact counterpart so everyone says, has just finished the high school, those who are intimate friends of the family say that Otto Lewis has been waiting for her and that there will be a wedding soon. Perhaps 'tis so, I know he has not forgotten Caroline, for whenever he comes to Louisville, he goes to Cave Hill cemetery and sits for hours beside a myrtle covered grave whose marble shaft bears the simple inscription:

CAROLINE:
ELDEST DAUGHTER OF ZEKE AND ANNE WATERS.
BORN 1867 DIED 1888.

"Greater love hath no man than this that a man lay down his life for his friends."

THE PREACHER
AT HILL STATION

Sunday morning in a little Virginia town nestling among the mountains. A crowd of Negro men and women, coming out of the little Methodist Chapel, discussing in their shrewd humorous manner the new preacher sent to Hill Station Chapel a month previous.

There was plenty of evidence of genuine emotion upon the faces of many of the recent worshippers. Those who enjoyed religion best by shouting were still rejoicing, and their fervent "Praise de Lawds" and "Hallelujahs" seemed but to deepen the troubled looks that were observed upon the faces of several of the "sinnahs" as the impenitent were called.

"Well, Aunt Jennie, do you still think our little elder can't preach?" said Robert Jones, a quiet, little yellow man whose eyes were even now wet with tears to a large black woman with a comely face who chanced to be walking his way.

"Hush, Jones, don' say a word! Ain't I gone an' shouted myse'f cl'ar out of bref, I nebber did feel so much lak flyin' as I did dis mawnin'. Ef it jes' hadn' ben for Mose an' de chillen, I'd ben willin' fer ole Marse to let down his golden chariot an' let me step on bo'd. Oh, glory!"

"De elder certn'y was in de sperit," remarked Jones, meditatively.

"An' ter think how I wo'ked against dat blessed man 'case ole Lias done tole me dat our minister was one ob dem edjercated fools, an' when he come to de chapel we ole folks gwine be put back in de corner."

A.M.E. Church Review 19 (Jan. 1903): 634–43.

"It was certn'y a wonderful sermon," said Jones, "I've hearn Ward, Wayman,—some ob de bigges' guns in de chu'ch, an' I aint nebber hearn a feelinger sermon dan I hearn dis mawnin'. Well, I guess I'll tu'n off heah."

"Tu'n off nothin'; come rite along home wid me. I prepahed dinnah fo' de elder ter day, but he couldn't come an somebody's got to he'p eat dat chicken an' apple-dumplin's 'sides Mose an' de chillen?"

The fame of Aunt Jennie's cooking was too well assured for Jones to think of refusing the invitation, so he walked on with her saying gently, "I'm so full ob de sperit that I don' feel a bit hungry. Smith was out dis mawnin'; he mus' felt mighty cheap after sayin' roun' so big to evahbody he never spec' to put his foot inside de chapel agin."

"De bird nevah fly so high but what he hab to come down to de groun fer his feed," said Aunt Jennie oracularly. "Lias Smith got to be sich a good Baptis' inside ob de four weeks dat he hab lef our chu'ch. Why he come to my house a few days ago an' tried to tu'n me, an' I've ben raised on Methodis' doctrine all my days. De Baptis' preacher, Elder Smiles, was wid him; they dropped in 'bout noon an' ob co'se I gib 'em bof dinnah. Seemed lak when Smith's mouth 'gin to close down on de biscuits an' fried bacon I had fer dinnah, dat it 'gan to loosen his tongue. Says he to me, 'Sis Jennie, you'd better come ober to de Baptis' chu'ch an' jine us, you'll get de rite kin of feed. 'Sides dat Elder Smiles dun proved it in de Bible dat dey aint no sich church as de Methodis' chu'ch in de Bible, nor dey aint any chu'ch mentioned, but de Baptis! Aint I rite Elder?' 'You's puffe'ly rite,' says Elder Smiles. Well, I was mad as a hornet, but I held in bes' I could an' says, 'How you make dat out, Elder Siles?' 'Well, Sis' Jennie,' he says, 'it's jes' dis way; you knows all de churches 'cep de Baptis' is called Peter Baptist. Now sarch de Bible from kiver to kiver, an' ef you fin' any Peter Baptist, or any other Baptis', 'cep'n one man, John de Baptis' I'll jine yo' chu'ch nex' Sunday.' Well, Jones, it made me mad to think he was settin' thar' at my table, eatin' my grub an' callin' me an' my chu'ch Peter Baptis. Says I, 'Elder Smiles, I want you an' ole two-faced Lias Smith to know dat

> I am Methodis' bred
> An' Methodis' born,
> An' when I'm dead,
> Thar's a Methodis' gone.'

"I told 'em what I thought of them bofe, an' dey lef' in a hurry, I tell you.

"You know, 'cause you'se my class leader, dat I ain't been doing my duty fo' de longes' an' my heart riz in my mouf, when I saw Elder Clark comin' fas' as he could.

"He come in, shook han's an axed me what I'se so mad about, an' den I up an' tole him de whole thing, from start to finish. Jones, you orter seen de Elder; I thought he'd split hisse'f laffin.

"He hah-hahed an' I got to laffin' too, an' I mos' killed myse'f. Den he sot down an' 'splained de whole mattah 'bout Christ bein' de chief cornah stone ob de chu'ch an' all de members belongin' to one family, till I actually felt sorry fer 'Lias an' his preacher, case I believe Elder Smiles is a good kin' ob a man, but ob cose he ain't got de edjercation our Elder's got.

"I was kinder skittish at fus' dat Elder Clark done come to git aftah me bout not comin' to Chu'ch, but he didn'. He come to see ef I'se willin' to let de chillen come to his school he gwine sta't sence he foun' out the white foks din' 'low us but three months' school.

"Den fo' he lef he tole me 'bout his ole mother down in

Washington dat was a slave heah in Virginny jes' lak me an' how dat woman lived in de wash-tub, till he got out ob school, so he could he'p her school de res'. Well, heah we is at last an' I reckon de chillens got evah thing ready by de away de grubs smellin'," and the twain went in to enjoy the feast of good things for which Aunt Jennie's Sunday table was justly famous.

When Clark came to Hill Station, he found the little Methodist Chapel divided into two distinct factions; one formidable and aggressive, led by 'Lias Smith, an unprincipled old Negro, with an intense desire to be known as the "bigges' man in de chu'ch."

This faction was composed of the majority of the older members, who, of course, were the financial strength of the church. The other faction was led by Robert Jones, a man respected alike by black and white for his excellent traits of character. Jones' followers were principally the younger people, who resented 'Lias Smith's coarse bullying manner and demanded a church carried on "lak de white fo'ks carry deirs on."

Aunt Jennie, one of the very strongest pillars of the Chapel, was with Jones at first; but finally fell a victim to the specious wiles of the enemy, becoming a staunch supporter of the Smith faction, which declared that the Bishop need not send them a man from the schools to quench their spirits. They refused to support such a minister; they demanded a man that didn't think he "kno mo' dan fo'ks dat hab ben professin' twenty an' thirty yeahs."

More than that, they demanded a preacher who could preach upon such startling subjects as "Dry Bones in the Valley," "The Sea of Glass" and "Lazarus in Abraham's Bosom"; "For," added 'Lias, "stir dese fo'ks up an' you'll git money, an' ef you don' you won'." He even went so far as to send a badly scrawled petition to the Bishop, describing the kind of a preacher that in *his* opinion, Hill Station required.

Perhaps Jones got some of the young people who taught in the Sunday School to write a petition describing the kind of a preacher that the young people thought was needed. I know not how it was, but the Bishop sent to Hill Station a man fresh from one of the largest and best known of our Negro institutions, a man small and insignificant in stature and withal not very prepossessing in looks; but large of soul, and very much in earnest concerning the needs, bodily and spiritual, of the tiny parish that had been assigned to him.

By persistent kindness, and a refusal to listen to the idle tales of either faction Clark had won the hearts of all of Smith's faction to such an extent that they had, with a few exceptions the most notable of which was 'Lias Smith himself, come back to the church and renewed their allegiance to her courts.

Finding himself defeated and unable, like Lucifer, to draw the third part of the elect with him, the old man took his family from the church and Sunday School, and joined the Rock Daniel Baptist Church which had obtained this queer name from a peculiar custom of this church which required its members to meet at stated intervals and sing and rock Daniel with clasped hands and swaying bodies until they were ready to drop from sheer exhaustion.

In order to combat this and other foolish customs and superstitions, Clark gathered the people together one night in each week and read to them stories of the superstitions of other people, and the way science had made mere bugaboos of them. He read to them stories from ancient mythology, bits of interesting history and short poems, commenting upon them in words that the most ignorant could not fail to comprehend; and when he felt that he had almost exhausted his resources, he called upon several of the white pastors for help and his appeal met with a hearty response.

They, in turn, filled one evening at the Chapel for several weeks, with bright earnest talks upon homely subjects which affected the everyday life of the people; and they were always greeted with an eager appreciative audience.

The week before the delivery of the sermon which had made such an impression upon its hearers, while Clark was returning at four o'clock in the morning from the sick bed of one of his flock, he saw a Negro boy sneaking out of the back gate of one of the white citizens of the place, with a large white rooster.

"Why, why, my boy, what are you up to?" he said, laying his hands upon the boy's shoulder.

"None yer bizness," replied the boy sullenly, with an ugly scowl on his dark face.

"Little brother," said Clark gently, "you are doing wrong; put that rooster back."

"Doin' wrong to take from white fo'ks?" echoed the boy incredulously. "You don' kno' what yer talkin' 'bout; you lemme go."

"Not till you do what is right. Stealing is stealing and it's just as wrong to steal from white folks as it is to steal from black ones. Put it back, and if you are hungry I'll give you money to buy meat," said Clark, willing to sacrifice the meat for his own meagre breakfast in order to enforce a lesson in morals.

"It's a lie; 'tain't wrong to steal from white fo'ks, you ole white fo'ks' nigger," said the boy, and wrenching himself from the minister's grasp, he gave Clark a brutal blow in the face and then ran.

The minister gave chase until he saw the boy disappear in

the rear of a house where he had been told his old enemy
'Lias Smith lived. He knocked, and after awhile 'Lias came
to the door. "Brother Smith, I came to tell you that your boy
is getting into trouble." "How' dat, Elder? Set down."

Clark sat down and related the circumstances. 'Lias looked
relieved. "I thought he'd been caught," he said. "See heah,
Elder, I mus' say you'se took a heap on yo'se'f to come an'
tell me afteh de way I done leff de chu'ch, an' I thank you
fer it, but, Elder, you can't make any ob dese ole heds dat
went thro' slavery believe dat any thing we takes from white
fo'ks is stealing! Whar did dese Virginny white fo'ks from
Gawdge Washerton down get what dey got? Dey stole de
black fo'ks time an' labor, an' made it off ob dem: dat's whar
dey got it."

The minister tried to reason, but apparently with no avail.
"Think of the disgrace of your boy being put in prison, if
you will not think of his sin," said Clark as he rose to leave,
"Sho, dey ain't nevah gwine cotch lil' 'Lias. He's too slick
for dat."

But we all know what happened to the pitcher that was
carried to the well once too often. A similar fate befell 'Lias,
Jr., for he was caught red-handed a few days later, while
making an early morning trip to a neighboring hen-house,
and in spite of his tears and protestations of innocence, landed
in the city jail.

Knowing the kind of moral training that the boy had received, Clark again counselled with the white pastors, and
persuaded them to assist him in getting 'Lias out of jail.
Through their united interposition, 'Lias was released, upon
the payment of a fine, his accusers refusing to appear against
him, after having been visited by Clark, and 'Lias returned
to his home a sadder and, thanks to Clark, a wiser boy.

Clark took the boy and his parents into a quiet place and

made them acknowledge their sin and promise to try to raise the other children differently.

That incident was the turning point, the pivotal epoch of young 'Lias life. He looked at the scar on Clark's face which his brutal blow had left, and he seemed to feel that he never could do enough by way of atonement.

He entered Clark's day school, next his Sunday School and a year later his church—but I anticipate; melted down by the incidents referred to and the sermon, the subject of which on that memorable Sunday morning was "Brotherhood," 'Lias came back to the church soon after, bringing his family with him, and for the first time in the history of the church membership, gave some slight evidence of having accepted the teachings of Christ.

Clark had been at the Chapel four years, and according to the rule of his ecclesiastical body, had stayed his time out, and was preparing to leave for good.

He could look back with a certain amount of satisfaction upon his labors at Hill Station. From being a place of purely noisy demonstration of the spirit, either of the good or the evil, the Chapel had grown to be a recognized center for all good enterprise. A six months term of school, a circulating library, and something more than a parrot form of knowledge of the Ten Commandments had been secured.

The membership of the Chapel was trebled, and in addition to the wiping out of their traditional church debt, under Clark's direction, several of the members had succeeded in clearing the titles to their own little homes.

And Clark had grown to love his work, he was constantly being surprised by the nobility he found in the lives of many of the newly freed. Among them was an orphan girl, with a thirst for books, whom he had helped off to school, and who had just returned, after a three years' absence, transformed from a shy country girl into a beautiful woman, not unlike some of the nice girls that Clark had known at Washington.

He was thinking of one of them now, a teacher in the public schools there, and of Ora May, his *protégé*, who gravely assured him that she wanted to go to Africa as a missionary. How pleasant it would be to have Ora as—when suddenly.

"Elder Clark! Elder Clark!" Ora's voice: He opened the door hastily. Ora stood there with wide-open eyes and parted lips, "Polls,—election—riot—'Lias shot!" she gasped. Clark threw on his coat and almost flew past her.

"To think I forgot it was the hour for the election, for the first time in four years! I might have known." The place where the polls were held was a good half mile. Clark ran till he got in sight of the place, then he stopped and a groan of horror burst from his lips.

A party of young white men, considerably the worse for drink, were trying to drive the Negro voters from the polls. The Negroes had refused to go and 'Lias, Jr., had been wounded by one of the drunken fellows. A large number of both black and white were coming upon the scene, and the situation grew more serious each moment.

As if emboldened by the presence of more of their kind the young white fellows began to yell "Down with the niggers!" "Don't let them vote." "We'll run them from the polls."

"Don't leave the polls; if we die, let's die like men. Out of one blood hath God created all the nations of the earth. If you are fired upon while doing your duty as American citizens, you must protect yourselves," and placing himself in the lead, Clark led the way to the polls and the Negro men followed him and cast their votes amid derisive yells and a perfect shower of stones. "Kill 'em!" shouted one of the drunken bullies.

"Friends," said Clark, mounting an old box that stood near, "Let me speak."

"Go on, let's hear the nigger preacher!"

"Let my people go home peaceably. They are only doing their duty as freed men and as voters. Who would not despise any man, black or white, who held this great privilege and would not try to use it. Friends, John Brown is dead, but his truth is marching on."

A cheer went up from the black men's throats, but it ended in a wail of anger and despair, for a bullet aimed at Clark's head struck him in his right arm and he fell.

Then, as if the sight of their wounded leader had infused into them a new-born courage, the black men charged upon their enemies, and drove them from the place with sticks, stones, and any weapon that chanced to be available.

Of course, there was a cry of riot and a call for troops to prevent the Negroes from murdering all of the whites, but the better class of Hill Station's white citizens, those who had become intimately acquainted with Clark's work, and knew that he was no politician trying to use his own struggling people as a mere stepping-stone to his ambition, believed Clark's version of the affair, and condemned the white marauders so strongly that some of them left Hill Station for good, and that was the first and last riot that took place in that vicinity.

Neither 'Lias nor the minister was dangerously wounded, and what with the careful nursing Clark received from Aunt Jennie and Ora, and the nursing and petting 'Lias got from his mother and the Chapel girls, they were inclined to think themselves lucky fellows.

Some eight weeks later Clark walked into his Annual Conference amid cheers, that brought tears to his eyes. He brought two trophies that were worthy of the occasion—Ora, the sweetest bride Hill Station ever saw, and 'Lias, as a new messenger of the gospel.

DRAMA

❧ ❧ ❧

AUNT BETSY'S
THANKSGIVING

CHARACTERS

AUNT BETSY
CA'LINE   *Her granddaughter*
SPARKS   *A Lawyer*
NELLIE RODNEY   *Aunt Betsy's daughter*
MR. RODNEY   *Nellie's husband*

SCENE I

(A cabin plainly furnished; family portraits on the wall; Aunt Betsy sits pipe in mouth)

AUNT BETSY.—Little did I think I'd eber come to dis: Heah I am nigh on to seventy yeahs ole and not a soul to care whether I lib or die, cepn 'tis Ca'line, my Nellie's lil gal. Lil Ca'line is a mighty heap of company for me, but I spect I'll hab to let 'em take her to de po' house, long side of me, fore many mo' suns'll rise an' set. Long as I could get roun' an' work de garden, I could get 'long all right, but since I done fell down an' broke my leg, I ain't been no 'count tall, cepn to patch, an' to save my life I can't make enuf to git grub an' cloes for me an' Ca'line. Ef I had to pay

Originally published by the A. M. E. Book Concern (Philadelphia, n.d.). Reproduced in this volume by courtesy of the Moorland-Spingarn Research Center, Howard University, Washington, D.C.

301

rent for dis cabin I jes' gib up rite now an' go off to de po'
house without a word, case I'd jes-kno' I couldn't do it, but
I've libed heah now, nigh on to fifteen yeahs an' dey ain't
nebber axed me fo' no rent, an' I guess surely dey ain't gwine
gin now.

(Enter Ca'line with a basket.)

CA'LINE.—Oh, grammer, what you reckon? I met a cullud lady on de street down in town, an' she look at me as
hard an' axe me my name an' how ole I was, an' den she said
she knowed you when she's a lil gal lak me an' she gwine to
sen' you a present an' she went in Mr. Paul's sto' an' got dese
things I'se brought home. *(Points to basket of parcels which
she has set on the table.)*

AUNT Betsy *(rising)*—Ca'line Johnson, am you lying? You
ain't done gone an' stole fo' de fus' time in yo' lil life is you?
What lady gib you de things? Talk quick, an' ef you's took
what didn't belong to you, dars gwine be trouble 'tween me
an' you, dats all!

CA'LINE *(shrinkingly)*—Oh grammer, cose I ain't lying, I
dunno who 'twas. 'Twas a yaller lady all dressed up fine, and
she talked nice and soft like, an' she kissed me, too. Ef you
don't believe me you can axe Mrs. Price's Ella.

AUNT B.—Shut your mouf Ca'line. Hits all rite. De Lawd
hab pervided, dats all. I was an unfaithful servant to doubt
Him for a moment. Didn't He feed 'Lijah when he was in
the wilderness, an' aint He promised to feed His children.
God bless dat cullud woman who eber she is. I hope I'll fin'
out who she is an' whar she's from.

CA'LINE—Bread, tea, sugar, bacon, eggs, butter and oh
Lordy, grammer, here's a silver dollar! *(Capers around.)*

AUNT B.—Praise de Lawd fo' His mercies. Now I'se gwine
git you a new pair of shoes fo' yo' po' lil feet so you can go

to Sunday school. Po' lil lamb, if yo' po' mamma hadn't been taken from yo', you'd been a heap different chile.

CA'LINE—Grandma, where is my mamma now?

AUNT B.—Well, lil Ca'line, I'll tell you 'bout Nellie. You'se twelve yeahs ole now an' ought to know. When Ben Johnson married my Nellie she was counted de prettiest cullad gal in Buckner county. I didn't want her to hab Ben Johnson, but she said she loved him an' after they married he led her a dog's life. He was always drinking and carrying on, an' one night, in one of his drunken fits he threw you outen de cradle an' Nellie sprung on him like a wil' cat, an' he'd a killed her ef some men hadn't cum in an' stopped him. Nellie ran away that night, thinking that you was dead an' she ain't nebber come back. I heard once dat she was dead an' again dat she was traveling with a show. I brought you home dat night an' I'se kept you eber since. Ben drank himself to death, an' I was glad when he was gone, do' I nursed him while he was sick an' tried to pint him to de Lamb dat takes away de sins of the world.

CA'LINE *(softly)*—Was he afraid to die grammer?

AUNT B.—No honey, he said dat God had forgive him an' he hoped to meet Nellie in heaben an' tell her how sorry he was fo' de way he treated her.

CA'LINE.—Oh grammer, if mammy'd only come back an' live with us, wouldn't it be nice? You'd have someone to take care of you, an' I'd have nice dresses like Mrs. Price's Ella, an' go to school every day. I'm going to pray to God to fin' her an' sen' her home.

AUNT B.—He's the one to pray to lil Ca'line. I don' kno' whether Nellie is living or not, God knows an' I pray every day dat ef she is He'll sen' her home. Set dese things in de cupboard Ca'line, an' den we'll read a chapter an' go to bed.

(Aunt Betsy opens the Bible for Ca'line. Ca'line seated on a stool at her grammer's feet opens her mouth as if to read. Aunt Betsy listens attentively.)
Curtain falls.

SCENE II

(Same as first. Aunt Betsy is darning.)

AUNT B.—A week don' pas' an' gone an' dat cullud woman ain't showed herself yet. I wonder who she was. I kinder thought maybe it was Nellie, but surely she wouldn't come that close 'thout coming to de house. Dem groceries dat woman sent is mos' gone an' de money on Ca'line's feet, but I ain't gwine worry. Don't de lawd allus pervide.

(Someone raps.)

AUNT B.—Come in. Hope dats somebody bringing me some mo' patchin'.

(Enters Lawyer Sparks.)

LAWYER S.—Howdy, Aunt Betsy. *(Shakes hands.)* *(Aside.)* (I hate to tell her.) How are you faring these hard times?

AUNT B.—Pretty well, sah, Mr. Sparks, considering my age an' condition. How's yo' family, sah?

LAWYER S.—All well, thank you, Aunt Betsy. *(Aside.)* (It's a nasty job.) The fact is, Aunt Betsy, I've come to tell you that Colonel Harrington has sold this cabin and the ground it's on and you will have to give it up at once as the owner will doubtless build.

AUNT B. *(rising)*—Dis cabin sol' an' heah I'se libed fifteen yeahs. What on earth is I to do? *(Cries.)*

LAWYER S.—I am sorry, but those are my orders from Colonel Herrington's agent. Perhaps if you write Colonel

Herrington, it might do some good. I'll see you again. Good day.

(Exit Sparks.)

AUNT B. *(still crying)*—De hour hab come at las', Po' lil Ca'line an' me mus' go to de po' house to be cuffed aroun' like all de res' of de po' outcasts dat am gathered there.

(Enters Ca'line.)

CA'LINE—What's de matter grammer, does yo' leg pain you?

AUNT B.—No, it's my heart. De cabin's sol' an' we ain't got no place to go. Colonel Herrington done sold de roof over his ole mammy's hed after promising I'd always hab a home.

CA'LINE—I don' believe Colonel Herrington done it grammer. Dat Mr. Sparks done it case he kno's Colonel Herrington is in Europe. Don't cry grammer, I'll be growed up soon an' I'll work an' buy you another cabin a heap nicer dan dis ole shack! Who bought it, grammer?

AUNT B.—I didn't axe. It was enuf to kno' dat it was sol'. Hush, ain't dat somebody knockin'?

(Re-enter Lawyer Sparks.)

LAWYER S.—Well, Aunt Betsy I'm here again. I have some more news fo' you. I just met my boy with my mail and I waylaid him and made him give it up. I find a very important bit of news for you in one of the letters.

AUNT B. *(in despair)*—Does we have to go to-day?

LAWYER S.—No, no, my good woman, listen while I read this letter.

(Opens letter, reads.)

Lawyer Sparks:—
    Dear Sir:—
    I learn that you are Colonel Herrington's attorney and I desire you to act for me in reference to the property that I

have purchased of him. I understand that there is an excellent old lady on the place and I don't wish her disturbed during the fall and winter months at least.

AUNT B.—Amen!
(Lawyer Sparks smiles and resumes reading.)

I want four good rooms built on in modern style and the room now standing to be used as a kitchen. The expense of building must not exceed $250.00. Also you can draw on me for $3.00 a month to pay the old lady for taking care of the place until I come.

Respectfully,
Sylvia Deane.

AUNT B.—Praise de Lawd. Glory to de King! Does you hear that, lil Ca'line. We don' hab to move. I'm dat happy I could shout.

LAWYER S.—Here are your first three dollars and I will add two more to help fix Ca'line for school. I have a heart somewhere about me if I am a lawyer.

CA'LINE *(jumping up and down)*—Oh goody, goody, goody!

SCENE III

(Prettily furnished sitting room; bird in window, books, pictures. Aunt Betsy in pretty flowered dress is darning, Ca'line pores over her school books.)

AUNT B.—Well, well, dese las' few months jes' pas' by lak a dream. I'se had plenty flour, plenty meat an' plenty fire. God bless dat Miss Deane an' now this is Thanksgiving eve an' to-morrow she's gwine come to see how we's getting along.

CA'LINE—She mus' hab lots of money. Don' built dis nice parlor wid de big winder fo' flowers an' sent all dis nice furniture to fix up de house, an' a box of clothes 'sides.

AUNT B.—I'se tried to keep de furniture jes' lak she sent it.

CA'LINE—You certny keep it kivered up good grammer, I ain't never knowed what color de sofar was till to-night.

AUNT B.—I guess not, case I sewed de kivers all down an' I jes took 'em off to-day, so everything'd look peart when she come to-morrow, an' I'm jes dressed up an' setting in here to-night to kinder practice an' know how to act to-morrow. I 'clare I feel as good as white folks.

CA'LINE—You is as good as dey is. All of us is if we behave ourselves! Teacher said so.

AUNT B.—Dat teacher better be careful what he says 'bout white folks. Never mind whether we's as good as dey is or not. Git all de learning an' de sense dat you kin git, an' you'll be all right. Don't kno' what Miss Deane might do fo' you ef she takes a likin' to you.

CA'LINE—I heard that Colonel Everly done give some smart colored man groun' enuf to build a college here at Everly fo' de cullud folks.

AUNT B.—Hi yi, dats good news. I hope I'll git you in Ca'line. Well, I'se sleepy. Guess I'll nod a bit. (*Aunt B. nods.*)

(*Door opens. Enters Mr. Rodney with a large basket, from which turkey feathers protrude. Nellie Rodney follows him carrying a valise. Ca'line starts and stares with open eyes. Nellie stoops over Aunt Betsy and kisses her, then kisses Ca'line, then rushes again to Aunt Betsy.*)

MRS. RODNEY—Mother, oh mother, here is your child, your long lost Nellie, come home at last, and oh Caroline, my precious child!

AUNT B. *(waking up and staring)*—Is dis you Mis' Deane? We's powerful glad to see you. Lawd hab mercy, it's my own Nellie, glory, glory, glory. Praise de lamb. *(Hugs her and cries for joy.)* Where you been all dis time, Nellie, an' who dis man wid you?

MRS. R.—This is Harry Rodney, my husband, mother. He is very smart and is going to build a college here for colored boys and girls.

CA'LINE—Grammer, dis is de lady gib me dem groceries an' dat dollar.

NELLIE—Mother, forgive me, it was I. I had given you up as dead long ago, in fact I had been told that you was, and of course I thought Caroline was dead. Colonel Everly had given Mr. Rodney some land for a school here at Everly. I had worked hard for years for a home of my own and had bought this land through a white friend from the North, not knowing that you lived on it or lived anywhere on earth. When I saw Caroline that day, the truth flashed on my mind, but knowing the prejudice against colored people getting good property, by the advice of my white friend, Mrs. Sylvia Deane, I went away without seeing you until now. I cannot tell you all my story now, but I am here to be with you and Caroline always.

MR. RODNEY—We worked to give our mother and daughter this happy surprise. We have got home in time eat our Thanksgiving turkey with our loved ones. Nellie had more patience than I to wait two whole months without seeing you after knowing of your whereabouts, but that was best for us all. Our white friends did not object to Aunt Betsy's cabin, but many of them will object to Aunt Betsy's cottage furnished, as it will be, with all modern improvements. Dear mother, believe me when I say, I have come to be a son to you, in your old age and a father to Caroline.

Curtain falls.

HEIRS OF SLAVERY
A Little Drama of To-day

DRAMATIS PERSONAE

HERO: *A Negro youth attired as an American citizen.*

FATHER TIME: *An old man leaning on his staff, with an hour-glass in his hand.*

HISTORY: *A tall, beautiful woman in a robe of purple velvet, with a crown upon her head and an Aladdin's lamp in her left hand.*

MIRIAM: *Jewish maiden in national costume.*

GLADIATOR: *A Greek in a Greek garb.*

VIRGINIA: *A maid in ancient Roman attire.*

ANGLO-SAXON DIGGER: *A man in workman's garb of early English period. Yoke around his neck and spade in one hand.*

SLAVE WOMAN: *A beautiful Negro woman in a costume of rich fantastic colors.*

POESY: *A slender girl in robe of delicate pink and green, flowers in her hair and scroll in left hand.*

ART: *A girl in dark crimson robe, cream colored girdle and roses, which she carries in her left hand.*

CHORUS OF SINGING GIRLS: *White robes with long, flowing sleeves. Wreaths upon their heads.*

HEIRS OF SLAVERY

SCENE: *A beautiful wood. A rustic seat appears in the background. Soft music is heard in the distance.*

A. M. E. Church Review 17 (Jan. 1901): 199–203.

(Enter Hero.)
HERO:
Tired out with life and color-blinded men,
I'll rest me in the shade of this attractive glen
And think, what brought me to this restful place,
And of the woes of my unhappy race.
Born of a race of slaves, my father paid
Our ransom and us freemen made;
And when great Lincoln signed the Black Man free,
We northward came to breathe true liberty,
And upward ever have we struggled since,
Our world of snarling critics to convince
Man's merit on no color's shade depends;
And here and there, we've found some honest friends.
Up from the depths and studious nights I've come,
No loud acclaims proclaimed my welcome home,
The little children cry me on the street,
And taunting words my tingling ears must greet.
In market-place, in courts and all by-ways
The Negro-hater dams my gates of praise;
In every way, our foe this thought would teach:
Manhood in highest forms above the Negro's reach,
Then why should I contend when all seems vain?
I'm down, why struggle sore to rise again?
My state, my hue, my race, all keep me back
From equal chance with others on life's track.
        (Hero sinks down on seat and falls asleep.)
        (Enter Father Time.)
    FATHER TIME:
Hot-blooded youth must have some time to cool.
I'll patience have with this misguided fool,
And flag his spirits with historic wine—
Till light upon his struggling soul shall shine.

(Time stamps on ground. Enter History.)
TIME:
History, thou glittering torchlight of the Age,
My idle whims must for the time engage,
Show to this youth of sunny Afric race
What other nations have been made to face.
Discouraged by his seeming sad young fate,
Teach him himself at proper worth to rate,
Disadvantages proudly to despise
And to the utmost heights in spite of all to rise;
For I have been e'er since existed Man,
And e'en before, and I know his race can
Prove to the world, despite their lowly birth,
Of one blood, hath God made all nations of the earth.
HISTORY:
Thy wish my law, oh, Father Time,
Man's history in every clime
I keep alone, and he shall see
Some other heirs of slavery.
(History rubs lamp. Enter Miriam.)
MIRIAM:
Upon the Nile we've laid our pretty boy,
Our little Moses of our hearts the joy;
Oh, woe to us, proud Egypt's daily scorn,
Oh, woe that e'er an Israelite is born;
Abused and scourged, with backs kept raw,
We now must make bricks, without straw.
(Miriam goes out weeping. Enter Gladiator.)
GLADIATOR:
Alas! that I, a freedom-loving Greek,
Must now of shameful ignominy speak.
Rome's wretched slave I at Nero's behest
Must stake my life; strength against strength must test.

'Mid scenes of slaughter all my days are sped,
When shall I reach the realms of the dead?
The gods attend my unpropitious life
And grant this day may end its bloody strife!
(Gladiator goes out. Enters Virginia.)
    VIRGINIA:
A slave! Oh, Venus, hear; I'm Marcus' slave.
Oh dark the hour that birth unto me gave.
Oh Father, haste Virginia's cries to hear;
Oh haste thee and relieve Virginia's nameless fear!
    (Virginia rushes out. Enter Saxon.)
    SAXON DIGGER:
'Neath Norman yoke, the Anglo-Saxons bend
Their homes, their lives upon their lords depend,
Sad to relate, four oxen equal all
The value of the life of an unhappy thrall!
    (Saxon goes out. Enter Slave Woman.)
    SLAVE WOMAN:
All gone, my children gone,
And I am left alone;
All auctioned off for gold—
May curses deep untold
Fall on this Slavery's cursed mart
That tears me from my own apart.
    (Slave Woman goes out weeping. Enter Poesy.)
    POESY:
I inspired song of Miriam's heart
When Jordan's waters rolled apart
I guided David's gracious song,
And dwelt with patient Job full long;
From classic hills of Greece and Rome
Homer and Sappho's strains have come;
In England, Shakespeare's soul I filled

Till he the passing years had stilled;
Longfellow and Whittier well I loved,
Their poet-hearts 'gainst Wrong I moved;
And I have not forgotten thee—
The Negro's harps of minstrelsy
Shall ring with strength throughout the land
Till laurel-crowned thy poets stand.

> *(Poesy remains standing over Hero. Enter Art, who scatters*
> *roses over Hero as she speaks.)*

ART:

Egypt, Rome and mighty Greece
The fabled land of Golden fleece—
Their marble pillars, temples grand
Despairing joy of every land,
The painting of old masters great,
The works of man ancient and late,
Are due to Art's inspiring love.
And now thy petty fears remove,
I love thy bright warm-hearted race,
And higher o'er all thy name shall trace.

> *(Art steps beside Poesy. Enter Chorus of Singing Girls, who*
> *form a circle around Hero and chant.)*

SINGING GIRLS:

Arouse, oh youth, from thy slumber deep,
Too long have ye lain in enchanted sleep,
Arouse to conquest, great and vast,
Arouse, for thou the power hast.

> *(All leave. Hero starts up and yawns.)*

HERO:

In faith, I've had a long and curious dream,
For it somehow to me in sleep did seem
I saw Semitic slaves 'neath Hamite rule!
Romans and Greeks I saw in Slavery's school.

And much do I despise my childish speech.
If we to loftiest heights aspire to reach,
We must both toil and suffer; 'tis the way
All nations conquered in the heated fray.
Allen and Douglass shame my sorry plight
Toussaint and Dumas star my gloomy night.
Resolved am I no little part to play;
Upon our night must dawn a fairer day.
I'll do my best, proving where'er I can
Despite his skin, a man is but a man!

(CURTAIN.)

THIRTY YEARS OF FREEDOM
A Drama in Four Acts

ACT I

SCENE 1.— *(Interior of a rude Southern cabin, table, several wooden chairs, stools, old-fashioned cupboard displaying a few dishes. Pictures of Lincoln, Grant and Frederick Douglass, on the wall. Flower-pots in the window. Aunt Savannah in faded calico dress, red handkerchief, pipe in mouth, discovered darning.)*

AUNT S.—Well, well, well! My little Ella libin'; married, an' got two chillen. 'Pears lak I can't get it through my ole he'd. My little Ella dat was sole away frum me w'en she was jes big 'nuff to toddle 'cross de flo'! Sole rite heah on dis bery plantashun whar I was bred en bo'n, whar my ole man and the yether chillen are buried. Oh, how many nites has I laid 'wake an' wept case dey done sole my baby gal away. Po' cullud folks, dey's had a hard time! All dese years dey's been forced to toil fo' dere masters in de cane-breakers, in de c'on fields an' on de cotton plantashun, an' what hab been dere reward? Sometimes dey's bin treated lik' human' an' sometimes lik' brutes! But, thank God, more'n thirty yeahs ago dey dun heah dat bugle note ob freedom echo'in ober dis lan', and Marse Lincoln war de man dat blowed de bugle. One t'ing 'sides makes me powe'ful glad, an' dat is, I's sabed up de money dat I urned nussin' since de war fo' dis berry

Originally published by the A.M.E. Book Concern (Philadelphia, 1902). Reproduced in this volume by courtesy of the Moorland-Spingarn Research Center, Howard University, Washington, D.C.

hour. I bo't dis cabin home, thinkin' ef eber I foun' my chile, she'd had a home. Lawyer Graham, one ob de bes' white men on de face ob de 'hole earth, he holp me fin' my chile. I 'clar' sence I dun nussed dat man an' his baby thro' yaller fever, 'pears lik' he thinks he neber can do 'nuff fo' ole Aunt Savannah, an' I'se gwine up to de Norf to see my chile.

(Bab raps at the door.)

AUNT S.—Cum. *(Enter Bab, calico dress, sun bonnet, apron sleeves rolled up.)*

BAB.—See heah, Aunt Savannah, Jim Peters said dat Aunt Marie Jones said Uncle Moses told Aunt Martha's Annie, that you war thinkin' ob goin' up Norf, an' I tooken my han's rite outen de wash-tub an' ran ober heah to see ef it was so.

AUNT S.—*(Rises in wrathful surprise.)* Dese Georgy collud fo'ks is de knowin'est collud fo'ks I'se eber did see in all my bo'n days. What dey know 'bout my business, huh?

BAB.—De Black Despatch allus does hab de lates' news. But sholy, Aunt Savannah, yo' don't mind tellin' of me. Is yo' gwine to de Norf sho 'nuff?

AUNT S.—Wal, yes, Bab, jes 'tween me an' yo' an' de gate post, I'se gwine norf jes soon's I kin git ready, but I didn' 'low to tell a sole 'til I was ready to start.

BAB.—Wat fer yo' gwine, Aunt Savannah, to hunt a husban'?

AUNT S.—Bab, dose yo' 'low to 'sult me? I 'lowed no man to look at me sence Gawge Wash'ngton Linkum Peabody died, an' never 'spec's to long's my hed's level. No, I dun heerd tell of lettle Ella, my baby gal dat was sole 'way in slabery times an' I'se gwine Norf to see her.

BAB.—Well, I do mus' say. Did yo' eber heah tell of sich good luck? How'd yo' eber cum to fin' whar she is? I know'd I'se gwine heah news ob somekin', case my rite eye's bin eachin' all day. Sho sign ob news. And what's gwine cum ob po' Elder Jonah?

AUNT S.—Sho I ain't got Elder Jonah to ste'dy 'bout. Lawyer Graham dun adve'tised in sum collud paper—de *Christian Recorder,* I b'lieve-an' foun' whar my chile is. She's a widow, an' got two grown-up chillen, a boy an' a gal. But see heah Bab, yo says yi' jes cum outen de washtub, dars a big pot ob greens bilin' on de kitch'n stove an' a pan ob co'n dodgers in de oben; is yo' hungry?

BAB.—Jes sho me dat pot o' greens an' dat pan o' co'n dodgers, an' I'll sho yo ef I'se hungry or not.

(Exit Aunt Savannah and Bab. Music. Reenter Aunt Savannah and Bab.)

BAB.—Now, Aunt Savannah, youse gwine cum down to de holler to de Voodoo meetin' tonight, ain't yo'?

AUNT S.—But wat's de use ob my goin'? I dun tole yo' dat I don' b'liebe in dat Voodoo no mo'. Ef yo' collud fo'ks could do so much Voodooism an' Hoodooism to each odder, why didn' yo' hoodoo de white fo'ks w'en dey's layin' de lash on yo' back in slabery times an' let yo' own color 'lone.

BAB.—Youse got pow'ful wise all ob a sudden. Don' yo know I cud have yo' walkin' on yo' hed ef I'se mine to? Ef yo' ain't feared ob me youse de only nigger in Georgy dat ain't. Is yo' cumin' down, or not?

AUNT S.—I'll be down dar to bid yo' all good-bye ef nothin' mo'.

BAB.—Good-bye; I'se gwine. *(Exit Bab.)*

AUNT S.—*(Follows her to the door then sits down and resumes her darning. A knock is heard. Enter Vesta Carrol attired in neat walking costume; also James Harris.)*

JAMES H.—Good evening, Aunt Savannah. We heard that you were going away, and we came over to tell you goodbye. *(Aunt S. shakes hands with them and seats them.)*

AUNT S.—Well, ef dat don' beat de Jews! Some fo'ks couldn't keep a secret ef dere lives depended on it. Yes, I'se gwine Norf to see my darter dat youse hearn me speak ob dat wuz sole erway. My darter tells me dat de collud fo'ks has a chance to get up in de Norf. Yo' an' Vesta better cum an' go 'long, case youse a mighty po' chance heah.

VESTA.—What, Aunt Savannah, give up the glorious work of teaching among my own people? No; with all the prejudice and its attendant hardships, I prefer to live in my own sunny Southland and devote my life to the elevation of my people. Could I teach school in the North, Aunt Savannah?

AUNT S.—Lawd noes, gal, fer I don't. But one t'ing I do no, dey nebber has no Klu-Klux nor lynchin' ob cullud men fer white men's meanness. But den youse rite. Stay whar yo' t'inks yo' kin do de mos' good, an' may de Lawd bless yo'. How's it wid yo' an' Jim? I ain't gwine ter 'say Doctor Harris, caze I'se nussed yo' w'en yo' warnt five minute ole, an' you'll allus be Jim ter me.

JIM.—(*Aside.*) Vesta is certainly a darling girl. I wouldn't let her go if she wanted to. (*Aloud.*) Aunt Savannah, you have been like a mother to Vesta and myself. You've helped us since we were little, motherless tots, and always taught us to labor for the elevation of our people. We hate to see you leave us. We thought you could bake our wedding cake, but here where we were born and bred, and where for two hundred and fifty years our parents tilled the soil and caused the sunny South to blossom as the rose, here where they once 'dwelt as slaves, we will stay like men and labor for the redemption of the rising sons and daughters of Ham.

AUNT S.—Amen. (*A knock is heard.*)

AUNT S.—Cum. (*Enter Chas. S. Wayman.*)

CHAS. S.—Good evening, Aunt Savannah, is it possible that you are going to leave us?

AUNT S.—Yes, Charles Summer, Aunt Savannah's gwine

lef' soon fo' de Norf to see her chile an' gran'-chillen. My ole heart's achin' fo' a sight ob dere faces. Forty yeahs is a long time to be separated frum yo' only livin' chile. 'Peers lak ef I had wings, I'd fly dar dis berry minit, so long, so long.

CHAS.—God was good to spare you to see this day, Aunt Savannah.

AUNT S.—Chillen, my God is able! He brought me out ob 'de cruel days ob slavery, an' He's dun took keer ob me ebber sence. Sing me a song, chillen, one ob dem good ole fashioned meetin' songs. *(They sing some Jubilee melody in which Aunt S. joins.)*

JAMES.—Well, Vesta, we must go. When do you start, Aunt Savannah?

AUNT S.—Not fo' nex' Thursday.

VESTA.—Where does your daughter live?

AUNT S.—Let me see, camel, elephant, geeraff, some-whar in New York.

VESTA.—*(Laughing.)* I guess you mean Buffalo, Aunt Savannah.

AUNT S.—Datt's it zacklyy. Nuffin lak habin' edification. Ef I had yo' edification, Vesta, I wouldn't stay heah nor no whar else.

JAMES.—Good night! We'll see you before you start.

CHAS.—I must go too. Good night.

AUNT S.—Good night, chillen. *(Another rap is heard.)*

AUNT S.—Cum. *(Enter Elder Jonah, attired in a well-worn clergyman's suit, battered stove-pipe hat. Walks as if a little lame, using a cane.)*

ELDER JONAH.—Good evening. Miss Peabody, how does de wedder progress you dis afternoon?

AUNT S.——Only tolable, tolable, only. Hab a cheer, Elder Jonah. What am de last' news ob Possum Holler?

ELDER JONAH.—De lates' news am dat you'se gwine tek

yo' depa'ture frum us, en it hab flustrated de action ob my heart so dat I ain't bin able to partake ob my reg'lar repas'.

AUNT S.—O g'long, Elder Jonah, g'long.

ELDER JONAH.—I thought I'd drap in dis afternoon en lebe yo' a little token ob my unadulterated affeckshun.

AUNT S.—What am it?

ELDER JONAH.—*(Producing a parcel wrapped in a brown paper and tied with cord.)* Hit am sum ob de fines' terbacker dat is growed in de State ob Georgy, en knowin' dat yo' had a slight presentment fur de weed, I brung it ober.

AUNT S.—*(With evident hesitation.)* Dat may hab bin de case in de pas', but my darter am a dressmaker, en bof ob my gran'chillen dun bin graduated 'long side ob de riches' white chillen in de Norf, en I don' spose to go dar a'disgracin' ob dem by smokin'; 'sides dat, my niece, Cinthy Ann Jones, dat went Norf wid de white fo'ks, tells me dat de cullud people puts on lots ob style. Dey has carpets on de flo', lace curtains at de winders, organs en pranners, en do' bells on de do'. Yes, en my darter Ella says dat sum ob de cullud fo'ks has 'vanced so far dat dey hires white hep to do de work. Ain't dat scrumptous?

ELDER JONAH.—Scrumptous sartin. De cullud fo'ks am sartinly cumin'.

AUNT S.—Sho, dey ain't cumin', dey dun cum.

ELDER JONAH.—See heah, Savannah, I'se bin terrubul sturbed sense I heerd you'se gwine lebe. Can't I 'swade yo' ter cum back arter yo' seen yo' darter? Why can't yo' 'en me hitch up? Yo' knowed Almiry, fust wife; yo' knowed Betsy, yo' knowed Lizy, Susan, Jane en Hannah, en yo' know I put dem all erway hansum. All de chillen dun growed up outen de way, en de littel cabin in de lane am lonely. What do yo' say, Savannah.

AUNT S.—*(Rises in marked wrath.)* Elder Jonah, I hab de

greates' respeck fur preachers in dere places, but ef yo' cum heah to cote, yo' might as well go, caze I made up my mine twenty yeahs ago, when Gawge Washin'on Peabody died, dat I'd nebber marry agin. Does yo' realize dat I'se turn'd sixty? Dar's no fool lak a ole fool, I'se often heerd, en I belebes it.

ELDER JONAH.—All rite, Miss Peabody, no 'fence 'tended, ma'am, no 'fence. I'll call agin. Good day. (*Elder Jonah makes an old-fashioned courtesy and departs. Curtain falls. Music.*)

ACT II

SCENE 1.—(*Midnight in the woods. A censer of alcohol burning in the centre of a group of masked women and men in white or black robes with Babette in the centre. The Voodoo spirit glides in and all prostrate themselves.*)

ACT III

SCENE 1.—(*Same as at first. Aunt S. dressed for her departure.*)

AUNT S.—In spite ob all dat's cum en gone, I hates to lebe dis ole cabin. 'Peers lak hit am de sweetes' spot on de face ob de 'hole erf. Ef Ella would only cum heah en lib, how happy I'd be; but den, she's bin bro't up in de Norf, en she says she cudn't cum Souf en take what we takes dat stays. I know sum ob us has it purty ruff in dis lan ob freedum. We has a mighty po' sho' in sum respeks, yet sum ob de culled fo'ks doin' mighty well down heah in de Souf. Any how it mos' breaks my heart ter go, but I mus'. I's gwine too. I ain't gwine tell dem chillens dat I'se got nine hundred dollars in de bank en gwine to git three hundred mo' fer dis cabin en de lan' its on. Ef dey lubs me, et gwine ter be fer what I is, not fer what I'se got. Ef ebrything turns out lak I hopes it will, Is gwine 'vide dat money 'tween Ella en de chillen; ef dey don', I'se gwine cum back heah en spen' de res' ob my days.

(Voices outside sing, "Get you ready, there's a meeting here tonight," and Elder Jonah, Babette, Vesta and James Harris, Chas. Sumner, Babette's Grandchildren, the Georgia Quartette, and remainder of the company, dressed very plainly, come ladened with bundles.)

AUNT S.—Glory en onner, what duz all dis mean?

CHAS. S.—Take this seat, Aunt Savannah, and I will tell you.

(Aunt S. sits in the centre of room.)

CHAS. S.—It means, Aunt Savannah, that a few of your friends whom you have helped in so many ways, have come to cheer your heart by humble gifts. May your Northern life be one of joy. Tell your friends in the North that as they boast of their greater freedom and larger opportunities, we of the Southland expect to hear of greater advancement than we are able to make. Tell them we are planting churches and school houses on every hilltop, and that we are filling the valleys with banks, groceries and other places of business. In spite of our ostracism, we are gaining ground and look forward to a bright future. On behalf of my friends and myself, I present you with this watch, which we trust you will wear in remembrance of us.

AUNT S.—*(Takes watch.)* Well, ef dis ain't de out-dunes' s'prise I ebber saw in all my bo'n days. T'ank you, sah. *(Each advances and presents gifts. The children bring flowers.)* I 'clare I dunno what ter say, chillen, I hates to lebe wus'n eber now. T'ank yo' fer dese presents; in de 'hole roun' worl' I no dey ain't a finer set ob cullud people dan dere is in

'Possum Holler. *(Georgic Quartette sings, and whole company join in singing, "Good-Bye, My Dear Old Southern Home.")* *(Curtain.)*

Music, Swannee River, with variations.

ACT III

SCENE 2.—*(A tasteful sitting room at Graves'. Ella Graves a matron of forty-two, sewing. Winona Graves at the piano. Marie Plummer examining new music, Robert Graves studying law.)*

MRS. GRAVES.—How long before train time, Robert?

ROBERT.—Two hours yet, if she comes in on the Erie road. Try to have patience, mother.

MRS. G.—I have waited so long, Robert. Forty years have passed over my head since I looked into mother's face.

WINONA—*(Aside to Marie.)* I am awfully sorry she is coming. It will be such a nuisance to have such an old hand-kerchief head, as grandmother is sure to be, always around in the way. Besides we have so little room. I don't know where she will sleep.

MARIE.—*(Aside.)* It is just too horrid for anything. *(Aloud.)* Where will your mother sleep, Mrs. Graves?

MRS. G.—She will have to share Winona's room for the present, as mine is too small.

WINONA—Oh, horrors! *(Door bell rings: Winona admits Tony Plummer.)*

TONY—Good evening. I hope I find you all well. What, Robert, poring over a book as usual? Bah, it makes my head ache to look at a book.

WINONA—Yes, Robert is a perfect nuisance. He just reads all the time, and such stupid, dry books! The books that I like, such as, "The Outlaw's Bride," and "The Fatal Marriage," he won't even look at.

ROBERT.—I can't afford to fill my mind with such trash. I have an object in life. I look forward to the day when "Robert Graves, Attorney-at-Law," shall swing in the breeze, and mother's mortgage shall be a thing of the past.

TONY—What?

WINONA—Yes, it is the dream of Robert's life to be a lawyer. Massman, for whom he worked so long, promised to take him into his office, but, as you know, Lawyer Massman died quite suddenly, and Robert's hopes were blighted.

TONY—*(Tragically.)* What's the use of a colored man trying to be anything or do anything in this country? This is the white man's country and everything in it is his. Over the doorway of every honorable profession he has written in letters of fire "No Negroes Need Apply." You find prejudice against the Negro in the theatres and hotels, on the railroads of the South, and, yes, even in the churches. A black face shuts you from everything but the menial drudgery that the white man does not care to perform. I had some sort of a silly notion of being an artist once, and I was patted on the back by my white professor and told that my work gave promise of great things, but when I applied for aid, I was offered a position as cook in the Artist's Club, and I accepted. There's no use trying, I tell you.

ROBERT.—*(Rises.)* But I say there is use in trying. What would Benjamin Banneker, the black astronomer; Toussaint L'Ouverture, the hero of Haiti; Richard Allen, the founder of the A. M. E. Church; Frederick Douglass, the orator; and Daniel Payne, the friend of Negro education, have accomplished without making a brave struggle to rise against the disastrous wave of prejudice. I care not if it be true, that "No Negro Need Apply" be written over the door of every profession, there are Negroes of genius who will not stop until they have reached the top of the ladder. It will be in the Negro's case as in the case of the people who have preceded him—a survival of the fittest.

WINONA.—I'm like Mr. Plummer. When I graduated from the High School I tried to get a school, just as my white classmates did, but the authorities informed me that if I wanted to teach school I would have to go South; then I applied for a clerkship, but the proprietors said that all of the girls would leave if the firm employed a colored girl, so I gave up the struggle and concluded to enjoy life as best I could in the depths of which my color had consigned me.

MARIE.—As this seems to have developed into an experience meeting, I'll give my testimony. When I finished school, several of my girl friends entered the business college and learned to be bookkeepers and stenographers; well, I saved up and took both courses, but, just as Winona says, I found no one brave enough to employ a colored girl. Some have given me job work, but no one would take me into an office on account of this hateful American prejudice that sometimes makes me wish that I was anything but an American. No use trying to be anything in this country.

MRS. G.—Do not despair, children; there's a better day coming. Rome was not build in a day.

ROBERT.—If you go in to win, you'll win, but you must have grit and determination if you keep step with the Caucasian race. *(Door bell rings. Winona admits Lucille Woodbury.)*

LUCILLE.—Robert, Mrs. Graves, all of you, I have received such good news today that I ran over to share it with you at once. I have been elected as teacher of the seventh grade at No. 2. My Principal says that I passed the highest examination of any of the applicants. He says he is personally acquainted with Afro-American teachers in New York, Brooklyn, Boston and Chicago, who are doing a similar work in the mixed schools, and he is glad that I shall have an opportunity to prove what I can do. This hour more than repays me for my years of toilsome drudgery. Excuse me, friends, these are tears of joy. *(Wipes eyes.)* There is not an Afro-American child in attendance at No. 2. Who says American prejuduce is not dying? Shall this not inspire me to do my best and thus prove to the Board that the Negro blood which flows in my veins does not lower the standard of the instruction I shall give? It shall, I am determined to succeed!

ROBERT.—Hurrah for our new school marm! *(All clap hands. Door bell rings loudly.)*

MRS. G.—*(Looking at her watch.)* It's five minutes past train time, Robert? What if that should be your grandmother and no one to meet her. *(Winona admits Aunt S.)*

MRS. G.—Thank heaven! At last! *(Attempts to embrace Aunt S., and faints.)* Curtain falls. Music, "Old Black Joe," with variations.

ACT III

SCENE 3.—*(Sitting-room at Graves'. Winona in evening dress. Enter Tony Plummer dressed in exquisite taste.)*

TONY—What, waiting, Winona? Oh, you are indeed charming this evening. Of all the girls at the reception tonight, you will be the sweetest. To think that I shall have the pleasure of escorting the belle of the city?

WINONA.—Tony, stop your nonsense. Suppose you rehearse that song you are going to sing in the concert while we wait for Marie.

TONY.—All right; anything to please the girls. *(Winona hands him the music. Tony sings.) Solo.*

WINONA.—Isn't that sweet?

TONY.—Not half so sweet as you are Winona. Say, Winona, I ask you for the forty-fifth time, will you marry me? I earn a good salary, and you shall have everything [your] heart can wish; go to all the theatres and balls you like, and be the gayest of the gay. I know you must be sick and tired of this stupid life you now live, with your folks always scolding because you are young and like to have a good time.

WINONA.—Yes, I do get tired of it. I sew all day, and then at night if I want to have a bit of fun, I get a lecture. Yes, I'll have you, Tony.

TONY.—*(Taking her hand and attempting to kiss her.)* But do you love me, Winona? I love you madly, passionately.

WINONA.—Why, yes, I suppose I do, but I do not want you to kiss me just yet; wait until I get accustomed to the idea.

TONY.—Perhaps this little gift will enable you to realize it more quickly. *(Pulls out a diamond ring and places it on her finger.)*

WINONA.—Just what I have longed for all my life! How the girls will envy me! What a perfectly magnificent ring. You deserve a dozen kisses.

Curtain. Music.

ACT III

SCENE 4.—*(Sitting-room at Graves'. Table in centre. Mrs. Graves and Aunt Savannah sewing; enter Lucille Woodbury.)*

LUCILLE.—Good evening, how are you both?

MRS. G.—Quite well, thank you, Lucille. Sit down.

LUCILLE.—Well, Aunt Savannah, how do you like the North by this time?

AUNT S.—Fust strate, chile, fust strate. Dar's lots ob difference in de two places, dat's sartin. I hain't hed a 'spectable sweet tater nor watermillion sence I lef' de State ob Georgy; but den, tak' hit all togedder, de Norf am de bes' place fur we po' cullud fo'ks. More free an'—up heah.

LUCILLE.—*(Laughing.)* More free an'—Aunt Savannah, you have such an amusing way of stating things. Mrs. Graves, did Robert succeed in getting into Lawyer Graham's office?

MRS. G.—No, Lawyer Graham told him that he could give him a job as coachman, but as for practicing law in his office, it was out of the question.

LUCILLE.—And yet, Lawyer Graham is called the colored man's friend, and when he wants office he never fails to solicit the colored man's vote.

AUNT S.—What Lawyer Graham is yo' all talkin' 'bout? I used to know a Lawyer Graham 'way down in Georgy.

MRS. G.—I think this one moved here from the South since you came. He and his wife are both lawyers. I sew for his wife.

AUNT S.—Hab dey eny chillen? I mos' sho I knows 'em. *(Aside.)* Aunt Savannah's gwine pay Lawyer Graham a visit. Won't take my gran'son in his office caze he's black. Well, we'll see.

MRS. G.—Poor Robert, I feel sorry for him; he works all day in the blacksmith shop, and at night he sits up and pores over his studies until past midnight. Everyone says he is talented, but no one seems willing to give him a chance. It's so hard. I have struggled so long and so hard to educate my children, and now that they are fit only for hewers of wood and drawers of water. Then, too, our mortgage falls due in one month and not a cent to pay on it. I economize in every way, but—*(Sobs, and lays her head on the table.)*

LUCILLE.—Dear Mrs. Graves, don't cry, something will turn up in your favor. I'm sure.

AUNT S.—No; don't cry, Ella, you'se gwine cum out at de big en' ob de horn. Jes put yo' trus' in de good Lawd. Yo' old mammy am needer a fortune teller nor a prophet, but she proph'sies dat mortgage gwine be lifted fo' de time, en Lawyer Graham gwine change his mine.

LUCILLE.—Oh, kind heaven, grant that your prophecy may come true! Now come downstairs and see what a nice cake I have baked in honor of Aunt Savannah's first anniversary with us.

AUNT S.—Laws a' massey! Has I bin heah a yeah? Le's go down an see what kin' ob a cook Lucille am. *(Enter Robert, who walks agitatedly up and down the floor.)*

ROBERT.—Almost I am persuaded to give up this unequal struggle. I started out bouyant and hopeful to get into the office of some able lawyer, but I have been repulsed so many times that I have almost come to Tony's conclusion that there is no use trying. What chance have I with a black face and an empty purse to reach the goal for which I seek? But I will not despair.

> "Lives of great men oft remind us,
>   We can make our lives sublime,
> And departing, leave behind us
>   Footprints on the sands of time."

Since my color is my misfortune. I will wear it worthily. Milton wrote his masterpiece after the world had become dark to him. No victory without arms. Oh, those who cruelly thrust the Negro aside on account of his color do not know how painful are the wounds that are inflicted by the poisoned arrows of prejudice. *(Enter Lucille.)*

LUCILLE.—Robert, I have come to ask a favor of you. Here is a hundred dollars of my salary that I have saved, and I want you to take it and pay on that hateful mortgage that is breaking your mother's heart. Do not let her know until it is done. Here is the money.

ROBERT.—No, no, Lucille, bless your womanly heart, I would rather bestow a kingdom upon you than to take one penny of your hard-earned salary.

LUCILLE.—*(Aside.)* And I would rather reign over his good, kind heart than reign over the richest kingdom on earth. *(Aloud.)* But, I insist upon it, Robert. I shall never know a moment's peace until it is done.

ROBERT.—Is it possible that you, too, are hardened by the weight of that fatal mortgage? Are you so fond of my mother, Lucille?

LUCILLE.—Why shouldn't I be? She has been just like a mother to me ever since mine died.

ROBERT.—*(Drawing near.)* And I have been just like a brother to you, but if I were in better circumstances I would ask to be admitted into a closer relation.

LUCILLE.—*(Tenderly.)* Coward!

ROBERT.—*(Drawing her to him.)* Who's a coward? Darling, will you be my wife some sweet day, when I am able to take care of you? Can it be possible that I have won the priceless jewel of your love?

LUCILLE.—Yes (if you grant my request).

ROBERT.—I'm the luckiest fellow in the world. Succeed! Of course, I will succeed with the thought of claiming you to inspire me. I will run through troops and leap walls for your dear sake. *(Curtain. Music.)*

[ACT] IV

SCENE 1.—*(Interior of Lawyer Graham's office. Caesar dusting chairs; Lawyer Graham at desk. A knock. Caesar goes to door.)*

CAESAR.—A lady at de do', Lawyer Graham.

LAWYER GRAHAM.—Show her in.

CAESAR.—Cum in. Law me, if it ain't—

AUNT S.—Sh. Sh.

LAWYER GRAHAM.—Well, my good woman, what can I do for you this morning?

AUNT S.—Well, thar's sev'ral t'ings Lawyer Graham kin do fer me, ef he's min' to. Does yo' rehcermember who I is?

LAWYER G.—Well, bless me, if it isn't Aunt Savannah. *(Rises and shakes her hand.)* Caesar, bring her a rocker. There now, sit down, and tell me where you came from. You gave me the wrong address and I lost track of you. Are you getting along all right?

AUNT S.—I jes cum frum my darter's, Ella Graves is her name. She sews fer yo' wife.

LAWYER G.—Is she your daughter? Well, I know you are proud of her, for she is a splendid woman.

AUNT S.—I sartinly is, but yo' axed me how I's getting 'long. I ain't getting 'long 'tall; I's mos' worried to def. I's jes' stedied till I's mos' heartbroken.

LAWYER G.—Worried to death? Heartbroken? What do you mean, Aunt Savannah?

AUNT S.—I means dat yo' ain't treatin' my fo'ks rite. W'at did yo' promise me, Lawyer Graham, when I nursed yo' chile through de yellah feber, ater de doctah dun gib her up?

LAWYER GRAHAM.—I told you that whenever you wanted me to do you a favor, not to hesitate a moment, if it was to give you a check for a thousand dollars, and I mean it.

AUNT S.—Well, den I want yo' to take my gran'son, Robert Graves, into yo' office, so's he kin l'arn to be a lawyer same's any white boy.

LAWYER G.—*(Laughing.)* Yes, Aunt Savannah, but you see, there's so much prejudice against the colored men entering the profession. It might injure me.

AUNT S.—Ain't yo' rich's cream? How's de cullud man eber gwine clim' ober dem two hundred en fifty yeahs ob fo'ced serbitude, ter edgercate yo' white fo'ks ef yo' don' he'p him ober?

LAWYER G.—Well, I haven't any serious objections against taking your grandson myself, but I don't know what Mrs. Graham would say; we are partners, you know. *(Enter Mrs. Graham in jaunty costume, befitting the new woman.)*

MRS. G.—Mrs. Graham is here to speak for herself. What is it? I have just got back from Detroit. I won my case, I've had a good dinner, and I'm in excellent humor. Don't be afraid to speak out; if you are begging for your church, put me down for ten dollars. Here, Caesar, take my wraps.

LAWYER G.—Mrs. Graham, this is Aunt Savannah, who saved Lillian's life when she was so ill in Georgia.

MRS. G.—*(Embracing Aunt S.)* I am so glad to see you. Caesar, take her things; she's going to stay to dinner. How delighted Lillian will be. She never tires of talking of Aunt Savannah. She is on her way now. I'll call her. *(Goes to the door.)* Lillian! Lillian! Lillian! *(From without.)* I'm coming, mother, dear. *(Enter.)*

LILLIAN.—O, Caesar, I missed you so much; I brought you a lovely book.

LAWYER G.—Do you know who this is?

LILLIAN.—Oh, if it ain't my darling Aunt Savannah. *(Embraces her.)* Did you come to live with us? You know you said perhaps you would.

AUNT S.—Bless my lam', Aunt Savannah pow'ful glad to see her chile.

LAWYER G.—Lillian, that tall young man who has been haunting my office for the past three weeks is Aunt Savannah's grandson. She wants me to take him into my office so he can complete his law studies. I will leave it to you and mamma to decide. What do you say?

LILLIAN.—*(Throwing her arms about Lawyer G.'s neck.)* Oh, take him, papa; give him a chance for Aunt Savannah's sake.

LAWYER G.—What do you say, Mrs. Graham?

MRS. G.—Is there anything in him? I don't want to offend you, Aunt Savannah, but young people sometimes mistake inclination for talent. The profession of law, like other professions, means hard work. There is no royal road to success. I have helped colored girls through school and am willing to extend a helping hand to your grandson. If taking him into our office will help him most, I am willing to do that, if Lawyer Graham thinks it's expedient.

LAWYER G.—Robert Graves is really a fine young man, my dear; well educated, studious, courteous and refined. He is very deserving. Altogether, there's nothing against him, except his color.

AUNT S.—Dat's all; dar's not'in again him 'cept his color, en his fo'parents brought dat long ago frum Africa wid em', en couldn't never git rid of it.

MRS. G.—Then I say, take him. What if I had educated my children by hard work and every avenue of success was closed in their faces because of their race, how dreadful would it be. We open our doors to the Jew, the Irishman, the Chinaman, Indian, Russian, German and every nation on the globe, and why should we be so hostile to this peaceful, industrious people who are striving so earnestly to rise. Aunt

Savannah, I will do everything within my power to aid your grandson.

LAWYER G.—History contains no record of any race of people who have made the progress that these people have made since Abraham Lincoln issued that immortal document known as the Emancipation Proclamation. Thirty years ago ignorant slaves enriching the soil of the sunny South by their labor, deprived of homes, of wealth, of education, in fact, deprived of everything that is essential to the life of a civilized man, and today able to boast of an orator like Frederick Douglass, educators like Daniel A. Payne and Booker T. Washington, ministers of the gospel like Richard Allen, legislators like Benjamin W. Arnett, to say nothing of their artists like Henry O. Tanner, as well as their poets like Paul Laurence Dunbar, and inventors. It is wonderful. Had I not willfully closed my eyes to these, no doubt I should have accepted Robert at once.

MRS. G.—You forget to mention that this race has also made their way into law and medicine; Judge Straker, of Michigan, and Lawyer Waring, of Maryland, are lights in the legal profession; and Dr. McKinney, of New York; Dr. Williams, of Chicago, Dr. N. F. Mossell, of Philadelphia, and Dr. Purvis, of Washington, are succeeding in medical lines.

AUNT S.—Caesar, gimme my hat. You'll hab to 'scuse me terday. I'se gwine home to spread de joyful news; 'peers lak my ole heart mos' bustin' wif joy; dis am de day my po' fader en modder prayed fer down in de cotton fields ob Georgy. Dey's fou't de good fite en gone on to glory, en dere pray'r is bein' ans'ered. Goodbye, may de Lawd bless yo' en yorn fer de kine words yo' has spoken.

LAWYER G.—Tell Robert he may come up at once.

CAESAR.—*(Attempting a somersault.)* Golly, I gwine be

sumpin myse'f. I don' belebe I'se got brain enuf to be a lawyer; guess I'll look to'ard de legislatu'. *Curtain. Music.*

ACT IV

SCENE 2.—*(Street. Aunt Savannah hurrying home encounters Elder Jonah on the street corner dressed in new Prince Albert suit, cane and telescope.)*

ELDER J.—Good afternoon, Mrs. Peabody, how does yo' comporosity seem ta gassiate dis afternoon?

AUNT S.—Why, law me, Elder Jonah, what yo' doin' heah? I tho't you's a thousand miles frum heah.

ELDER J.—Sho I's cum to lib heah. Gwine to start a little canny sto' on de corner whar I kin see yo' ebery time yo' pass, en I'se gwine keep pesterin' you' till yo' says "yess."

[Dialogue from Aunt S. missing from original text.]

ELDER J.—Lef' 'em well. Jim Harris dun made his fo'tune curin' sum rich white 'oman dat de odder doctahs gib up, en he en Vesta married en libin' on de fat o' de pot. Charles Sumner gradgerated frum college en got one ob de bigges' churches in Georgy. Dey all sen' lub en Charlie say he gwine cum up heah en cote yo' gran'darter sence he saw de pick-sture yo' sent Vesta.

AUNT S.—Well, ef dem culled fo'ks ain't flyin' dere kite high, I'll gib up. What's Babette doin'?

ELDER J.—Diggin' conjeration roots en throwin' dus' in sum po' ignorant pusson's eyes as usual. Lawd, how skeered dem cullud fo'ks is ob Babette. Savannah, am dere eny chance fer me?

AUNT S.—Law me, Elder Jonah, I'se got so many free 'sponsibilities on my mine dat I couldn't tawk ob sech a thing.

My gran'son gwin to be a law'er en I's nussen gittin' $10.00
a week. I aint got no cause ter marry.

ELDER J.—I see you's jes es hard-hearted es eber. Well,
will yo' 'cept ob a fine Georgy watahmillion da I'v dun brung
fer yo.'

AUNT S.—A Georgy million, cos I 'cepts ob it; I 'clar' I
feel 'bliged to yo.'

ELDER J.—*(Grins with joy.)* Well den, I'll walk fur es
yo' domicile en lebe it. *(Aside.)* Yo' fish won't bite one kine
ob bait, put on another kind. *(Curtain. Elder Jonah sings.)*

ACT IV

SCENE 3.—*(Sitting-room at Mrs. Graves'.)*

MRS. G.—*(Walking the floor with a letter in her hand.)*
Will troubles never end. Winona, my heart's idol, says in
this letter that she has gone off to be married to that reckless
Tony Plummer. Robert has gone in search of her and should
he and Robert meet there will be trouble. Oh, I pray heaven
no harm will befall my darling child. And then today the
mortgage falls due. It seems that my heart will break. Mother
is the only one who seems cheerful and I suppose she holds
up for our sake. Let come what will, Robert and I have
determined to provide her a home as long as she lives. *(Enter
Robert almost breathless with excitement.)* Robert, have you
found my child?

ROBERT.—No, I have not, mother, but I have placed the
matter in the hands of a detective and I will renew my own
search as soon as I have acquainted you with a strange piece
of news. Grandmother has interceded wtih Lawyer Graham
and secured me the position I so longed for, and Mrs. Gra-

ham thinks of employing Marie Plummer as her private secretary.

MRS. G.—Your grandmother! How in the world could she influence Lawyer Graham to do such a thing?

ROBERT.—Grandmother was Lawyer Graham's mammy or foster mother; grandmother has known him for years, and upon one occasion saved the life of his only child, Lillian. Lawyer Graham says he can deny her nothing; grandmother came home yesterday with the intention of telling you, but you were gone and soon after she was called away to see after a patient.

MRS. G.—Wonderful, wonderful; now if my mind were only at ease about Winona, I believe the mortgage foreclosure would cease to worry me.

(Enter Winona, followed by Aunt Savannah, Lucille and Elder Jonah.)

WINONA.—*(Falling at her mother's feet.)* Oh, mother, forgive me, I have been so ungrateful; from henceforth, mother, I will endeavor to be as good a daughter as Robert is a son.

ROBERT.—Did Plummer dare to wrong you? If he has his life shall pay the forfeit.

AUNT S.—*(Laying her hand on Robert's arm.)* Don' be hasty, young man; Winona's alright; Lucille en me's kep trac' ob her eber sence she lef' de house. She en Tony did go befo' de justis ob de peace to be married, but while dey's waiting fer him to cum in de police cum in ater dat diamont ring Tony had gib her. Jes es it happen' Tony had dat ring in his ves' pocket, else Winona's allus bin 'shamed ob her ole Georgy gran'mother, but she'll lib ter thank me yit fer sabin' her frum marryin' dat bundle ob tailor's clo'es wid no mo' principle 'bout him dan a rat.

ELDER J.—Dese youn' fo'ks don' git nuff strop ile; stop ile's what dey needs.

WINONA.—*(Rising.)* Oh, grandmother, I thank you now. I plainly see I never loved him. I was only dazzled by his manners and sweet words. I feel as if grandmother's hand had pulled me back from the brink of an awful precipice.

(Enter Marie Crying.)

MARIE.—My poor brother has been arrested. It was all Winona's fault; she was always wishing for a diamond ring and Tony could deny her nothing. Mrs. Graham promised to make me her secretary, and now our family is disgraced forever. Oh, what shall I do.

LUCILLE.—Be composed, Marie. Mrs. Graham knows all about it. She does not condemn you for Tony's crime.

AUNT S.—Chillens, it's a hard lesson, but one bof ob yo' gals needed. I ain't got no edification to speak, do I kin read en scratch a little wid de pen, but I has allus foun' dis to be true, dat de youn' fo'ks, bof black en white, dat spen's dey precious hours readin' dese trashy books dey calls nobels, en frequen'in' wine rooms, dancin' halls en gamblen dens, en dressin' finer dan dey kin 'ford, neber cums to no good en'. Yo' youn' fo'ks has all de chance in de worl' to be useful men en women, en I want yo' to spread yo' wings en see how yo' kin fly, caze de hope ob de cullud race lies in dis youn' generashun.

ELDER J.—Mrs. Peabody, you'se a'cumin'; I couldn't sed dat bettah mysef'.

LUCILLE.—Aunt Savannah, your words have the sound of true wisdom. Winona as a dressmaker, Robert as a lawyer, Marie as a stenographer, and myself as a school teacher, will prove to the world that we are going onward and upward. *(A knock is heard and Winona admits Lawyer Graham with papers in hand.)*

LAWYER GRAHAM.—Good morning, Aunt Savannah, I have good news for you; part of it is, that this being Tony

Plummer's first offence, and Mrs. Berry refusing to prosecute him, he will get a very light sentence. The other part is, I have secured you a pension of $10.00 a month and a thousand dollars back pension; this with the money you have out at interest, makes you worth in the neighborhood of $2,000.

AUNT S.—*(Clapping her hands.)* Glory en onner. I jes wonder'd ef I's gwine hab 'nuff fer dese chillren without strappin' myse'f glory en onner.

ELDER J.—*(Aside.)* No chance fo' dis darkey now.

MRS. G.—Why, mother, I didn't know that you had a cent of money except what you earned nursing; why didn't you tell me?

AUNT S.—Wanted to s'prise yo', dat's why; don' belebe en tellin' yo' insides no how. Lawyer Graham, write Ella out a check for $500 so she kin pay off dis mor'gage en build de house ober in King Anne style that Winona's allus ta'kin' 'bout, en gib Robert en Winona each a hundred dollars, en write out a check fer de hundred dollars dat Lucille len' Robert to pay on de mor'gage.

LUCILLE.—*(Blushing.)* Robert, who told her?

AUNT S.—Foun' out myse'f. I'se a new 'oman lak Mrs. Graham. Marie, I's gwine present yo' wid one o' dem pranners yo' write letters on, bein' you' en Winona's sech fren's, en I spects to heah ob yo' makin' a fine 'oman ob yo'se'f; en when eny ob yo' marry I'se gwine he'p yo' all I kin. Glory en onner, dis am a proud hour ter me.

MRS. G.—Saved! Saved! My home and my child. *(Cries.)*

LAWYER G.—Excuse me, good day. *(Exit Lawyer Graham.)*

ROBERT.—Grandmother, you have acted the part of a good angel in our home. You have made the best possible use of your Thirty Years of Freedom. May we profit by your ex-

ample and prove alike to enemies and friends that we are as
worthy of freedom as any race of people on God's green globe,
and that, though surrounded by ostracism, we will continue
to educate, to accumulate wealth, to cultivate the principles
of morality and to worship the God who hath delivered us
from bondage until all men everywhere shall know that
Ethiopia hath stretched forth her hand unto God!

ELDER J.—Amen.

Curtain. Tableaux.

TABLEAU

*Robert and Lucille before Rev. Charles S. Wayman; Winona
and Marie, Maids of Honor; Elder Jonah, Aunt Savannah,
Mrs. Graves, Vesta Carroll, Dr. Harris, Babette, Lawyer
Graham, Mrs. Graham and Lillian, all interested spectators. A
wedding march is played very softly. Colored light. Curtain.*

FIFTY YEARS OF FREEDOM
OR
FROM CABIN TO CONGRESS
A Drama in Five Acts

CHARACTERS

BENJAMIN BANNEKER HOUSTON
An Ambitious Young Kentuckian
AUNT RHODA   *A Southern Mammy*
LINDY   *Aunt Rhoda's Ward*
JAKE   *A Trifling Husband*
SUE ⎫
LOUPHENIA ⎬ *Aunt Rhoda's Daughters*
PANSY ⎭
LIGE ⎫
GLADSTONE ⎬ *Aunt Rhoda's Sons*
COLONEL WHITE   *A Gentleman of the South*
MISS LOU   *His Beautiful Daughter*
ROBERT WHITE   *Her Suitor*
RUTH PENN   *A Quaker Teacher*
PRESIDENT NORTON   *President Bayview University*
ARTHUR NORTON   *His Son*
PROF. COX ⎫
PROF. WEIR ⎬
PROF. MINOR ⎬ *Members of the Faculty*
PROF. WARD ⎭

Originally published by the A.M.E. Book Concern (Philadelphia, 1910). Reproduced in this volume, by courtesy of Brown University Library, Providence, RI.

341

VAN WERT ⎫
OGDEN ⎪ *Students*
STEWART ⎬
POWELL ⎭

GEORGE NEIL   *A Successful Negro Lawyer*
EDITH NEIL   *His Young Daughter*
MRS. NEIL   *His Wife*
IDA CAMPBELL ⎫ *Friends of Edith*
JULIA STORM ⎭
MAID
GUESTS AT THE RECEPTION.

ACT I

SCENE 1.—*(Interior of Aunt Rhoda's cabin, calico curtains at window, Bible on center table, family portraits on wall, portraits of Douglass, Lincoln, Bruce. Aunt Rhoda, a pleasant-faced woman of perhaps 45, is stirring cake in an old-fashioned yellow crock. Lindy, a pretty girl of 12, is holding Gladstone, and at the same time, attempting to read. Pansy, a girl of 8, is singing a plantation ditty. Louphenia, 10, is clapping her hands in time to the tune, and Lige barely 7, is watching the cake bowl with hungry longings.)*

PANSY (sings).—

> "Juber dis and juber dat,
> Juber killed a yaller cat;
> Ain' yo' 'shame, yo' dirty dog,
> Dance this juber."

AUNT RHODA—Why don' yo' children stop makin' so much noise? It's enough to wake up the dead, the way you uns go on. Why don' yo' clar out from under my feet anyhow. You allus as thick as flies when you're not wanted. I don' look for you uns to get a blessed thing Chrismus 'cause you so hard-harded.

LIGE *(whiningly)*.—I want the bowl when you through with it Mammy, Pansy had it the las' time.

PANSY *(indignantly)*.—I didn't 'tall, Mammy, Lige had it his own self, didn't he Louphenia?

LOUPHENIA *(witheringly)*.—Cose he did.

AUNT RHODA.—Here Lindy, put dat book down and get dese children out do's befo dey drive me plum crazy. Here's Miss Lou spectin' company fo' Chrismus, and dat trifling Sue ain' got mo'n haf the cakes baked. I clar to gracious, Sue can't get aroun' haf as good as her ole mammy wid all de rheumatism I got in my jints. *(Lindy tries to get the children out, when a rap is heard. Lindy opens the door and a bare-footed boy of fourteen staggers in. He has a bundle tied in red 'kerchief on his shoulders and around his hat is a band of black calico).*

AUNT R.—Great head of the church, who is this? *(Sets cake bowl on table.)*

BEN.—Is this my Aunt Rhoda? *(He sinks down in a chair as if exhausted.)*

AUNT R. *(rushes to him and lifts his head. He is a well-developed lad, with a handsome face and speaks better English than the average colored Southern boy)*.—It's Ben, my Sister Lucy Ann's baby boy, her only living child. I see the favor. Lindy han' me de cordial quick. Po' chile 's he's jus' played out. *(Pours cordial down Ben's throat. He revives).* There now, he's comin' 'roun' alright. *(Hugs Ben.)* Yes this is yo' Aunt Rhoda. You favor Lucy Ann, up an' down. They say that a boy that favors his mammy is bo'n fo' good luck. How is Sister Lucy Ann anyhow, an' why didn't you sen word you's comin'? I clar to goodness, you mos' took my bref, comin' in on me so sudden.

BEN.—Mother's dead, Aunt Rhoda, and I haven't got anybody in the world but you. *(Wipes eyes on coat sleeve.)*

AUNT R.—Lucy Ann dead? *(Begins to cry. The children join her, except Lindy, who tries to quiet them.)* Po' lam', tain't no mo' an' could be expected. She never was strong an she's been ailing a long time. When did she die?

BEN.—*(wipes eyes again on coat sleeve).*—She's been dead three weeks to-day. She suffered like everything. She called me to the bed before she died and told me if they didn't treat me right, after she was dead, I could come to you.

AUNT R.—Course you can stay with your Aunt Rhoda. I'm po' as Job's turkey, an' he was so po' he had to lean agin the fence to balance hisse'f, but long as me an' the chillens got a piece of bread I'll divide it with you, an' what I lack the Lord who's promised to look ofter the orphans, will make up.

BEN (puts hand in bosom and draws out a package).— Aunt Rhody, mother sent you her ear-rings and breastpin an' a quilt she pieced while she's sick. There were some more of her things I could have brought but Aunt Millie, the house-keeper and the rest of them took them and I couldn't get hold of them.

AUNT R.— *(examining things).*—I aint much han' fo' jewelry, but I'm goin' to wear these ear-bobs out of respect for Sister Lucy Ann. Po' Lucy Ann, I wish I'd a been there, when they was going through her things, an' he'ping themse'ves.

BEN.—Oh my poor head how it aches, I walked so far and I feel so faint.

AUNT R.—*(suspiciously).*—Walked? Did you tramp all the way here from Lucy Ann's? You run away that's what you's done. What you run away for? It's a blessin' twasn't cold or you'd froze to death sure.

BEN.—'Cause mother told me to come to you if I wasn't treated right. Col. Thomas beat me like a dog for nothing and I ran off.

AUNT R.—What did he beat you fo', I hope you didn't do nothin' mean and ornery?

BEN.—Why Aunt Rhody, I been working for Col. Thomas up at the big house long before mother got sick, waiting on him and tending to his horse, and he seemed to think a heap of me and always gave me his old papers and magazines when he was through with them, and Aunt Millie used to let me read some of the books out of the book-case when she was in a good humor.

AUNT R.—Well, hurry up chile, for the lan's sake an' tell the res'. Don' go all aroun' Robin's Hood's barn befo' you tell what happened, yo' remin' me of yo' Uncle Jake's prayin'. He goes way to Jerusalem an' back befo' he gets through.

BEN.—Well, 'twasn't nothin' for him to get mad at anyhow. You know mother was always crazy about schooling herself and she's always urged me to study hard as I could at school, and I did and I always stood head of my classes. Well, 'twas a day or two after mother died and I picked up one of Col. Thomas's old newspapers and I read where some young colored man went from the South and worked his way through one of the biggest white colleges in the North and now he's a rich lawyer practicing in Michigan and the paper said how everybody black and white was proud of him, because he worked his way up from the bottom, and all at once something seemed to say to me, "Why don't you do that, Ben? You're not afraid of hard work," and it seemed like I could hear mother saying to me like she used, "Ben learn all you can and never be too lazy to work and you'll get through the world, even if your poor mother does have to die and leave you alone."

AUNT R. *(wiping her eyes.)*—Ben Houston ain't you never coming to the point?

BEN.—Yes'm, I'm most through. I was telling Aunt Millie and some of the rest of them about what I'd read and what I'd like to do, and they told Col. Thomas that I was thinking about running off and he called me up to the house and asked me about it, and when I told him Id like to go, because I though I'd have a better chance to get an education he got mad and said that all education was good for was to spoil Negroes for work, and we wasn't worth our salt anyhow, since Freedom. He asked me what good education would do me, and I said it would make a man of me, and then he said I was giving him impudence and he took the buggy whip and whipped me like everything, and he never had touched me when mother was living, and I knew he didn't have any right to whip me when I hadn't done anything, so I watched my chance and ran away.

AUNT R.—That wasn't nothin' to beat yo' for if that was all, but you know there's plenty of white folks everywhere thinks just like him, that education spoils colored fo'ks fo' work an' I guess it do spoil some of 'em same's it does white folks. You was right to come, you don't have to stay no where you don't want to unless you're bound out by the law. We're free now, thank God! I don't know how you're going to get any schoolin' because the colored fo'ks haven't got any school round here 'cep'n de Sunday school Miss Lou carries on here in my cabin every Sunday, but Lindy ain't been to no other school and she reads to beat the band.

BEN.—That would hardly do for me, Aunt Rhody, because I finished the school at home last year, and could have got a school to teach if mother had been well enough to leave.

AUNT RHODA.—Sake's alive, you sho' is sma't. Done finished school an' talkin' about goin' to college.

LINDY.—Aunt Rhoda, don't you think cousin Ben ought to have something to eat.

AUNT R.—That's the born truth! Get that piece of hog jole out of the cupboard and the sweet taters out of the ashes and see if the hoe-cake ain't brown *(Lindy goes out)*. Heah,

Pansy, Lou, Pheny, Lige and Gladstone shake hands with your cousin Ben *(the children advance bashfully. Ben takes Gladstone on his knee).* Now you's seen all the family 'cep'n yo' Uncle Jake, and my oldest girl Sue who works at the big house for Miss Lou and Colonel White. Set up Ben and eat. *(Ben goes to the table and eats.)* Heah, children, take dis bread and clear out *(gives bread to children, exit all but Lindy, who sets more plates on the table and remains interested in the conversation).*

BEN.—Isn't Lindy my cousin too?

AUNT R.—No, Lindy is Jake's niece, Celia's girl. Her mother's dead and she ain't got nobody to look after her but me, but you can call her cousin jes' the same as you do the res' de chillen.

LINDY. *(throwing her arms around Aunt R's neck).*—And Aunt Rhoda is so good to me.

BEN.—Aunt Rhody, you've got a big heart! *(Voice is heard outside singing. Enters Jake.)*

JAKE.—Hello, there ole woman, didn' you forgit to blow a dinner horn?

AUNT R.—Couldn't you tell whether the horn was blowed or not?

JAKE.—De way my insides feel it orter blowed whether it did or not.

AUNT R.—You'll never die in debt to your stomach Jake Jones, you don't study 'bout a livin' thing but eatin' an' possum huntin'.

JAKE.—Possum mighty good ole lady and when you bring him out of de oven, he's cooked good enuf fo' de president of the United States to eat *(see Ben).* Why who's this?

AUNT R. (mollified).—It's Lucy Ann's boy Ben. Po' Lucy Ann's dead and he's come to stay with us. Jus' think my po' sister's gone and I didn't know a thing about it *(wipes eyes).*

JAKE.—Dat's what dat dog's been doin' a howlin' 'round

dis place fo' de las' month, well she suffered a long time, sho' Ben, chile, you're welcome to our po' cabin. We'll try to fin' you a bite to eat and a bunk at night as long as you's willing to stay.

BEN.—Thank you, Uncle Jake, all I want is a chance to go to school and learn something. I'll try not to give you and Aunt Rhody any trouble, I can do lots of work.

JAKE *(aside)*.—He is de boy, I'm lookin' fo' for Colonel White certny do impose on my constitution, making me work so hard. Dat's a good sperit, Ben, and if you feel rested enuf you might come out to de fiel' dis afternoon.

AUNT R.—'Deed he ain't going to no fiel' to-day. Don't you see the chile's all played out tramping all the way from Henry County way heah?

JAKE.—Alright Rhoda, I didn't mean no harm *(walks to table, sits and helps himself)*. By de way, Rhody, I hearn a pow'ful piece of news to-day.

AUNT R.—You don't say, I hope none of the colored folks got in any trouble.

JAKE.—Oh, no, it's good news, or you'll say so anyhow. A Quaker lady is here frum de North and going to start a school heah for de cullud fo'ks.

LINDY. *(jumps up)*.—Oh I am so glad.

BEN.—Just what I was wishing.

AUNT R.—Who's a telling you, Jake?

JAKE.—Why St. Nichols, Aunt Mandy's daughter's boy Ike.

AUNT R.—Well his mouth ain't no prayer-book, but it may be so. Where they think they going to have it?

JAKE.—Dey don't know but dey wants to have it at de Cross Road's Church.

AUNT R. *(meditatively)*.—I wonder if they's asked the white fo'ks if they kin start the school. Kinder late in de season too, right heah at Christmas.

JAKE *(gesticulating)*.—What dey gwine ask de white fo'ks fo'? Ain't we culled fo'ks free? Is de 'Mancipation Proclamation passed in Congress or not? Ain't we free same as de white fo'ks? Catch me askin' a white man whether I can do anything or not?

(Col. White from outside thunders) Jake. *(Jake jumps up from the table with astonishing alacrity.)*

JAKE.—Suh?

COL. WHITE *(calls)*.—You get that field finished up this afternoon, you hear, you lazy, black rascal?

JAKE.—Yes, suh, yes, suh, I'm comin' Colonel *(starts out in a hurry)*.

AUNT R.—Land sakes alive! I ain't got that cake baked. *(Hurries around and begins to stir the cake.)* Clar out from here, de las' one of you, or I'll skin you alive! *(Children scamper right and left.)*

(A rap is heard.)

(Aunt R. runs out with cake-bowl, comes back wiping her hands.) I wonder who on earth's comin' here now. *(Opens door, Ruth Penn the Quaker teacher stands on the threshold. She is attired in the gray Quaker garb and is a sweet-faced woman of 30.)*

RUTH.—This is Friend Rhoda, I know.

AUNT R.—Yes, ma'am, I'se a friend to everybody, sho's you bo'n, and you're de Quaker lady the Lord has sent to lead us po' cullud fo'ks from darkness into light. Come in.

(Ruth comes in. Sits down. Dusts rocker with her apron.) The good Lord knows, I hope and trust that the school will be started. There's just a few colored fo'ks aroun' here an' all of 'em po' an' not able to pay a teacher, an' so we ain't had no school.

RUTH.—Yes, I am Ruth Penn, and I have come from my home in New England to labor here among your people. I know that our work is apt to meet with opposition and I

thought perhaps thee could give me some advice. This is
Friend White's land, thee is on is it not?

AUNT R.—Yes, ma'am, almost far as you kin see looking
toward the South is Col. White's lan' and me an m'os' all my
fo'ks used to belong to the Whites, and I was the chillen's
nurse after mammy died and I never could make up my min'
to leave the old place. Course I might leave an' do better an'
then again I mightn't.

RUTH.—So thee has been in the family all thy life and
nursed the children.? Are they all living?

AUNT R.—No, there's just two chillen left, the one they
call Lady Mary and our Miss Lou.

RUTH.—Lady Mary? Are they English?

AUNT R.—Mistress was English born and bred, and after
she died one of her English cousins came over here and married Miss Mary, and after his brother died, it made her a
Lady Mary, and they call him Lord Clyde but I think that's
downright heathenish to call any body Lord here on earth,
and I've always been expecting to hear of something dreadful
to happen to him for taking the Lord's name that way.

RUTH *(smiling)*—Thee must be a little bit of a Quaker,
Friend Rhoda. We do not use titles for ourselves or others.
So the mistress died. Were there any sons?

AUNT R.—Yes, she died heart-broken over losing her two
boys, master Louis and master John, the two handsomest boys
in the whole country, chillen I'd nursed ever since they were
born, got killed the same day fighting in the Rebel Army.
Mistress was always good as an angel and she hoped and
prayed all the time that the colored fo'ks would all be free
without any war, and when the word came and they was
killed she went to bed and never got up.

RUTH.—Time brings about many sad changes. I asked
not from idle curiosity but because I would know the dispo-

sition of the people before I appeal to them in aid of the school.

Aunt R.—Yes, there's just three left, Lady Mary in England, Col. White who's head's fas' blossomin' fo' the grave, and Miss Lou, the baby chile, dat I'd give my last drop of blood for, she's so dear to me.

Ruth.—Do you think I can enlist their efforts in starting the school?

Aunt R.—Miss Lou's all right. She's just like mistress. She loves the colored people an' she'd go right in and teach herself if Col. White would let her. She could do it too, 'cause she went off to New Orleans to school when she wasn't out of short dresses jes 'bout 13 or 14 years old, and she's got a big education! She can do two or three kinds of talkin' 'sides what she talks to us, and she's always talkin' about helpin' de colored fo'ks but Col. White, it's accordin' how you catch him. Sometimes he's good as pie and 'nother time he rears and pitches like a lion he do.

Ruth.—You still work for them.

Aunt R.—Yes'm. I does the washing and mending for the rent of the cabin and a garden patch, and Jake my ole man and my daughter Sue, they's hired by the month. They don't get much though, 'cause all Col. White's got is some land and the rent he gets frum it don't hardly keep 'em going. Miss Lou she done got a little money of her own left from mistress' private fortune, but la me nothin' ain't like it used to be befo' the war. Why Christmas the big house would be full of company and down in the colored fo'ks quarters there'd be as much fun as up at the big house.

Ruth.—Well, friend Rhoda, I think thee had better go and speak to Friend White first and ask if we may have the school here on his land and I will follow on later and see what he says, will thee do this?

AUNT R.—It'll be mos' like Daniel going in the lion's den I 'spect, but I'll go, and you pray that the Lord of Hosts go with me.

RUTH.—If anybody can win him it will be thee, my good woman, his children's nurse and trusted friend. Never fear, the Lord of Hosts shall arm the Right!

(Exit Aunt R. and Ruth, enter Lindy and Ben.)

LINDY.—That's the Quaker lady who's going to start the school.

BEN.—Yes, I've seen pictures of them in books. They used to carry slaves over the underground railroad when they were running away from the South.

LINDY *(coming close to Ben)*.—What, did they have a railroad under the ground?

BEN.—It wasn't a sure enough railroad, it was just kind white people like the Quaker teacher who took poor colored people in who were running away from slavery and helped them on their way.

LINDY.—I love kind people don't you Cousin Ben?

BEN.—Yes, that's why I love you. The rose is red, the violets blue, sugar's sweet and so are you.

LINDY.—Oh Cousin Ben, do you love me already? I love you too, and I'm sorry for you.

BEN.—Yes, I mean it Lindy. I'm only a poor colored boy, but I am going to work hard, study hard and make a man of myself so I can help my people.

LINDY.—Oh, Cousin Ben, like Frederick Douglass?

BEN.—Yes, and like Senator Bruce, Bishop Turner and other great Negroes. I had a colored teacher at home who used to talk to me about them all the time. I don't think I'll get much chance here, and if I get a chance I'm going to the North and find the college that colored lawyer graduated from.

LINDY.—Oh, what would I do, Cousin Ben. You promised to help me with my books.

BEN.—Stay here with Aunt Rhoda and learn all you can little Cabin Princess. Girls don't have to know as much as boys and when I get through school I'll come back and take you away with me. Do you want to wear my mother's ring so you won't forget.

LINDY.—Yes, Cousin Ben. *(Ben puts ring on Lindy's finger.)*

AUNT R. *(calls).*—Lindy.

LINDY *(runs out).*—Yes'm.

CURTAIN

ACT II

SCENE II.—*(Colonel White's dining room, with a view of the kitchen when the door opens in the back-ground. Sue, a neat looking girl of eighteen in white sewing apron and cap is setting the breakfast table. Colonel White is at his desk reading the morning paper. Enters Aunt Rhoda in freshly laundered dress and apron, with tray on which are two covered dishes.)*

AUNT R. *(curtsying).*—Good mornin', good mornin', Colonel. How you feelin' this fine mornin'? You's lookin' mighty fine sure.

COL. W.—Pretty well, pretty well, Rhoda, for an old fellow. How's your rheumatism. Sit down there. Sue does well, but we miss you in the kitchen, nobody can beat your cooking, Rhoda.

AUNT R.—Thank you suh. Cooking allus did come handy to me some how *(sits down).*

COL. W.—Well, when it comes to cooking and singing, your folks are hard to beat.

AUNT R.—My rhematism ain't bothered me much fo' the las' day or two, an' I's feelin' so spry this mornin' that I got up a little earlier, and fixed up something a little extra fo' yo' breakfast. Heah, Sue put these dishes in the warming oven, I didn't know you'd be so late with yo' breakfast. Keep them hot till the Colonel is ready for his breakfast. *(Exit Sue with dishes.)*

COL. W.—What did you fix for me Rhoda?

AUNT R.—Oh, 'twant much. I jes' fried you a young chicken with the cream gravy you liked and baked you a pan of light rolls.

COL. W.—Why Rhoda that was very kind of you I am sure. Is there anything I can do for you? Children all well?

AUNT R. *(curtsies again)*.—Yes, suh, all well an' able to eat all they kin git.

COL. W.—I repeat Rhoda, is there anything you wish. Is Jake in any new trouble?

AUNT R. *(tossing her head angrily)*.—Nothing but what I can settle. He went to town and came back full as a tick, but I waited till he went to bed and then I used the cloes stick on him until he was sober as anybody.

COL. W. *(laughs heartily)*.—Rhoda, you are a great disciplinarian.

AUNT R. *(stiffly)*.—What's that you callin' me? I hope you ain't callin' me names 'bout that triflin' Jake Jones.

COL. W. *(laughing more heartily than ever)*.—No indeed, I'm complimenting you, Rhody, I mean that you manage Jake and the children well, but are you sure there isn't something I can do for you this morning? Lou was telling me you wanted a new red table-cloth and knives and forks for Christmas. Is that what's worrying?

AUNT R.—No, suh, the Lord knows I ain't got that red table-cloth to study 'bout, I needs it, but I won't die if I don't get it. But now I come to think of it, there is something I might as well as ask you about while I'm up here.

COL. W.—I knew you wanted something Rhody, you was always a first class diplomat. Alright, what is it.

AUNT R.—Who owns the lan' the Cross Road's Church's on, Colonel White, you or Mr. Robert White?

COL. W.—Why I own it of course. I though you knew that years ago. It's just this side of the boundary line, you may thank your stars for it, for Mr. Robert never would have let you had a church on his land. He's not a churchman and don't believe in churches.

AUNT R.—I always thanked my stars that my folks belong to your family instead of Mr. Robert's. Well, then if you own the lan' I know it will be alright.

COL. W. *(looking up from his paper).*—What will be alright, Rhoda?

AUNT R.—Why a school for the colored people that a Quaker lady's come from the North to start for the colored people.

COL. W.—Quaker lady nothing! Do you suppose ladies of any kind are going to leave their homes and come and live among Negroes to teach them? No, they have better sense. No, I'm not going to have any school started here. The Negroes don't need any school, they're not worth the powder and lead it would take to blow them up with, now. We don't need any educated niggers around here. *(Stalks about room in a passion.)* We need Negroes to work the land, that's what we need!

AUNT R. *(starts to speak and wipes eyes on apron. Sue comes to door peeps in and listens anxiously. Enters Miss Lou. She a girl of fragile build with brown hair and eyes. She wears a*

riding habit and has roses in her hands. She is pretty and re-
fined.)

MISS LOU.—Good morning, papa *(kisses him).* Isn't it a
glorious morning. The birds are singing in the hedges and
all the world seems happy. I had a splendid ride. Birdie still
goes a little stiff but she can't help it, poor thing. Too bad
she got that fall while I was in New Orleans. Am I late?
Well, here is my peace offering. Aren't they beautiful? *(Holds
out flowers.)* Out of the conservatory. Oh, how I love flowers. *(Goes back of center and calls Sue.)* Sue, bring me some
roses so that I can arrange these flowers.

SUE *(pokes her head in from kitchen).*—Yes, Miss Lou.

MISS LOU *(suddenly perceives Aunt R.).*—Oh, here's
mammy. *(Hugs her.)* Why, what's the matter with you,
mammy?

COL. W.—She's pouting because I told her I wasn't going
to have some meddling Quaker woman here from the North
starting a school for the lazy niggers around here, on my
land. Sue bring in the breakfast *(Sue brings in breakfast.)*

MISS LOU. *(placing flowers in vases).*—Oh, papa, it must
be right if mammy wants it, I never knew mammy to make
a mistake. I've often wished I had time to start a day school
for them. The years I spent at the school in New Orleans
convinced me that education is good for everybody.

AUNT R.—I don't want my children to grow up in ig-
'nance if they ain't white. I expected the Draines and the
Peterses and all of the res' of the po' trash 'roun heah to be
against having the school, but I didn't expect it of Colonel
White, faithful as his colored fo'ks always been to him.

SUE.—Breakfast is ready, if you please, sir. *(Col. W. and
Miss Lou seat themselves, bow their heads for a silent grace and
begin to eat. As Col. White looks at the dishes, Rhoda has prepared for him, his sternness relaxes.)*

COL. W.—Oh, I don't care, have the school if you want to, but don't think any of you are going to slack work to go, and me paying you wages.

AUNT R.—Thank the Lord!

MISS LOU.—Papa, you're a darling.

AUNT R.—Good mornin', I must be getting back to the cabin.

COL. W. *(tossing her a half dollar)*.—Here treat yourself, Rhoda, you gained your point as I expected you would.

AUNT R. *(smiling and slipping the coin in her pocket)*.— Thank you, Colonel, you made me feel mighty dubious sir, mighty dubious, I tell you.

MISS LOU.—How are you getting along with the Christmas baking mammy? I couldn't help you and Sue any yesterday. I was so busy with my Christmas gifts. It's a burden to have so many relatives and friends at holiday times.

AUNT R.—Everything baked but the pound cake. When the fo'ks comin'?

MISS LOU.—Oh, I guess they'll be here in time for dinner tomorrow. Cousin Robert sent word that he would be here in time for breakfast, but the others will come later. Here take this candy to Gladstone. *(Reaches plate from table. Aunt R. takes it and departs. A rap is heard. Sue goes to door at left of stage.)*

SUE.—Colonel White, there's a lady to see you.

COL. W.—Who is it?

SUE.—I don't know, sir. She's a strange looking lady.

COL. W.—Tell her to come in. *(Enters Ruth Penn. Col. W. and Miss Lou rise. Col. W. bows gallantly.)*

COL. W.—I am Colonel White, and you are—

RUTH.—Ruth Penn, if thee please. I am sorry to disturb thee at thy breakfast hour.

MISS LOU *(extending hand)*.—Oh, never mind that! I am

the Colonel's daughter Louise. Won't you sit up and have breakfast with us?

RUTH.—Oh no, I will sit here while you finish. I am glad to know thee both.

COL. W.—You wished to see me?

RUTH.—Yes, if thee please; I came to thank thee for thy kind permission to start a school for the colored people here on thy land. Friend Rhoda has just told me the good news!

COL. W. *(angrily)*.—I never could get around letting Rhoda have her own way, but I'm not in favor of the school. The Negroes need hoes and rakes more than they do spelling books.

RUTH.—Friend White, have not these people souls?

COL. W.—I don't know whether they have or not, madam; there are those who say not.

RUTH.—But thee does not believe such a wicked thing, I am sure. Thou knowest that they are human beings like ourselves, and that, having been turned adrift without education, money or friends, they need kind Christian people to live with them and teach them.

MISS LOU.—Oh, yes, that is true. So my dear mother used to speak. We shall be friends, I know.

COL. W.—And, Miss Penn, those who associate with the Negroes here in the South, for any purpose whatever, should realize, before doing so, that such a course of action ostracises them from the society of Southern people.

RUTH.—We Quakers follow Christ, and our work often leads us among the lowly. Your sweet daughter believes this, for I learn that she has started a Sunday-school among the poor colored people. Again I thank thee for the opportunity to open the school.

COL. W.—I gave my word to Rhoda to satisfy her; but, madam, I have no sympathy for those who come from the

North to teach us our duty to our Negroes. I am a plain man, and I speak as I feel.

Ruth *(gently)*.—Thou art blinded by the gods of this world. Thee will see differently some day. *(She glides out.)*

Col. W. *(pushing back his plate)*.—Another Northerner down here on a fool's errand, wanting Negroes sent to school and put on an equality with the whites. Before the war it was against our law to teach them to read and write even, and thus we kept them in their places.

Miss Lou.—But, papa, listen. The colored people were brought to this country against their will and made to toil like beasts of the field, to educate us, clothe us and keep us in luxury, while they were kept in ignorance and poverty; and I think that the South owes the colored people a chance, and a fair one at that!

Col. W.—Lou, you're getting beside yourself. Much learning doth make thee mad. Are these the principles you imbibed while off at school? Whose Negroes were better treated than mine? I believe in treating the Negro well as long as he behaves himself, just as I do my horse, my dog or any other animal.

Miss Lou.—Oh, papa, you are wrong to speak so! Does not the Bible say, "Out of one blood God created all the nations of the earth"? Is not the Negro our brother?

Col. W.—Here, Lou, this is enough of your impertinence! Don't presume on my love and try me too far! The idea of your thinking that a Negro could ever be equal to a white man! Out of one blood indeed! And is the proud Anglo-Saxon blood indeed the same as that of the inferior African? Haven't the Negroes owned the continent of Africa for centuries, and do they not still live there in an uncivilized state?

Miss Lou.—History tells us of a time when the Angles

and Saxons were equally rude and barbarous. It was Christianity that tamed the wild Saxons and Angles. Let us give the Negro all of the advantages of Christian civilization before we say that he is incapable of reaching the same heights.

COL. W.—That I should have lived to hear a daughter of mine express such views! I'll not stay here to be insulted so. *(Starts off.)*

MISS LOU.—Oh, papa, do not be angry with me! I beg your pardon if I have offended you.

COL. W.—Say no more, miss; say no more! *(Goes out and slams the door.)*

MISS LOU *(sadly).*—What have I gained but my father's deep displeasure? He is unreasonable on this question. Sue, you may clear away the table now.

(Enters Sue, who removes dishes quickly and puts cover on the table.)

MISS LOU.—Bring my sewing basket, Sue. To-morrow is Christmas, you know, and I have some gifts to finish. *(Sue brings basket. Miss Lou takes out sewing and begins to sew.)* Have you finished that book I lent you, Sue?

SUE.—Yes'm. It was a fine book, Miss Lou.

MISS LOU.—Yes, it is a prime love story, St. Elmo. I read it twice in New Orleans. I don't think I could love a man like St. Elmo; could you, Sue?

SUE.—Law me! I don't know; I ain't never been in company.

MISS LOU *(sighing).*—Too bad there aren't some nice young fellows around. I'll have to hunt you a beau.

SUE.—I don't need none. I want to go to school and learn to be a teacher.

MISS LOU.—A teacher? Why, Sue, you'll have to study hard. I'll help you nights before we go to sleep. I'll do my own hair while you study.

SUE.—No'm, I love to do your hair. You've got a beau. I reckon he'll be over bright and early to-morrow.

MISS LOU.—My Cousin Robert? Yes, I s'pose he will. Papa and Uncle Robert are dead set on our marrying, but every time I see Robert I get more out of the notion.

SUE.—Mr. Robert's nice-looking, but they say he's got a bad temper.

MISS LOU.—Yes, the White temper. I know all about it. But it isn't that that keeps me from liking him. I like somebody else.

SUE.—Why, Miss Lou! Who?

MISS LOU.—I don't know so much about him, only that his father is the president of a big college in Michigan, and the young man was the youngest professor in the faculty. He was a nephew of our president at the New Orleans school.

SUE.—What's his name, Miss Lou?

MISS LOU.—Don't you ever tell, Sue. His name is Arthur Norton.

SUE.—Where do he live?

MISS LOU.—At Bayview, Michigan. I only saw him a few times, but he seemed to like me. But oh, well, I don't suppose we'll ever meet again! *(Sighs.)*

SUE.—Was he good-looking, Miss Lou?

MISS LOU.—Handsome! He had such kind gray eyes and such polished manners. But my! papa would never allow him to come here. All his folks were abolitionists.

SUE.—You don't say.

(Footsteps are heard.)

MISS LOU.—Sue, you can have that sprigged lawn of mine. I think it will just fit you. *(Lays finger on lips.)* Remember!

SUE.—Yes'm.

(Enter Col. W. and Robert W. Exit Sue.)

COL. W. *(in good humor, apparently; rubbing his hands to-*

gether).—I met Robert coming over, and I returned back with him. Make yourself at home, Robert. I'm going to hunt Sue and order up your breakfast. *(Exit Col. W.)*

ROBERT *(crosses over to Lou; takes her hands).*—And how is my fair cousin this Christmas Eve morning? The roses in your conservatory are not more fair to my eyes—

MISS LOU.—Fie, Cousin Robert! You were ever an arch flatterer.

ROBERT.—A man may not flatter when his whole being throbs with love, as mine does for you.

MISS LOU *(withdraws hands).*—Have I not told you it is in vain for you to speak thus? It can never be as you wish.

ROBERT.—Oh, say not never, dear cousin. Let me wait awhile. Answer me not now. You have changed since you went to New Orleans. I thought once you like me.

MISS LOU.—Oh, Cousin Robert, I do; you are all the brother I have; but that is all. Rachel Draine is single yet. Why not court her?

ROBERT.—Lou, do not trifle with me. I have your father's consent, and I will marry you in spite of yourself.

(Enters Col. White; sits at desk; takes up letters and begins to read.)

COL. W. *(looks up from letter in his hand).*—Ah, here is a letter from Colonel Thomas, asking about a Negro boy who ran away from his place a short time ago, and his whereabouts have been made known by some of the servants. He says the fellow is very rude and impudent, by reason of too much schooling, but he wishes him returned and he will be responsible for the cost. *(The door leading into the kitchen is ajar, and Sue listens.)* He says further that the boy was given to him by his mother, who is dead, and he can claim him by law.

Miss Lou.—It is Ben, mammy's nephew.

Robert.—And do you keep here such a character?

Col. W.—I see little of the boy. He has been working around here with Jake, but I liked his appearance and had thought to hire him to help Sue about the house and accompany Lou on her drives.

Miss Lou.—That would be well. Ben is not rude and impudent. He is mammy's own sister's child, and came to her at her sister's dying request.

Robert.—But surely you will oblige Colonel Thomas, our richest and most influential neighbor, and return the boy? His son John visits me, comes New Year's. Send the boy back by him.

Col. W.—It may be the best thing to do. Colonel Thomas and I have business interests, and it is useless to quarrel about such a thing as sending the boy home. *(Sue disappears.)*

Miss Lou.—I think he could not have been well treated. He was bruised from being beaten, ragged from head to foot, and half dead from his weary journey.

Robert.—Well, what would you, fair cousin—that he should come robed in a velvet gown, riding on a white charger? Do not rags and lashings belong to those of his class?

Miss Lou.—Cousin Robert!

Col. W.—You will never win Lou by talking thus. She has strange notions about Negroes and the way they should be treated.

Robert.—She has been shut up in school too long. When she has been home longer she will again think as we do.

Miss Lou.—I never thought as you do.

Robert.—Well, do not let us quarrel in the season of Christmas cheer and good will. Are you as fond of riding as you used to be?

MISS LOU.—Yes, if anything, more so.

ROBERT.—I hope, then, my Christmas present to you has not been ill chosen. I've a pretty mare outside awaiting your inspection. Will you come out and see her?

COL. W.—Of course she will. Come. I'm going to take another peep at her myself.

(Exit all. Enter Ben and Sue.)

BEN.—So Mr. John is to take me back to Colonel Thomas' at New Year's. Well, he won't find me here to take. I'm going on to the North. I hate to leave Aunt Rhoda and you and Lindy and the rest of the children and Miss Lou, but mother used to say where there's a will there's a way, and if you trust in God and do right you'll come out all right. I've got to try that mare for Miss Lou, and maybe that will be my chance. *(Exit Ben hurriedly.)*

SUE.—I'll tell mammy first chance I get. It's mighty resky for Ben to go so far from home.

(Re-enter Col. W., Robert and Miss Lou.)

ROBERT.—Since you have refused my gift, I think I had better relieve you of my presence also.

MISS LOU.—I am sorry, Cousin, but I could not accept it. But you must stay. It's a pretty sight to see mammy and her family come in after their Christmas gifts in the early morning, each one yelling, "Chrismus gif', Colonel! Chrismus gif', Miss Lou!"

COL. W.—Yes, it is fun to see them, though it brings back sad old memories of other days.

ROBERT.—I hardly think I shall stay. What about the boy? Will you send him back by me? I have a notion to spend the day with John Thomas.

MISS LOU.—Oh, no!

COL. W.—Why not, if he is to go at all? You are hard to please to-day.

MISS LOU.—'Tis not right.

COL. W.—I'll call him in and question him. *(Exit Col. W.)*

ROBERT.—Promise you will try to love me, and all shall be as you will. I will leave the boy.

MISS LOU.—I am a White too, Cousin Robert, and I have a mind and will of my own, and I say, once and for all, No!

CURTAIN

ACT III

SCENE III.—*(Bayview College. President's office. Prof. Norton, Secretary of the Faculty, is at his desk. Ben raps on the door.)*

PROF. N.—Come! *(Enters Ben, in poor but clean clothing. He carries his few old shabby books.)* Well, my lad, what can I do for you to-day?

BEN.—If you please, sir, I came to enter the university.

PROF. N. *(astonished).*—You don't mean it!

BEN.—Yes, sir. I heard about this school down in Kentucky a short time ago, and I made up my mind to graduate from this school if I lived.

PROF. N. *(smiling).*—I feel complimented by your selecting my alma mater. How did you happen to settle on the school, did you say?

BEN.—It's almost like a fairy tale, sir. I just happened to pick up a piece of old newspaper that told about a young colored fellow that had worked his way here from the South and graduated from this college, and how proud everybody was of him, and how he became a successful lawyer.

PROF. N.—You mean George Neil. Yes, the university is justly proud of him. We hope to see him a judge some day. He is a credit to us.

BEN.—The paper said the white people was as proud of him as the colored ones, and that is what inspired me to want to come. I want to be something too.

PROF. N.—Good! But seriously, my boy, sit down here and let me talk to you. How old are you, and what is your name?

BEN.—Ben Houston, sir; and since Miss Lou told me about Benjamin Banneker, the Black astronomer, I thought I'd call my name Benjamin Banneker Houston, if you don't mind.

PROF. N. *(starting).*—Miss Lou—who—No, I have no objection to that name, I am sure. And your age?

BEN.—Going on sixteen now, sir. Miss Lou and Aunt Rhoda both said I was so big for my age nobody'd hardly believe I wan't older. I was fourteen when I left Colonel White's place to come here.

PROF. N.—Colonel White! I have heard of the Whites of Kentucky. Ben, it takes a number of years and a good deal of money to go through a school like this, and there would be a lot of preparatory work before you could begin to work for a degree.

BEN.—All I want is just a chance, sir. I don't care how hard I have to work. Couldn't I work my way through, sir?

PROF. N.—I don't know. I must talk with father. If the faculty is willing to admit you, it means that you must have a great deal of help to enter even the lowest classes of such a university as ours, with a view to graduating. However, a boy with your grit should be encouraged. Have you had any Latin, algebra or physics?

BEN.—Yes, sir, I've had a pretty fair start in all three. They didn't have it in our school at home, but our teacher had been through the book and he helped me nights.

PROF. N.—Good for him, and you too! Here! *(Hands examination sheets.)* Take these blanks *(writes hurriedly)* and this note, and go to that house over there across from the campus, and my mother will give you some dinner; and after you have eaten, write out the answers to these questions and bring them back to me. *(Exit Ben.)* Such perseverance would do credit to the proudest Anglo-Saxon blood. Heard of this university down there in Kentucky, and came here seeking an education. Poor, despised African race, there must be something great in you, or you would not in the face of such discouraging circumstances make such heroic attempts to rise! Kept in a state of abject slavery for more than two centuries, the moment the pressure is removed, up they spring, inquiring the way to the light of civilization. Truly we owe this people a chance! Miss Lou! Can Ben's Miss Lou be the beautiful Southern girl I met at New Orleans three years ago? She was very young then, but had a mind as beautiful as her face. Her friends took pains to tell me that she was engaged to her cousin, and I have tried to forget her; but alas! "Her bright smile haunts me still." It must be my Miss Lou, for she lived out from Louisville and her father's name was White. I'll see the boy again and question him. Poor lad! I know that father will be willing to admit him if he can pass the preliminary examination, but I know not how it will be with the rest of the faculty. Some of the students made it unpleasant for Neil. Such a fine fellow, too!

(Enters President Norton. He is a fine-looking old gentleman of sixty, with a saintly face. He carries a cane.)

Pres.—Well, Arthur, my son, any new applications?

Prof. N.—Yes, a poor colored lad, who heard of our university down in Kentucky, and worked his way here in the hope of graduating from this university.

Pres.—He had pluck, all right. I'm afraid we'll have a fight on hand, but I'll do what I can for him, for I'll never be the man to shut the door of opportunity in the black man's face. *(Recites.)*

> Howe'er it be, it seems to me
> 'Tis only noble to be good.
> Kind hearts are more than coronets,
> And simple faith than Norman blood.

Tennyson never said a truer thing, to my mind.

Prof. N.—I'm with you, father. My sympathies are always with the under dog.

Pres.—Where is the candidate?

Prof. N.—I sent him over home for some dinner.

(Ben raps.)

Pres.—Come!

Prof. N.—Here he is, father. You look like another boy since you've had your dinner. Let me have the examination sheets I gave you.

Ben *(hands them)*.—I hope they're all right, sir.

Prof. N. *(examines paper)*.—Excellent! Look here, father. How's this?

[Pres.] *(adjusts glasses, looks over papers)*.—He's been studying. His answers show considerable knowledge of these subjects. I'd be willing to admit him on the strength of these answers. *(To Ben.)* And so, my lad, you're very anxious to be admitted to this university, and you have no money, and came here in the hope of working your way through?

Ben.—Yes, sir.

PRES.—Arthur, I think I'll step over to Professor Cox's room. Several of the faculty are there. *(Exit Pres.)*

PROF. N.—Ben, tell me about your Miss Lou. What kind of a looking young lady is she?

BEN. —Oh, she looks exactly like an angel, only prettier. She has long brown curls and big brown eyes, and the sweetest smile coming and going over her face all the time, and when she's talking to you her voice makes you think of the little singing birds in the woods.

PROF. N.—Why, Ben, that's quite poetical. Did you say that she is Colonel White's daughter?

BEN.—Yes, sir, Colonel White's her father, and Mr. Robert White, her cousin, is the one she's to marry. Aunt Rhoda says she never saw the man that was good enough to marry Miss Lou, but Mr. Robert White's folks and Colonel White always been dead set for him and Miss Lou to marry. *(Steps are heard.)*

PROF. N. *(sharply).*—The faculty! *(Throws open door to left.)* Sit in here, Ben, and look over the magazines until they are through.

(Exit Ben. Enter Pres. and members of the faculty.)

PROF. COX.—President Norton, I repeat, it is an outrage to admit another Negro to an institution like ours. We lost five students the last year Neil was here. I'm one of the oldest members of the faculty, and I think my opinion ought to have some weight.

PROF. WEIR.—It seems a shame to turn away any who seek higher education, but I am somewhat of Professor Cox's opinion.

PROF. MINOR.—It does not seem to me that the time has yet arrived for Negroes to graduate from our best institutions.

PROF. WARD.—Professor Norton will speak for the rest of us.

PROF. N.—Gentlemen of the faculty of Michigan's noblest institution, I am here to plead the cause of the humblest and most helpless client an advocate could have. My client is a Negro lad, born in adversity and nurtured in poverty. From a Kentucky cabin he has worked his way hence and knocks at our doors for admittance. Should we admit him and allow his intellectual thirst to be quenched at our fountains of knowledge? He has nothing to offer us of this world's goods, for his ancestors gave to ours over two and a half centuries of unrequited toil. What contrast to our white students, who, for the most part, come to us from homes of wealth and culture, the sons of parents who do all within their power to stimulate them toward the goal of the highest type of citizenship; but my young client, without educated parents, or favorable environment, starts out to seek the same grand heights! Will you close the door of hope in his face? Will you deny him his chance? Gentlemen, it was but yesterday that the shackles were burst from his limbs. Shall we refuse to unshackle his mind!

(Part of the Professors say, "No!")

PRES.—Is there any one else who wishes to speak? I will say that the young man passed a very creditable preliminary examination. I will now take a vote. All who are willing to admit the Negro boy rise.

PROF. COX *(to Prof. Weir)*.—The Nortons run everything. I won't be obstinate.

(All rise.)

PROF. N. *(shakes hands with all)*.—Thank you, gentlemen, thank you!

PRES.—Aye, you voted like men. It reminded me of the days of Garrison and Sumner in dear old New England.

PROF. N. *(opens door of outer room)*.—Ben! *(Enters Ben.)*

PRES.—Gentlemen of the faculty, the student you have voted to admit. What is your name, sir?

BEN.—Benjamin Banneker Houston.
PROF. N.—Mr. Houston, gentlemen.

CURTAIN

ACT IV

SCENE IV.—*(College campus. Group of students with textbooks under their arms, among them Harry Van Wert, Robert Ogden, Richard Stewart.)*

VAN WERT.—I say, it's a beastly shame to have that nigger here in the university with us. We don't stand for anything like that in Texas, I tell you.

OGDEN.—Well, we don't like it any better in Massachusetts than you do in Texas—that is, a whole lot of us.

STEWART.—Hush! here he comes now.

(Enters Ben with books under his arm.)

VAN WERT.—The dark clouds are gathering. I guess it's going to rain.

OGDEN.—Hello, coon!

STEWART.—Oh, say, now, fellows, don't be so rough.

VAN WERT.—I suppose you think you're white because you're here. I wouldn't say where I wasn't wanted.

(Ben stops, looks at him quietly, then starts to go on.)

VAN WERT.—Don't look at me that way, Negro, or I'll let you know who I am.

BEN.—I know who you are now, Van Wert.

VAN WERT.—Pray let us have the benefit of your opinion.

BEN.—You are a cheap bully.

VAN WERT.—You dare insult me like this! *(Strikes him. The other two do likewise, and Ben is knocked down. Students come running. Some cry "Shame!" Ben gets up. Stewart and*

Ogden run. Ben pounds Van Wert. President Norton comes up. Other students disappear.)

PRES.—Gentlemen, what is the meaning of this disgraceful scene?

VAN WERT *(pointing to Ben).*—This coon insulted me.

PRES.—Calm yourself, Van Wert; such language is not permitted here. Ben, I am surprised to hear such a complaint of you.

OGDEN.—That's what comes of having a Negro in the university.

STEWART.—I hope he'll be expelled at once.

PRES.—Rest assured, gentlemen, the matter shall be thoroughly investigated. Come to the office with me, Houston.

(Exit President and Ben.)

VAN WERT.—I guess we've got him in a pretty scrape at last. We must stick together and get him expelled if we can.

OGDEN.—Yes he's getting entirely too prominent around here. Professor Norton makes a regular fool of him.

STEWART.—It will never do for him to know that we started the trouble. Come on, let's go.

(Exit students. Enter Ben with Powell, a student friend.)

BEN.—It looks pretty dark for me. I am afraid that President Norton thinks I was in the wrong. I have tried so hard to be patient under the insults of the last six years, but my persecutions grow worse.

POWELL.—I don't believe Professor Norton will fail you. He thinks so much of you. And I'll stick by you for the sake of old Kentucky, if for nothing else.

BEN.—Yes, as poor as I am, I would have, perhaps, given up the idea of graduating from this institution had it not been for the encouragement given me by Professor Norton and his father. Whenever the Professor meets me he has an encouraging word; and then he has been so kind in getting me work to pay my expenses. *(Enter Professor Norton.)*

PROF. N.—Good morning. Powell, I wish to see Houston a few moments.

(Powell lifts hat and walks off. Professor Norton takes Ben's arm.)

PROF. N.—Benjamin Banneker Houston, what's this I hear of you? You've actually been in a row, insulted his Lordship Van Wert, and made a brutal attack upon him besides.

BEN.—Professor Norton, do you believe Van Wert?

PROF. N.—Not often. Tell me about the whole thing, Ben.

BEN.—Van Wert's been after me ever since I've been here. He and his friends have lost no opportunity to taunt me about my race, color and poverty. I have borne it patiently. To-day on my way to the astronomy class, Van Wert made remarks about a dark cloud gathering as I came up. Ogden called me a coon. I didn't say anything. I simply looked Van Wert in the eye, and he resented it, and then I called him a cheap bully and he struck me, and the other fellows jumped on me too. Of course I defended myself the best I could, and I can't say but what I was enjoying the situation, when Professor Norton arrived.

PROF. N. *(laughs.)*—Just about what I thought. Van Wert's father is very rich and Van Wert tries to take advantage of this fact to do as he likes. A set of cheap bullies is a fit term for him and his associates, for money doesn't make men. Ben, it's character. Don't you worry, Ben; you've done good work since you've been here, and father and I are going to see you through. Who else saw the affair?

BEN.—Powell and Hart were there.

PROF. N.—I'll see them. I think I can depend on them to tell the truth. *(Exit Professor Norton.)*

(Ben walks slowly and seems depressed. Enters Lawyer Neil; slaps Ben on the back.)

BEN.—Why, Mr. Neil, how did you happen over to-day?

NEIL.—Oh, I must get over once in a while and see how my Kentucky lad is making out. The fact of the matter is Ben, that all of us here at Bayview are proud of the record you have made, and we wish to do something to show our appreciation, and I thought I'd start the ball a-rolling by extending a reception to you at our home Thursday evening; and, oh, yes, Mrs. Neil and Edith will expect you to dinner at six on the same evening. If Edith were older, and you hadn't talked so much of that little Lindy you left down in old Kentucky, I might be afraid to have you over so much. By the way, have you heard from home lately? I've been so busy I've neglected you like everything this year.

BEN.—Yes I hear from Aunt Rhoda and Miss Lou and them regularly. Colonel White, where Aunt Rhoda lived, is dead, my Uncle Jake is dead, my Cousin Sue's married, Miss Lou's beau, Mr. Robert White, is married, and Miss Lou and my little Cousin Lindy are in England visiting "Lady Mary" as Aunt Rhoda calls her.

NEIL *(whistles)*.— Whew! Why, Ben, you're indirectly connected with the English nobility, aren't you? You spoke of the colored people building a college there at your home. Is it completed?

BEN.—Yes, sir. They've put up a fine brick building with stone foundations on the very spot where the Ku-klux burnt down the old Cross Roads Church where the Quaker teacher taught, and, strange to say, she is back teaching colored children on the very spot where she suffered persecution.

NEIL.—Don't call it strange, Ben. When "truth gets a hearing" mighty changes take place; and when any people have it in their hearts to rise as strongly as the Negro race, God will raise up friends for them on every hand, and victory will be theirs. But I must be going.

BEN.—I wanted to speak to you about a little trouble I am in.

NEIL.—Trouble? Come up to your room and tell me all about it. That's the way we lawyers make our living, you know—off of other people's troubles.

CURTAIN

ACT IV

SCENE V. *(Parlors of Lawyer Neil's beautiful home arranged for a reception. Palms conceal an orchestra. Piano and other appropriate furnishings. Ben discovered alone. He is in a well-fitting suit. Looks well. Enters Edith Neil in a reception gown. She is barely sixteen.)*

BEN *(rising).*—Well, Miss Edith, have you come at last?

EDITH.—Alone, Mr. Houston? Hasn't papa come yet? Too bad he had to miss dinner, when he had planned to have such a nice hour with you. Oh, the life of a professional man! I wouldn't marry one for anything. You can never depend on having them when you want them.

BEN.—I don't think I'd be hard to find. It's been so long since I've had a home, I think I'd wish to stay all the time.

EDITH.—That's what you say now, but men change after they are married.

BEN.—Do they, little Miss Worldly Wise? I can't imagine any one changing toward you.

EDITH.—Can't you? Don't try to flirt with me, sir. You college boys are dreadful. Papa told me he believed you were engaged to a girl in Kentucky.

BEN.—Did you believe it? *(Enters Neil.)*

NEIL *(shakes hands heartily with Ben; kisses Edith).*—Run away, little girl. I wish to see Houston privately. *(Exit Edith pouting.)*

NEIL.—Well, Ben, my boy, you came out all right. I told

you you would, didn't I? Those fellows have had a bad record ever since they landed here. Professor Norton 'phoned me about it this morning. He was very anxious about the outcome.

BEN.—I know he was, but not half so much as I, right here on the eve of my graduation. Fortunately, Powell and Hart couldn't be bribed by Van Wert's money, and what they said exonerated me from serious fault. I lost my temper, all right, and, as I told Professor Norton, when Professor Norton came up and I had Van Wert down, I was enjoying the situation.

NEIL.—It was time to lose your temper, I think, when three fellows had you down, pounding the life out of you. I went in for athletics a good deal when I was in college, and I was always in good trim for the boys. *(Laughs.)* Say, Ben, as long as you have selected law as your profession, I may take you in as a partner some day if you decide to settle here.

BEN.—Thank you, Mr. Neil. This is more than I deserve.

(Bell rings. Enters neat-looking maid.)

MAID.—A gentleman to see Mr. Houston.

NEIL.—Tell him to come in. Come up to my den when your caller has gone, Ben, and let's finish building our air castles.

(Exit Neil. Maid admits Professor Norton.)

PROF. N.—*(looks around).*—First time I was ever in Neil's. Hang it! he's got everything in excellent taste. *(Looks at pictures.)* He's got some good pictures.

BEN *(who has risen).*—Good evening. Nothing wrong with Professor Norton, is there? He wasn't feeling so well this morning.

PROF. N. *(shaking Ben's hand).*—No, nothing wrong with us, but a telegram came for you, and, knowing how attached you are to that old auntie of yours, as it was on my way, I stopped in with it. I hope there's nothing wrong with her, or Mrs. White, or any of them.

BEN.—Thank you, Professor. It was very kind of you. *(Takes telegram and tears it open nervously and reads. Smiles.)* It's the best news I ever got in my life! Miss Lou and Lindy are back in America! They're in New York. Some one of Miss Lou's English relations has left her a fortune, and they're coming to my graduation, and they're going to bring Aunt Rhoda too!

PROF. N.—Is Miss Lou's husband with her? I mean Mrs. White, of course.

BEN.—Who said Miss Lou was married? They like to tormented [sic] the life out of her to have Mr. Robert White, but she wouldn't do it, and Aunt Rhoda told me he'd married one of the Draine girls, and certainly had his match.

PROF. N.—Miss Lou not married! Then why didn't you say so, you idiot?

BEN *(in surprise)*.—Why, Professor Norton, you don't know Miss Lou? *(Aside.)* I wonder if dear old Professor has lost his mind.

PROF. N.—I know her so well that I never would have stayed away from her all of these years had I not thought that she belonged to some one else. Miss Lou, my sweet little Southern rose! I met her in New Orleans, Ben, when she was just out of short dresses, and I loved her from the first time I laid eyes on her. I was only restrained from speaking by a sense of honor. I was told that she loved her Cousin Robert, that they were engaged and would be married when she returned. When you first came and I asked you a few questions concerning her, your answers confirmed my worst fears.

BEN.—Great Caesar! what a plaything fate makes of us.

This is certainly a great surprise to me. I hope you'll win her yet. I don't know any other man on earth who's good enough for Miss Lou. She's sent me money several times since I've been in college, and said it was a debt she owned Aunt Rhoda. Aunt Rhoda is her mammy, you know.

PROF. N.—No, I didn't know that. When will they get here?

BEN.—The telegram does not say. It is from Lindy Roberts, my cousin, who went to England with Miss Lou. She says they will let us know when they arrive. Unless they wire again, I won't know what train to meet.

PROF. N.—Oh, what cruel suspense! If it were not Commencement time I'd leave for New York to-night. Well, I must go.

(Exit Professor Norton.)

BEN.—Oh, yes; I must go up to the den.

(Exit Ben. Enter Edith Neil, Julia Storm, Ida Campbell.)

EDITH.—My first reception! Oh, I know I shall enjoy myself to-night. Say, girls, how sweet you both look! It was nice of you to come early. We've had such a time to-day. I told mama it was a blessing she had taught me to work. The girl left last night and we had a time finding someone to serve dinner. You know we had Mr. Houston for dinner to-night.

IDA.—Oh, did you? That's why he couldn't come to play tennis.

JULIA.—Edith, you mustn't set your cap for Mr. Houston. You're just coming out. You're too young. You must give Ida and me a chance.

EDITH.—I'd set my cap for him if I thought 'twas any use. Papa's just crazy about him, but I'm afraid a Southern girl has cut us out. He was talking about her at the dinner table. She's in England traveling with a white lady.

IDA.—The idea! Nothing but a servant girl. I should think he'd look higher. *(Bell rings several times. Music strikes up.)*

EDITH.—Oh, our guests are arriving! Come, girls, let's see if everything is ready. *(Exit girls.)*

(Enter Mr. and Mrs. Neil, with Ben. Girls come back and form a receiving line. Enter guests.)

EDITH.—Dr. and Mrs. Lynch, Mr. Houston.

IDA.—Rev. and Mrs. Berry.

JULIA.—Judge and Mrs. Carroll.

EDITH.—Mr. Albert Carroll, our poet.

JULIA.—Madame Delphine Lewis, our vocalist.

EDITH.—And here is Mrs. Craig, whose new book is making her so famous.

JULIA.—Professor Gibbs, the artist.

(Guests come forward as they are introduced, and seat themselves.)

NEIL.—Friends, it affords me much pleasure to-night to have you meet our young guest. Mr. Benjamin Banneker Houston, for whom I predict a seat in Congress if he keeps on as he has begun. *(Subdued applause.)* We who have watched Mr. Houston from the time that he entered the doors of our great university know that he was in every sense of the word at the foot of the ladder. His only assets were honesty, love of learning and a willingness to work hard. Scorned by many of the students, he went quietly on his way doing good work in all of his classes and sustaining throughout his college career an unimpeachable record. Not only has he conquered the prejudice of the faculty and students, but for the most part he has won their respect and admiration as well, and he will represent his university in the coming State oratorical contest this fall. *(Applause.)* This being the eve of Mr. Houston's graduation, I have asked you here to meet him and to rejoice with me that we have a young man of our race

so earnest, so persistent, so eloquent. I will now ask Mr.
Houston to say a word. *(Applause.)*

BEN.—Honored Host, Ladies and Gentlemen; From Cabin
to Congress is a long stretch, but if Mr. Neil's predictions
are ever verified, that is the distance it will mean for me. I
confess that my aspirations have not soared so high as that.
When I entered the doors of your great university, I simply
obeyed the intolerable longing for knowledge that had arisen
in my soul, and sought to assuage it. It seems strange, but it
is true, that it was the account of Lawyer Neil's own graduation, that I read in an old newspaper in Kentucky, that gave
me the determination to get a college education. *(Applause.)*
The measure of success that has so far attended my humble
endeavors I owe to the teachings of my mother in our little
Kentucky cabin. I wish no higher life than the opportunity
to serve my fellows. I thank Lawyer Neil for this opportunity to meet some of the most cultured and gifted of my own
people, and I pledge myself to-night to press forward toward
the highest achievements within my reach. *(Applause.)*

NEIL.—How do you like the ring of my Congressional
timber? We will now be favored with a song by Madame
Delphine Lewis.

(Madame Lewis sings. Applause.)

NEIL.—Miss Storm and Miss Campbell will favor us with
a duet, I am sure.

(Julia and Ida play.)

NEIL.—Will Professor Harris give us a song?

(Professor Harris sings.)

BEN.—I am not taking the place of the master of ceremonies, but if Miss Edith would sing—

MRS. NEIL.—Sing my favorite, Edith.

NEIL.—Certainly she will sing. *(Edith plays and sings.)*
And now if the orchestra will favor us with a march, we will

go to the dining room. Mr. Houston, will you take Miss Neil?

(Guests fall in line while march is being played, and follow Neil, Mrs. Neil, Ben and Edith off stage.)

CURTAIN

ACT V

SCENE VI.—*(A private sitting room in a hotel. Miss Lou in a black tailor-made gown, hat and black mourning veil is standing at the window. She is prettier than ever. Lindy, grown very pretty, is stylishly gowned. She walks nervously around the room and occasionally looks in the glass.)*

LINDY.—Oh, Miss Lou, I'm so nervous! Just think, it's been almost seven years since I saw Ben. Suppose he don't like me when he sees me, after being with all these pretty girls here in the North. Do you think I look as well as I did when he left home? He called me his little sweetheart Lindy the day he left.

MISS LOU.—Is it possible that you don't realize that time and training have made you a very handsome girl? You foolish Lindy! And then, if you were homely, your disposition would make you loved anyway. If Ben doesn't appreciate you after the way you've worked and studied to educate yourself and be a fit companion for him, I shall be disappointed in him, that's all.

(Enters Aunt Rhoda with various articles of clothing in her hand.)

AUNT R.—Miss Lou, I jus' wish you'd come up to my room and see how them ornery uniform men done tu'n my bran new trunk upside down and got my bes' black dress and everything else all mussed up. They ought to be arrested for such doings.

MISS LOU.—I'll be there in a minute, mammy. Don't worry. The porters didn't mean to be so rough, I'm sure.

AUNT R.—'Course they meant it. They jus' natchually hate to see a colored person have a trunk like that. *(Marches out angrily.)*

LINDY.—Oh, my heart beats!

MISS LOU.—That's love, Lindy. That was the way my heart did when Mr. Norton used to come to the school to see his cousins.

LINDY.—Mr. Norton! What Mr. Norton?

MISS LOU.—Oh, a handsome young professor from the North that I met at the school in New Orleans.

LINDY.—Norton! Where have I heard that name? Oh, President Norton and Professor Norton, Ben's friends.

MISS LOU.—This was Professor Norton too, but it isn't likely that he is related in any way with Ben's friends. I see Ben didn't lose any time. Here he comes now.

LINDY.—Oh, Miss Lou!

(Exit Miss Lou. Enter Ben. He gives one look at Lindy.)

BEN.—Whew! but you're a stunner! *(Kisses her repeatedly.)* My cabin princess, why didn't you tell me how handsome you had grown, so I would have known what to expect? Always writing that I would be disappointed when I saw you! You little hypocrite!

LINDY. *(looking up into his face).*—And you are really not disappointed in me?

BEN.—Yes, I am disappointed. I didn't expect you to be half so pretty and so well dressed. *(Kisses her again.)*

LINDY.—I'm so happy, Ben. I have thought of you night and day and the years seemed so long.

(Enters Aunt Rhoda.)

AUNT R.—I know you two ain't half through kissing, but maybe you'll get another chance. Howdy, Ben, Howdy! *(Hugs him.)* Oh, if Lucy Ann could see you now! *(cries for joy.)*
(Messenger boy raps. Hands Ben message. He reads it.)

BEN *(to boy).*—All right. There's no answer. Aunt Rhoda, you don't know how happy it makes me to see you. You're all the mother I've got, you know.

AUNT R.—You've been more like a son to me than anything else. When you would send me money I always told Miss Lou that I knew you were robbing yourself.

(Enter Miss Lou. She goes up and takes both of Ben's hands.)

MISS LOU.—Ben Houston, what a splendid specimen of manhood you are! I am proud of you!

BEN.—Ah, Miss Lou, I owe so much to you!

MISS LOU.—Nonsense! Be good to this foolish Lindy, who has tormented herself all the way from England with the thought that she would not meet your expectations.

BEN *(Looks at watch and then at window).*—I think she's in a better frame of mind already, Miss Lou. Miss Lou, excuse us a few minutes. I want to take Aunt Rhoda and Lindy around the block.

MISS LOU.—Certainly. Make it as pleasant for them as you can. Don't get the engagement ring yet. I bought one in London that I think you will like.

BEN.—All right, Miss Lou. I forgot to tell you that you're looking fine. You're as rosy as a Kentucky peach. The sea voyage did you good.

MISS LOU.—It did us both good, and in more ways than one. My mother's brother took such a liking to me that he made me his heiress, and when my Lindy marries I shall give her a nice little sum for herself. Run on now. No time for pretty speeches.

BEN *(Looks out window).*—No, we must go at once.

(Miss Lou seats herself at piano and removes hat and veil and begins to play. Maid enters with card. Miss Lou takes card.)

MISS LOU.—Arthur Norton! Can it be—I will see the gentleman here. *(Exit maid, enter Professor Norton.)*

PROF. N. *(extending hand).*—Miss Lou, have you forgotten me?

MISS LOU.—No, but you have changed. Your eyes are sad and you have a moustache.

PROF. N.—And you wore your hair down and not up. Oh, dearest, to think I have known Ben since the day he first came and never knew until he received your telegram that you did not marry your cousin Robert.

MISS LOU.—Did you care?

PROF. N.—Did I care! Oh, my sweet shy southern rose, yes; because I love you, and have since I first saw you and I want you for my own. Now that I have you on my own territory you shall not escape me again. You don't love anyone else, do you dear?

MISS LOU. *(throws arms about his neck).*—I loved you too since that happy day in New Orleans, that is why I could not please my father and wed my Cousin Robert.

PROF. N. *(kisses her hands).*—I can hardly believe my ears. I have been hopeless so long. Listen. If you will consent we will be married at once. My parents will call and take you to their home this evening.

MISS LOU.—Married right away? What will I do with Lindy and Aunt Rhoda?

PROF. N.—Ben graduates to-morrow night. Fine fellow Ben. He has crowded eight years' work into his six years' chance. He'll be wanting to marry pretty soon himself, and in the meantime your humble friends can make their home with us.

MISS LOU.—Oh, how nice you are. That is just what I

would like. Out of the fortune left me I had resolved to give each of these three loyal friends sufficient to give them a start. Mammy I shall want near me as long as she lives. Her children would have to come here or she'd never stay.

PROF. N.—I will buy her a little place to-morrow, and I'll send Ben after the children. He needs a vacation. How will that do? Now will you name the day?

MISS LOU.—I am at your mercy, sir, any time you please.

CURTAIN

ACT V

SCENE VII.—*(Ben's living room. He is at his desk, Lindy is reading. Aunt Rhody is piecing a quilt with blocks on the floor.)*

LINDY.—How's your rheumatism to-night Aunt Rhoda?

AUNT R.—It don't bother me a bit, that medicine Lige give me helps me more'n anything I ever tried.

LINDY.—Lige is doing so well in his practice you should be proud of him. It's nice to have a Dr. White in the family.

AUNT R.—Yes, yes that part's alright, but it's the first time I ever took any of his medicine in my insides. Being proud of a doctor in the family and letting him experiment on you like these young doctors do is two different things. But I sure have got lots to be thankful for anyhow. Sue's married to the minister and in her own home, Pansy and Louphenia's is teaching and Lige is doctoring. Gladstone says that he's going to graduate from his Cousin Ben's college and he's going to stay with Miss Lou 'til he graduate.

BEN.—Wise Gladstone. Prof. Norton will certainly see him through.

LINDY.—The way Lige and Edith act I think there'll be a wedding before long.

AUNT R.—Can she cook? Lige is just as greedy 'bout eating as ever.

LINDY *(mischievously)*.—I don't know, ask Ben; she was his girl before I came.

BEN.—Don't you believe her Aunt Rhoda, Lindy was the only girl I ever had. Yes, she can cook of course not like you and Lindy.

AUNT R.—Well, I can stand it if Lige can.

LINDY.—Hasn't Miss Lou got three beautiful children?

AUNT R.—What's the matter with yours?

LINDY.—Benjamin Jr. and Lucy! Nothing, they are as sweet as they can be. I just put them to bed, precious darlings. Ben, do you know what day this is? It's our tenth marriage anniversary!

AUNT R.—Great head of the church, why didn't you say something about it, so you could have had a brass wedding?

LINDY.—Tin wedding, Aunt Rhoda. *(Ben laughs.)*

AUNT R. *(stiffly)*.—Well, what's the difference? I'm sure brass is worth more than tin.

BEN.—Lindy, I confess I have been so busy during the last presidential campaign that I might have forgotten that I was married at all if you had neglected any of your wifely lectures.

LINDY.—Almost forgot you were married did you? *(pulls his ears.)* Shame on you.

(Bell rings. Maid goes to door.)

LINDY.—I wonder who's coming. Turn on the lights, Mary. *(Enters Prof. Norton, Miss Lou, Lawyer Neil and those who were at the reception at Neils'.)*

BEN.—Why come in friends this is an unexpected pleasure, I am sure. Have seats. *(Shakes hands with all.)*

PROF. N.—Yes, be seated, I have a word to say:

Friends, some seventeen years ago, when our distinguished orator and fellow townsman arrived at Bayview, fresh from a Kentucky cabin I had to plead to get him admitted to our University. Step by step he has made his way, until he is acknowledged to be one of the most polished orators of the day. Not only does he excel in oratory, but his services in municipal and state affairs have proven him to be a man of deeds as well. He has thrown himself into every work of reform and shown himself a leader of men, it is therefore a very great pleasure to me to say to you that Mr. Benjamin Banneker Houston will represent us in Congress. *(Cheers.)*

> "Honor and shame from
> No condition rise,
> But we build the ladder by
> Which we rise,
> From the lowly earth to the
> Vaulted skies, and we climb
> The ladder round by round."

(Cheers.)

MISS LOU.—Ben, Lindy, I am so glad for you.

GUESTS.—Speech, speech!

BEN.—Friends, fellow citizens, I would not be human if at this hour I did not feel my breast throbbing with patriotic pleasure at being chosen by my fellow-men to represent them in some of the affairs of state. I feel unworthy of the great honor conferred upon me, but since you have bestowed it, I will try to show my gratitude by good hard earnest work. I feel that I have a threefold part to play, first as a representative of more than ten millions of Negro citizens, struggling for life, liberty and the pursuit of happiness, next as an American representing the entire boundary of the United

States, and then as a part of the law-making bodies of the grandest republic on earth. *(Cheers.)*

(Band plays America.)

BEN. *(wipes eyes).*—And my fellow-citizens, I thank you for the recognition that you have given me as a black man. We love our country. When she is in danger our men march to the front and bare their bosoms to the enemy's as freely as do the white men, and in times of peace we are equally as law abiding, all we ask is a man's chance and we will prove to you that we have within us all of the elements that go to make up the highest type of American citizenship. As I look around me to-night. I look in the faces of several who have helped to shape the current of my life. Aunt Rhoda who took me in, and shared her cabin fare of bacon and hoe-cakes with a motherless lad, Miss Lou, who was my Sunday school teacher and friend, my wife who has inspired within me the deepest reverence for the women of my race, and Prof. Norton and his father and Lawyer Neil, who made it possible for me to go through college.

I would say to the young men of my race that there is hope for them. No matter how discouraging things may look at times, honesty of purpose and hard work will win out. The Providence which takes me from the cabin to Congress will smile on all who put their trust in God and do the Right.

CURTAIN

THE SPIRIT OF ALLEN
A Pageant of African Methodism

CHARACTERS AND SUGGESTED COSTUMES
IN ORDER OF APPEARANCE FOR PAGEANT

[SCENE I]

MISTRESS OF PAGEANT—*Grecian costume of pink with pink over drapery.*

KING COTTON—*White robe with flowing sleeves cut square in neck over drapery to train in back bordered with purple. Silver crown of tin foil. White sandals.*

COURTIERS—*Knee breeches, cut away coats of sateen, lace frills and cuffs, white stockings, low shoes, long sateen vests with buttons.*

PAGE—*Knee breeches of red, white stockings, slippers, cutaway coat.*

ABOLITION—*White robe, flowing sleeves.*

SLAVES—*Female—Plain calico or gingham dresses, handkerchiefs, turbans, Male—In blue shirts and blue trousers.*

SCENE II

OVERSEER—*Wide brimmed hat, cheap suit.*

WIFE AND CHILDREN—*Dressed very plainly. Children are bare footed. Spectators, ordinary clothing of the period.*

SCENE III

COLONIAL GROUP—*Ladies' hair dressed high and with curls, powdered hair, white caps, waists and skirts made full of flowered material, silkolene, etc. fans, elbow sleeves, ruffles.*

389

PH[I]LLIS WHEATLEY—*Slender dark girl, wears dark blue with white kerchief and cap, blue stockings and slippers.*

SCENE IV

GROUP OF CHURCH GOERS—*Gray or black dresses made full, white kerchiefs and caps, large fans.*

SCENE V

WHITE WORSHIPPERS—*Women wear black dresses made full, wear black and gray silk. Men—black suits.*

NEGRO WORSHIPPERS—*Men wear same only poorer quality.*

SCENE VI

RICHARD ALLEN—Black clerical suit, white shirt and tie, worshippers dressed as in Scene V.

SCENE VII

RICHARD ALLEN—*Wears suit of broadcloth. Elders wear black suit, white shirts.*

SCENE VIII

SCIPIO BEAN AND H. ROBERTS—*Shabby black suits, old fashioned satchels, bibles.*

SCENE IX and SCENES X through XIX

EASTER DAY—*White robe decorated with names of mission fields cut out of thin cardboard, wears a golden cross. The words "EASTER" appear on a pasteboard crown of same material, hair worn low.*

CHILDREN'S DAY—*Blue robe, white stockings, slippers, sash, hair in curls. "Children's Day" is on her crown and banner.*

EDUCATION—*Wears college cap and gown. "Education" appears on front of cap, carries banner.*

ALLEN'S DAY—*Wears Clerical garb, banner says "Allen's Day."*

SCHOOLS—*Wear college caps and gowns and pennants on their sleeves with names of their respective schools.*

MISSION FIELDS—*Islanders wear white bordered with bright colors, sandals, large white hats.*

BUSH GIRL—*Robe of blue extending to ankles, bracelets on arms and legs, sandals.*

SOUTH AFRICAN MOTHER—*Skirt to ankles, drapery about waist, yellow cloth, babe naked save for loin cloth.*

SOUTH AMERICAN—*Rich robe of red, slippers, flowers in hair.*

CANADA—*Silk robe of lavender, jewels. Each character carries a banner which is held aloft in parade.*

PRESIDENTS—*Women's Mite Missionary and President Women's Home and Foreign Missionary—Black dresses, white lace collars and cuffs.*

CHURCH PERIODICALS—*Christian Recorder and all except Women's Recorder wear costumes of white cambric, knee breeches, cutaway coats, white stockings, slippers, they have pens over ears, wear high hats, carry pennants with name of periodical inscribed.*

WOMEN'S RECORDER—*Wears evening gown of white paper sateen or silk, white stockings, slippers, carries a globe of the world or may [carry] a banner with name of paper on it.*

JUDGE—*Black suit or gown.*

CLERK—*Black sack suit or brown.*

SUNDAY SCHOOL CHILDREN—*White for girls, dark blue or brown for boys.*

LEAGUERS—*White with blue sashes for girls, dark suits for boys. All carry banners with names of their department.*

EPISCOPAL BELLES—*Evening gowns, jewel vanity boxes.*

CONFERENCE—*May wear dress to represent state products, wisdom, handsome robe.*

BISHOPS—*May wear robes or clerical garb.*

GENERAL OFFICERS—*Business suits.*
BISHOPS' WIVES AND OTHER WOMEN—*Evening gowns.*
CRADLE ROLLERS—*may appear in buggies decorated as floats.*
GROUPS OF LEAGUERS—*wear modern costume.*

THE SPIRIT OF ALLEN
A Pageant of African Methodism
Written by Katherine D. Tillman

PROLOGUE

Three loud blasts are heard on a trumpet. The Mistress of
the Pageant steps before the curtain and says:

When the bugle soundeth clear,
Then the Pageant draweth near,
Begun in Slavery's cruel reign
When bound beneath an iron chain,
The Negro for three hundred years
Suffered in agony and tears.

SCENE 1.   THE SPIRIT OF SLAVERY

*Time, 1793, appears in background. A haughty king gorgeously
robed sits on a throne attended by courtiers. At his feet kneel two
slaves with baskets of picked cotton. (An overseer stands with
whip in hand over them.)*
    Enters Spirit of Abolition.
    SPIRIT OF ABOLITION—*(advances toward the throne*—May
I have audience with thee, King?

KING—I like thee not, thou has made much trouble in England through that fanatic Wilberforce. What wouldst thou here, be brief.

ABOLITION—Justice, oh King, I plead for the millions of unhappy Negroes in Africa, in America and wherever oppressed, for out of one blood hath God declared He made all nations of the earth. They are our brethren. Too long have they suffered bonds and afflictions in this blue land and gospel country. They have toiled willingly for their oppressors since the Dutch ship landed at Jamestown with its first cargo of slaves. They have made the land to blossom as the rose from one end to the other, but how have they been repaid? They are bought and sold as cattle; they and their children are kept in ignorance and poverty and they have no rights that a white man is bound to respect. Can you not hear their piteous cries tonight from a thousand cotton plantations, from a million humble cabins and from all their tortured souls and bodies as they pray for freedom. Pity them, oh King, and set them free!

KING *(rises)*—Never! Always the strong must serve the weak. That is the law of the ages. The Negroes must remain slaves in America that the whites may have gold for themselves and their children. I, King Cotton, so decree. Ever must more and more slaves be brought from Africa to supply the demand. Freedom for the slaves! Ha, ha! That would mean menial labor for us and our children. I will hear no more of this nonsense. Away with this traitor. Silence him by force for I hereby proclaim that forever and forever Slavery shall exist and Cotton shall reign as King.

Courtiers seize Abolitions and bind him. Curtain.

Chorus in Plantation costumes appears and sings "And I Couldn't Hear Nobody Pray."

SCENE 2.   THE AUCTION BLOCK

(An auction block appears. On it stands a Negro Slave with his hands chained. His wife with three children crying and clinging to her extends her arms toward her husband in a last good bye. A prospective buyer looks on carelessly with hands thrust in his pockets. Several white and Negro spectators appear in background.)
    Chorus—sings behind curtain "Old Kentucky Home."

SCENE 3.   AT MISTRESS WHEATLEY'S
IN BOSTON

Time appears in background, 1776.
    Mistress Adams and Mistress Clark are visiting in Mistress Wheatley's parlor. They are knitting.

MISTRESS ADAMS—Tell me, somewhat, Mistress Wheatley, of this African maid of yours who has written a book of poems that has astonished the good people of Boston.

MISTRESS CLARK—Yes, do, Mistress Wheatley, for we have been abroad so long it is hard to realize that your sickly appearing little black girl has grown into such a remarkable genius that even President Washington acknowledged with a personal letter a poem written by her in his honor.

MISTRESS WHEATLEY—Well to make a long story short, I wanted to get a young colored maid to fetch and carry for me when I get feeble, and one morning when one of the big slavers moored in Boston Bay I went aboard. I found one poor delicate little thing of eight or nine years, naked except for a cloth about her loins. Her weakened condition aroused my sympathy and I purchased her and brought her home.

MISTRESS CLARK—And your daughter taught her?

MISTRESS WHEATLEY—*(smiling)*—We all had a hand at that.

MISTRESS CLARK—I have heard say that she was the aptest girl you ever saw and we have always been taught to consider Negroes ignorant and stupid.

MISTRESS WHEATLEY—My Ph[i]llis was never like that. Although so young she remembered that in Africa, she saw her mother pour a basin of water on the ground in worship of the sun. She indeed learned fast and became so skilled in latin that she translated Ovid's stories. Her book of poems recently published is the first literature ever produced by an American slave outside of the almanac of Benjamin Banneker the black astronomer.

MISTRESS ADAMS—Wonderful! And is it true that she will go to England for her health?

MISTRESS WHEATLEY *(sadly)*—Yes, in the hope of strengthening her constitution. Ph[i]llis has never been strong.

MISTRESS CLARK—I would, we might see her if it be not too much to ask.

MISTRESS WHEATLEY— *(rings bells, enters small Negro boy in livery)*—Tell Miss Ph[i]llis to come to the parlor. *(Boy bows and retires.)*

(Enters Ph[i]llis. Slender dark girl in colonial costume and cap, a quill pen sticks in her hair and she carries a book. She moves toward her mistress with a world of affection in her face.)

MISTRESS WHEATLEY *(rising and placing her arm about Ph[i]llis)*—Ladies, my dearly beloved adopted daughter. Curtain.

Chorus Ethiopia—Munday.

SCENE 4.   ON THE WAY TO ST.
GEORGE'S CHURCH
IN PHILADELPHIA.

Time, 1786. (A group of Negro women meet outside the door of the home of good Mary Lee. They are on their way to church.)

SISTER JANE—Is my bonnet on straight, Sister Ann?

SISTER ANN—*(adjusts bonnet)*—See if my skirt is hanging. I just wish we were going anywhere except to old Saint George's church this morning.

OTHER SISTERS—*(shocked)*—Why Sister Ann, for shame to talk that way about the house of God.

SISTER ANN—*(tosses her head)*—That's just the way I feel. It's the white folks' house of God and the white folks don't want us and I don't want to be with them because I just can't feel the spirit when I know I'm not wanted.

SISTER MARTHA—*(dreamily)*—Have patience, Sisters, I've been having wonderful visions in my sleep. I believe that God's looking down on us and He's going to move the hindering cause. Oh, Glory! *(clasps hands)* Glory, Glory, Glory!

SISTER MARY—Yes, and I believe He's going to move it through Preacher Richard Allen. Seems like God has just raised up that young man to be a leader for his people.

SISTER ANN—I wish I could hear him preach every time I got to church and I wish we could have a church of our own where we could serve God to ourselves and not be a disturbance to anybody.

SISTER MARY—If we did it would be the first time the colored people of Philadelphia ever had a church of their own.

SISTER MARTHA—Yes, we have been wandering as sheep

without a shepherd, but God's going to give us a church of our own because we love Him and He's going to give us shepherds from among our own people to lead us. Oh, glory!
  Curtain.
  Chorus behind curtain sings "Every Time I Feel the Spirit."
  Mistress of Pageant steps before curtain.

Wouldst know the history of the Church,
Come, gaze about with me,
And see where Richard Allen rose,
And struck for liberty.

Within the old St. George's church,
While black men bowed in prayer,
Behold them dragged up from their knees
Scorned and insulted there.

And as brave Allen left St. George
With lifted hand he vowed,
That 'neath their own fig tree and vine,
His Race should worship God!

SCENE 5

Time, 1786, appears in golden letters in background of set. (George's church, Philadelphia. It is the hour of worship, and among the white worshippers we find the group of colored women in Scene 4 and Richard Allen, Absalom Jones, Doris Ginnings and William White. They sing "Blest Be the Tie that Binds." Some of the white worshippers are not in the spirit of the hymn for they keep turning and frowning at the colored worshippers. They look indignantly at the colored people and as they kneel in prayer one of the white officers lays hold of Jones.
  OFFICER—You must get up, you must not kneel here.

JONES—Wait until prayer is over.

OFFICER—No you must get up now or I will call for aid and force you away.

RICHARD ALLEN—Wait until prayer is over and we will get up and trouble you no more.

(Trustee beckons to another officer. They drag the colored men from their knees. Allen goes out with uplifted face and hand.)
Curtain.
Mistress of Pageant appears.

In this dark hour the people cried
   To God in earnest prayer,
And oft was heard these good old hymns
   Upon the midnight air.

Chorus behind curtain sings "Steal Away to Jesus."

SCENE 6—SPIRIT OF FREEDOM

Time, 1794, appears in golden letters. First A. M. E. Church. The Blacksmith Shop. Richard Allen is in the pulpit. Several brothers and sisters sit opposite each other in the "amen corner." The worshippers come in all ages, some comically dressed, some dressed well. An old man hobbles in on his cane. An old woman shouts all the way to her seat. They sing, "Oh, When the Rocks and the Mountains Shall All Flee Away. You shall have a new hiding place that day."

RICHARD ALLEN—*(rising)*—Brothers and sisters, hear me. I said to our accusers, "We are Methodists *(voices cry amen)* and willing to abide by the discipline of the Methodist church but we were dragged off our knees in St. George's church and treated worse than heathen and we determined to seek

for ourselves the Lord being our helper. When they threatened to [l]ead us out I said, "If you deny us your name you
cannot seal up the scriptures from us and deny us a name in
heaven. We believe heaven is free for all who worship in
spirit and in truth. We are determined to go on God being
our helper. We believe if we will put our trust in God He
will stand by us" *(amens are heard)*.
    We will sing our opening hymn:

> Oh God our help in ages past
>   Our hope for years to come
> Our shelter from the stormy blast,
>   And our eternal home.
>
> Under the shadow of Thy throne
>   Still may we dwell secure,
> Sufficient is Thine arm alone,
>   And our defense is sure.

Curtain.
Enters Mistress of Pageant.

> The Southland brought her tribute great,
>   Of churches, schools and stalwart men,
> And men from north and east and west,
>   Joined in the everlengthening train.
> The women brought their sweet
>   Their graces, wealth of soul and mind,
> Their children their most precious gems
>   A place in Bethel's ranks to find,
> We now come to the holy hour
>   When Richard Allen with head bowed
> Is consecrated by just men
>   A bishop in the church of God.

SCENE 7

Time 1816, appears in background. Place, Philadelphia Bethel
A. M. E. Church. The First Negro Bishop in America.
*   Richard Allen kneels before the altar. The elders have their*
hands upon his head and he has his hands on the bible.
*   Curtain.*
*   Chorus sings "The Church Is Moving On."*
*   Enters Mistress of Pageant.*

> And now this church still weak in might
> Obeys the Master's blest command
> And sends its first two messengers,
> With tidings to a foreign land.

SCENE 8

First Two Foreign Missionaries. Their names, Scipio Bean and
H. Roberts appear in background. Each carries an old fashioned
satchel and bible and stands before the altar. Chorus sings "Hark
the Voice of Jesus Crying."

SCENE 9—THE SPIRIT OF SERVICE

Time, 1922. Missionary Headquarters at New York Bible House.
*   In the background appears in center, Parent Home and For-*
eign Missionary Society organized 1864. Secretary of Missions
Dr. Rankins sits in center. To right appears Parent Women's
Mite Missionary Society, organized 1874. President Mrs. Mary
F. Handy sits at right. To left appear Women's Home and For-

eign Missionary Society, organized 1893. Mrs. S. G. Simmons, president, sits at left of secretary of missions.

SECRETARY OF MISSIONS—I am very glad to have with me today the president of the Parent Women's Mite Missionary Society, Mrs. Mary F. Handy, and the President of the Women's Home and Foreign Missionary Society, Mrs. S. G. Simmons, whose organizations have aided so materially in the development of our old and new mission fields for I have been informed that we are to have a visit from each of them at this time.

Chorus sings:

> Hark, hark my soul angel's songs are swelling
> O'er earth's green fields and oceans wave beat shore.
> How sweet the truth those blessed strains are telling
> Of that new life when sin shall be no more.
>
> Angels sing on, your faithful watches keeping.
> Sing us sweet fragments of the songs above
> Till morning's joy shall end the night of weeping
> And life's long shadows bread in cloudless love.

Enter—West African Bush Girl, Liberian, Haitian Girl, South African Mother and Babe, San Domingo, Jamaican, South American, Canadian, Bermudan—each bears a burden.

BERMUDA—We thank God for Sister Nora F. Taylor, who brought the light to us. We need more evangelists in our island.

BUSH GIRL—I come to thank you all for the good bishops and missionaries your church has sent us, but oh, there are not enough to tell us about Jesus and how to live, there are so many of us. Help us we pray.

LIBERIAN BOY—I am proud of my country, but Liberians need help to work the resources of our land; we want the Christians of your church to lie here among us and train us.

HAITIAN GIRL—Many in our beautiful island do not know God. Send us more preachers and teachers we pray.

SOUTH AFRICAN MOTHER AND BABE—Help the poor mothers of South Africa that they might become great women like the good bishops' wives who have come to us.

SAN DOMINGO—Our faithful missionary Rev. James, asks help that the A. M. E. Church shall send more teachers and preachers.

CANADA—We come to thank our church mother for what she has done in bringing the gospel to Canada and pray for more laborers in the vineyard.

SOUTH AMERICAN GIRL—We are so glad you are sending laborers into our beautiful country where many do not know Christ. We want a chance to be trained here. HELP! HELP!

(All kneel before Secretary.)

SECRETARY—Dear Sisters, do you realize now why we must call upon you so earnestly for aid and can I count on you to help answer these pleading prayers?

PARENT MITE MISSIONARY PRESIDENT—It is the joy of our heart to spread the gospel. By God's grace we will not fail you. Since 1874 we have served at your call. Our Young People's Department will aid you with South America.

W. H. AND F. MISSIONARY—Your daughters' hearts beat in unison with yours, dear Mother of the Parent body—we are pledged to labor while life lasts that our mission fields may be maintained and new fields developed until in some far sweet hour a redeemed world shall clasp hands and join in singing.

> All hail the power of JESUS' name
> Let angel prostrate fall
> Bring forth the royal diadem
> And crown HIM LORD OF ALL.

SECRETARY—In the name of the Triune God the A. M. E. Church accepts the challenge, look up by faith and see salvation in the blessed cross of Christ.

Chorus, "Over Jordan"—Hilbert Stewart.

SCENE 10—CONNECTIONAL DAYS

Time, 1922. Easter Day, Children's Day, Educational Day, Allen's Day meet.

CHILDREN'S DAY—Please, dear Lady, who are you? I just got in from Nashville where our Sunday school building is located and I wish to get acquainted right away so I can have a real good time while I am in this big city.

EASTER DAY—*(bows graciously)*—I am Easter Day, I celebrate the most sacred festival of the church. All loyal ministers and followers hold me in reverence. The altars are radiant with bloom of flowers and the message of Easter is explained to the people and they give an offering for the mission fields. Only I am sorry to admit, that many who come to church decked in a fine Easter outfit give nothing but pennies, nickels or dimes on this holy day. A dollar is a small enough offering for Easter Day but if our entire church would give even a dollar on Easter Day how happy our Secretary of Missions and the missionaries would be. Only a dollar on Easter day.

> Only a Dollar on Easter Day,
> Just a dollar from you and me,
> For the barren places in need at Home,
> And our missions across the sea.

And our brethren in West Coast Africa
   Bowing to stick and stone,
Might be led with their wives and little ones,
   To trust in the true God alone.

And down in South Africa
   Into the humble heathen kraal
We could carry the blessed news of Him,
   For whom in vain they call.

And souls in South America
   Still bound by chains of sin,
Set free by the sacred words of truth
   Might be tenderly gathered in.

Yea and all the little isles of the sea,
   Might hear the glad news and rejoice,
If we will give just as we pray,
   Obeying the Master's voice.

And those at Home who need our help
   Will have their cup of cheer
If we today will do our part,
   And help the load to bear.

Only a Dollar, the price of a toy,
   Oh, will we not willingly give,
That those for whom the Saviour died
   Might hear of him and live?

CHILDREN'S DAY—I will give a dollar every Easter Day after this, just see if I don't.

EASTER DAY—Now that is just the way the Missionary Department feels from the Bishop down. I tell you Easter Day is a very important day in the A. M. E. Church. When we fail to give liberally and report promptly the poor missionaries are bound to suffer. Ah here come our Mission Fields now. Let me introduce them to you. *(Calls each field by name, each bows.)* Sit down and make your selves at home. Now little lady tell [the] men who you are.

CHILDREN'S DAY—Oh, Miss Easter Day I know you know me! I have been a part of the church since 1883. You ought to get Bishop Smith started about me. He's our church historian you know. He knew me when I wasn't knee high to a duck. In fact I wasn't here at all. Then Bishop Chappelle and Dr. Bryant worked on me and trained me until I'm one of the most important days of the church. Talk about flowers! You ought to see the flowers the children bring to church on Children's Day? Why its the gladdest day in the whole year. We have birds singing in the church too. My but we have a good time and you ought to see how we give money. Why the children built that big Sunday school building at Nashville. Here's a piece a lady wrote about me.

CHILDREN'S DAY

Why are we so happy, the flowers seem to say,
Why sing the birds' sweet songs, why this is Children's Day!
Christ loved the little ones and our church loves them too
We have a whole day of the year to show what we can do.
We bring in birds and flowers and decorate that day,
And then we bring our gifts and on the altar lay.
We speak pretty pieces sing our sweetest songs,
The best must go to Jesus the best to Him belongs.
I do not know what you about the Days will say
But seems to me the best, is our own Children's Day!
Oh hear come the children now. I told them to wait for the others,
(enter children singing "We are the children of the church.")
We are the children of the church our mothers reared by prayer,
The Church our fathers fortified by faith and manly care.

CHORUS

Our father's church, our mother's church
 Is just the church for me,

Our father's church, our mother's church
  Mine evermore shall be.
                    Bishop L. J. Coppin, A. M. E. Hymnal 131.

Easter Day, Education Day applaud as children conclude waving their banners and exit.

EDUCATION DAY—*(steps up to Children's Day)*—Pardon me, but allow me to congratulate you, Children's Day and you too, Miss Easter Day. I suppose you know me. Our Secretary, Dr. Jackson, talks about me so much that lots of folks think I'm just the biggest day in the church. However, I'm not in vain. Let me tell you though, Wisdom is the principal thing, therefore get Wisdom and with all thy getting get understanding. Put a man or a people amidst the greatest resources of the earth and without knowledge they are powerless to use them; give a man merely material knowledge and you but increase his power for evil, but in our church schools the heart, the head and the hand, we educate and that is why we have been able to furnish the church and the race with so many leaders. One day in the year every loyal churchman and churchwoman, for we always believe in women having an equal right to give an offering for Christian education. When we put over our Five Million Dollar Drive we are going to have a jubilee for all of my children will be out of debt. Here they are: *(enter church schools)*. I'm not a bit of a poet but I wrote a few rhymes of introduction *(schools give yells)*.

EDUCATION—Well, well, that will do.

Hurrah we cry for Wilberforce
  Allen and Morris Brown
Paul Quinn and Kittrell next we name,
  As they are written down.
Edward Waters and Western U,
  And Shorter College, too,

Payne Seminary, Wilberforce,
   Will teach you what to do.

Our Campbell College and Payne U.
   Wayman in Kentucky
If you can get in either one,
   I think you'll be lucky.
Turner Normal in Tennessee
   Payne Institute also,
And Lampton College doors ajar,
   To all who wish to go.

And last but not least you see,
   In Oklahoma Flipper-Key
Monrovia Training School, West Coast,
   West Africa doth pride,
While Bethel in Cape Town we hope,
   Forever shall abide.

Schools sing "The Friends of Education call"—Bishop Coppin, A. M. E. Hymnal 738.

WILBERFORCE—Please excuse us, our President, Dr. Gregg wants to entertain all of the schools at a reception. See you later *(exit schools)*.

EASTER DAY—And who is this young man. I think I have seen him before, somewhere.

ALLEN'S DAY—Ha, ha! If that doesn't beat all. If it hadn't been for me or what I represent there wouldn't be any Connectional days, because there wouldn't be any connection! I am beloved, Allen's Day, I am to my church what Washington and Lincoln's birthday are to the country. On my day, every progressive pastor and church celebrates the birthday of the founder of the African Methodist Episcopal Church so that all from the least to the greatest may know why it exists and may hear of its wonderful achievements for God and humanity. For

'Twas Richard Allen whose brave heart
　Beneath a sable skin concealed
A love of Liberty and Right
　As great as hero e'er revealed.

'Twas he who, in the Quaker Town
　Sounded our Independence Bell
That in its strong melodious notes
　Of Freedom for all men did tell.

And in a humble blacksmith's shop
　Arose a Bethel to God's praise,
Whose incense floating from her shrine
　Doth perfume all the passing days.

You heard what Children's Day said. The Sunday School is doing marvelous work but we found out with Father Clark that we needed a training school for young Christians, something to help save them from the vicious influences of the pool halls, modern dance halls and card tables. In 1900 the Allen C. E. League was organized at Wilmington, N. C. Dr. B. W. Arnett was our first Secretary, then Dr. Gregg, then Dr. Julian C. Caldwell and now we have Dr. S. S. Morris. I really don't believe Dr. Morris has thought of anything but the Allen League work since we elected him at St. Louis. He's on the job day and night and the League is growing in importance everywhere he goes and hundreds of young people are being reached. They're passing here now on the way to the mass meeting *(enter Leaguers with pennants)*. They sing "Shout, Oh Shout, We're Coming, Allen's Sons," A. M. E. Hymnal 737.

CHILDREN'S DAY—Hurrah for the Leaguers, for they like us are the Church of tomorrow!
Curtain!

SCENE 11. THE FUTURE CHURCH SUNDAY SCHOOL CHILDREN AND LEAGUERS PERFORM A SIMPLE DRILL WITH FLAGS.

SCENE 12—AT THE COURT OF LITERATURE, 1922

In background on a large scroll appear names of Church authors. Underneath is a large want ad. "Readers Wanted for These Books. Inquire at A. M. E. Book Concern, 631 Pine St., Phila.": Richard Allen, Daniel Payne, B. T. Tanner, H. M. Turner, Alexander Wayman, James A. Handy, C. S. Smith, W. H. Heard, L. J. Coppin, A. Grant, W. J. Gaines, J. C. Embry, J. C. Caldwell, Amanda Smith, C. W. Roman, R. R. Downs, A. E. Waddleton, A. Whitman, D. H. Butler, R. R. Wright, Jr., W. S. Scarborough, J. W. Rankin, Paul Laurence Dunbar, Amanda Smith, I. M. Burgan, R. C. Ransom, Josephine D. Heard, Effie Lee Newsome, T. G. Stewart, Christine Smith, Clara Bookter Thompson, Isabel T. Temple, Fannie J. Coppin.

(Judge on bench; Clerk at desk.)

Enter Christian Recorder, Southern Recorder, Western Recorder, Voice of Missions, A. M. E. Review, Women's Missionary Recorder, Allenite, Allen C. E. Star.

JUDGE—Well, what is before us this morning?

CLERK—If it please your honor all these plaintiffs have a case against the A. M. E. Church for non-support.

JUDGE—What is the charge?

CLERK—Lack of support.

JUDGE—Who represents them?

CHRISTIAN RECORDER—If it please your Honor, we are too poor to hire a lawyer, and we will plead our own case.

JUDGE—Swear him in.

Clerk swears him in.

JUDGE—You may proceed.

CHRISTIAN RECORDER—I am the Christian Recorder, a weekly newspaper published by the A. M. E. Church at the Book Concern in Philadelphia. I am the oldest Negro newspaper in the United States, but I do not let my age hinder me in getting around with the news. I seek to serve the interest of the home and church, and I ask that you hereby order under penalty of a fine that every member of the A. M. E. Church be a paid up subscriber.

SOUTHERN RECORDER—May I speak your honor.

JUDGE *(smiles)*—I suppose I'll have to hear from each of you.

SOUTHERN RECORDER—I am the Southern Recorder. I, too, am a weekly visitor. I am published at the Sunday School Union building in Nashville. Our people don't read enough and those who do read always want to borrow their neighbor's paper, and we poor papers can't live that way. I want you to order that every member who knows about the Southern Recorder and don't take it and pay for it, be fined $50. If they want the news they will get it in the Southern Recorder.

WESTERN RECORDER—Judge, I am the Western Recorder, and it sure keeps me hustling to keep in circulation. I give the latest church news and plenty of live wire editorials, but I am younger than my brethren and sometimes I am slighted. However, I am growing in popularity all the time and if you will just order that anybody in the ranks of the A. M. E. Church who slights me is liable to a fine.

VOICE OF MISSIONS—I am the Voice of Missions, Judge, your honor, and I want you to make a ruling that since the supreme business of the Church is the spreading of the Gospel, every member be compelled to take the Voice. I am published in New York. I am the best looking journal in the church.

A. M. E. REVIEW—How these fellows do talk, Judge. I am the A. M. E. Review, the cream jug of the Church. We appeal to the best in our readers and we never lower our standard. We only publish quarterly, but our matter cannot be excelled and we ask you to rule that no minister or layman be allowed to lay claim to intelligence unless he takes the Review.

WOMEN'S MISSIONARY RECORDER—I have waited for my brethren to speak because they are older and wiser. I represent the Women's Missionary Recorder, published monthly at Fort Scott, Kansas. We record the doings of the Missionary Societies all over the connection and publish articles and cuts direct from our African Mission Fields each month. Since we are doing this the Societies are doubling and trebling their missionary funds and we want you to rule that in the discipline and in the conferences the Women's Recorder be placed on an equal basis with the other church papers and that no woman in the A. M. E. church, or widower or bachelor, be considered in good standing who is not a paid up subscriber to the Women's Recorder.

ALLENITE—Judge, I'm a little fellow as you see, but there's lots of weight to me. I've struck some pretty big blows in my life and some I struck haven't revived yet. Please rule that I am not to be ignored.

ALLEN C. E. STAR—I'm a brand new church organ, but
I don't want to be overlooked, for I am the organ of the
Allen League. The Allenite is the voice of the Sunday School.
Don't we make a nice team?

CHRISTIAN RECORDER—Decision, Judge. We all are invited to take part in a monster church parade, and it will not
be complete with the Christian Recorder left out.

JUDGE—Well, I have been listening carefully to all you
have said and I have been weighing you and I must say you
are a fine looking set of church periodicals. One can scarcely
realize that you have but little over fifty years of opportunity
behind you. No race and no church can afford to be ashamed
of you or slight you. Reading maketh a ready man and the
Court hereby orders under penalty of the stigma of ignorance
being placed upon each delinquent that every member of the
A. M. E. Church who desires to be considered intelligent
and progressive, who is not now a subscriber to each of these
church journals, shall at once take the proper steps to remedy
this fault and any attempt to evade this law shall be promptly
brought to the knowledge of this court.

PERIODICALS—Hurrah, we are saved!

Curtain.

MISTRESS OF PAGEANT—

And in our world tragedy
  The Negro played his part
With courage and with sacrifice,
  And with a loyal heart.

And when we give honor
  To whom honor is due
We'll own that the Negro
  Is American clear through.

SCENE 15—AT THE COURT OF PATRIOTISM *

A group of soldiers at the recruiting station. Group of Red Cross workers making bandages. Two nurses bending over wounded soldier. Soldier bidding gray-haired mother good bye.
   Music of Star Spangled Banner is played softly throughout. Curtain.
   MISTRESS OF PAGEANT—

Makers and Founders of the Church
   Many have gone before
Who for the sake of God and Church
   The heaviest burdens bore.

Thank God they lived we come to say.
   And then we thank Him, too,
For noble souls yet left on earth,
   The work of God to do.

Red roses for the living
   And for the dead, the white
Heroes and heroines of faith
   Stars in this dark world's night.

SCENE 16—IN MEMORIAM—SCROLLS OF BISHOPS

Richard Allen, Morris Brown, Edward Waters, Paul Quinn, Willis Nazery, Daniel A. Payne, Alexander Wayman, Jabez

*The original text is incomplete; it jumps from Scene 12 to 15.

P. Campbell, James A. Shorter, Thomas D. Ward, James M. Brown, Henry B. Turner, William F. Dickerson, Richard H. Cain, Richard R. Disney, Wesley J. Gains, Benjamin F. Lee, Moses B. Salter, James A. Handy, William B. Derrick.

Joseph H. Armstrong, Evan Tyree, M. M. Moore, Charles S. Smith, Cornelius T. Shaffer, Levi J. Coppin, E. W. Lampton, H. B. Parks, J. S. Flipper, J. A. Johnson, W. H. Heard, John Hurst, W. D. Chappelle, J. H. Jones, J. M. Connor, W. W. Beckett, I. N. Ross, W. D. Johnson, A. J. Carey, W. T. Vernon, W. Sampson Brooks, Wm. A. Fountain.

(Music of "Lead Kindly Light," is played.) Curtain.

SCENE 17—THE BELLES OF THE 18 EPISCOPAL DISTRICTS

(Wisdom, a beautiful woman, is attired in a handsome robe with train. She wears a crown of jewels. Pages attend her. Music is played softly throughout this scene. Jingle of bells is heard.)

PAGE—*(Enters. Bows low to Wisdom.)*

WISDOM—Well, what wilt thou?

PAGE *(bowing again)*—The Belles of the Eighteen Episcopal Districts desire audience with thee.

WISDOM—Districts of what?

PAGE *(bowing again)*—Of the African Methodist Church.

WISDOM—You may admit them.

(Enter eighteen handsomely gowned women with pennants bearing the name of the Bishop and the number of the District she represents.)

WISDOM *(kindly)*—Well, ladies, how can I serve thee?

ALL *(kneeling)*—Which of us is greatest?

WISDOM—Rise and let me hear from each in turn.

BELLE OF FIRST *(bowing low)*—I am entitled to speak first. I represent the First Episcopal District of which Bishop Heard is Chief Pastor. Our District as you see is a famous one. Our conferences are Philadelphia, New Jersey, New York and New England conferences *(these conferences represented by men and women or both, enter, bow as name is called and stand back of District belle.)* Our District is noted as the scene of the rise of African Methodism in the old Blacksmith shop. In Bethel Church, Philadelphia, we have Richard Allen's tomb. In the same city we have the historic Book Concern, the home of the Christian Recorder and of our hymnals and disciplines and all kinds of good literature. In this city also lives Bishop Tanner, Bishop Coppin, Bishop J. Albert Johnson and Bishop Heard. Josephine D. Heard, the poet, Dr. Evelyn Coppin, the lecturer, Mrs. Emily Kinch, the Missionary, and Mrs. M. S. C. Beckett, the talented Corresponding Secretary of the Parent Mite, Dr. R. R. Wright, the brilliant editor and author, and Dr. Baxter, business manager. In New York we have our Missionary Headquarters with Dr. J. W. Rankin as our Secretary, Editor of the Voice of Missions, and at Oceanport, New Jersey, Dr. R. C. Ransom, popular editor of the A. M. E. Review and Mrs. Emma S. Ransom, writer and social worker. Are we not first and greatest?

WISDOM—How many Episcopal Districts has the A. M. E. Church?

ALL—Eighteen, Wisdom, eighteen.

SECOND DISTRICT—I represent the Second District of which Bishop J. A. Albert Johnson is the head. Our conferences are Baltimore, Virginia, North Carolina, Western North Carolina conferences *(conferences enter and bow as named.)* In the Baltimore Conference we have the Financial Headquarters of the Church with Dr. Hawkins our Financial Secretary in charge to take care of Dollar Money. Did you ever see the fellow. He is the fellow who makes all of the preachers hustle at conference time. Here he is *(enter Dollar Money. He wears a costume covered with silver dollars and carries a banner of Financial Department.)* In our District live Bishop Hurst, Bishop I. N. Ross, Mrs. K. Bertha Hurst, treasurer of our Parent Mite, Bishop W. Sampson Brooks, Dr. B. F. Watson, secretary of our Extension Department. Do you know what the Extension Department does. It saves our churches from the sheriff's hammer.

Mrs. Mary F. Handy, the beloved president of the Parent Mite lives in Baltimore and Dr. S. S. Morris, our League secretary, in Virginia, and in Greensboro lives the talented Associate Editor of the Women's Missionary Recorder, Mrs. Susie B. Dudley. I am sure that we ought to be first.

THIRD DISTRICT—I represent the Third District and I tell you we are proud of our District. Our conferences are Ohio, North Ohio, Pittsburgh and West Virginia. Our chief Pastor is Bishop Joshua H. Jones. I'm sure we are the greatest for our District is the seat of Wilberforce University, the oldest school of the Church, founded in 1856. Wilberforce has furnished several bishops and General officers to the church, and other able leaders, including Miss Hallie Q. Brown, president of the National Association of Colored Women's Clubs.

FOURTH DISTRICT—Most Gracious, do not let that bell ring all night, there are fifteen others waiting for a hearing.

—Our Chief Pastor is Bishop Levi J. Coppin. Our conferences are Indiana, Illinois, Chicago and Northwestern. Aren't they good looking? Among our many attractions are the churches in our hostess city, Chicago, second city in the

United States, the Preacher's paradise, the place he never wants to leave until the Lord calls him from labor to reward. Well here are the Churches (Mother Quinn, Bethel, Institutional, Wayman Chapel, St. Stephens, Grant Chapel, St. Johns, St. Marys, Coppin Mission, Trinity, etc.) Scores of strong young men have gone from these churches into the ministry of the A. M. E. Church. In our District is the home of the late Bishop Shaffer and of Bishop H. B. Parks and Bishop A. J. Carey and of Mrs. Nora F. Taylor and Miss Mary Evans, evangelists.

BELLE OF FIFTH DISTRICT—Our chieftain is Bishop H. B. Parks. Our conferences are Missouri, North Missouri, Southwest Missouri, of the "Show Me" State, Kansas, Nebraska and Colorado. (Upon the land conquered by Paul Quinn for Jesus, great churches have arisen. St. Paul in St. Louis, Allen Chapel in Kansas City, St. John in Omaha and Shorter Chapel in Denver.) Then there is our Western University standing like a lighthouse on the banks of the Missouri, Douglas Hospital in Kansas City, Kansas. In our District lives Bishop W. T. Vernon, Dr. J. D. Barksdale, editor of the Western Christian Recorder, and at Fort Scott we find the headquarters of the "Women's Missionary Recorder," with Mrs. Katherine D. Tillman, editor and manager.

(Belles ring loudly.)

BELLE OF SIXTH DISTRICT—Dear Wisdom, just forget what these other girls have said for this is the Sixth District ringing for your attention. Bishop Joseph S. Flipper is our Chief Pastor, and conferences are: Georgia, North Georgia, Macon, Georgia, Southwest Georgia, Atlanta, Georgia, South Georgia, Augusta, Georgia. Seven, and all Georgia. Our District is made sacred by the past labors of Bishop Turner and Mrs. Laura Turner, founder of the Woman's Recorder.

It is the present home of Bishop Flipper and Bishop Fountain and Bishop W. D. Johnson. Our crowning joy is Morris Brown University, established 1885, at Atlanta, Georgia.

BELLE OF THE SEVENTH DISTRICT—Please don't do all of the talking, leave me something to tell, for we are doing all the things that you are doing. Our Chieftain is Bishop William D. Chappelle. Our conferences are South Carolina, Columbia, Northeast South Carolina, Piedmont and Palmetto. We have historic churches and a loyal people. Perhaps our greatest monument is Allen University where our Bishop once served as President. I know you have heard of our great educational drive. The Bishop's Council meets with us next winter; don't you think we are the greatest?

BELLE OF THE EIGHTH DISTRICT—Look out! Here comes the Eighth District, Bishop W. W. Beckett is our leader. Our conferences are: Mississippi, North Mississippi, East Mississippi, Central Mississippi, Central Mississippi and Northwest Mississippi. Lots of Misses and good looking like me. This is the home of Campbell College and of famous Mound Bayou Negro town founded by a lawman of the A. M. E. Church and of Mrs. Clara Bookter Thompson, connectional Superintendent of the Juvenile Department, writer and lecturer.

BELLE OF THE NINTH DISTRICT—I represent the Ninth District. I am sure we are the greatest because we have the Senior Bishop B. F. Lee as our Bishop. Our conferences are: Alabama, North Alabama, Central Alabama and South Alabama. Our district is the seat of Selma University.

BELLE OF THE TENTH DISTRICT—The Tenth is getting restless. RING OFF PLEASE. Our chief pastor is Bishop William D. Johnson, whom we call "OUR BIG BROTHER." Our conferences are Texas, Central Texas, Northeast Texas, North Texas, and the Republic of Mexico.

I think you will agree that we are the largest thing on the map. Our State is the largest in the United States, and we have a whole Republic annexed to us. Our District is the home of Paul Quinn College at Waco, established in 1881, and of that live wire Secretary of Education, Professor A. S. Jackson.

BELLE OF ELEVENTH DISTRICT—Most gracious, do you like oranges and pineapples and flowers. In our District, presided over by Bishop John Hurst, oranges are common as apples and if you give us the banner we will send you a whole carload. Our conferences are: Florida, East Florida, South Florida, Central Florida, West Florida and Middle Florida. Our district is the home of Edwards Waters College and of Mrs. Mary McLeod Bethune.

BELLE OF THE TWELFTH DISTRICT—I am from the Twelfth District. Bishop L. N. Ross is our chief pastor. Our conferences are: Arkansas, West Arkansas, East Arkansas, South Arkansas and Central Arkansas—all kinds of arks and each one like Noah's ark, a symbol of safety. Our district is the seat of Shorter College established at Argenta.

BELLE OF THE THIRTEENTH DISTRICT—Although our beloved Bishop Tyree fell at his post to Bishop Parks was assigned Chieftain of Oklahoma, Central Oklahoma and Northeast Oklahoma, and our work went nobly on. Our District is the seat of Flipper-Key University. The other half of our district was assigned to Bishop Fountain, Louisiana, North Louisiana, Central Louisiana Lampton College at Alexandria, established 1890 by Bishop Grant, is prospering under Bishop Fountain.

(Belles ring loudly.)

BELLE OF FOURTEENTH DISTRICT—I represent the Fourteenth District, Bishop A. J. Carey is our chief pastor. Our conferences are: Tennessee, West Tennessee, East Tennessee, Kentucky and West Kentucky conferences. Our greatest pride is centered in our two educational institutions, Turner College and Wayman Institute. So important is our District that it has been selected as the seat of the next general conference.

BELLE OF THE FIFTEENTH DISTRICT—I represent the Fifteenth District, Bishop James Connor, chief pastor. Our district is both home and foreign for our conferences are: Michigan, Ontario, Nova Scotia, and Bermuda. In our District lives the church historian, Bishop C. S. Smith and the superintendent of the Young People's Department of the Parent Mite, Mrs. Christine S. Smith, in Detroit. Bethel and Ebenezer are great centers for the thousands of our people who come from the South. In Canada and Bermuda we are building up a loyal membership.

BELLE OF THE SIXTEENTH DISTRICT—I am representing West Africa. Our Chieftain is Bishop W. Sampson Brooks. Our conferences are: Liberia, and Sierra Leone. I was a humble Bush girl and knew nothing of Christianity or civilization but GOD sent our good Bishop Brooks and his missionaries to rescue me. I am a product of the Monrovia Day School for Girls, taught by Mrs. Martha Ridley. My mother helped me to escape from the Bush because the heathen women of West Africa have a hard life. Now that I know about Jesus I want to study at the new school Bishop Brooks is building at Monrovia so I can teach my people.

BELLE OF THE SEVENTEENTH DISTRICT—I am a native woman of Africa and I have the great honor to represent the Seventeenth District. Bishop W. T. Vernon is our Bishop. He and his dear wife came 10,000 miles across the seas to help us. Cape Colony, Transvaal, Orange River, Zambesi and Natal are our conferences. Aren't you glad to see us?

Wei, Gahts. How you like I speak to you? In South Africa some of the Dutch and some the English. How you like I speak to you?

WISDOM—We speak English in this country.

BELLE OF THE SEVENTEENTH DISTRICT—Oh, how we need help in our country. You have seen in the Women's Recorder how we live in humble kraals. We have pleasure to tell you of our school, Bethel Institute, at Cape Town, and of what the Parent Mite Missionary has sent us all along and of the beautiful memorial church the Women's Home and Foreign Missionary Society is going to build there.

BELLE OF THE EIGHTEENTH DISTRICT—Well, I am ringing to call your attention to the Eighteenth District. I may be last, but goodness knows our District is not the least. Bishop William Fountain is our leader. California Puget Sound, South America and West Indies are our conferences. I tell you we have a mighty big job on hand working on two continents. As for home, everybody knows that Puget Sound and California are two great conferences. To my mind, according to numerical strength, they lead the connection.

BELLES—Wisdom, a decision. Which is the greatest?

WISDOM—Fair Belles, you have so delighted my mind and so dazzled my vision that I cannot think. I must ask for more time. (*Enters Messenger Boy, hands a telegram to Wisdom. Reading.*) I am told to inform you that you are urged to retire at once as preparations are being made for the triumphal march of the church of Allen and you are expected to retire at once and prepare to march with your Districts.

BELLES—Oh, goodness girls, let's hurry. (*They powder noses.*)

Exit all. Curtain.

MISTRESS OF PAGEANT—

Into the idle listless lives
  Of the young people of today
The Allen League is brought to save
  And lift them in the higher way.

SCENE 18

A modern sitting room: 3 boys and 2 girls are present. Doris 15, is at the piano; Harold, 16; Philip, 14; John 15, are playing checkers and smoking cigarettes. Genevieve, 15, is looking out of the window. Doris is playing a jazz melody.

Costumes modern.

GENIVIEVE—Sunday is sure a tiresome day at this house, I'll say it is.

PHILIP—Oh, don't say that about your home.

GENIVIEVE—Well, it is; you know it is. We can't play cards or dance here, and we can at almost everybody else's house we go to. Aunt Lou is a regular old fossil about such things.

DORIS—Why, Genevieve, your Aunt Lou is a darling. She is strict, but she has let us have lots of good times.

GENEVIEVE—I want dancing and cards and plenty of excitement. There's nothing else to go to. She won't let us go to Sunday shows. Just wait till I'm grown up. I'll have some fun on Sundays.

HAROLD—Oh, let us, Genevieve. Where is Eleanor?

JOHN—Yes, where is Eleanor? If she was here singing for us we'd forget our troubles.

GENEVIEVE—You'd never guess? You know that big national Young People's League Congress is here—you saw the posters? Well one of the delegates was Eleanor's chum at

Wilberforce. She called up for Eleanor and they've gone to the mass meeting.

HAROLD *(groans)*—Deliver me from a convention. They wear me out.

JOHN—I say they do.

PHILIP—What do the old folks do? Make speeches a yard long and pass a big string of resolutions that never amount to anything.

GENEVIEVE—No; goosey—its different somehow. It's mostly young people like us. Why, there are young people expected from everywhere.

DORIS—I don't care a rap about the convention. I'm sure it would be dry as a stick, but I want Eleanor. She is so lively, and we can always have a good time when she's here. She's always full of fun.

(Enter Eleanor, 18 high school senior.)

ELEANOR—What you looking so glum about, having a funeral?

ALL—Oh, Eleanor! So glad you've come. You've saved our lives. *(They crowd around her.)*

ELEANOR—I'm so glad to hear it. Get your hats; we're going out.

ALL—Where? Where?

ELEANOR—To see the biggest sight of your lives.

ALL—What is it?

ELEANOR—The triumphal march of the Allen League parade. A thousand young people of our own race will be in line with Bibles, banners and music.

GENEVIEVE—Marching for what, Eleanor?

ELEANOR—For Christ and His Church.

DORIS—Who are they?

ELEANOR—The young people of the African Methodist

Church led by their General Secretary, Dr. Morris, who has travelled thousands of miles arousing the young people of the Church to train for Christian service and help save other young people. Oh, they had a wonderful service this afternoon. I wish you could have heard Dr. Morris.

GENEVIEVE—What's the matter with you Eleanor? I never saw you look that way before.

HAROLD *(laughs)*—Maybe she hit the trail and got converted this afternoon like they do in Billy Sunday's meetings.

JOHN—The idea of jolly Eleanor being converted. I don't want her to be converted. It will spoil our good times.

GENEVIEVE—No danger of that is there, Eleanor, old pal. She never wants to go to church. She always gets her Latin on Sundays.

Quartette or Chorus sings: "Since Jesus Came into My Heart."

ELEANOR—That's the secret. Jesus came into my heart this afternoon. I am not only a Christian, but I signed the pledge as a Leaguer, and I'm going to fall in line with the rest of the parade. I brought the Association cards along so you can sign them and march with us. Will you come, dear little sister? You know our dead mother said I must not leave you, and you young people, who like myself, have been wasting your Sunday afternoons, with jazz music and idle jesting, will you not join the A. M. E. League of young people who are working for Christ and the Church?

Chorus: "Since Jesus Came Into My Heart." Orchestra accompanies.

They sign hurriedly.

Mistress of Pageant enters—

A hundred years and more,
    Have passed since Allen's Day
But Allen's spirit still alive
    His followers doth sway.

And under God they proudly march
  Keeping the Cross in view
Counting no sacrifice to dear
  His blessed will to do.

SCENE 19—THE SPIRIT OF ALLEN
VIEWING
THE TRIUMPHAL MARCH OF THE
CHURCH

In the background one hundred and six stars appear, representing the years of the Church. Above the stars blazes a luminous Cross. On a pedestal the spirit of Allen looks down. Music of: "Onward, Christian Soldier" is heard as procession of all characters in Pageant, except King Cotton passes.

CURTAIN

ANTHOLOGY

~ ~ ~

QUOTATIONS FROM
NEGRO AUTHORS

"Life is a fighting game against the powers of sin"—GEORGE
M. TILLMAN.

"It is all very well to say that every one will live till his
time comes. You need to remember that your time is like
India rubber; you can stretch it or shorten it by the amount
of pull you put upon it."—H. T. KEALING.

"Morning hours are the wings of the day, and wings are
suggestive of elasticity, buoyancy, hopefulness, ambition, aspiration."—JULIAN C. CALDWELL.

"We must war eternally with ignorance, mankind's cease-
less foe."—W. T. VERNON.

"There is no lesson that Negro boys and girls so need to
master as that of the necessity of work, of the hell of idleness.
Work in the face of obstacles and adversity is the school that
makes men, women and angels."—W. E. B. DU BOIS

"You will never convince anyone of the essential equality
of the races except by the practical argument of achievement."—CHARLES W. CHESTNUTT.

"When I am gone above me raise,
   No lofty stone perfect in human handicraft
   Say this of me and I shall be content,

That in the Master's work my life was spent
Say not that I was either great or good,
But Mary-like she has done what she could."
                                —JOSEPHINE D. HEARD.

"Can Afric's muse forgetful prove,
Or can such friendship fail to move
    A tender human heart.
Immortal friendship laurel-crowned
The smiling graces all surround
With heavenly art."—PH[I]LLIS WHEATLEY.

"A woman must labor to be dressed with purity, crowned
with wisdom and adorned with the jewels of patience and
perseverance"—M. F. PITTS.

"The man who is strong to fight his fight
    And whose will no front can daunt
If the Truth be truth and the right be right
    Is the man the ages want.
Though he fall and die in grim defeat
    Yet he has not fled the strife,
And the house of earth will seem more sweet
    For the perfume of his life."
                                —PAUL LAURENCE DUNBAR.

"Upon the nation's blackboard before their united intelligence Africa and Africans shall yet rewrite their own history
and the world shall yet recognize them as brethren."—WIL-
LIAM SAMPSON BROOKS.

"The black man must write for the black men and give
them proper or mental rank among the historic peoples of
the earth."—CHARLES HENRY PARRISH.

"He had no great accumulations, but left posterity a rich heritage of melody."—HALLIE Q. BROWN.

"Our boys and girls must stand,
As giants in the land
   With torches high,
Come, rouse from sluggard sleep,
And help the vigil keep;
What tho' the clouds hang low
There's blue beyond.
                    —EVA CARTER BUCKNER.

"The Negro is neither angelic nor diabolical but merely human and should be treated as such."—KELLY MILLER.

"One can only guide genius or talent where it exists to surmount difficulties and how to work to the best advantage."—SAMUEL COLERIDGE TAYLOR.

"And we with sable faces pent
   Move with the Vanguard line
Shod with a faith that Springtime keeps,
   And all the stars enshrine."
                    —GEORGIA D. JOHNSON.

"Disease and death draw no color line."—GEORGE HAYNES.

"The liberators of humanity, Jesus, Paul, Tindale, Luther, Wesley, Allen, Garrison and Lincoln were all men of splendid and indiscribable loyalty to truth."—A. B. COOPER.

"To realize the best for yourself consecrate yourself to something outside of yourself."—R. R. WRIGHT, JR.

"Hail land of the Palmetto and the Pine,
From Blue Ridge Mountain down to Mexic's sea;
Sweet with magnolia and cape jessamine,
And thrilled with song-thou art the land for me."
—ALBERY A. WHITMAN.

"Be strong my son, the weakling never can secure the thing for which he strives, for he who rests, and there supinely waits for some change guerdon of reward but waits in vain. Be strong! Be strong!"—B. B. CHURCH.

"Symbolic mother, we thy myriad sons
Pounding our stubborn hearts on Freedom's bars,
Clutching our birthright, fight with faces set,
Visioning the stars"—JESSIE FAUSET.

"Your race is calling you to carry on its good name and with that, the voice of humanity is calling to us all." — ALICE D. NELSON.

"Clean life, serene life,
Life that knows no shame,
Life that's writ in service
On the scroll of fame."—JOSEPH S. COTTER.

"I ask no rich reward, I only crave
A spirit singing to the lashing rain,
A lifted heart that never knows defeat,
God help me to be strong: God make me brave."
—ANNA M. HENDERSON.

"We shall prosper in proportion as we learn to dignify and glorify common labor and put brains and skill into the common occupations of life.—BOOKER T. WASHINGTON.

"The women of a race should be its pride,
We glory in the strength our mothers had,
We glory that this strength was not denied
To labor nobly, bravely and be glad"
—PAUL LAURENCE DUNBAR.

"All I ask for the Negro is fair play. Give him this and I have no fear for his future."—FREDERICK DOUGLASS.

"A race like an individual, lifts itself by lifting others up."—BOOKER T. WASHINGTON.

"The distance of years lends not only enchantment but sobriety to the view."—WILLIAM PICKENS.

"The price of liberty cannot come too high nor its safeguards be maintained with a courage and vigilance too sleepless and unyielding."—REVERDY C. RANSOM.

"In every walk of life prove yourself a hundred per cent patriotic and useful."—BISHOP HENRY BLANTON PARKS.

"Truth has never been the exclusive inheritance of any one nation."—R. R. DOWNS.

"We can reach our highest attainment, only in so far as we stoop to reach the man beneath us."—EMILY CHRISTMAS KINCH.

"The work of the colored woman's Club is to teach the race the lesson of self-control revolutionizing communities and bringing about their moral and civic salvation."—MRS. BOOKER T. WASHINGTON.

"You will never come into your own until you put at the service of the Almighty all of your powers-mind, body and soul. You will never know what happiness is until you have a large share in making others happy."—NANNIE H. BURROUGHS.

"We realize that to day is the psychological moment for us as women to show our true worth, and prove that the Negro woman of to-day measures up to those strong sainted women of our race who passed through the fire of slavery and its galling remembrances."—MARY B. TALBERT.

"We must have trained guardians for the home whether they be natural mothers or selected ones."—MRS. S. JOE BROWN.

"A landless race is like a ship without a rudder."—BOOKER T. WASHINGTON.

"I have learned that success is to be measured not so much by the position one has reached in Life, as by the obstacles which he has overcome while trying to succeed."[No author given in original.]

"We trace the power of Death from tomb to tomb,
And his are all the ages yet to come."
　　　　　　　—PH[I]LLIS WHEATLEY.

"Still wondrous youth each noble path pursue
On deathless glories fix thine ardent view."
　　　　　　　—PH[I]LLIS WHEATLEY.

"In Flanders field where poppies blow,
　Beneath the crosses row on row,
We blacks an endless vigil keep.

Yea we though dead can never sleep,
  Ingratitude has made it so.
Africa long ages sleeping,
  Oh my Motherland awake,
In the East the clouds glow crimson.
  With the new dawn that is breaking,
And its golden glory fills the western skies."
         —CLAUDE MCKAY.

"Since Poets have told of sunsets
  What is left for me to tell?
Can only say that I saw the day press
  Crimson lips to horizon gray."—EFFIE LEE.

"Sky, seas, and mountains wonders are
  And chartless winds or fierce or mild,
But still I think God's masterpiece,
  Is just a little child."—ETHEL CAUTION.

QUOTATIONS FROM
KATHERINE D. TILLMAN

"For Oh how much of happiness,
  A humble hut can hold,
Such joys as misers cannot buy,
  With all their hoarded gold."

"Say not that you have no chance,
  Read the Negro's thrilling past,
See what he has done and dared,
  Then go on to conquest vast."

"We call our visions madness,
  And cast our ideals away,

And are ever less than we should be,
   Had we had our visions stay."

"John Brown was hanged for Freedom's cause
   By man-made freedom-hating laws,
But he had won his God's applause,
   And where his martyr's blood was spilled,
The seed of freedom were instilled
   And men with new-born courage filled."

"On through the long night of oppression and wrong,
   On with a smile and on with a song,
Where darkness is deepest then follows the dawn;
   Then soul of my soul go upward and on.

"So rich so pure her jeweled womanhood
So consecrated to her fellow's good
   That on and on
Shall shine her life in other happier spheres.

Undimmed for'er by mortal ills and tears
   Through years unborn."

"Ring out the Bells of gladsome Easter time,
   In celebration of event divine,
With resurrection joys the music swells,
   While multitudes now seek the Saviour's shrine."

"In workman's shop or the "Front"
   The Negro soldier does his stunt
Proving a patriot, loyal, true
   To his country's flag "red, white and blue."

"For do you not think, it may be the homes we build for
     eternity,
Are built of the kindness, cheer and love,

Our lives send on to the heav'n above?"

"I serve my Lord the King,
    No greater post I ask,
No matter where for Him I serve,
    So honor crown the task."

"Give if you like wreaths for the dead but
    Long as I on earth shall tread,
And grief the human heart shall bow,
    I'd rather give my flowers now."

"Our times are in God's hands,
    Our lives are in His care,
The Old Year served from Him,
    Our heaven allotted share,
And after all we had more sunshine than of shade.

    So welcome the New Year with hearts with courage lade."

"Within the church that happy Christmas day
    Where holly berries on the chancel lay
The little children carolled forth the praise
    Of Christ the Prince of Peace, Ancient of Days."